Leo Kestenberg and Franz W. Beidler
Complete Correspondence 1933-1956

translated and edited by

Philip A. Maxwell

online press

Victoria, BC, Canada

ISBN: 978-0-9920618-1-4

online press

Table of Contents

"Germany in the 1920s, Weimar Germany, that was actually the peak of western civilization. In the sciences, the arts.... It was a model of democracy, [had] a huge labour movement, a lot of political activism. In 1928, in those elections, the Nazis had only a few percent of the vote. In 1933, they were so powerful that Hindenburg, the President, was compelled to select Hitler as his Chancellor; he hated him, he had contempt for him, class contempt ... but there was just too much popular support. Well, within ten years, Germany went from the peak of western civilization to the depths of barbarism in modern history and the fundamental reason is that the centre collapsed. People lost any respect... for the major political parties...Germany really was the absolute peak of western civilization [before Hitler] and descended to the ultimate barbarism in a short time."

Naom Chomsky

speaking with Tom Ashbrook

NPR On Point

September 28, 2010

Introduction

No written work has yet been able to capture the totality of the Nazi transgression against humanity. We are left to do what we can, piece by piece, to comprehend even a part of what happened. The present collection of letters is a chink in the written mosaic. It illustrates what the Nazis did to their own country, their own countrymen and to the world, and how the luckier victims, those destined to survive, coped with the hellish legacy of the evil done them.

This book contains the collected letters to each other of two men who achieved much during the Weimar Republic, the decade-long experiment with democracy that Germany engaged in after the Great War of 1914-1918. Leo Kestenberg was a key figure in the cultural landscape of the Weimar Republic (1918-1932). Franz Beidler, Kestenberg's right-hand man, although the first-born grandson of Richard Wagner, broke with the rest of the Wagners in embracing socialism, marrying a Jew, and rejecting Hitler. Both Kestenberg and Beidler were Germans-of-choice who had to leave Germany in 1933 to escape Hitler soon after he had crushed the country's first democracy. Had there been more Germans like Kestenberg and Beidler before the First World War, the great catastrophe of World War I probably would never have occurred. As it was, the War and the peace that followed set the stage for their efforts to build and fortify democracy and humanistic culture in Germany. Sadly, the War and its aftermath also set the stage for the rise of Hitler and his barbaric followers.

To many conservatives, the world seemed to come to an end after the First World War. The Hohenzollern, Hapsburg, and Romanov Imperial Dynasties collapsed, as did Imperial Germany, the Austro-Hungarian Empire and Imperial Russia. Revolution engulfed Russia and threatened to bring chaos not only to Germany but to the component nations of the former Austro-Hungarian Empire. Years of semi-absolutist rule, of wartime death and deprivation, ended all at once. Pent-up, creative intellectual and artistic energies found release all over Europe and beyond. The temporary disappearance from the political field of the discredited and defeated conservative elites, left a vacuum that the Social Democrats and other leftists filled, with élan. Artists, writers, and musicians of every sort took part in the renaissance. They gloried in the new atmosphere of liberation which invigorated their lives with reawakened vitality and meaning.

Leo Kestenberg (born 1882) was one of these artists, one who was also an arts organizer, and teacher. A piano virtuoso, he was a protegé of Feruccio Busoni[1] and apostle of Franz Liszt. In 1914, Kestenberg had left the non-pacifist Social Democratic Party to join the strongly anti-war Independent Social Democrats. Starting in 1915, Kestenberg organized numerous workers' concerts in the newly-built Theatre-on-Bülowplatz in Berlin, the building of which was financed with workers' donations. The opening concert featured Artur Schnabel playing Beethoven's "Emperor" Piano Concerto. [2] Besides performances of orchestral pieces of all eras, Kestenberg organized excellent chamber concerts (e.g. with the Havemann Quartet[3]), solo performances (Landowska,[4] d'Albert,[5] Fischer[6]), and choral concerts featuring many distinguised artists. He also organized afternoon dance performances featuring avant-garde artists such as Mary Wigman.[7] These examples give only an inkling of the breadth and energy of Kestenberg's activities during the war, which he eluded as a result of life-long ocular affliction.

In 1916 Kestenberg took over additional duties as editor of *Bildermann*, a progressive periodical for the visual arts published by Paul Cassirer [8]. The first issue of this publication, which ran for eight intense months, appeared at the beginning of April with original

---

[1] Ferruccio **Busoni** (1866-1924) - composer, pianist, writer, teacher, conductor. Kestenberg was a veritable apostle of Busoni. For several years, he often functioned as Busoni's secretary and musical copyist. His life-long, Kestenberg's teaching and philosophy were animated and inspired by Busoni's visionary approach to music, the arts, and philosophy. For Kestenberg, only Franz Liszt stood on the same heights as Busoni.

[2] Artur **Schnabel** - (1882-1951) - piano virtuoso and teacher; leading interpreter of Beethoven and Schubert.

[3] **Havemann Quartet** - String quartet named after its founder, Gustav Havemann (1882-1960, German violinist). It played classical and avant-garde music.

[4] Wanda **Landowska** - (1879-1959) - Polish-born, brilliant harpsichordist who inspired a renaissance of the instrument and studies into music written for harpsichord. In 1931, she made the first complete recording with harpsichord of Bach's *Goldberg Variations*.

[5] Eugen **d'Albert** - (1864-1932) - Concert pianist who studied with Franz Liszt. Composer of the opera, *Tiefland* (Prague, 1903) and 20 other operas.

[6] Edwin **Fischer** - (1886-1960) - Renowned Swiss concert pianist, conductor and teacher. Among his students: Paul Badura-Skoda, Daniel Barenboim, Alfred Brendel, Jörg Demus,

[7] Mary **Wigman** - (1886-1973) - German pioneer of modern dance and expressionism as well as dance therapy.

[8] Paul **Cassirer** - (1871-1926) - Jewish German publisher and gallery owner. The Paul Cassirer publishing house started in 1908 and died with the Nazi takeover in 1933. Cassirer published contemporary writers and artists of the highest quality in projects of great creativity.

lithographs by Slevogt,[1] Kollwitz,[2] Liebermann,[3] Barlach,[4] Kokoschka,[5] and Kirchner,[6] among other prominent artists. After the end of *Bildermann*, Kestenberg continued his work with Cassirer. Together they continued to publish Barlach and Kokoschka, and works by such writers as Elsa Lasker-Schüller,[7] and Rosa Luxemburg[8] as well as Eduard Bernstein's twelve-volume edition of Ferdinand Lassalle's writings.[9] Most of these projects had been directly inspired by Kestenberg.

Before 1914, it would have been unthinkable for a man like Kestenberg, to become a civil servant in a Prussian government. He was, after all, an ethnic German of Czech origin, a Jew, and a pacifist Social Democrat. But in November of 1918, amid disturbances following the collapse of the monarchy, Germany was declared a republic. Only weeks later, on Dec. 1, 1918, Leo Kestenberg took up his duties as the top advisor on all matters musical in the Prussian Ministry of Science, Art and Education (previously called Ministry of Culture). The two ministers responsible for this department knew and valued Kestenberg's work at the Bülowplatz Theatre (*Volksbühne*) and also with unions and workers' educational committees. They gave Kestenberg a free hand to initiate and carry out reformist projects that had waited four long years for the war to end.

---

[1] Max **Slevogt** - (1868-1932) - German painter (impressionist) and illustrator.

[2] Käthe **Kollwitz** - (1867-1945) - Major German pacifist painter, illustrator, and sculptor.

[3] Max **Liebermann** - (1847-1935) - Leading German impressionist painter and printmaker.

[4] Ernst **Barlach** - (1870-1938) - German expressionist sculptor, printmaker and writer.

[5] Oskar **Kokoschka** - (1886-1980) - Austrian expressionist artist and poet. In 1934, because of Nazi threats, Kokoschka fled Austria for Prague. When the Nazis made preparations to invade Czechoslovakia, he emigrated to the United Kingdom. Kokoschka painted an impressive portrait of Kestenberg.

[6] Ernst Ludwig **Kirchner** - (1880-1938) - German expressionist painter and printmaker.
A founder of the expressionist group *Die Brücke*.

[7] Else **Lasker-Schüller** - (1869-1945) - Jewish-German poet and playwright. Fled to Palestine to escape Nazi persecution.

[8] Rosa **Luxemburg** - (1871-1919) - Marxist theorist and activist, co-founder of the Communist Party of Germany.

[9] *Gesammelte Reden und Schriften* (ed. Eduard Bernstein). Cassirer, Berlin 1919/20; 12 volumes and a supplementary vol. [*Collected Speeches and Writings of Ferdinand Lassalle*, ed. Eduard Bernstein]
Ferdinand **Lassalle** (1825-1864) - founder of international socialism in Germany
Eduard **Bernstein** (1850-1932) - major figure in the German social democratic movement and party. From 1878 to 1890, when the Social Democratic Party was banned in Germany, he wrote articles in *Der Sozialdemokrat* under the pseudonym Leo.

Kestenberg's first priority in 1919 was to attract leading teachers, musicologists, composers, and musicians to fill teaching positions which had become vacant over the years. He wanted younger people than had been the case previously and ones who were active in and committed to modern German developments. His first big appointment was Feruccio Busoni to replace Richard Strauss as head of the master class in composition at the State Academy of the Arts. In his further appointments, Kestenberg dispensed with the earlier system of seniority-based appointments. In going his own way, based on talent, achievement, and ability, Kestenberg met some resistance and earned himself such epithets as "music dictator," "music Pope" and *Kultur* Pope.

Over time, Kestenberg rejuvenated the Berlin *Hochschule* [Music Faculty, Berlin University] by appointing Artur Schnabel and EgonPetri[1] as professors of piano, Carl Flesch[2] and Gustav Havemann for violin, Lula Mysz-Gmeiner[3] and Julius von Raatz-Brockmann[4] for voice. Kestenberg named Walter Braunfels[5] director of the municipal conservatory of Cologne. Other significant appointments included the pianist Eduard Erdmann[6] and the cellist Emmanuel Feuermann.[7] He also began a thorough plan of reform and new appointments at the State theatres of Wiesbaden and Kassel and the State music institutes of Königsberg and Breslau. In seeking a new director of the Berlin University Faculty of Music, Kestenberg brought in the then-celebrated Viennese opera composer, Franz

---

[1] Egon **Petri** - (1881 Hannover-1962 Berkeley) - Famous keyboard virtuoso and teacher. Student of Busoni. His students included Earl **Wild** and John **Ogden**.

[2] Carl **Flesch** - (1873-1944) - Hungarian-born violinist and pedagogue. Although arrested by the Gestapo in 1939, he was able to move to Lucerne, where he died.

[3] Lula **Mysz-Gmeiner** - (1876-1948) - Austro-Hungarian contralto and teacher. Her students included Elisabeth **Schwarzkopf** and Lula's son-in-law, Peter **Anders**.

[4] Julius von **Raatz-Brockmann** - (1870-1944) - German baritone. His students included Hans-Hermann Nissen and soprano Frida Leider who wrote, "For some time I had not felt at all comfortable in my lower register and here Prof. Raatz-Brocmann was able to help me." Leider, *Playing My Part*, General Publishing, 1966).

[5] Walter **Braunfels** - (1882-1954) - German composer, pianist and music teacher.

[6] Eduard **Erdmann** - (1896-1958) - German pianist and composer.

[7] Emanuel **Feuermann** - (1902-1942) - famous, internationally active cellist. Professor in Berlin 1929-1933. He died in New York.

Schreker.[1] Kestenberg also had Georg Schünemann[2] appointed as deputy-director. He was a well-known and capable musicologist, critic, and writer and a favourite of his students.

Schünemann played an important rôle in helping Kestenberg to realize his goal of improving music education in Germany by means of a comprehensive and methodical reform of every aspect of musical education. The Kestenberg reform, as he planned it, would improve the teaching not only of students, both in schools and privately, but also the education of music teachers and the organization of music schooling from kindergartens to universities. Musical education was also to include the use of music as a therapeutic tool in educating children with disabilities. Church musicians and their teachers were also to be included in the reformed schooling system as were musicians involved in the burgeoning youth movement which featured folk music.

Kestenberg made use of the newly created Central Institute of Education and Teaching to reach some of his ends, especially establishing widespread standards for music teachers, including adequate pay, and also introducing benchmarks for testing and grading students. Under the aegis of the Central Institute, Kestenberg started a series of annual "School Music Weeks." Starting in 1921, these conferences attracted increasing participation of musicians and teachers. There were 200 participants at the first conference in 1921, in Berlin. By 1928, 1,200 people attended. After the first conference, the subsequent "School Music Weeks" took place in Cologne (1922), Breslau (1923), Hamburg (1924), Darmstadt (1925), Munich (1926), and Hannover (1928). Each conference dealt with a specific aspect of the greater reform. The 1923 School Week, for instance, was dedicated to plans for the reform of musical teaching in public schools. In 1925, the year in which Kestenberg introduced governmental re-organization of private music tuition

---

[1] Franz **Schreker** - (1878-1934) - Austrian opera composer, conductor, and teacher. Although the Nazis often attacked him as a Jew, Schreker was born a Christian, played organ in churches in his younger years, and probably never set foot in a synagogue. Nothwistanding, in 1933, he was banned from teaching, composing or conducting. His works were banned from performance. (see: Michael Haas, *Forbidden Music* (Yale, 2013).

[2] Georg **Schünemann** - (1884-1945) - Musicologist and teacher. Deputy Director of the Music Faculty, University of Berlin during the 1920s. He worked closely with Kestenberg in advancing the reform of the institutional and private teaching of music. After the Nazi takeover, he became a member of the Nazi Party. During the war, he worked in the area of de-Jewifying opera libretti in German translation. He also worked for the Nazi star, Alfred Rosenberg, in nazifying culture and organizing the theft of musical treasures from conquered countries. Kestenberg seems to have destroyed Schünemann's letters to him, probably as a result of Schünemann's Nazi activities.

("Education towards humanism with and through music"), the School Week dealt with church music. With these conferences, Kestenberg gained the contact and exchange of ideas that he needed in order to achieve his impressive reform of musical education in Germany which was unprecedented in scope and ambition.

This great reform was a significant part of Kestenberg's overall plans. Beyond this, he intended not only to reorganize and improve music education but also to enrich and invigorate the whole of musical life in Germany. In 1922, he began to develop a plan to renovate the so-called Kroll Opera which had fallen on bad days. From the start Kestenberg viewed his Kroll Opera plans as "by far his greatest and most daring" venture. [1] His intention was to create an opera house that would be dedicated to modern musical performances, scenery, stage direction, and programming. Typically, Kestenberg was able to convince the necessary government people, including the financial planners that his idea was viable and of value. The Kroll Opera opened in 1927 with a production of Beethoven's *Fidelio* which, in every respect, broke from tradition and routine. The conductor Otto Klemperer delivered a dynamic interpretation of the score while the youthful and willowy soprano Rose Pauly provided a Leonore more youthful, active and compelling than had ever been seen on a German stage up to that time.[2]

The event of 1927 which was of central importance for this book was the start of Kestenberg's working relationship and friendship with the grandson of Richard Wagner, Franz W. Beidler. Kestenberg was not all that interested in Beidler's Wagnerian lineage (son of Wagner's daughter, Isolde and her husband Franz Philipp Beidler). Far more interesting to Kestenberg was that Beidler was the great-grandson of Franz Liszt.

For several other reasons, Beidler intrigued Kestenberg. Beidler was an avid member of the Social Democratic Party, something that pleased Kestenberg as much as it horrified the ultra-conservatives of Beidler's family in Bayreuth. As Kestenberg got to know Beidler better, he also came to like and respect Beidler's wife Ellen, born Gottschalk. Not so with Beidler's Wagner relatives. They viewed Isolde's son as the black sheep of the family, for he had committed the unforgivable sin of falling in love with a Jewish woman, and, worse still, marrying her. Never mind that Ellen came from a prominent Berlin famiy. She was

---

[1] Kestenberg, *Bewegte Zeiten*, p.66.

[2] Rose **Pauly** - (1894-1975) - Born in Hungary of Jewish parents, she was a soprano who became an international star, especially in lead rôles in works by Wagner and Richard Strauss. At the Kroll Opera, she sang in Ernst Kreneks, *Der Diktator*, and in the world premiere of Paul Hindemith's *Neues vom Tage*. In 1937, she emigrated to the USA because of persecution by the Nazis. She sang leading rôles at the Metropolitan Opera until 1942 when an accident put an end to her career. After that, she settled in Israel, where she died in 1975.

the daughter of Prof. Dr. Sigmund Gottschalk, a renowned gynecological researcher and teacher in Berlin, author of books, and hospital administrator.

For the Wagners, social and academic status were things that could be of real interest only among pure Aryans. In 1927, formally or informally, all of the Wagners already had been supporters or members of the National Socialist Party for as much as eight years.[1] For Beidler, the political and racist radicalism of his family was disgusting. Their rejection of him and his wife merely strengthened his certainty that he was on a sound ethical and political path. Kestenberg had great respect for the strength of Beidler's convictions, all the more unique in a member of a family that was a proto-Nazi vanguard unit long before the birth of Hitler's party.

In 1927, after receiving his doctorate in Berlin, Beidler (and his wife Ellen) joined Kestenberg in the Prussian Ministry of Culture. They researched and created a yearbook, in which every aspect of musical life in the whole of Germany was recorded in impressive detail. The Beidlers were a great team. In their special project, her knowledge as a political economist and his as a writer, researcher, and statistician supplemented and amplified their individual gifts.

Down to small places in the remotest corners of Germany, the Beidlers compiled activities, participants, goals and contact information for musicians and ensembles throughout the whole country. They worked tirelessly in beginning and building an archive which, they assumed, would form a research basis for the creation of further yearbooks. Published in 1931, the one yearbook remains a model of how to research and present such yearbooks and continues to be a valuable source for historians seeking information on musical life in the Weimar years. In addition to his work on the Yearbook, Beidler became Kestenberg's personal secretary and right-hand man. Franz and Ellen also became close friends with Kestenberg's family.

The Yearbook of 1931 turned out to be one of the last of Kestenberg's great achievements in Germany and an equally great one for the Beidlers. But by the end of 1931, when the Yearbook was published, the writing was on the wall for Kestenberg and his progressive reforms. As extreme conservatives of various stripes gained ever more power on both the federal and state levels, leftists like Kestenberg gradually came to the realization that their days in government were numbered. Even Kestenberg and the Beidlers, however, would have been surprised to learn that the first Yearbook would also

---

[1] In Wahnfried, the Wagners' villa in Bayreuth, Hitler was already regarded as the coming German saviour and redeemer in 1919. This was before the founding the Nazi Party which grew out of the German Workers' Party (DAP) a year later.

be the last.

In hindsight, the collapse of democracy and of Kestenberg's reforms in Germany began, in embryonic form shortly after Kestenberg took up his government position at the end of 1918. In 1919, summoned to testify at a parliamentary inquiry into the Great War, General Field Marshall Hindenburg (1847-1934) maintained that Germany had been on the point of winning the war when traitorous forces on the home front betrayed the fatherland by surrendering, thereby stabbing Germany in the back. For many Germans who still worshipped Hindenburg as a hero, his invention of the myth of the national betrayal by a back-stabbing, seemed credible. After all, no enemy forces had ever entered Germany until after the peace which seemed all the more shameful and incomprehensible.

Adolf Hitler took up the legend of the dagger in the back and used it for his own purposes by elaborating on exactly who the forces were that had stabbed Germany in the back. It was the Jews, he screamed, as only he could, and the Socialists, Communists, and pacificsts. Having swallowed Hindenburg's lie, which was so comforting, many Germans also swallowed Hitler's, whose Nazi publications churned out endless attacks on Jews, leftists, pacifists, democratic thinkers and politicians and anyone who could be associated with the traitorous dagger. Gradually, through constant repetition of the lie, as well as harping on the ostensible injustice of the Versailles Peace Treaty, the Nazis convinced more and more people that the Weimar Republic was part of the betrayal of Germany.[1] These people came to see Hitler as the saviour who would bring down democracy and restore Germany to its pre-war glory.

As part of their campaign to bring down "the Weimar System," the Nazis attacked and slandered all writers, poets, composers, theatre people, and artists who regretted the First World War or who had not joined the army to fight in it. Under the Nazi term "as-

---

[1] During the Weimar Republic, conservative complaints about the Versailles Treaty were as fictional as the stab-in-the-back fable. It was the Bismarck who had established the precedent of heavy war reparations in 1871 after defeating the French. Instead of complaining, the French got down to paying off the onerous reparations and were done with them within a few years' time. Again, in March, 1918, the Germans imposed harsh terms on the defeated Russians in the Treaty of Brest-Litovsk. In his book on Germany's war aims, the German historian Fritz Fischer drew attention to the severe German plans with regard to the Benelux countries after the assumed German victory in the west. Even to this day, there are still German and non-German historians who give credence to the myth that the Versailles Treaty was unprecedented in its unfairness.

phalt literati" such contemporary writers as Stefan Zweig,[1] Max Brod,[2] Maximilian Harden,[3] Alfred Döblin,[4] and Bertholt Brecht[5] found themselves being accused by Hitler of being not only degenerates but also Jews, whether they were or not. Kurt Weill, the composer, and Brecht's co-creator of *The Three Penny Opera* of 1928 was a favourite target of the Nazis, both as Jew and as "degenerate" modernist.[6] Another prominent recipient of Nazi hatred was Heinrich Mann, whose outspoken support of the Weimar Republic so angered the Nazis that they declared him a Jew for the simple reason that only a Jew

---

[1] Stefan **Zweig** - (1881-1942) - Austrian-Jewish writer of great distinction. A strong pacifist, he eluded army service in World War I. After the war, he became an outspoken opponent of nationalism and an early proponent of a united Europe. In 1933, he wrote the libretto for Richard Strauss' opera, *Die Schweigsame Frau*. After the Nazis took power in 1933, they added Zweig's writings to the book-burning and *verboten* lists. He emigrated, first to England, then to Brazil, where he and his wife committed suicide in 1942.

[2] Max **Brod** - (1884-1968) - Born in Prague, Brod was a writer engaged in Jewish subjects including Zionism. His great passions were Franz Kafka and Leoš Janáček about both of whom he wrote many articles and several books. After the Nazi takeover in 1933, when he was added to the *verboten* list, he worked in Prague. In 1939, he emigrated to Palestine. His brother, writer Otto Brod (1888-1942) was murdered in Auschwitz.

[3] Maximilian **Harden** - (1861-1927) - Born in Berlin, Felix Ernst Witkowski, to a Jewish family; Protestant convert, 1878. He first dedicated himself to the theatre, doing significant work with Max Reinhardt in Berlin. After 1900, he increasingly wrote on contemporary affairs and became a prominent yellow journalist. Starting in 1906, he began outing in print the homosexual circle surrounding Kaiser Wilhelm II. This resulted in a series of court cases that brought Harden into the public limelight. In 1913-14, Franz W. Beidler's mother Isolde sought to prove in court that Richard Wagner rather then Hans von Bülow had been her natural father. Harden became involved in the scandal by pointing in print to the homosexuality of Isolde's brother Siegfried. The start of the war in 1914 and Siegfried's marriage in 1915 put a damper on the scandal.

[4] Alfred **Döblin** - (1878-1957) - German social critic, writer, and medical doctor. He wrote *Berlin Alexanderplatz*, one of the most famous German novels of the 20th century. He was active as a left-leaning member of the Social-Democrats. In 1933, he fled to Zurich, then Paris. He ended in the USA, working for MGM in Hollywood. After converting from Judaism to Catholicism in the USA, he returned to Europe after the War.

[5] Bertholt **Brecht** - (1898-1956) - Born a Protestant in Augsburg, he became the leading Marxist theatre director and author. After the Nazi takeover, Brecht moved to Denmark, then Finland, and the USA. He returned to (East) Berlin after the war. His international influence on 20th-century theatre was enormous.

[6] Kurt **Weill** - (1900-1950) - Like Kestenberg, Weill was the son of a cantor (in Dessau). He studied composition with Feruccio Busoni, 1921-1923. After the Nazi takeover, Weill fled first to Paris, then the USA, where he became an American citizen. He created a large number of works in many genres, some of them with great success.

would be capable of favouring the postwar Weimar democracy established in Germany.[1] Nobel Prize winners such as Albert Einstein and Thomas Mann also felt the Nazi lash, the former for espousing "Jewish science" and the latter for finding good things to say about democracy and about the Jews after he visited Palestine in 1930.

Among all these Nazi pariahs, Leo Kestenberg occupied a prominent place. They were driven to distraction by the fact that a Jew could have the power to reform the Prussian system of musical education while daring to advance the German folk-music sector and appointing modernist composers to teaching positions in Prussian universities and starting up the Kroll Opera House as a place for progressive, modernist, operatic productions. They also denounced Kestenberg's activities as a promoter of workers' concerts. Soloists at the Kroll Opera and in the workers' concerts invariably got anti-Semitic reviews from the Nazi house propaganda organ, *Völkischer Beobachter*, whether they were Jews or not. The mere fact of association with Kestenberg and his ideas got people labelled as Jews. This was the unanswerable, double-whammy which the Nazis always turned to in their scream-machine publications when other weapons seemed lacking in expolosive force.

Hitler and his movement did not limit themselves to attacking living figures such as Einstein and Mann, or Kestenberg. They launched all-out attacks on great Jewish writers and composers such as Heinrich Heine and Felix Mendelssohn, the same men whose works were burned in bonfires after the Nazis came to power. In attacking these great men of German culture, Hitler used the arguments developed by Richard Wagner in his anti-Jewish writings. As Jews, neither Heine nor Mendelssohn could be real Germans. They did not have that special German profundity of soul. Their racially inferior blood damned them to superficiality which both Wagner and the Nazis claimed to find in their masterworks.

As opposed to these Jewish artists, the Nazis claimed to find that the greats of German culture, figures such as Goethe, Schiller, and Beethoven, were creators whose souls were full of teutonic, Nazi-like depth and soulfulness. Like the Nazis, so claimed the Nazis, the Germanic artistic icons were in favour of unifying all German-speaking areas into one country. They were ready to support wars to achieve this noble goal. They despised Judaism and democracy and would have been followers of Hitler had they lived long enough. In effect, the Nazis sought to weaponize the heroes of German culture. Hitler tried to use the deputized Nazi heroes, Goethe, Schiller, and Beethoven, among others, as

---

[1] Heinrich **Mann** - (1871-1950) - Writer. Elder brother of Thomas Mann. His works contained biting social satire and criticism, and support for democracy. After the Nazi takeover he fled Germany and ended in Santa Monica, California, where Thomas Mann also made his home.

pillars upon which to build an edifice of nazified, purely Aryan culture which was as much a mirage as Hindenburg's legend of the dagger-in the back.

Obviously, fitting Goethe, Schiller, and Beethoven into the Nazi *Weltanschauung* was arduous work even for a Hitler or a Goebbels. Where they found a perfect fit in every way, however, was with Richard Wagner, the Wagner family, and Wagner's followers. Wagner's writings and those of his son-in-law Houston Stewart Chamberlain were prime sources for the theory of blood-racism so beloved of and crucial to the Nazi fanatics. The Wagnerites' decades-long radical racism was fertile ground for the acceptance and advocacy of the Nazi world view. The Wagnerites despised democracy, and, of course, rejected the Weimar Republic. Bayreuth's house writers, such as Paul Pretsch, Otto Daube, and many others of the Wahnfried Circle, were to be found in articles published by *Völkischer Beobchter*. As early as 1923, membership in the Nazi Party was higher in Bayreuth than almost anywhere else in Germany.

We know how intense Hitler's interest in Bayreuth was. We also know how uncomfortable the lot was of the few Jewish singers who performed in Bayreuth after 1924 — great artists such as Alexander Kipnis and Friedrich Schorr. We also know how total was Winifred Wagners's adherence to Hitler, Nazi fascism and the führer principle. As early as 1919, she and the rest of Wahnfried saw Hitler as Germany's saviour-to-be. Her loyalty only increased as the years went by and even continued almost unchanged after World War II.

Bayreuth, Wagner, the Wagners and their followers were one and the same as the Nazis, a perfect two-way street and a perfect fit with each other in every important respect. It will not do the pass off this connection by simply saying that Wagner had merely been used by Hitler. Wagnerism and Nazism breathed and moved with each other, were identical twins and clung to each other in an uncanny, symbiotic, loving embrace, like Tristan and Isolde: to the end and beyond.

In 1933, after Hitler became Chancellor and then won the last democratic election in Germany until after the war, Franz W. Beidler felt almost as driven to leave Germany as did Kestenberg. That is the point at which this correspondence begins. The exchange continues through the whole of the Third Reich and ends in the mid-1950s.

How many important and substantial Jewish and other anti-Nazi German citizens lost all hope after the rise to power of Adolf Hitler, who made it clear that Jews, Slavs, Roma, leftists, and gays were mere vermin? Like Kestenberg and Beidler, those leftists with high profiles in the Weimar Republic were immediately aware that their former lives had come to a full stop. They were like ants, stepped upon by a big boot from above. After a time, many simply waited in Germany for things to get better while they only got worse. Others fled, only to commit suicide in desperation at their inability to establish new lives in far-flung, foreign countries.

. Our two correspondents had advantages of birth, accomplishment, and inner strength which they were able to put to use in building new lives outside of Hitler's Germany, Kestenberg in Czechoslovakia, Beidler in Switzerland. Kestenberg had been born in Austria-Hungary and could therefore reclaim Czech citizenship. Beidler's father had been born in Switzerland. Franz W. was therefore a Swiss citizen. In addition, Kestenberg was a figure of international renown. The Kestenberg Reform was known and highly praised in the musical capitals of Europe. As Wagner's grandson and Liszt's great-grandson, Franz W. Beidler was also a public figure in Europe and abroad.

Both men fled Germany in 1933, Kestenberg only weeks after Hitler became Chancellor, Beidler some months later. The ways they coped with their difficult situations are gripping. Kestenberg almost immediately formed a plan and sought backing for a new international organization for the improvement and reform of musical pedagogy. He gained support from the Czechoslovakian government and applied his enormous energy to organizing international conferences, publications, and interchanges.

Beidler left for France in the summer of 1933, where he first spent some time with Thomas Mann, the Mann family and their circle of friends, all in exile. Beidler and his wife then left for Paris where they spent months trying to build a basis for a new working life. Beidler's letters bear witness to his energy in networking. As Beidler himself reported, everyone who was anyone in Parisian musical life opened their doors to this Wagner. But he was unable to make real inroads into the staid arrogance, inertia, and insularity of the Parisian musical establishment of 1933. In the end, Beidler had to seek a new life in Switzerland, the land of his paternal ancestors.

Throughout the correspondence of Kestenberg and Beidler, hundreds of prominent refugees are mentioned, each one with a different fate, each with a different strategy for survival. Also mentioned are the cultural quislings, the former co-workers in the Kestenberg reform, now Nazified apparatchiks. Kestenberg often mentions his special heroes, Feruccio Busoni, and Franz Liszt. For his part, Beidler often enough mentions his own family, the Wagners of Bayreuth and the Liszt descendants in Paris. Understandably, his remarks about the Wagners are coloured by his rejection of the Nazis.

One key aspect of life shared by both Kestenberg and Beidler was the central role of Judaism in both their lives. For Kestenberg, this was natural. His father had been a cantor in the two most important synagogues of Czechoslovakia, one in Prague, the other in

Reichenberg. Already as a child, Kestenberg was not only thoroughly conversant with Jewish customs and beliefs, but also avid about them. At the same time, like his father, Kestenberg developed a profound love of German music and literature. Once he was at home in Germany, however, he had to become thoroughly private about his Judaism. As already mentioned, the Nazis had declared open season on Kestenberg.

Like Albert Einstein and other Jewish intellectuals, Kestenberg, while supporting the Zionist cause, had qualms about Zionism and the chances of establishing a Jewish state in the Middle East. He was, after all, a convinced pacifist and universalist, someone who avoided all forms of particularism. Little could he imagine in 1933 how intensively his fate would be bound up with that of the Jewish state to come, the Land of Israel.

For his part, Beidler came from one of the most thoroughly anti-Semitic families in history. His grandfather, Richard Wagner, author of the influential anti-Jewish screed, *Jewry in Music* (1850, re-issued 1869), had been the most prestigious outright proponent of blood racism in Germany. He described Jewish blood as an "alkali" and played with the idea of the destruction of all Jews.

The line from Wagner to Hitler via his second wife Cosima and son-in-law Houston Stewart Chamberlain was direct. Not long before the failed *Putsch* of 1923, Hitler made a pilgrimage to Bayreuth and kneeled before Wagner's grave after paying a visit to Chamberlain. Beidler's mother, Isolde, was no less anti-Semitic and anti-democratic than any of the other Wagners. Despite that, Franz W. Beidler calmly and intellectually became a leftist, a democrat and a philosemite. As already stated, he married a Jewish intellectual in 1923, the same year that Winifred, Daniela Thode, and Eva Chamberlain and their circle became card-carrying members of the Nazi Party.

Beidler's letters to Kestenberg show his disdain for his family's political immaturity and the ever-greater crimes of the Nazis. While his family in Bayreuth rejoiced in their Führer and his misdeeds, Beidler expressed to Kestenberg his disgust and sometimes even his despair at the fate of humanity. Kestenberg was more controlled and circumspect in his letters. Even he, however, occasionally could not refrain from shooting a poison shaft in the direction of enthusiastic Nazis who had formerly been "guests at Pope Leo's table," as Kestenberg put it.

Through the ever-tighter strangulation of freedom perpetrated by the Nazis during the 1930s and after, Kestenberg and Beidler gave support and sustenance to each other in coping with the calamity and surviving in a poisoned world. Their correspondence mirrors the growing uneasiness and even panic caused them by Hitler and the other Jew-haters. Their letters are presented here in a faithful and complete English translation as a memorial to two fine exemplars of the greatness of German culture at a time when that culture was being defiled and destroyed by tyrants and thugs.

After the war, in 1953, when survivors were picking up the pieces and rebuilding Europe, international teachers of music in co-operation with UNESCO, decided to create the **International Society for Music Education**. Its first President, Arnold Walter[1] of Toronto, Canada, was a friend of Kestenberg's. In his activities as an academic and administrator, he proved himself Kestenbergish, as Beidler liked to say. In fact the whole idea of the ISME was Kestenbergish. The organization was built on Kestenberg's work, and, in recognition, the ISME made him its first honorary president.

Today, many members of the ISME know little of Kestenberg. A reading of his correspondence with Franz W. Beidler will provide ISME members with a detailed account of the gestation of the ISME, its pre-history, and its conception. The correspondence also shines a new and bright light on Franz W. Beidler's contribution to Kestenberg's work in staging three international conferences of music educators, in 1936 (Prague), 1937 (Paris), and 1938 (Switzerland). That these letters are available in English will allow ISME members and others easy access to the many insights contained in them about an aspect of organizational history that has never before been available to them, in English, in such detail. The legacy of Leo Kestenberg and Franz W. Beidler is very much alive today. In both style and content, their correspondence is of historic value and significance.

---

[1] Arnold **Walter** - (1902-1973) - musicologist, teacher, administrator, writer, founder of the Canadian Opera Company (Toronto) and Director of the Music Faculty, University of Toronto, 1952-1968.

Editor's Preface

I first met Franz W. Beidler in the summer of 1980. Friedelind Wagner had suggested that I contact him. "He's a funny, old guy who lives in Zurich, Isolde's son. You should talk to him," Friedelind said in her slyly uninformative, probingly ironic and willfully wrong-headed way. "Phone his daughter. Her name is Dagny. It's supposed to be Norse or something. Naming children with Norse names was all the rage back then."

She said Norse, I heard "Aryan". She said "back then," I heard "World War II." As I say, provocatively wrong-headed. In fact, Beidler had named his daughter after a close Norwegian friend, Dagny Sautreau,[1] something that Friedelind probably knew.

After having spent a year doing research in the Richard Wagner archive in Bayreuth as well as other archives, I was focused, among other things, on the story of the so-called *Beidler Prozess*, the court case brought in 1913 by Beidler's mother, Isolde, against her mother, Cosima Wagner, to prove that her father was Richard Wagner and not Hans von Bülow. Mostly, I wanted to hear what he had to say about his mother, whose birth in 1865 proved to be at least as fraught with unanswered questions as the birth in 1813 of one Richard Geyer.

At the time I visited Beidler in Zurich, I viewed his mother as not much more than a crazed Cassandra dominated by uncontrollable emotion. He did not see her that way. Asked to describe her, he more than once came back to the term "exotic." "I always saw her as a sort of enormous, lush, exotic plant," he said, gesturing upwards and outward with his hands to make me see the dimensions of this astounding plant. At the time, I only partially understood what he meant.

Beidler's parents were both highly emotional. His father was a masterful conductor, virtuoso pianist, and accomplished accompanist. Both technically and emotionally, he was an excellent interpreter of Liszt, Wagner, and other romantics. Beidler's parents had fallen in love while Beidler Sr. was coaching Isolde, who had taken singing lessons. Cupid's arrows found their mark while Beidler accompanied Isolde in Act One of her father's *Die Walküre*. She was a fiery Wagnerian, fully into the role of Sieglinde. He was a full-blooded musician. The rest, as some might say, is hysteria.

---

[1] Dagny **Sautreau** - (1876-1974) - née Dagny Bjørnson, daughter of Bjørnstjerne Martinius Bjørnson (1832-1910), Norwegian writer, winner of the 1903 Nobel Prize for Literature. Dagny Sautreau was an author in her own right. Beidler's daughter was born on April 20, 1942 and named Dagny Ricarda Beidler. Dagny carried the meaning "a new day."

After their marriage in 1900, both of Franz W. Beidler's parents often let their emotions run far ahead of their thinking. This resulted in any number of problems and "scenes." Perhaps because Franz W., who was an only child, was more in the company of adults than is usual, and because of his native intelligence, he rapidly realized that the way his parents lived their lives was not the way he intended to live his. His letters to his parents show a child who was more rational and intellectually organized than his parents. After his mother's death in 1919, Beidler completed his secondary education and continued on to earn a doctorate at the University of Berlin.

Many of my questions to Beidler in 1980 were about the court case of 1913-1914. Like most everyone else, he condemned his mother and her lawyer for taking up a legal battle that they had no chance of winning. What he never seemed to consider, or talk about, was that, in some ways, he was more the central figure in the case than his mother or his grandmother. It was his future and Bayreuth's that the court confrontation was meant to influence. In the end, German justice ruled against him.

The court decided, wrongly, that Cosima had conceived her daughter Isolde with Hans von Bülow rather than Richard Wagner.[1] With this stroke of juridical misjudgment, Franz W Beidler formally and legally lost his status as a Wagner. Nonetheless, Isolde's sister and brother, Eva and Siegfried, both born out of wedlock to the same father as Isolde, were treated as Wagners rather than von Bülows. Something was askew about this. It remains legally uncorrected to this day.

Both Beidler's pedigree as a Wagner and that of his daughter have been ignored by other, "more legitimate" Wagners on the basis of a court decision which they all knew,

---

[1] Of course, whatever the court decided was "right" and binding — legally. If it had ruled that Isolde was the child of Richard and Cosima, that would have been just as legally right. What was fact, rather than juridical right, was that Wagner was Isolde's natural father. That was shown in 1903 by Carl Friedrich Glasenapp (1847-1915) who, in the third volume of his Wagner biography, published a definitive assertion that Isolde was Wagner's child. What he wrote was definitive because it came from Cosima Wagner; after Wagner's death, she had played a strong editorial role in his work on all important questions. She even financed his project. In May of 1903 Glasenapp sent Cosima, who was in Lucerne, the galley proofs of his third volume for her approval. Her allowing the information about Isolde's lineage to remain can be traced back to a desire to legitimize Franz W. Beidler as a possible successor for Siegfried Wagner should he remain childless. By the mid-1990s, after the Festival Foundation had been in place for two decades, even Wolfgang Wagner referred to Isolde as "the first child that Richard Wagner and Cosima von Bülow had together." [*Akte*, p.60]. In deliberately lying to a court of law in 1914 (Isolde a von Bülow), the Wagners disgraced themselves forever, doubling their past infamy in cuckolding Hans von Bülow while shamelessly deceiving and making a fool of Wagner's great benefactor, King Ludwig II of Bavaria.

and still know, to have been wrong. When the offspring of Siegfried Wagner received around 13 million DM in "selling" their share of the Wagner cultural inheritance to the national and state governments of Germany, it did not enter the mind of a single one of them that Isolde's granddaughter, Dagny Beidler, Franz's daughter, might also have a claim to consideration in the settlement.

In the mid-1970s, when the structure of the Festival Foundation was hammered out, seats on the governing council were allotted to the descendants of Siegfried Wagner but none to the living descendants of his sister Isolde. In this, the Wagner family once again refused to accept their moral obligation to recognize Isolde and her progeny as Wagners with same rights as the other Wagners. By reliving the lies and betrayals of 1865, 1866, and 1914, the Wagners voluntarily descended deeper into the moral abyss in which they had wallowed for so long. As the ignominy of their behaviour becomes better known, the ethical dissonances in their story will continue to taint them almost as much as their shameful record during the Third Reich.

After Friedelind Wagner's death in 1991, a council seat was allowed to pass from Friedelind to a complete family outsider, her heir, who happened to be a British subject and an artists' agent, and therefore someone with a possible conflict of interest. Apparently, he was deemed to count more as a Wagner than Isolde, Isolde's son or her granddaughter. In many other respects, Dagny R. Beidler's Wagner relatives have treated her as a sort of Wagnerian asteroid, one that appears occasionally when the constellation is in Beidlerian alignment but which can otherwise be ignored on the basis of age-old lies and lack of familial rectitude.

If, in the 1950s, the Wagners who ruled in Bayreuth, the brothers Wieland and Wolfgang, had been more in tune with the Beidlerian alignment, they would have tried harder to fulfill their responsibility to a wounded nation which needed the Bayreuth Festival to cleanse itself of the political and racist sins it had committed before and during the Third Reich.

Beidler was different from most of his relatives. As far as the Nazi guilt of the Wagners was concerned, he had none. He was an intellectual, a well-educated historian of music, a life-long socialist, and a democrat. He weighed his words carefully and seemed a man very much in possession of his ideas and his emotions. Clearly, he was dedicated to clear thinking. He loved music, had a vast experience of it, wrote a lot about it, and gave many radio lectures on it. Entirely unlike his mother, Franz did not seem to be the type of person who could get carried away by emotion. Because of his calm and thoughtful demeanor, I was all the more impressed by three surges of controlled emotion that I witnessed while talking with him.

One of these outbursts was about the way, after the war, that Siegfried's children and their shoal of "formerly fascist" Wagnerians were allowed to continue their rule over the Festival in dynastic fashion, despite their intimacy with Hitler, his "movement," and the band of war criminals who were his followers. As we, unlike Beidler, now know, Wieland had a cushy "job" for a few months, in Bayreuth, in a satellite annex to the Flossenbürg concentration camp. This position was a *pro-forma* sinecure, invented for Wieland by his brother-in-law Bodo Lafferentz, husband of Friedelind's younger sister, Verena, to allow Wieland to stay in Bayreuth and continue avoiding military service during the last months of the war.

Beidler did not know this aspect of Wieland's biography, but he did express great disgust that, throughout Germany, and especially in Bavaria, old Nazis were permitted to continue in positions of power after the war as if nothing had changed. At the very least, Wieland had undergone a superficial personal experience of the concentration-camp apparatus. Perhaps it was this that motivated him, in the 1950s and 1960s, to confront more seriously his family's Nazi past than did brother Wolfgang, who seemed governed mostly by a desire to smother in silence any mention of his family's historical disgrace.

Another of Beidler's flareups occurred while he was talking about the time after the Nazis came to power. He described how, in mid-1933, he had received notice from the Nazi authorities, that he had been dismissed summarily from his job in the Prussian Ministry of Culture and would have no right to do any of the work he had previously done. To make matters worse, two years later, after he made a formal demand to the Nazi government to be relieved of his German citizenship, the Nazi authorities classified him as an *Ostjude*, a category of person applied mostly to Jews from Poland or Russia.

When he told me of this, Beidler seemed literally to implode in indignation and disgust. This threw me off completely because I knew that he was born a Protestant and remained so, officially, although practically an agnostic. What also confused me was that his enormous indignation seemed to apply more to his having been classified as an *Ostjude* than to the injustice of his being termed a Jewish German by the Nazis. He also seemed to expect me to understand his indignation over being classified as an Eastern Jew and to participate in this indignation.[1]

As I learned later, Beidler had left himself open to Nazi chicanery by marrying a Jew in 1923. While attending university in Berlin, he had rented rooms in the house of Prof. Dr. Sigmund Gottschalk. Not without historical precedent, Beidler had ended up falling in love with Sigmund's elder daughter, Ellen, who was a brilliant university student, specializing in political economy. In the Gottschalk home, Beidler found a real family for the first time in his life. The Gottschalks embraced him for what he was and he became a son, one with a positive understanding of Jewishness.

Why did Beidler react so strongly to the memory of this injustice, this gross libelling of him as an *Ostjude*? After reading his correspondence, especially with Jews, I observed how deep his feelings were — for his wife, for her family, and for their fellow Jews. On the other hand, the Gottschalks were anything but *Ostjuden*. They were a completely assimilated German family of an elevated academic background. As already mentioned, these were not refugees from the shtetls and ghettos of Poland but members of the upper crust of the Berlin medical and university establishments. Part of an upper-crust Jewish family, Beidler may have taken on a feeling common among many German Jews that they were a cut above their eastern co-religionists, both in culture (German) and language.

The third and most powerful of Beidler's explosions came when I mentioned Friedelind Wagner. "*Eine scherrrrreckliche Frrrrau,*" [a horrrible woman!] he roared with an intonation that seemed to start in the ground beneath him and rise like lava in a volcano, picking up speed and force as it rose. When I asked him why he felt such disdain for Friedelind, he attacked the book that she had published in 1944, *The Royal Family of Bayreuth* [entitled *Heritage of Fire* in the USA]. He found it an entirely despicable piece of trash and made no bones about his scorn for the author and her book. He found Friedelind's attacks on her family beneath contempt and unfair and her presentation flippant and lacking in any trace of style or cultivation.

I did my best to defend Friedelind. I had read the book before ever meeting her and

---

[1] Beidler's daughter, **Dagny R. Beidler**, has said that her father was listed as an *Ostjude* because the Nazis did not want a grandson of Richard Wagner to appear in the list of expatriated German Jews, something which would be read by many and might cause consternation. Rather, by putting him in the list of *Ostjuden*, which most Germans would not peruse, the authorities expected that his decertifiction as a German would go unnoticed. Furthermore, according to Dagny R. Beidler, her father actively applied to the German authorities to be relieved of his German citizenship because he was so disgusted at what had become of Germany under the Nazi regime. He wanted nothing more to do with it and celebrated when the German denaturalization was complete. (Personal communication, Dagny R. Beidler to Philip A. Maxwell.)

had loved her for the book, despite its obvious stylistic weaknesses. It was, after all, something of a propaganda tool on behalf of the Allied cause. But, with the exception of Ernest Newman's epic, four-volume biography of Wagner, Friedelind's book was the first piece of writing about the Wagners or by them that rang true to me in significant ways. I was grateful to her for revealing the intimacy of the Wagners with Hitler and the Nazis. I admired her for so bravely defecting to the Allies and for abandoning so fully her anti-Semitic upbringing, for trading the unique advantages of the Wagners in Germany for the life of an impecunious . Later I learned that Friedelind's book had actually underplayed the the intimacy of the family with Hitler and the Nazis in many significant respects.

On the one hand, Beidler, born in 1901 was a whole generation older than Friedelind (born in 1918). He was a product of a university education and much discipline, a product of an earlier world, one where manners, self-discipline, and noble comportment were personal priorities and points of honour. He had personal memories of his grandmother Cosima, and took her as a paragon of bearing and self-control, one to be emulated. Friedelind grew up in the more liberated era after World War I, without good examples to model herself on. She was wild, spoiled and unevenly schooled for most of her childhood. Even as a child, as already mentioned, Beidler was the most rational and clear-thinking member of his family. Friedelind was the most chaotic. Beidler had many good reasons to despise her. But I loved her for both her virtues and her failings, both obviously on display in her book. She could do no wrong as far as I was concerned, despite her predilection for doing so.

Despite their differences, Franz and Friedelind were united by their fixation on the downtrodden, the "underdogs," including the Jews. They both rejected many of their ancestors and those ancestors' belief in a mighty Jewish world conspiracy. Both chose difficult paths in following their convictions. They delved more or less deeply into the origins of anti-Semitism in Germany and into the Jew-hating psyche of Richard Wagner. Both Franz and Friedelind renounced personal benefit in turning their backs on the Nazis. After the war, they both continued to make sacrifices by swimming against the stream, drawing attention to the continuing presence of Nazis in high places. They demanded a reckoning with the past but did not often receive much satisfaction in this effort, not excepting from other members of the Wagner clan and its hangers-on.

Some years ago, Dagny R. Beidler allowed me access to her father's correspondence with Leo Kestenberg. (The collection consists of original Kestenberg letters and Beidler's carbon copies of his own letters.) I came to realize that these letters were of interest and significance. While reading, transcribing, absorbing, and translating this correspondence, I was greatly impressed. These were men who were dealing with the stresses of creating new lives outside Germany and coping with increasing Nazi threats to themselves and the world. They both approached their problematic existences with systematic concentration and inner strength. Their style of writing inspired me. Both were men of great culture and education. Both relied on each other for help and sustenance in difficult times. As the Nazi juggernaut grew tighter, their friendship deepened.

I had encountered Leo Kestenberg's name in accounts of the Weimar Republic. But from his personal letters to Franz W. Beidler, I came to know, respect, and even love a man whom I grew to see as a great German, a strong and immensely talented musician who epitomized those things that were unique and noble in German culture, those profound qualities that were ridiculed and despoiled by Austrian and German barbarians between 1933 and 1945. Kestenberg's letters also showed me that he was a magnificent Jew, the sort of man who personified the strengths and virtues of his co-religionists and their contributions to the culture not only of Germany but of the rest of the world.

That such a man could be hounded and persecuted by the Nazis would seem tragic, if it were not for the mass and scope of the Nazi crimes against other Jews and for the fact that Kestenberg and his family were able to escape the Nazi invasion of Czechoslovakia and find yet another new home, in Palestine. There is so much depth of feeling amid tremendous stress in these letters, so much deep friendship, and so much interplay of the great German and Jewish virtues, that I never cease to be moved profoundly by the written dialogue of these two men.

When I contacted Rachel Epstein, Kestenberg's granddaughter, who is an Israeli, I informed her that I intended to publish the correspondence in the original German and then in English translation. She expressed a preference that the work be published first in English, a wish that I was happy to respect. Through my work on her grandfather's letters, I feel that I have come close to a man whom I wish I had known personally. Through these letters, I am hoping that others will also come to know both these unique men, Kestenberg and his close friend and associate, Franz W. Beidler — as people, as musicians and musicologists, as survivors, as good Germans, as Jew and as philo-semite, as men who did not succumb to Nazi-induced desperation but who went on to live new lives in new countries and to find their places in a new world where they made new contributions to the lives of new people.

Abbreviations

Leo Kestenberg = Kbg

Franz W. Beidler = FWB

Richard Wagner Archive = RWA

1. 1933.05.11 — Kbg (Prague) to FWB (Berlin)

[handwritten]

Background:

Both Kestenberg's and Beidler's lives in Germany began to crumble months before Hitler's takeover of the government. Things took their first turn for the worse when Franz Papen (1879-1969) became Chancellor at the end of May, 1932. Although he remained in office for only half a year, he restored the right of Nazis to wear their uniforms publicly and roam the streets as they wished, violently when they felt the urge, which was often. Papen also virtually putsched the state government of Prussia, making himself the Commander of Prussia, the most important of the German states. Before being forced to resign, because even he was not reactionary enough, Papen eliminated the Art portion of the Ministry of Science, Art, and Education in which Kestenberg worked. On Dec. 1, four days after his 50th birthday, Kestenberg received notice that he had been retired, "until further notice," which, under the circumstances, meant "forever."

On the occasion of his birthday, Kestenberg received a panegyrical testimonial from Prof. Dr. C.H. Becker,[1] formerly Minister of Science, Art, and Education, and Kestenberg's immediate superior:

> ...The purpose of appointing you to the Ministry was to create a new, expanded, living environment for music in all its forms and renderings, with the help of government subsidies. With completely unprecedented scope, the cultivation of music was to become a state priority. With you, as with your [Social Democratic] Party colleagues, there were socializing tendencies present. But you did not give primacy to fulfilling longstanding Party goals. Rather you wanted to see the incomparable treasures and inspirational power of music, especially German music, made available to the broadest segments of the nation in the best possible performances. The whole panoply of diverse Ministry measures arising from this approach owe their existence to your initiatives: the reform of our higher institutions of musical learning, especially the Academy of Church and School-Music; the creation of an artistic examination authority; the greater emphasis on musical education of our young people in all possible schools; the governmental promotion of folk music (choral societies, popular concerts, the youth movement); the

[1] Carl Heinrich **Becker** -(1878-1933) - An expert on Islamic civilization an history, Becker was a Professor at various universities. From 1916 on, he served in various capacities in the Prussian Ministry of Culture, including as cultural cabinet minister (1921, 1925-1930). His humanistic goals and methods were a perfect match with Kestenberg's. Reform and liberalization of university education was one of his priorities.

founding of the National School Music Weeks; and the highly controversial regulation of private music instruction. In every area, you unavoidably had to engage in clashes with existing powers, traditions, and tendencies, a fate that no reformer can ever escape.

A man like you, was able to recommend to his Minister for appointment to leading positions such profoundly different composers, conductors and musical pedagogues as Schreker and Pfitzner [1] or Klemperer[2] and Furtwängler[3] or Jöde[4] and Moser.[5] In doing this, you demonstrated that, while recognizing all the political, artistic or pedagogical differences of opinion, what counted for you in serving the larger cause was solely the quality of the people to be appointed. …

For more than a decade, I was able to observe the efficiency of your organizational and artistic work in the Ministry. Certainly, as an artistic personality, you

---

[1] Hans Erich **Pfitzner** - (1869-1949) - Anti-modernist, German composer. He wrote the opera, *Palestrina* (1917). Although Pfitzner was very conservative, Kestenberg obtained a teaching position in Berlin for Pfitzner in order to achieve balance among the teachers of composition between the ultra-modern and more conservative tendencies of the time. Kestenberg recommended Pfitzner although he was an severe anti-Semite because he valued his ability as a composer.

[2] Otto **Klemperer** - (1885-1973) - Renowned German conductor of Jewish origin (converted to Catholicism, 1919). He was a protegé of Gustav Mahler and served as conductor and administrative director in various opera houses and orchestras. He was musical director of the Kroll Opera 1927-1931, where he performed contemporary works such as Schoenberg's "*Die glückliche Hand*, Janacek's *Aus einem Totenhaus*, Stravinsky's *Oedipus Res*, and Hindemith's *Cardillac*. He fled Germany in 1933 and became the conductor of the Los Angeles Philharmonic Oechestra. After the war he became famous for his recordings with the Philharmonia Orchestra of London. I his last years he returned to being a practising Jew.

[3] Wilhelm **Furtwängler** - (1886-1954) - One of the great conductors of all time. After World War I, having made steady career progress, he began reaching pinnacles in Vienna and Berlin. In 1922, he was appointed a permanent conductor of the Berlin Philharmonic. In 1931 he became musical director of the Bayreuth Festival. Unfortunately, Winifred Wagner fell out with him and shifted these responsibilities to Heinz Tietjen. Unlike many other of the best German conductors, he remained in Germany during the Third Reich, something which caused him some difficulty after the war even though there was not much love lost between him and Nazis such as Dr. Goebbels.

[4] Fritz **Jöde** - (1887-1970) - A musical pedagogue dedicated to involving young people in music. He took as his mission to create "singing youth," and "a singing population." He tried to instill in young people the belief that making music themselves was better than merely hearing it.

[5] Hans Joachim **Moser** - (1889-1967) - musicologist, musician, author (non-fiction and fiction). Father of soprano, Edda Moser. He lost his academic jobs in 1933 because the Nazi regime regarded him as politically suspect. By 1940, however, he gained a high administrative position in the Nazi propaganda ministry. He was a prolific writer on music as well as an active singer.

> had an individual approach and personal views. But in your official briefing of the Minister, you put your personal tastes aside in the general interest of a State that must exercise care in all possible directions. To single out only one factual example, you tried to support the artistic world as energetically as the folk music movement.
>
> During all of your efforts, you held true to a very specific, ever-present pedagogical ideal, one which you learned from the life and work of your master Busoni. I would describe it with words from the decree of May 25, 1925: "Education towards humanity with and through music." [quoted by Kestenberg, in *Bewegte Zeiten*, pp.78-79]

What Becker could justifiably have underlined in his letter was that Kestenberg had kept political and confessional criteria to one side in recommending appointments. In the case of the composer Pfitzner, for instance, Kestenberg recommended him for a teaching post despite Pfitzner's well-known radically anti-Semitic views. Kestenberg valued the composer's abilities as a musician; these abilities were paramount in deciding on his appointment.

Removed from his job at 50, and without any prospects in a Germany that was becoming increasingly inhospitable, Kestenberg took solace in his Minister's glowing praise. "With this letter in my pocket," wrote Kestenberg, "it was no longer so depressing to be left out in the cold." He turned back to practising diligently on the piano and polished up Liszt's B-major sonata, which he performed for the first time at the end of December at a benefit concert in support of the emigration of Jewish children to Palestine.

Only one month later, on Jan. 30, 1933, Hitler took office as Chancellor. "From then on," wrote Kestenberg, "night after night, I no longer slept at home. I had to request friends to allow me to sleep at their place because I received threatening letters every day and was subjected to verbal abuse by telephone and on the radio. In short, my life was no longer safe in Germany." [*Bewegte Zeiten*, p.79] As the famous piano-maker, Edwin Bechstein,[1] remarked in a letter to his Nazi friends in Bayreuth, relatives of Franz W. Beidler's: "What I hear is that all the Jews have already left Berlin."[2] Those Jews with foresight but not able to leave yet were packing their belongings in readiness for worse. Kestenberg was one of these. Franz W. Beidler and his wife were also active in ways that will become clear.

---

[1] Edwin **Bechstein** - (1859-1934) - One of the leading manufacturers of pianos. He and his wife Helene were early supporters of Hitler.

[2] From a letter of Winifred Wagner's secretary, Liselotte Schmidt, to her parents, Jan. 31, 1933.[RWA]

Throughout Germany, all the old Nazis celebrated wildly. Beidler's aunts, Eva Chamberlain and Daniela Thode, both members of the Party since 1923, were in ecstasy. Daniela sent the Führer a telegram: "God bless the great German moral victory."[1] Eva Chamberlain, widow of Houston Stewart Chamberlain, prophet of Nazi racism, wrote to a friend, "We want to greet the great event for Germany as a providential turning-point. ... Ach, if only the whole of Germany - including the Ostmark [Austria, Sudetenland, etc.] — will "awake" and we may see "the day" approaching." The "day" was indeed approaching. Hitler dissolved the Reichstag and called an election for March 5. People began to die in the streets as political violence rose, more than 70 dead by the election.

By mid-February, Hermann Goering, who had taken over control of "security" in Prussia, was directing the Prussian police to use their pistols against Communists. "Police who fire their revolvers in the execution of their duties, will be protected by me...but those who hesitate to shoot will be punished according to regulations."[2] Meanwhile, meeting with the 25 wealthiest industrialists on Feb. 20, Hitler proclaimed: "We are about to hold the last election." If he lost the election, he warned, he would remain in office "by other means...with other weapons."[3] Hermann Goering, at whose residence the meeting took place, chimed in: "...The election of March 5 will be the last for ten years, in all likelihood, indeed, for 100 years." As Goering made no secret of these sentiments to other highly-placed people, it is likely that Kestenberg was informed of just how deadly his situation was becoming. Only a week later, the immolation of the Reichstag by Nazis led to a further tightening of their death-grip on Germany. Berthold Brecht wisely fled to Vienna the next day, the same day that President von Hindenburg signed a decree curtailing civil rights. Only days before the election, Hitler's storm troops engaged in an orgy of violence. In Frankfurt, only two days before the election Goering announced: "My measures will not be crippled by any bureaucracy. I won't have to worry about justice, my mission is only to destroy and exterminate."[4]

After the Nazi victory on March 5, it was only four days before an anti-Jewish boycott was enacted. Communists and Social Democrats were brutally repressed. As Thomas Mann wrote to René Schickele on March 13, "How extraordinary! One leaves one's country to lecture on Richard Wagner in Amsterdam and Paris, and when one wishes to return, it has run away." Kestenberg observed matters worsening with dizzying rapidity.

---

[1] Daniela **Thode** [RWA]

[2] James Poole, *Hitler and His Secret Partners*, Atria, 1998, p.29.

[3] Manchester, William, *The Arms of Krupp 1587-1968*, Bantam, p.407.

[4] Toland, John, *Adolf Hitler*. Garden City, N.Y., 1976, p.303,

On the 17th, Jewish doctors were dismissed from Berlin hospitals. Jewish judges and lawyers were summarily shoved aside in Berlin and Breslau. "I simply couldn't bear [not being there]," wrote Winifred Wagner on the 20th, "and I had the good fortune of seeing Hitler twice — once I had a cozy meal with him. Fabulous how he is finally getting to take over."[1] The next day, she was a guest of honour at the enormous "reconciliation" show put on in Potsdam, a Kaiser-sized schmooze-fest between the old royalists and the new Nazis, between the Hohenzollern and the Sturm troops, between von Hindenburg and Hitler. What the royalists did not realize is that it was their last gasp. The Bayreuth Festival choir was there to make it all sound suitably harmonious, ecstatic, and almost believable.[2]

The last straw broke for Kestenberg on March 22, when he heard a speech on the radio. It was Goering as he opened the Prussian State Parliament. Goering's bullishly bellowing voice so disgusted Kestenberg that he decided there and then to take the next train over the border, to Czechoslovakia, the land of his birth and the home of his mother and some relatives. His wife and his younger daughter Rahel[3] were to arrive later. His older daughter, Ruth,[4] and her fiancé, Tunja Gladstein [17] soon decided to leave for Amsterdam, a dangerous undertaking because Tunja, as a stateless Russian, had no identification papers. In Prague, Kestenberg immediately set about laying the groundwork for a new international organization for musical pedagogues. Meanwhile, in Berlin, his wife Grete, together with friends, including the Beidlers, packed up the Kestenberg furniture and possessions so that they could be transported to Prague.

It was almost two months after his escape from Berlin that Kestenberg wrote his first letter to Beidler. The latter did not respond with any regularity, probably because it was best for him and his Jewish wife to remain as inconspicuous as possible, so as not to come to the attention of the Jew-baiters and mail openers.

---

[1] Hamann, Brigitte, *Winifred Wagner oder Hitlers Bayreuth*, München, 2002, p.234.

[2] Hamann, *Winifred*, p.236.

[3] Rahel **Kestenberg** - Leo's daughter, later Raquel Kestenberg-Vieira da Cunha (b.18 Jan. 1918, Berlin-2002)

[4] Ruth **Kestenberg**, later **Gladstein** (25.10.1910, Berlin-28 Feb. 2002, Haifa), eldest daughter of Leo and Grete Kestenberg.

1933.05.11 — Kestenberg to Beidler

[handwritten]

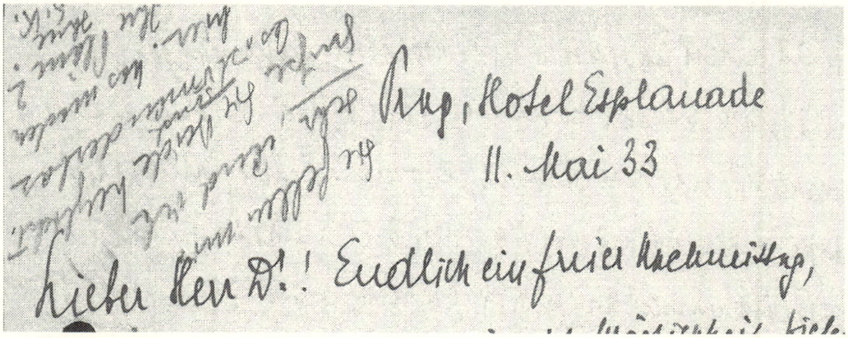
Prag, Hotel Esplanade
11. Mai 33
Lieber Herr D!! Endlich ein freier Nachmittag,

Prague, Hotel Esplanade
11 May 33

Dear Herr D !! [Doctor] Finally an afternoon free, offering the first, long-awaited opportunity to write to you — in tranquility and in ample detail. First of all, many thanks for your generous help in getting us moved out and winding up our affairs. Our things have been here for quite a while and are awaiting resurrection. Yesterday we found a flat where my mother lives. Of course, it will have to be finished first, since the building is completely new. As soon as we have changed our address, we will notify you immediately. — I'd like to save all general remarks for another, more favourable occasion; anyway, they would hardly offer anything original. — Still, I am very happy that our specialized organizational and pedagogical experiences of the last years can give me a certain basis for a new area of work. Here, too, the "Yearbook", with all its positive and negative features, may prove useful.

Naturally, as soon as my plans take on a really tangible form, I will give you more detail — the contours are already beginning to come into focus. Perhaps both of you [Franz and Ellen Beidler] will even be able to be of assistance again in the future; admittedly, still just a somewhat vague music-of-the-future idea. And that reminds me of your request for a letter of reference. I think that I'll have to wait until I have a typewriter to ensure that the impression made by the document is a bit more impersonal. In doing this, I intend to give recognition to everything that you achieved since 1927 and to go into the truly brilliant ability that you demonstrated as executive secretary [*Privatsekretär*], under all circumstances. Please write me whether you require the reference very soon or if it still has two weeks. — In Amsterdam things are unfortunately not alright since T's [Tunja[1]] residency does not seem secure yet. We are waiting on pins and needles to hear news that we hope will be favourable. Please send Prof. Alois Hába[2], Podvitami 68i, Prague-Kuste, the amount that my mother owes him (200 Marks) and which our friend, Hedwig S., will give you immediately. The only thing I ask is that you take care of this right away because Hába is waiting for it in urgent anticipation.

How are all our friends doing? What is Schünemann[3] up to and Hindemith, Moser and Jöde and my other "creatures"?[4] I would also like to know how Anneliese Landauer & Frl. Dr. [Isabella] Amster are. I'm also very glad to hear news about the rest as well. My wife asks Frl. Dr. Amster to forgive her for her somewhat unfriendly hastiness on the telephone. Frl. Dr. Amster will most likely have learned from you the particulars of what was happening. – I certainly do hope that you will come here one day, perhaps for work, or also sight-seeing. — Have you read the essay about Wagner by Thomas Mann?[5] I have seldom been so excited as by the way he formulates things here, even though there is plenty to criticize. When I have a chance, I won't miss the opportunity to treat Mann to a research seminar on Liszt's creative powers, on which, it becomes apparent from an incidental remark, he seems to cast a great deal of doubt. – But this brings me to the sorest spot of my otherwise very enjoyable existence here, so full of hope, so youthful and good-humoured: the lack of a piano for more than 2 months is very severely undermining my plan for autumn to give lectures on Liszt and I shall have to do a lot of catching up to regain my earlier, hard-earned technical level (unfortunately, we may not yet speak of a "pinnacle"). – My wife tells me just now that there could still be a few copies of Bückens "Handbook of Musicology"[6] at Mr. Katz' (bookstore), Kleist St. 29. [*marginal note*: They

---

[1] Tunia **Gladstein** - (Dec.25, 1905-Aug. 4, 1970) later married Ruth Kestenberg.

[2] Alois **Hába** (1893-1973) - Czech composer of microtonal pieces; teacher (quarter-tone scale specialist).

[3] Georg **Schünemann** (1884-1945) - worked closely with Kestenberg during the 1920s, especially on reforming music education in Germany. See note in Introduction.

[4] Kestenberg had appointed many of these people and others to important teaching positions in Berlin.

[5] "Sorrows and Grandeur of Richard Wagner." Delivered by **Mann** in February in Munich, Amsterdam, Brussels, and Paris. Its anti-Nazi content led to a strong, pro-Nazi public outcry and threats against Mann. Mann responded by removing himself and his family, permanently, from Germany, an action which made a strong international impression.

[6] Ernst **Bücken** (1884-1949) - music historian, university professor, editor of the Handbuch der Musikwissenschaft 1927-1934.

landed by mistake in the whole mess that he was so kind to take. Please tell him that after we have unpacked, we will think of his Lassalle[1]; that both crates still have not arrived at Amsterdam; that I am very anxious!!!] Have him give you these and say hello from us and put the whole work aside for me until it can be bound. After that we shall come to an agreement on where it will reside. With a thousand very sincere greetings to your dear wife and to you

Your old

LeoKbg

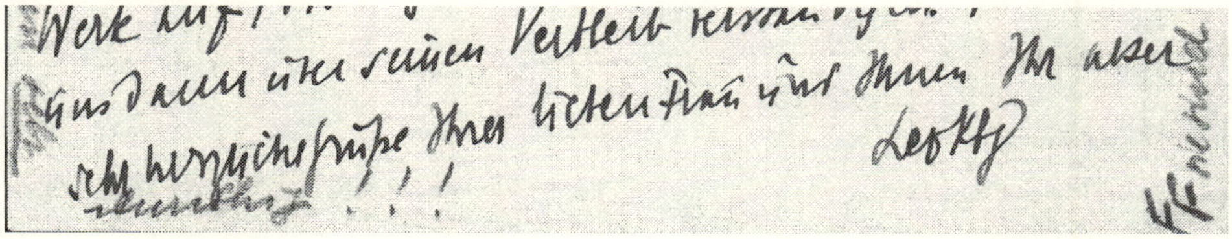

[In upper left corner of p.1, added diagonally by Kestenberg's wife, Grete, in pencil] I miss you very much and I send you both much love. Outside of that, it is wonderful here [in Prague]. How are your plans looking? Your G.K. [Grete Kestenberg]

1. KBG to FWB — 1933.05.11

[1] Ferdinand **Lassalle** (1825-1864) - founder of international socialism in Germany.

2. 1933.06.02 — Kbg (Prague) to FWB (Berlin)

[handwritten]

[printed letterhead]: Ministry Section Head i.e.R. Kestenberg

~~Berlin W8~~
~~Unter den Linden~~

Prague XIX — Dejvice č. 1646
19.VI.33

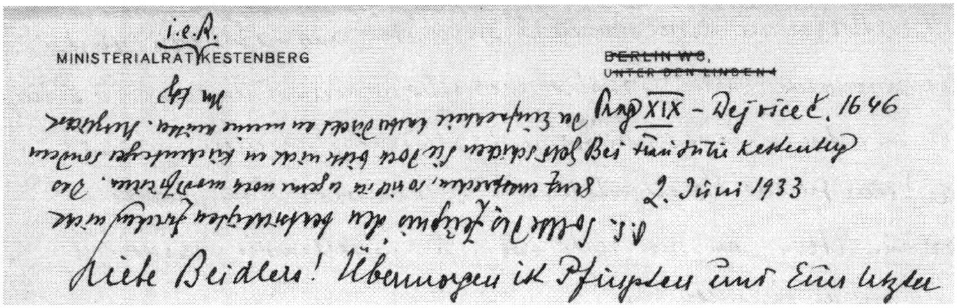
i.e.R.
MINISTERIALRAT KESTENBERG
~~BERLIN W8,~~
~~UNTER DEN LINDEN~~
Prag XIX – Dejvice č. 1646
2. Juni 1933
Liebe Beidlers! Übermorgen ist Pfingsten und Euer letzter

Dear Beidlers! The day after tomorrow is Whitsun and your last letter was from Easter! [not extant] Once again, I've got that feeling of helplessness, of the yearbook editor, who is unable to comprehend the inexcusably unpunctual work methods of others and, crying out for help, turns to the metaphysical terminology of race and blood in an attempt to find at least an excuse for such slothful writing habits. — But seriously, I am angry at you for paying so little attention to our solidarity and that all my efforts have been for nought. Through Hedw. and Elfriede I repeatedly had you reminded to write. Now, with this supremely personal, hand-written letter, I am again attempting to blow you out of your laziness as letter-writers. Ruth has been complaining energetically that she has heard nothing from you.

It could be that there is little to report. And the little that there is may not be of much interest. Presumably, there will not be much chance for us to meet in the near future. So I would find it very good of you if you would just write and say how you are doing personally, what you are up to, whether you are nearing completion of your Wagner book [Cosima biography] or if other plans have encroached.

Here, we are living in a very nice suburban area that is growing into a quarter for scholars, with an archiepiscopal seminary, technical academies, and student housing. Tomorrow, I shall finally get a piano so that I can once again practice and prepare my Liszt lectures. Otherwise, everything is still unclear and unsure. The plans that initially seemed on the point of realization, have now been set on a more generalized path and therefore have been pushed back somewhat.[1] Nonetheless, I am quite happy and only seldom afflicted by moods of depression.

And the archive?[2] How has the academy plan developed? Has the plan for rescue via Geneva been taken seriously? I believe that Matzke[3] in Breslau probably would be likely to do everything possible to make expendable the work that has been done up to now. I have received no recent news at all. Neither about Heinz[4] nor about our George[5] nor Hans Joachim.[6] But I assume that all of them are more or less fitting in.

A few days ago, we attended a really interesting opera premiere here, "*Dream Betrothal*" [*Verlobung im Traum*] by Krasa.[7] It seemed to come from a lineage that reminded us

---

[1] The "plans" Kestenberg refers to relate to starting up an international organization uniting all those, except citizens of Nazi Germany, who were involved in all aspects of teaching music.

[2] "Archive" refers to the collection of musical documents started by the Beidlers as part of creating the Yearbook of German Music. The further of existence of such an archive, created by socialists as it was, could only be uncertain, at best, in the Third Reich.

[3] Hermann **Matzke** (1890-1976) - music professor in Breslau - main interest: unifying the work of musicians and acoustic technicians.

[4] Heinz **Tietjen** (1881-1967) - in 1920s, became theatre general manager with the help of Kestenberg, in Breslau, then, 1925 Berlin (Deutsche Oper, 1926 Unter den Linden, Kroll Oper, 1927 all state theatres of Prussia). Artistic Director Bayreuth Festival, 1931-1944. Stage Director, administrator, and conductor.

[5] Georg **Schünemann**.

[6] Hans Joachim **Moser**.

[7] Hans **Krasa** (1899-1944) - Czech composer - died in Auschwitz. Composer of the opera, *Brundibár*, about the moral victory and existential horrors of children in mortal danger - performed 55 times in the concentration camp Terezin (Theresienstadt).

of the best years of the Kleiber[1] and Kroll[2] times. Otherwise, in this country as elsewhere, that era remains unforgotten.

Grete, Julie[3] and Rahel are in very good spirits and send best greetings to all of you. Could you perhaps get Miss Elfriede's agreement to send quick payment of the remaining amount to mover, Richard Kirchenberger, Prague I, Dlouha Trida II° 25? He is waiting for it on pins and needles.

And now the most heartfelt greetings of your half scolding, half affectionate "boss" L.K.

[Grete handwriting] D.[Dear] Beidlers — bad people — I'm also sending you greetings, supremely handwritten, from heart to heart and mouth to mouth! And I gave you Ruth's keys, also by hand. Please, please, please answer her. She is completely distraught because she sent you all her papers which she needs urgently in order to apply for her thesis exam. Please it's very urgent! Your Grete K!

[Kestenberg handwriting] P.S. If the "reference" does not completely satisfy its intended purposes, I shall be happy to modify it. Please do not send the money to Kirchenberger but rather, because it's simpler, directly to my mother. With best wishes, your Kbg

2. KBG to FWB — 1933.06.02

---

[1] Erich **Kleiber** (1890-1956) - conductor, director of Berlin State Opera 1923-34 - progressive; anti-Nazi. Father of Carlos Kleiber.

[2] **Kroll** Opera. From 1927-1930, Kestenberg was instrumental in turning this theatre into one of the most progressive institutions in Germany and an internationally renowned setting for great operatic productions. Conductor Otto Klemperer was the Kroll's director. In only four years, there were forty-four new productions, many of works by contemporary composers (Stravinsky, Janáček, Hindemith et al).

[3] Julie **Kestenberg**, Leo's mother, née Fischer (21 Sept. 1856), Rosenberg.

3. 1933.06.19 — Kbg (Prague) to FWB (Berlin)

Background

It would seem evident from Kestenberg's remarks that he might not yet have been informed, in detail, about the changes which the Nazi regime was pushing through in Germany, especially its program of "*Gleichschaltung*," meaning Nazification or total synchronization of all aspects of life under Nazi ideology and rule and total organization according to the so-called *Führer* principle. Kestenberg, for instance, seemed to still harbour hopes that the Beidler Archive could be continued in one way or another, somewhere or other, but, as might be expected in hindsight, such an archive, originating in Kestenberg's section of the Ministry, had absolutely no chance of surviving in any form.

By June, it becomes evident, Kestenberg had received a letter from Beidler, unfortunately not preserved. Although Beidler's letter evidently informed Kestenberg of some events, concerning the fate of the archive, for example, Beidler would likely have remained circumspect, simply because the Nazi regime of fear and spying was already solidifying its grip on Germany. Correspondence from this period, especially between Germans in Germany and those outside Germany, must be read flexibly in order to determine what the correspondents sometimes were hinting at and if they really meant some of the things they wrote, for their partners or for a government reader.

1933.06.19 — Kestenberg to Beidler

[handwritten]

Prague XIX — Dejvice č. 1646
19.VI.33

My dear Beidlers! Your yearning to see perfection of form in all correspondence reminds me vividly of my similar strivings with regard to Busoni[1] (But you are much better at doing justice to this aspiration than I was back then.) And it also reminds me of your fastidiousness in writing copy for the yearbook and questionnaires; in short, your only too familiar "persnicketiness" [*Mäklichkeit*] — an expression as imperfect in form as it is appropriate — with regard to all written statements, whether originating from yourself or from outside. This exquisite sensitivity, this severe, discriminating criticism is admirable during times of peace and enjoyment of life. But today, in the relationships of closely

[1] Ferruccio **Busoni** (1866-1924) - see note in Introduction.

aligned friends who depend on one another, this fastidiousness seems to me to be somewhat out of place. But now you have made up for a lot of this and my last cry for help, which I hope that you did not hold back from Elfriede, was already out-of-date.

First of all, I'd like to respond to your news, all of which was very interesting to me. The history of how the archive came to an end is not sensational. In bureaucratic life, this sort of dissolution is not a fate that is unusual. I am pleased that in Breslau [present Wrocław; Matzke was there] there is not already a wish being expressed, much less heeded, for immediately coming up with someone to assume the hereditary mantle. Are you not in contact with Prof. Stein?[1] In the past (Congress of Associations [*Kongreß der Interessengemeinschaft*] in Essen, where I invited him to give a presentation, then also after my lecture at the U.D.M.V. in Königsberg) he acquitted himself very well. It would not surprise me if he showed an active interest in the continuation of the archive, and if he even were to stand up for keeping on the same staff. Do you think that I should write to him after a respectable grace period? — The plan which you developed, or rather sketched out in the letter to the S.R.R. in Zürich pretty much shocked me.[2] This is because a core demand closely corresponds to a synopsis that I drew up at the end of March and which presents an important basis for projects that are ripening at the moment. (You see that I am now paying attention to questions of priority.) If everything goes well, I long ago started to give a lot of thought to the continuation of our work — perhaps also of our staff — and the establishment of strongholds in Geneva or Paris would be a second stage of utmost importance in going down this legal road — as opposed to the questionable way other, transferred, facilities have arisen here. But I hope to be able to report more about this in a few weeks. I find the stance you have taken in all these matters to be singularly upstanding and completely in accord with the stance we had up to now. This could also bear fruit in the future.

I will gladly be of assistance to your further efforts. I'll be very happy to write to Relative Pronoun [Einstein] after you give me the full particulars concerning the direction your plans are heading. He seems to have a special interest in young intellectuals. I also will make direct contact with the un-doubting Thomas [Mann]. But you must tell me — soon and, I hope, informally — what your aims are. — I am very grateful for all greetings and for being kept in close contact. I like to think of the grim but oh so gentle Hagen [Wagner, *Götterdämmerung*]. I would also like to know what our close colleagues in the music commission are doing, especially the wheeping man and the directorate of the associa-

---

[1] Prof. **Stein** - [??]

[2] S.R.R. - Swiss Broadcasting Society.

tion, old Curt [Sachs][1] in particular. Your reports about Heinz [Tietjen] were also not surprising. But his situation should become more favourable because of the appointment of Wilhelm F. [Furtwängler] What does Luischen have to say? And please, please write soon about what you learned during the closed professional visits that have been announced.

There is not much to report about us. I am working very intensively on my Liszt evenings. We're feeling very well and hope the far-reaching plans will come to some decision-making, by autumn at the latest. By the way, a mutual understanding with Thea [Dispeker][2] & Elfriede, perhaps also with Hedwig might be very desirable, about a further appeal in the question of quarter-tonal music and about other questions that are current here. I would be grateful if this could be facilitated soon. And now, heartfelt greetings to you and, for your long-awaited letter, many thanks from me, who thinks often of you both, Beideler and Beidelest (this is the result of my Czech grammar lessons),

your old L.K.

3. KBG to FWB — 1933.06.19

[1] Curt **Sachs** (1881-1959) - German musicologist. Emigrated to USA 1937.

[2] Thea **Dispeker** (1902-2000) - b. Dorothea Schlesinger; emigrated to USA 1938, where she became an opera agent.

4. 1933.07.05 — Kbg (Prague) to Beidlers

~~Prague XIX — Dejvice č. 1646~~
~~5 July 33~~

Dear Beidlers, you are to be the first who I am informing of the founding, a few days ago, of a "Central Office for Music Education" — admittedly with a plea that you keep this strictly confidential. Initially, I am merely being co-opted by the directors and any sort of practical or material consequences are not yet visible. But I nonetheless believe that it will be possible to continue the organizational efforts of the last years, that it will be possible to expand and enhance the course-work with external participants in multifaceted forms. I found your allusion to Capek[1] very valuable. But, up to now, I could not do anything with it because, oddly enough, he does not seem to have any connection to musical questions. In the circle of music historians, composers, and teachers, with whom I have dealings, nobody knows him personally. At any rate, I would very much welcome further material since the special duties will require contact with the responsible commission in Geneva to be established very quickly. Presumably all of this will not be able to happen before autumn, since, initially, the internal preparatory work will have to be completed before the official announcement can be made. Therefore also my request for confidentiality, which I — one tone higher — I repeat with a raised index finger and Lohengrin-like severity.

A few days ago the newly wed Isabella Eisenstadt visited us with her husband and brother-in-law. In spite of everything, she was charming and likeable, which I could not claim about her opposite number, appearing as he did in duplicate. But unusual times do justify many a violation of the usual boundaries. And why not the erotic ones as well? — We are very happy about the further application of quarter-tone theory by Mr. von Schönfeld.[2] But, for the quarter-tone authorities, we are still hoping for more eclectic inroads along this not so laborious path. — I am very eager to hear about how your projects are progressing. No matter where you land, I hope that you will stay connected to my future work, one way or another. I am already putting together questionnaires and striving towards a synthesis of your addiction to ponderous thoroughness and my cursory volatility. The scrupulous precision in matters of punctuation and the pristine state of all materials are also to be faithfully adopted. Whether colleagues can be found here, who personify all these virtues at once seems questionable to me. Everything here centres more on content than form. — By the way, I am still true to your great-grandfather [Franz Liszt], whom I serve for 6-7 hours daily. Let's hope that he accepts this service benevolently and

---

[1] Karel **Čapek** (1890-1938) - Very influential, 20th-century Czech writer.

[2] Mr. von **Schönfeld** - [??]

blesses it with success for this work. The Czechs love Liszt "with the warmth that is innate to them," (as M.M.[1] would say); perhaps the dependence on Liszt of the national music god, Smetana[2] (who properly deserves the honour), might contribute to this success. Forgive this undefiant (-perhaps also brainless?) letter and accept heartfelt greetings from all of us

Your old lion

4. KBG to FWB — 1933.07.05

[1] Max von **Millenkovich** (1866-1945) - pseudonym Max Morold - Austrian writer on music; director of the *Burgtheater* in Vienna, 1917-1918. Nazi from 1930 on.

[2] Bedřich **Smetana** (1824-1884) - Czech composer, looked upon by Czechs as the father of their national music. *The Bartered Bride*.

5. 1933.07.13 - Kbg to Beidlers

Liebe Beidlers,

die von Ihnen mit Recht so hochgeschätzte Chronologie soll

von mir nicht mehr verletzt werden. Da ich mich jetzt Ihnen

Dear Beidlers!

I shall no longer be offensive about the chronology [1] that you are right to value so highly. Since, through possession of a typewriter, I now feel almost synchronized [Nazi jargon — *gleichgeschaltet*]. In the future, I shall be able to be very good and respond to all your messages. First of all, I want to respond to the complex: League of Nations-Commission and Intellectual Cooperation, which you touched upon in your letter of June 20. [letter not extant] Everything that I have heard of this up to now is as good as unusable for our work. When I visited Coeuroy[2] and Dr. Picht, naturally also Dr. Rotbart[3] in Paris in 1927, I spoke about these questions. All three told me that they had nothing to do with musical questions in an official capacity. Coeuroy works privately for an international archive for gramophone records. As far as I know, the League launched only one large inquiry which, if I am not mistaken, you drew my attention to at the time. I am not able to discover any relationship at all to the ideas which I had as sanatorium prior in Fürstenberg. So, I have to rest on my own grandeur, or, as my ancestors would have said: "Even if you explode!" ["*Und wenn Sie zerplatzen!*" - Yiddish] Now, too, I do not yet believe that anything serious is happening there and I still plan to work from here to win over these somewhat plodding blocks. Naturally, I will not omit putting into play the good relationships that function here with virtually automatic certainty.

But now for something personal: should I still write to Thomas [Mann] on your be-

---

[1] chronology: Kestenberg pokes fun at Beidler for the latter's supposedly prim concern about who owed whom a letter of response, whose turn it was to reply.

[2] André **Cœuroy** (Jean **Belime** - 1891-1976) - Studied with Max Reger. Founder of *Revue musicale*, with Henry Prunières, editor-in-chief 1920-1937. Head of the musical section of the League of Nations, 1929-1939. Author and translator (German to French) of many books on musical subjects. (*Music et littérature*, *Appels d'Orphée*, *Wagner et l'esprit romantique*) He was interested in modern developments, such as jazz on records and radio.

[3] Dr. **Picht**, Dr. Grete **Rotbart** - Like André Cœuroy, they worked in the German section at the League of Nations in Paris.

half? I don't understand your twists and turns with regard to this. Previously, when I wrote something about a relative pronoun, I was thinking of the relativity man [Einstein] and I wanted to hear from you if there was any sense in my writing to him on your behalf. But you did not even [last line runs off of the carbon copy]

By the way, I would like to say right off that I view Béla Bartok [1] as an extremely worthwhile collaborator and, as very important for my plans. Paul Bekker [2] already gave him information in Florence and he seems to be interested in the progress of my plans. He is also a very zealously active collector of Slovakian folk songs and, even from this standpoint alone, is very esteemed by authorities here.

I found your letter to Heinz [Tietjen], in its present form, not very heroic. You've known him long enough to know that he is marked by a sensitivity that is especially strongly developed and that he does not have the slightest tendency to actual or even pretended hooliganism; but even more to the point, that he, in any case, is incapable of asserting his will in his own workplace. So what is the point of reminding him of his own weakness by more or less gruffly poking him in the ribs? I am convinced that he suffers greatly from this sort of attack from a quarter that he viewed as benevolent, and this touches on the whole tangled mass of recriminations relating to the previous era [Weimar Republic] and which is connected to Hans J.'s [Moser] daily work and equally with Heinz' position. But there is no sense in always bringing up the question of the hen and the egg, disputes which seem to me at this moment of time no longer, or not yet, topical.

If there were a possibility here of establishing for you a viable livelihood, you could be my Number One here and also my best associate! I am preparing a work on the ideas of humanity in musical pedagogy (but please: do not say anything more about this, because of priority!), for which you would certainly be able to find wonderful materials in the libraries here and drag them over for me. So, as it is, I am forced to search for myself. I have already found various things that are of utmost importance to me. I hope that it will become a respectable work that also can have contemporary appeal, especially because we have to assume that my previous "loyal colleagues" will soon be bringing forth contrary evidence. I am looking forward to preempting them.

---

[1] Béla **Bartók** - (1881-1945) - important Hungarian composer, concert pianist, and ethnomusicologist.

[2] Paul **Bekker** - (1882-1937) - an influential German music critic and author, as well as a conductor and theatre director. In 1925, with the backing of Kestenberg, Bekker became director of the Kassel State Theatre, and was director of the State Theatre in Wiesbaden, 1927-1932. He left Germany in 1933 because of the Nazis. Author of many books, including a biography of Richard Wagner (1924). He died in New York.

I received Hilde's [1] letter and that of Schönfeldt [sic] with many thanks. But I am still awaiting more news! Naturally, I have a very lively interest in the Spanish Cultural Federation. I'd like to ask you to tell me more about it because I have heard absolutely nothing relating to it from anyone here. That is no miracle, however, since we live on the periphery, in a district of villas and know only Franz Liszt and Comenius[2] here, two good masters, but both long dead. Write very soon and in detail about everything, also about whether you have already made your visits to the musical people. I would very much like to learn how Dr. Böttcher[3] is doing. I really miss the various periodicals, especially his. It would also be very important for me to find out if anything at all has been changed in the edicts [*Erlassen*] or if there is any prospect of change.[4] I have also not yet heard who is now the Chairman of the State Examination Commission for private music teachers and what its present make-up is. Maybe it would also be possible to find out how many candidates participated last time and what the results of the examination were. I would find news about all of these questions, and generally about the whole complex very desirable. What I do know is about the [Nazi] synchronization [*Gleichschaltung*] of the Association, about the change of the directorate of the Association and that Ebel[5] has remained as one of the secretarial chairmen. Perhaps you could find out further details.

You recall the Bourgeois Gentilhomme and his moods with respect to assignments? I'm reminded of him now because my eminent benefactor and employer now wishes that, at the moment, I should refrain from writing about the humanity idea but rather about a theme which I had mentioned to him: about Franz Liszt in Czechoslovakia and about his influence on composing here. Your collaboration on this would be especially valuable. Can you tell me anything that relates to the relationship of Liszt and Smetana? I want to

---

[1] Hilde - probably Hilde **Grunwald-Groening**, secretary of the archive under Kestenberg's direction.

[2] John Amos **Comenius** - (1592-1670) - Jan Amos Komenský (Czech/Slovak), Johann Amos Comenius (German) - Czech teacher and author, considered the founder of modern education, therefore a Czech hero. He wrote *Didactica Magna.*

[3] Hans **Boettcher** - (1903-1945) - co-editor of the journal *Musik und Gesellschaft* which was published only in 1930. With Ernst-Lothar von Knorr, Boettcher directed the public music school at Neukölln in which Paul Hindemith taught on a voluntary basis.

[4] Kestenberg had brought in a series of decrees by which practices in all aspects of music pedagogy were reformed and standardized.

[5] Arnold **Ebel** - (1883-1963) - German composer and music padagogue. Member of Nazi Party 1937. Karajan conducted an overture by Ebel in 1937. Ebel wrote various marches and war songs for the military. After the War, he continued composing and belonged to the leadership of various musical organizations. The city of Leipzig awarded him its Mendelssohn(!) prize in 1959.

get everything available here in newspapers and journals about Liszt's concerts in Prague, Bratislava and Brno (1840 and 46). I also want to pursue the origins of the Hussite song and the Slavic hymn. Perhaps you can also get hold of some material. Orel[1] wrote a small book on Liszt in Bratislava. I shall get it here too. Maybe you will yet come up with things I do not know. Now I'm just waiting to hear that I am supposed to write about the humanity idea in musical pedagogy and Franz Liszt in Czechoslovakia at the same time!

Don't be critical of the lady typist, [marginal mark F]
most heartfelt regards
Your

LK

[Other handwriting] Sincerest greetings to both of you!

from the Palestine child.[2]

F [marginal note re: typist by Grete K] who I was not this time, but only "a stand-in." We are hoping that your plans succeed — much, much luck! Your old G.K.

Please give greetings from us to Frau Mama

5. KBG to FWB — 1933.07.13

[1] Dobroslav **Orel**, *Františék Liszt a Bratislava*, Univ. Komensky, Bratislava, 1925.

[2] **Palestine child - Rahel**, Kestenberg's younger daughter, an avid Zionist who would make the *aliyah* to Palestine in 1934.

6. 1933.07.17± [undated] — Kbg (Prague) to Beidlers

[on stationery of Esplanade Hotel, Prague]
Prague XIX - Dejvice č. 1646

Dear Beidlers!

Your melancholy but angry farewell to the archive brings back vivid memories of the time of its founding and the hopes that were tied to its creation. Like much of what I began, the "Yearbook" was a project meant for far-off in the future. Actually, it floated before us with clarity only as a "sketch", whereas, for me, its accomplishment did not worry me much at the time of its first draft. A crucial mistake, even though admittedly often an advantage: this saying B before thinking of, or, better, deliberating with clarity about A. This is what then generated the principal difficulties in carrying out the practical work; that and also the lack of a unified treatment of the material, which is to blame for what seems to me the compelling necessity for standards that are across-the-board for all of the material. But mistakes are present and they can be corrected next time. And I am convinced that one of us will have the opportunity for a similar work, even if under completely different conditions. The "male instinct to play," this mighty motor, the all-encompassing significance of which increasingly impresses me, will guarantee this. But for our archive, the fiction of a cohesive music-phalanx was also an implicit precondition and this cohesiveness and profound bond, born out of expediency as a free choice, [were] recognized and obeyed. This has now been outwardly accomplished. But I do not believe that there will be immediate success. It seems to me that for our work, and yours especially, everything is lacking. I cannot see anyone who wants to take up the intellectual legacy, who perceives and moulds the living, organizational context into an artistic form. Schünemann needs an idea-person; he would have what is needed to master it technically. Matzke would have neither the one nor the other. And all the others do not see what the words are meant to mean, let alone that these people should continue what we began. Perhaps H.J. [Hans Joachim Moser] could be considered, this whizz kid and know-it-all, who, however, would tackle such a thing only at the instigation of a publisher.

For better or worse, we shall have to get used to the archive, too, falling into a Sleeping-Beauty slumber until the mythical prince shows up to awaken it. Now, in this retrospective — you know that I have no talent for history, especially for that of the most recent past — the only thing remaining is to think with gratitude from the bottom of my heart for how you both came to terms with this work [the yearbook, the archive], how it very soon became "yours," with what glowing fervor you protected and raised the adopted child, against the frequent lack of comprehension of the often indifferent and negligent natural father. Admittedly, that was mostly just the outward appearance; for, essentially, it was a pet child which was only born in a harsh time, and much too late to grow up in accord with the original hope. Now that the "child" has been taken from us, all these thoughts must be silenced and, for the three of us, there should remain only a profound feeling of satisfaction that it was born at all and that we have its existence to thank for much profound enrichment and insight. I won't be intoning a "Requiem", because I have a staunch belief in a continued growth or a reawakening.

Someday, later, someone must put together the story of everything fundamental and almost historical and philosophical that stood as godfather to the Yearbook and the archive. Perhaps that is already the theme for the "preface" to an International Yearbook 193_?

And now everything else. I wrote immediately, in detail to the Relativity Man. I shall also contact Thomas [Mann] and everyone else on your behalf. As soon as my "position" here is secure and officially established, everything will be much easier. I hope to be able to help you in a much more energetic way. But we have to "count on" at least one transitional year. You need at least that long probably to readjust, spiritually and materially.

From Susanne Trautw.[1], I had a very detailed, worried letter from the Hague. It contained really interesting comments about professors. Please pass on my very warm greetings to Tiessen[2], Sachs [Curt], Wolff[3] and all the others who are still favourably disposed. So you think that I should write to Eb.Pr.? [Eberhard Preussner[4]] I would very much like to receive the "Musikpflege" here regularly. I did not find the volume that you sent at all terrible. Completely the opposite. The critique of "Katz" and other things actually excellent. Has the Allg. Musik Ztg. [*Allgemeine Musik Zeitung*] crossed your path? My life here, without the usual extreme attacks seems almost too English. [a pun: *engelisch*=angelic][5]

---

[1] Susanne **Trautwein** - (1886-1933) - music teacher.

[2] Heinz **Tiessen** - (1887-1971) - German composer, one of the talents appointed to teach in Berlin during the 1920s by Kestenberg - (others: Schreker, Busoni, Hindemith, Schönberg, Jöde, Pfitzner, Kaminski).

[3] possibly Theodor **Wolff** - (1868-1943) - editor-in-chief of the Berliner Tageblatt.
possibly Hermann **Wolff** - prominent agent for artists in the field of classical music
possibly Dr. Friedrich **Wolf** - (1888-1953) - medical doctor, writer, leftist politician.

[4] Eberhard **Preußner** - (1899-1964) - German in musical pedagogy. Editor of the publications, *Die Musik* and *Die Musikpflege*, Preußner worked with Kestenberg at the Berlin Central Institute for Education and Teaching.

[5] During the 1920s and early 1930s, when Kestenberg played a central role in German musical life, he was constantly exposed to threats and attacks by the Nazis.

I am very eager to hear what you gabbed about at Dr. Hans B.'s.[1] Perhaps you could arrange to have "his" publication sent to me — if it is still his. And since I am making such inquiries, I should like to give expression to a heart's desire. After I am once again in the money, I would love to stop up the veritably sinful gap in my library and obtain all the letters to and from Liszt, Wagner, and Bülow that have appeared in print. I have nothing, except Wagner-Liszt. If you ever hear of antiquarian bargains, please keep me informed. Actually, I am very grateful for every tip, every note, every piece of information. For the time being, I sit the whole day at the piano, read only ancient books and learn only the barest of details from the newspaper. Otherwise nothing. An exquisite situation, admittedly, but one which could stand some spicing up with a bit of salt and pepper.

For Ruth's *Exmatrikel*, many thanks. [The document given when a student leaves a university.] Painfully, Tunja's future is once again completely uncertain. Perhaps he will have to try to come here. We are waiting by the hour for a call from him. —

Today's official telegrams gave me lively reminders of our days in Bayreuth, of our friends from there, of proper and disguised canine [*hündisch* - also means "cringing"] escorts of the erstwhile Landgrave. [possibly a reference to a local Nazi] Are relations with the illustrious house [House of Wagner, Wahnfried] entirely dissolved or is Wini [Winifred Wagner] permitting herself to condescend to corresponding with illegal relatives?[2] But I have no wish to be indiscreet and do not wish to know anything of this with any precision. Please remain true to your resolution and confirm it immediately, at least via postcard to me, who sends you both very warm greetings

L. and G. [Leo and Grete]

P.S. So that there is no misunderstanding: to those named in your letter of July 15 [not extant], especially Bartok, I shall be writing to them in the very next days. I only want to wait for an interview that I'll be having here on the 24th of this month and because of which I have to contact him.

By the way: Did the meticulous archive also collect the personal statements in the press abut the "Chef" over the last years? Miss Rdf [Rudolf] sent me all the volumes that I had obtained in the pre-war years but which did not touch at all on my professional

---

[1] Hans **Boettcher** - the publication: probably *Musik und Gesellschaft* (1930).

[2] "**illegal relatives**" - Although Beidler was demonstrably a natural grandson of Richard Wagner, a German court ruled in 1914 that his mother Isolde had been the natural daughter of Hans von Bülow, Cosima's first husband. Because of this ruling, in the famous Beidler case, Franz W. Beidler lost legal claim to being a Wagner. Kestenberg could therefore call Beidler an "illegal relative" of Winifred Wagner's, in a joking way.

work during the "14 years". Irresponsibly, I did not bother about this at all and Frl. Rdf. never began or implemented anything without a direct order. Now I'm missing the friendly and hostile accompaniment parts. [*Begleitstimmen*] But perhaps you at least have the articles by H.H.S.[1] and A.E.,[2] which appeared in November. The A. M. Newspaper Collection [*A.M.Ztg.-Sammlung*] will have to be obtained sometime in the future.

6. KBG to FWB — 1933.07.17±

[1] likely Hans Heinz **Stuckenschmidt** - (1901-1988) - German music historian, critic, and composer.

[2] likely Alfred **Einstein** - (1880-1952) - German music historian, critic, editor, and influential writer.

7. 1933.08.19 — Kbg (Prague) to Beidlers

Prague XIX, 19.8.33.
Prague XIX Dějvice č 1646
[Kestenberg handwriting]

~~received 27.8.33. Sanary-sur-Mer~~
~~answ'd. 28.8.33~~
[Beidler handwriting]

Dear Beidlers,

In your last letter, which I received August 3rd [not extant], you held out the prospect, with some certainty, that you would make your departure "next week." You then outlined your travel schedule quite precisely and indicated that you wanted to stay in the vicinity of Thomas [Mann] for about 2 weeks and then be in Paris at the beginning of September. I therefore delayed answering your letter because I assumed with certainty that you would promptly inform me of your holiday address. Today, my wife received a card from Hedwig. It emerges from it that you are still in B.[erlin] and that you complained of not having received an answer to your letter. — I found your last letters [not extant] in particular to be extraordinarily valuable but I wanted to respond to them in detail and was waiting for the new address. So I make the urgent request that you write immediately to say if your travel plans have changed or whatever else is happening. — In the meantime, I received a very amiable letter from the relativity man [Einstein], one that, at any rate will be of great use to you. Naturally, he can put his help at your disposal only when a concrete position is in question, one for which he can recommend you. — It would be very good of you if you could write and say if State Secretary Lammers[1] is still in office. I would also like to have more detailed information about Dr. Weber[2], whom you mentioned as being friendly. Everything that you tell me about your future activity is of the utmost importance to me! — Here, I've had a very quiet and undisturbed working phase, that I indeed spend mostly at the piano. Almost everyone has left town and hardly anything will happen before the beginning of September. A few days ago, I received from Min. Rust[3] the official notification that, as of July 31, I am dismissed from the civil service and that a further directive should follow about my remuneration. This form-letter was to be expected as a

---

[1] Aloys **Lammers** - (1877-1966) - German lawyer and civil servant. From 1925 to 1933, he was Prussian State Secretary in the ministry of Science, Art, and Public Education

[2] perhaps Ludwig **Weber** - (1891-1947) - German composer who wrote music for the youth movement in the German music of the 1920s. Kestenberg was active in promoting this movement.

[3] Bernhard **Rust** - (1883-1945) - Joined the Nazi Party in 1922. Minister of Science, Education and National Culture in the Third Reich. The UN War Crimes commission indicted him for "human guinea pig" vivisection. Rust committed suicide.

result of the Law for the Restoration of the Professional Civil Service [*Berufsbeamtengesetz*].[1] — I am often asked here about literature concerning methods of teaching music in advanced institutions of learning. Teachers here believe that crucial books on modern forms of teaching have appeared in the last ten years. I regret so much having to disappoint them time and again in this matter, since everything that I have seen here of such methodical works (e.g. Rabson-Burkhard, Ast, etc.) does not contain what the people here expect. They just believe that a sort of literary Nuremberg funnel[2] has been created. If you should come across anything at all in this area, I would be very grateful if you would send me word about it. — I regret very much that I'm missing volume 52 of the Weidmann pocket edition of the little book that I edited entitled, *The Teaching of Music in Prussian Schools*. It contains the position paper of 1923 and the guidelines for the various categories of school. If you possess it or if you can get a hold of it anywhere, I would be much obliged if you could send it here. In the worst case, I might turn to the publisher for help. — The printed materials that have been sent me are doing excellent service, especially the volumes of the Composers' Association [*Tonkünstler-Verband*]. I have taken in, with concentrated comprehension, all the notes you marked. Many thanks! — I am reserving a more in-depth treatment of all more general questions for later, after I know your immediate plans. That is why I am asking you to excuse the somewhat provisional character of my letter. Later, I shall send you a lengthier outline of mine from which you will be able to learn fuller particulars. I am absolutely depending on you to send news of yourself immediately so that I can fill you in further.

With all the very best greetings, also from my wife and from Ruth and Rahel — also from Granny —

Your old
L Kbg

[Ruth handwriting] special greetings from Ruth,

I may stay here. T. [Tunja] may also come. It would be so fine to see you again.

7. KBG to FWB — 1933.08.19

---

[1] "**Professional Civil Service Law**" - enacted by the Nazis April 7, 1933. One of the first laws enacted in the Third Reich, this eliminated Jews and other "enemies" of the Nazis from the civil service and, in practice, beyond. Civil servants who could not prove pure Aryan lineage were fired or pensioned off. Pensions were soon enough reduced or eliminated.

[2] Nuremberg funnel. A joking metaphor for mechanical teaching and learning, consisting as it does, of connecting a funnel to a student's brain and filling the funnel with facts, theories and knowledge, all of which move effortlessly into the brain in question.

8. 1933.09.01 — Kbg (Prague) to Beidlers

1. IX.33.
Prague XIX, Dejvice č 1646. 1. IX.

My dear Beidlers,

Finally on the afternoon of August 29 the first long yearned-for news from you, from freedom, arrived! [not extant] And the joy that you too are in a safe place is stronger than the small annoyance over your bout of bluster, which, as usual, was absolutely groundless. However, for starters, I have by now learned enough from your historical objectivity to determine that in your long letter of August 1, you very emphatically wrote that you wanted to leave Germany in the same week etc. etc. — That is no longer current since, happily, we now have received from you the definitive explanation of your silence. I hope that, from now on, we shall be able to remain in close and uninterrupted contact.

I found the thorough and droll description of the prelude to your departure very interesting. The whole process shows that not every hope must of necessity disappear. Be that as it may, I am, at any rate, very happy that you were able to get out — half pulled, half pushed — because, without this unforeseen incident, you probably still wouldn't have made the decision to do it.[1]

It was a splendid idea of yours to set off immediately to Thomas Mann.[2] You know that I have held him in especially high esteem for an eternity. Without a doubt, he is the strongest and most significant spirit in contemporary Germany and it is for all of us a matter of special pride that he too lives outside the borders. I shall never forget an evening at Preetorius' in Munich[3], where Mann, together with wife and daughter, were present and where, for the first time, I had the opportunity to become acquainted at close

---

[1] The incident referred to is not known precisely. It may have related to Beidler's wife **Ellen** being Jewish.

[2] Thomas Mann's first stop as an exile was in **Sanary-sur-Mer**, in the south of France. The Mann family, including Thomas' wife Katja, brother Heinrich, and sons Golo and Klaus also took exile there, as did other illustrious fugitive artists, including Bertolt Brecht, Lion Feuchtwanger, Egon Kisch, Arthur Koestler, Annette Kolb, Katherine Mansfield, Ludwig Marcuse, Erwin Piscator, René Schikele, Ernst Toller, Franz Werfel, Alma Mahler-Werfel, and Arnold and Stefan Zweig - among others.

[3] Emil **Preetorius** - (1883-1973) - important German stage designer and graphic artist. Despite his anti-Nazi orientation, he was the Director of stage design at the Bayreuth Festival during the Third Reich. Denounced in 1942 as a "friend of Jews," he was arrested by the Gestapo. Hitler and, no doubt, Winifred Wagner, interceded to have him released quickly.

range with his stupendous knowledge and the ability for instant synthesis combined with a very rare, charming diffidence and nobility. I envy you very much the advantage you now have of being together with Mann and I would be very grateful if I could possibly receive a really detailed report about your talks with him. (There is one small complaint that I do not want to suppress. It arose from the otherwise wonderful essay about Richard Wagner. [*Sorrows and Grandeur of Richard Wagner*] In a small, almost inconspicuous sentence of no account, Mann casts doubts, in somewhat disparaging tone, on Liszt's productivity in comparison with Wagner's. I have often had the intention to write to Mann about this. Perhaps I shall do it someday, in this connection and very openly, since Mann merely says out loud what "the whole world" thinks about Liszt, although, admittedly, it especially pains me, in this one case, to have to identify Thomas Mann with "the whole world.")

But now to your plans and intentions! To start with, for your information, I'm sending you a copy of Einstein's letter. After you write me to say who Einstein should contact on your behalf, naturally I shall be very happy to write to him again. It is still not completely clear to me in which institute you would like to work. As far as I know, the League [of Nations] supports only the I.I.C.I.,[1] (paid for by the French government), in which André Coeuroy played a role; on the German side, Dr. Picht and Dr. Grete Rotbart were employed. At that time, General Director Krüss[2] also took a great interest in this institute — he was, after all, the proponent for all international affairs. Admittedly, I do not know how things are looking now. A while back, I wrote to Coeuroy, but have not yet received an answer. Robert Brussell, the managing director of the "French Association for Artistic Growth and Exchanges"[3] was no better; he failed to react to my second letter.

If you could gain a firm foothold in this "Association", I would consider it a very exceptional stroke of good luck. This is an institute that is built on the widest of bases, apparently has a lot of money at its disposal but seems to achieve next to nothing. A few

---

[1] **I.I.C.I.** - International Institute of Intellectual Cooperation (*Institut international de Coopération intellectuelle*) - a non-governmental institution established in 1926 under the auspices of the League of Nations.

[2] Generaldirektor Hugo Andres **Krüss** - (1879-1945) - During the mid and late 1920s, he was Albert **Einstein's** representative and proxy on the I.I.C.I., responsible for intellectual co-operation under the aegis of the League of Nations. Gradually, as Krüss showed growing affinity for Italian and German fascism, and anti-Semitism, Einstein distanced himself from and finally broke with Krüss. In October, 1933, when Germany quit the League of Nations, Krüss ended his interest in the I.I.C.I.

[3] Robert **Brussell** - (1874-1940) - a French writer, critic, and cultural bureaucrat. In 1922, he founded the *Association française d'expansion et déchanges artistiques*, which became the AFAA (*l'Association française d'action artistique*).

months ago, when I very carefully asked the German Fr. [sic] ambassador about this institute and about Brussell he answered me very undiplomatically with coarse invective against Brussell's intellectual abilities. He just called him an idiot. Although I am not able to embrace this opinion, I do believe that both of you [Ellen and Franz W. Beidler] would be able to work wonderfully in this institute and enjoy all your enthusiasms to the full. Unfortunately, I fear that they hire only French people. But, unless I am mistaken, the whole institute is divided into the various culture-states and there are special people assigned to work on each country. The institute is responsible to the Minstry for Foreign Affairs and the Ministry of Education. Some time ago, Brussell had a very industrious old Jewess (Madame Mendel) — from Romania, if I am not mistaken — removed, probably because she was too intelligent! You may be exaggerating the influence of Bartok. He is supposed to come to Prague in the next week or so. Naturally, I shall see him and then, of course, I shall talk to him about you.

As for the plan of your position-paper, I would very much like to provide various additions, if I could get an approximate summary from you. I have just received copies of my lecture from my dear wife. They are to go to all participants in the June 30 conference. Naturally, you will also receive a copy. You will then best be able to see the correlation of my work with plans regarding the position at the League. If you should have need of historical material, I refer you very emphatically to the musical pedagogue, Wilhem[1] who lived in Paris at the beginning of the nineteenth century and established and organized more there than everything else that was done in Prussia from Zelter[2] to Kestenberg. That would be a wonderful special area of work for you, that could become a treasure trove for us all and for which a publisher certainly could be easily be mustered. It would, additionally, be a small revenge against the gruesome arrogance of the Prussian musical pedagogues à la Dr. Münnich, Moser, etc.[3]

Your extensive description of how you are living at the moment, your home, what you are eating, and what you are doing, reminded me a bit of Goethe and delighted me. One really gets a very clear idea from it about your life and also your environment. How-

---

[1] Guillaume-Louis Bocquillon-**Wilhem** - (1781-1842) - French musician, teacher and choral conductor. He developed methods of teaching music which achieved great success and recognition in France (including the *Legion d'Honneur*) and influenced teaching in Germany and Switzerland.

[2] Carl Friedrich **Zelter** - (1758-1832) - German composer, conductor, and music teacher. Among Zelter's pupils: Mendelssohn, Meyerbeer, and Nicolai. Zelter contributed to a revival of J.S. Bach's music.

[3] Richard **Münnich** - (1877-1970), music teacher, co-editor of the *Zeitschrift für Schulmusik.* s**Moser** - H.J.Moser

ever, I would very much like to know if the little woman is also eating up all these delicious foods or if she leaves half of them uneaten. If the latter is the case, as I fear, I shall probably have to make up my mind to travel to the Côte d'Azur to cajole her to do otherwise, as in Bayreuth.[1]

During these weeks of summer it was completely quiet around here. Gradually, however, "one" does return and a few dreams may begin to blossom and mature. Our dear Rahel is presently in hospital because she had to have her appendix removed. Fortunately, she is doing very well, and she is completely serious in her wish to emigrate to Palestine at the end of this or beginning of next month. Ruth has decided to stay with us in Prague and to do her doctorate here, something which is terribly involved in Holland. Besides that, Prague is much less expensive than Amsterdam. For the time being, though, Tunja is still remaining in A., because he has received a one-year residence permit and also has made very good connections there. Being separated is, of course, very painful but bearable, one hopes, given all the great pain in the world.

Continuation on September 3

The explanation for the ignominious intermezzo [in Beidler's correspondence] came with your airmail letter of August 28! [not extant] I am very grateful to you for all your information, which is always very interesting and important to me. It also seems to me indispensable that we keep permanent and precise watch over our [past] professional domain in Germany and, keep ourselves up-to-date as far as is possible. It just occurred to me again that Comrade Grötsch,[2] who used to be features-page editor of the "Dresdener Volkszeitung" [*People's Paper of Dresden*], told me that the "Neue Vorwärts" [*New Forward*], i.e. Stampfer,[3] would very much like to have a feature about the theatre and the art scene in general in contemporary Germany. We immediately thought of you; first, because Stampfer certainly would like to publish something by you, and then because you have

---

[1] It is likely that the trip to the Bayreuth Festival, to which Kestenberg refers here and elsewhere, took place in 1930. During that Festival, Wagner's son Siegfried, Director of the Festival, died of a heart attack on August 4. Beidler was a pallbearer. There is a photograph which shows both Ellen and Franz standing at the grave during the burial.

[2] Robert **Groetsch** - (1878-1946) - Editor-in-Chief of the Social-Democratic newspaper, *Dresdner Volkszeitung*, 1908-1933. The Nazis invaded the offices of the paper in 1933. Groeltsch fled for his life. A fellow editor of his, Max Sachs was tortured to death in Sachsenburg concentration camp.

[3] Friedrich **Stampfer** - (1874-1957) - Austrian social-democratic journalist and politician. Editor-in-chief of *Vorwärts*, the party organ of the SPD (Social Democratic Party) until 1933, when he fled to Prague, later to Paris and then the USA. In Prague he was part of the leadership of the SPD-in-exile and published the *Neuen Vorwärts*. He was both an anti-Fascist and an anti-Communist.

been in Germany up to now and optimally informed about the nazified [*gleichgeschaltete*] repertoire. If I already can hear your objections against working on the "N.V.", I consider it my duty to inform you of this possibility, since I would think it wrong at present to be overly demure in choosing work. Besides, in this setting you can certainly include your opinion about the mistakes that were made [in the past]. But I can already imagine how, from the vantage-point of your austere judge's bench, my objectivity and tolerance will receive no mercy. — However you intend to decide about writing this feature, please write to me right away so that I can inform Com. Grötsch. I do not have any contact here with Stampfer and I also do not intend to seek him out. Of former P.V. [party veterans?], we see here only Dr. Hertz, [1] whom we find very congenial, and, for the rest, almost exclusively musicians. Most recently, Dr. Stiedry,[2] Mrs. Pisling,[3] Dr. Latzko,[4] Wolfes etc. etc. were here. Today, two students visited me, Hollitscher[5] and Baruch, who told us many interesting things about school and university.

A few weeks ago, a stage director, Walter Jacob,[6] whom I have known for a fairly long time (at present Paris 9e, 24 rue Fontaine, Hotel Lizeux), informed me that a committee had been formed in Paris a few weeks ago, "Bureau Central de la Musique et des Spectacles" [*Central Office for Music and Shows*] to which Dr. Altmann, Alexander Maass, Walter

---

[1] Paul **Hertz** - (1888-1961) - German politician, Jewish. He was a social-democratic member of the German parliament during the Weimar Republic. He fled Germany in 1933 and ended up in Prague. In 1939, he and his family were able to emigrate to the USA. After 1949, he was lured back to Germany by his old comrade, Ernst Reuter, then mayor of West Berlin. Hertz filled various political positions until his death in 1961.

[2] Fritz **Stiedry** - Austrian conductor. In 1933, he fled to Leningrad where he conducted the orchestra. In 1937, he was able to emigrate to the USA. After 1945, he conducted opera in Chicago and New York.

[3] Mrs. **Pisling** - probably Nora Pisling-Boas, a singer for whom Hindemith wrote a number of songs. She worked with Fritz Stiedry and Kurt Weill.

[4] Andreas **Latzko** - (1876-1943) - Hungarian pacifist writer who wrote several books and articles in German. His books were burned by the Nazis in 1933. He fled to the USA, where he died in poverty in 1943.

[5] probably Walter **Hollitscher** - (1911-1986) - Austrian philosopher, physicist, psychoanalyst, Communist.

[6] Paul Walter **Jacob** - (1905-1977) - German stage director and actor. In April 1933, he fled to Amsterdam and then to Prague. For the next few years he worked in Luxembourg and Prague. In April 1938, he fled, first to South Africa and then to Argentina. He returned to Germany after the war, despite most of his family having been murdered. He became director of the municipal theatres of Dortmund.

Jacob, Fürst, Mayer etc. belong.[1] This committee also seems to have given itself the job of collecting all the addresses of emigrants. Walter Jacob has written a short essay in a Dutch periodical; this motivated me to suggest making a presentation summarizing the cultural work done during the "disgraceful 14 years" [of the Weimar Republic]. I do not know, however, if he is the right man for this task — it is also conceivable that Paul Bekker, might feel drawn to this subject and, to start with, would write a continuation of his "German Musical Life" in a more comprehensive presentation. An "Opera Dramaturgie" by him will be appearing in Zurich (Orel Füssli publ.), which, according to his synopsis, must be very interesting since it expands on the whole history of opera from the point of view of the voice.

By the way, how is your Wagner manuscript[2] going? If you have a copy of it, I would love to get to know it. Have you not attempted to have it published somewhere? Or does it bear similarities to "the Kaiser's new clothes". [ref. to story by Hans Christian Anderson].

I shall accept your "form of address" if you allow me, to accept, like Grandmama, the whole regalia of the aggressive wolf, not for instance if you think of a toothless, senile vision of someone completely robbed of all fight and courage. I have nothing against devouring Red Riding Hood, if also no intention of doing so. On the contrary: I welcome red hats of every colour.

I am very disappointed that you've still not sent me any reports about your conversations with Thomas and, above all, about your intentions for the future. I've gained enormous respect for your morning excursions and hope that you'll also use your transformation into a morning type to reply to me very soon in the same vivid and humorous form.

With the most affectionate greetings, also from my four women —

Your old

LeoKbg

[in Grete's handwriting]

I enclose the letter of Mrs. I.-L. which I received some time ago. I kept it back until I had your new address.

8. KBG to FWB — 1933.09.01

---

[1] In a letter of Kestenberg's to Paul **Bekker** (August 1933), he connects the following people with areas about which they could write: Dr. Altmann with spoken theatre, Paris; Alexander Maass with theatre in Alsace; Walter Jacob with opera, operetta, and music; Fürst with film; and Mayer with cabaret, variety, and dance. - see Dietmar Schenk, ed. *Leo Kestenberg, Gesammelte Schriften*, Band 3.2. Rombach Verlag, Freiburg im Breisgau, 2012, 141-2.

[2] Beidler's biography of his grandmother, Cosima Wagner.

9. 1933.09.30 — Kbg (Prague) to Beidlers (Paris)

[postcard - handwritten]

1933.09.30 [Postmark on postcard has 2.X.33 Prague]

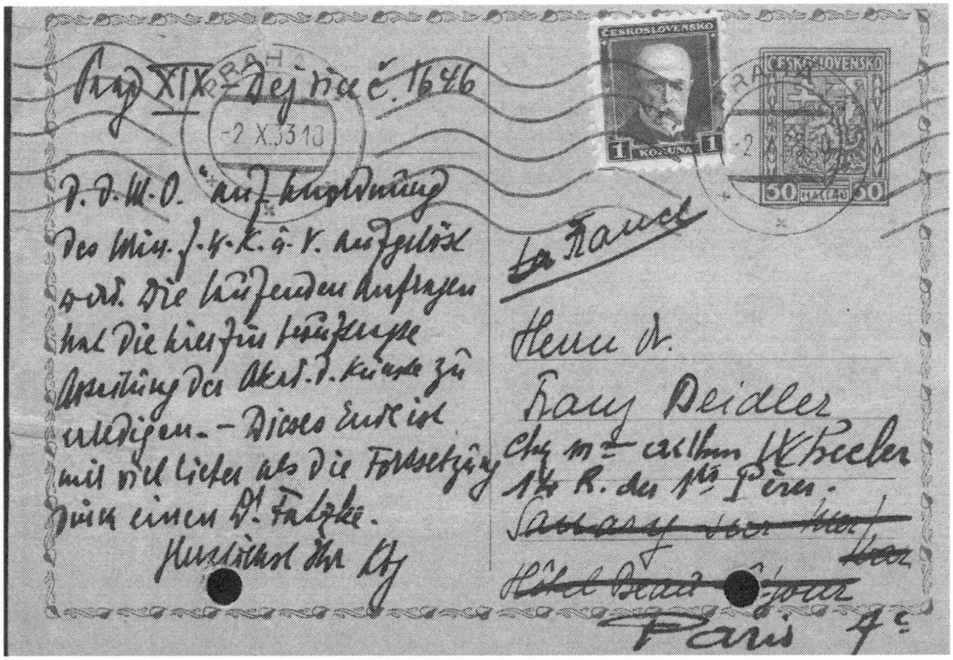

La France
Dr. Franz Beidler

Sanary sur Mer/Var
Hôtel Beau Séjour

c/o Mme Arthur Wheeler
14 R. des Sts Pères.
Paris 7e

[typed]

Dear Dr. Beidler,

Now it's time for me to take you to task again. It is completely incomprehensible to me that, after taking such a praiseworthy and energetic run at writing, you simply stopped for so long. I am just at an absolute loss to explain it and I ask you to tell me, as **immediately** as you can, even if only on a post card, what's doing with you. — As for me, nothing has changed, either for better or for worse. Some time ago, Schickele[1] asked me about you. Naturally I immediately gave him good news about you. Both of them send you fondest greetings — from the whole family as well.

Yours

[signed] LKbg

Prague XIX, Dejvice č 1646
30.9.33

[handwritten]

I just came across an official announcement in "Melos" saying that the "Archiv d.d.M.O." which is attached to the "Z.s.f.Z.u.K" will be broken up by order of the Ministry f.k.k.a.V. Ongoing inquiries are to be attended to by the division of the Acad. of Arts authorized to complete this task. I much prefer this ending to continuation under some Dr. Fatzke.[2]

With great affection,

Your

Kbge

9. KBG to FWB – 1933.09.30

---

[1] René **Schickele** - (1883-1940) - Alsatian writer of expressionist bent, who dedicated himself to the cause of better French-German relations. He wrote mostly in German.

[2] A pun poking fun at Dr. Hermann **Matzke**, for whom Kestenberg had little respect. The word Fatzke can be translated in English as "stuck-up twit" or "stuffed shirt".

10. 1933.10.26 — Kbg (Prague) to Beidlers

[handwritten]

Prague XIX - Dejvice č 1646

26.X

Dear Beidlers! Since I asked Tunja, who now lives with us, to describe for you the agitation set off in us by your eternal silence, I can simply pass over this unavoidable chapter in our dealings with you and only give expression to my satisfaction at your having become neither a Nazi princeling nor a corpse.

For the rest, I'm sending sincere greetings to you in your capacity as a Parisian. And now I do hope that some positive developments will take shape, whereby I am naturally taking for granted somewhat more reliability ("Even upon the Grave, he plants seeds of Hope.")! [Schiller][1]

Alright, to begin with, I request that you immediately contact Miss Susanne Friedburg, at Mrs. Saudi, Paris I, 38 rue du Mont-Thabor, because two days ago I asked her to pay visits for me to Brussel, Ceuroy [sic], and Döblin. Despite very understandable oppositional hints in their letters, the first two must be congenial to you since they also leave letters unanswered. But I take it that you, despite all objections, do not want to allow the momentous position of an accredited ambassador to be disputed and that, since, at any rate, Miss Friedburg will soon be leaving for England, probably it will be positively fine with her if she leaves these dealings to you. For England, I also have sufficient errands for Susanne F. to carry out.

Dr. Einstein already showed me the galley proofs of Schneider's critique a year ago, admittedly without the infamous name-castration, which, however, must be more mortifying to the perpetrators than to me. And Hans Joachim's [Moser] fate has long developed along ominous lines.[2] But the actuality is new and interesting to me. If only all those who

---

[1] From Schiller's poem Hope (***Hoffnung***) - "*Noch am Grabe pflanzt er - die Hoffnung auf.*"-

[2] At this point, in 1933, **Moser's** Nazi activities were not as "ominous" as they increasingly became, especially during World War II. There were many other musicologists, however, who went far further in Nazi fanaticism than Moser ever did.

were summoned to "dine" by "Pope Leo" were to "die," with Havemann[1] & Trapp[2] in the vanguard. And Heinz [Tietjen]?

Otherwise, everything is going relatively well. On November 11, I'm speaking in Amsterdam to the Association for School Music and on the 13th I'm playing in Hilversum great-grandfather works (among others "Lyon," a piece on the first silk weavers' insurrection, Valley of Obermann, Tell and both Franciscan Legends). Perhaps I shall combine this with lectures to the SPD [Social Democratic Party] Education Committee in Zurich. Aufhäuser,[3] who lives in our neighbourhood, is working on this. — Realization of the central office plans is making good progress. Dent[4] & Chantavoine[5] have responded very positively. Bartok not refusing but quite uninterested. Your information on this account seems incorrect.

Now I have heaped enough burning coals on your guilt-laden head, that the intercession of the ever angelic St.Elizabeth-Ellen will save me from purgatory and I am curious to find out the outcome. Overcome your vanity about form which, to me, is a bothersome, specious inheritance and obey the spontaneous. In the presence of adequate talent, a proper form is generated without a lot of thinking. But I'm not named Hans and you not Walther. [*Die Meistersinger*] What's the use of these morning-dream prescriptions!

With heartiest greetings and affection of old
Your LKbg

10. KBG to FWB — 1933.10.26

---

[1] Gustav **Havemann** - (1882-1960) - German violinist of leftist views until 1933; thereafter fanatic Nazi and director of the *Reichsmusikkammer*. On April 2, 1933, he wrote: „The Combat Group for German Culture [of which Havemann was a member] will know how to prevent any further trace of Jewish influence from remaining in the musical life of Germany." In 1935 Goebbels ejected Havemann from Nazi organizations because he had gone to bat for Hindemith.

[2] Max **Trapp** - (1887-1971) - German music teacher and composer. Member of the Nazi Party 1932.

[3] Siegfried **Aufhäuser** - (1884-1969) - German labour-union leader and Social-Democratic politician. 1921-1933, he was a member of the German parliament. In 1933, he fled to Prague. The Munich appeasement caused him to move to Paris and then, in 1939, to New York. He returned to Germany in 1951. He and his wife are buried in the Jewish cemetery in Freiburg/Breisgau.

[4] Edward **Dent** - (1876-1957) - English professor of music and writer. He was an active promoter of increased international co-operation between composers, musicians, and teachers of music.

[5] Jean **Chantavoine** - (1877-1952) - French musicologist. He was the Secretary General of the *Conservatoire National Supérieur de Musique* in Paris and published several papers on music of the Romantic period as well as biographies of Beethoven, Liszt, Saint-Saëns, and Mozart.

11. 1933.11.16 — FWB (Paris) to Kbg

Paris (18): 16.XI.33
Aviation-Hôtel,
27º rue Tholozé.

Dearest Fellow Social Democrat Kestenberg,

because I cannot really let you wait any longer, I am sending you at least a few lines in a hurry although, in the meantime, nothing permanent, definitive, or palpable has been attained on any section of the front.

To begin with — your last letter: Susanne will already have written to you that I have "acted under and expedited orders" and that I contacted her without delay. She was thus spared a visit to Brussel that, without doubt, would not have been very pleasant for her. We had already been at his place. That he is an idiot, I already knew and was therefore not surprised to be able to verify this. But that he is totally uninterested and, in addition, all but rude — I hadn't reckoned on that. He did not have even the slightest clue about us, not about the Yearbook, nor the archive. Little by little, he recalled a "jeune fille" [young girl], by which, it soon turned out, he meant Thea D. [Dispeker]. Factually, he indeed knew nothing about her; but her appearance seems to have left remnants of a faint impression in him. Do you know why he does not respond to you (naturally, I immediately asked him about this)? It is because he may not have a German correspondent in Prague, but only a Czech. It was embarrassing for him, however, to write this to you so directly — so he just didn't answer at all! Voilà. All the same, he put at our disposal the whole material of his office (particularly the publications which are otherwise difficult to obtain here), for day-to-day use, and he referred us to the "directress" of the German division (Mrs. Maurice), who is very charming and obliging. Starting up anything more with Brussel is out of the question. Perhaps it is possible by way of his directors. That is not apparent yet, but we will give it a try.

Before I make mention of Coeroy, a preliminary note, which is necessary because you cannot yet be aware of our intentions. Getting a position with the I.I.C.I., either immediately or later, is impossible. I'm aiming for an assignment (without a permanent contract) for introducing organizational, musical work within the framework of the I.I.C.I. A few days ago I submitted several positive proposals, more or less for selection, to a C.I.C.I.

member, whom I met through Fellerer,[1] who has been acquitting himself famously and truly like a good friend (rare thing!). Independently of this, two days ago I applied in writing to Henri Bonnet,[2] the director of the I.I.C.I., seeking to make his acquaintance (he knows of me through Thomas Mann) and to discuss with him questions of sourcing material for several private works. Whether the main topic can resonate during this first visit, directly, on my initiative, remains to be seen. I shall see Coeroy only after my visit with Bonnet; this sequence must be adhered to strictly. It will take about one more week. What would you like from Coeroy then? Susanne seemed to speak only of your wish that the forwarding of the "Revue musicale" to Prague be continued as before. Is that everything? I can hardly believe that! If possible, please supply me rapidly with some information about the "central office" and perhaps also a few immediate requests for the League! I know too little of what you actually expect from the I.I.C.I. to form an assumption that would allow me to step forward, even cautiously.

The way we have been received in Paris has phenomenally exceeded all expectations! I really had not believed that the [Wagner/Liszt] ancestry would cause all, and I do mean all, doors to open here as if on their own! One after the other, we are making the acquaintance of everyone of rank and distinction. I shall report to you in detail soon. Of course, I am going about it discreetly and gradually; and I am carefully scouting the whole terrain first in order not to commit any *faux pas*. Everything here takes terribly long. However, I hear from all quarters that the outlook for me, in a variety of directions, is not at all bad; I just have to stay very patient, because everything here needs time, a lot of time. Exceptionally charming and the best guides that you could wish for are Chantavoine, Lichtenberger,[3] and Expert.[4] Most likely tomorrow, my debut will take place at the

---

[1] Karl Gustav **Fellerer** - (1902-1984) - German musicologist. He taught at Münster University, from 1932 at Fribourg, Switzerland, and from 1939, the University of Cologne, where he was the Director of the Institute of Musicology. He co-operated increasingly with the Nazis, joining the Party in 1941. He participated in the Rosenberg Group, in which he travelled to occupied places such as Paris to organize thorough archival research to determine which valuable documents and other items would be confiscated for transport to Germany.

[2] Henri **Bonnet** (1888-1978) - French politician and diplomat. In 1931 he became Director of the I.I.C.I., the forerunner of UNESCO. He was the French ambassador to Washington from 1945 to 1954.

[3] Henri **Lichtenberger** - (1864-1941) - French music critic, author (including a book about Wagner), and a major specialist in German studies. After World War I, he worked for the healing of French-German relations.

[4] Henry **Expert** - (1882-1955) - French architect. He designed many public buildings, mostly in a classical Art Deco style. In 1950, he received the *Légion d'honneur*.

"French Society for Musicology". The list of people on our visiting list is endless and expands daily. Thank goodness! For a few days now, we've had here in Paris the three suitcases that we left behind in Berlin.

I have got an especially great amount to write you on the subject of Liszt — but not until one of the next opportunities. I have here the family Ollivier as *Meschpoche* [yiddish: clan, family considered as a joyous burden].[1] Daniel Ollivier, Blandine Liszt's son, received me right off as "cher cousin" [dear cousin] and I am already helping him with editing the second volume of the correspondence of Liszt and the Countess d'Agoult. The first volume appeared at the beginning of this year. Now I've got two quick questions for you. Do you know the following Liszt pieces: 1) "The Four Elements," and 2) "The Child Flavigny." We do not know them; that is, Ollivier and I. But, as you know, that is not saying much. If they exist, then you know them for sure. Then: a letter by Liszt begins with the attached excerpt from a song fragment. Do you know it? The letter is from the year 1841. From whom can this miserable declamation and simple "melody" come? Nobody here knows.

Incidentally: I am severely upset! If you are already in Holland, making propaganda for great-grandfather (what a shame that I cannot be there to hear you!) and then subsequently speak in Zurich, then, by God, you could travel by way of Paris. No, actually you must have done so, since I cannot fathom it — how can you take a different route from Holland to my homeland [Switzerland]?[2] I must say: we would have been enormously overjoyed to see you finally once again!

And finally: Your fantastically excellent allusion to Wilhem hammered down on me like a bomb — no, like lightning and "orage" [thunder]. I am beginning the work now and hope to achieve some results soon. This positively brilliant tip once again powerfully elevated my respect for you and I proclaim everywhere here with genuine pride that I am part of your circle and your work. (A propos: who actually belongs right now, who is new, to the Society of Friends of Kestenbergish projects? How do things stand with Eberhard?

---

[1] Beidler's **Ollivier Mischpoche** - Franz W. Beidler was related to the Olliviers through his grandmother Cosima Wagner (née Liszt). In 1857, Cosima's elder sister, Blandine (1835-1862) married the lawyer and politician (in 1870 he became the 30th Prime Minister of France) Emile Ollivier (1825-1913). Like Cosima, Blandine was the daughter of Franz Liszt and Countess Marie d'Agoult (1805-1876). D'Agoult had also had a son with Liszt, named Daniel (1839-1859). The Daniel referred to by Beidler was the son of Blandine and Emile. Daniel Ollivier (1862-1941) published books of correspondence - Liszt/d'Agoult and Liszt/Blandine.

[2] Beidler's father had been born in Switzerland, therefore making that country his son's homeland as well as his own - by Swiss usage.

[Preussner] Do you hear anything from him?) For the Wilhem tip, a thousand thank you's, and soon more about him! Aside from all the objectively interesting things for us, work on him will be very beneficial to my ambition to flesh out the [Wagner/Liszt] lineage with usable professional works of my own.

For today, sadly, the end. God, how much there could still be to describe, to recount, to argue! But you must finally have news! Please forgive mistakes in style and typing and all of you, be embraced and hailed, with all affection and cohesion of old,

Your

11. FWB to KBG — 1933.11.16

12. 1933.11.25 — FWB (Paris) to Kbg

[typed]

Paris (18): 25.XI.1933,
Aviation-Hôtel,
27, rue Tholozé.

Dear Comrade[1] Kestenberg,

among various other things on your 50th birthday, you received a congratulatory letter from a former government minister. Since then, the times have gone (temporarily?) bad. On your 51st birthday would you make do, among various other things, with the congratulations of a future government minister? For the time being, actually, that doesn't yet look likely; but more about that later. The most important thing is that Sancta Elisabetha [i.e. wife Ellen] and I, the latter much less holy, are, as always, united and in solidarity with wishes for you that come from the bottom of our hearts. We are making our appearance empty-handed, without a book and without a picture, as is appropriate for honourable emigrés. But with very hearty congratulations!

But not quite completely empty-handed. Can you still remember, from a distance, a Mr. Joachim Kuehn? The story — you should receive something, at least to laugh about. Last Sunday, there appeared in a local tabloid rag an interview with me that was completely and utterly falsified, including ostensible statements that I would never permit to leave my mouth, not even in the most trusted circles. Conjectures of a "resourceful" journalist. I used the provocation to write Mr. Kuehn a letter, a copy of which I am sending you today [not extant]. As a result of this dumb story, the "incognito" (better split: inkognito!) is now at an end.

In order to nip in the bud further, uncheckable newspaper articles, I have had to take the decision to give a real interview (also having to do with Wagner) to a local representative of the Hearst-Press (biggest newspaper concern in the world, from the USA — let's go whole hog!). That will make its way through the press in two weeks. It is measured in expression but acerbic and clear-cut. Let's hope you like it. I'm eagerly awaiting the consequences.

In the meantime, I was with Bonnet at the I.I.C.I. and made the acquaintance of Coeuroy at the same time. Two days earlier, he had just come back from Spain where he had spent almost two months. Right from the first moment, we got on very well with one another. I immediately turned over your request and gave him your address, which he

---

[1] Comrade = *Genosse* in German, a form of address used by Social Democrats to this day.

claimed not to know. Whether you really will receive the publication seems questionable to me. C. told me right off that they are finished financially and may, from January on, have to stop publication entirely. Yes, yes, that's the way things look here as well! Not encouraging. I shall soon find out more, in detail, from Prunières,[1] whom I shall see next week (this week he is in Holland).

What do you hear from our "homeland?"[Germany] I am well informed about the general state of affairs, via connections with various correspondents of local English papers. Also, even if you don't believe it: the secret document in the "Petit Parisien" is genuine! I also had not believed it but, since yesterday, I have become somewhat better informed. A few days ago old Oscar B.[2] wrote me (formerly B.B.C!): "I have completely lost my newspaper employment which means the loss of almost all my means of existence. We have no idea how we are supposed to continue.... To note: 70 years old and an ailing wife. Oh yes. Would you know of anyone there who might help me, to whom I could try to write?" Humor evaporates before such things. And I cannot bring the matter forward in a big way because it would put him in even greater danger! But naturally I am doing what I can on the quiet. For the time being — no results.

We are very much looking forward to receiving news from all of you. Warmest regards to everyone (incl. Tunja), we'll write again soon.

12. FWB to KBG — 1933.11.25

---

[1] Henry **Prunières** - (1886-1942) - French musicologist, proponent of international contemporary art, including music, dance, and painting, among others. He founded *La Revue Musicale* in 1920.

[2] Oskar **Bie** - (1864-1938) - German art historian and author, well-known and respected in Bayreuth. His works were forbidden by the Nazis.

13. 1933.12.21-ca — Kbgs (Prague) to Beidlers

[handwritten fragment]

[p.4 of letter 20.Dezember - 1933

P.S. The mailing of my letter got delayed after all and since your letter of today, sent to Grete, bears your Paris address, it makes me very happy. Your remarks about the position of Czechoslovakia stimulate detailed commentary, which, however, I shall set aside for another time. I've never been at one with the essentials of your optimism even though, just yesterday, Minister Krofta[1] and Prof. [Zdeněk] Nejedly,[2] Professor of Musicology, a splendid human being and an old communist, made very skeptical passing comments during our meeting. But it is wonderful that you are once again in Paris. Please give my most energetic regards to Chantavoine whom I shall soon want to invite to undertake presenting a paper at our congress. (One more reason for you to come.) And please write me what the legendary I.I.C.I. is doing! Are Dr. Picht and Miss Dr. Rotbart, still there, in assigned posts, and also Ceuroy [sic]? Paul Dessau[3] was here for a few weeks. A very nice person, but completely uninformed in the areas which are of interest to me. Do you see Prof. Sachs, Lichtenberger — and can you perhaps find out the address of Mersmann?[4] Please do not be annoyed with me for all these questions. It is as in the past; and, with ref-

---

[1] Kamil **Krofta** - (1876-1945) - Czech historian and diplomat. Krofta was a strong supporter of Czech President Edvard Beneš, playing a central role in determining the foreign policy of the Beneš administration. Krofta gave crucial support to Kestenberg and his project of creating an international organization to promote and improve musical pedagogy. Krofta, who was Czech Minister of Foreign Affairs from 1936 to 1938, ended up in the Theresienstadt concentration camp for his active participation in the resistance movement. Although liberated in May 1945, he died in August.

[2] Zdeněk **Nejedlý** - (1878-1962) - Czech scholar, musicologist, historian, and literary critic. Member of the Czech Communist Party from 1929 on. During World War II, he lived in the USSR. His special interest as a historian was in the Hussite revolutionary movement of the 15th century. He wrote several books, mostly on Czech subjects.

[3] Paul **Dessau** - (1894-1979) - German composer and conductor. As a Jew, he fled to France in 1933, leaving in 1939 for the USA, living first in New York, then in Hollywood where he composed music for films, including early Walt Disney works. After the war, he lived in East Germany. In 1954, he married the renowned East German stage director, Ruth Berghaus.

[4] Hans **Mersmann** - (1891-1971) - German musicologist greatly respected by Kestenberg. He was in charge of the respected publication *Melos* 1924-1933. Appointed professor at the Technical University in Berlin in 1926, he was relieved of his post in 1933 by the Nazis because he had so actively promoted contemporary music. He had to eke out a meagre existence as a private music teacher. In 1935 he was denounced by the Nazis as a bolshevik. From 1947 to 1957, he was the Rector of the Music Faculty of the University of Cologne.

erence to answers, I am as usual not all that confident, especially as concerns *tempo*. Or has the world changed, including the Beidler-Wagner-rhythm?

Affectionately yours,

LKbg

[additional page by Grete handwritten]

My dear comrades, I am very moved. I must admit that I missed your dear words on the 18th very much. I thought French schooling must have made you so chivalrous as to no longer congratulate an "old lady" on her birthday. And now that I want to see all my loved ones gathered around me on the 18th (or sadly now in letters), you may be the least of the missing, all the more since, happily, our correspondence is once again flowing. Because we all, unfortunately, are incapable of remembering birthday dates, (and the old calendars are missing), you both should receive all the best New Year's wishes that have been sent to Paris from my big old friend-loving heart. Gradually, I am beginning to recover from all the horrors. Sadly, the past is a heavy burden that I drag along behind me (and it does not want to let me loose). It would be wonderful to be able to see you again, an eye for an eye, tooth for a tooth (also a mouth for a mouth). And with that I want to close - - - .

With great affection! Your old G.K.

Grandmama sends loving greetings.

[Ruth handwriting] also from me, the best for you both! I often yearn for you, and especially for you in the Kalckreuthstrasse, and Tunia and I always imagine how we will make a big trip and visit you, at least for one night-long yack [*bequatchen*] about <u>everything</u>. Write sometime to Tunia. Your Ruth.

13. KBG to FWB — 1933.11.21±

14. 1933.12.24 — Kbg (Prague) to Beidlers

[handwritten]

~~Ministerialrat~~ Kestenberg

~~Berlin W8, Unter den Linden~~

Prague, in the night that the people
of our time and the countries
in which we dwell call "holy"
and in the year that belies this
holiness even more than any other.

Dear Beidlers! You are right: the Old-Testament tooth for a tooth and unanswered letter for unanswered letter took command of me during the last weeks, in relation to you. But this vengeful feeling, already overcome and sated, is not solely to blame for the long break in our correspondence. After my Holland trip, I was in great demand because of my first public concert, which took place here on the 4th of this month, as well as being kept on my toes by lectures, meetings, and all the other endeavours that are supposed to help to establish a new existence in both intellectual and material form. Now, thanks to a long meeting that was held on the 22nd, i.e. last Friday, all that has reached a certain new era and I can thank you for you letters, all of which arrived punctually, although I do so with something of a guilty conscience because I have to deliver an important article which is not yet begun. Admittedly I am still in the dark about a lot of information that would be important to me. For instance, I would very much like to know what you were doing this summer. After your first precise and stimulating reports, you uttered not one single additional word about the Manns, Schickele, and the others. [at Sanary] And I would have been very happy to hear much more about them. In addition, you announced that an article by you would be appearing in the December issue of "Sammlung." But things have sunk into silence again about this. I am all the happier about the hints you gave that you have entered close connections to Ollivier and your Liszt relatives. At the moment, I am reading the first volume of the [Franz Liszt] letters to the Countess [d'A-goult], which the publisher, S.Fischer, sent me here, and through which I am once again locked into this magic milieu. so refreshing and so beyond time. Unfortunately I do not know the compositions which you named, nor the excerpt that you attached. Here and now, there is so much to do for the already published and half-known works of Liszt that the search for missing ones seems non-essential. Among the Germans here, also the Jews, downright hatred for Liszt is noticeable; it is based on a complete ignorance of the *oeuvre*, a hatred that receives ever greater nourishment from the pseudomodern trend with its false polyphony. On the other hand, I hope to find in the Czechs, for Liszt, as for every-thing else, a rich resonance. The personal relationship [of Liszt] to Smetana in itself commits them to gratitude. These historical reminiscences play a large role here. — How do things stand with the living Liszts in Paris? I have the impression that there, too, there is no real understanding to be found for the religious works or the works stemming from the Geneva period. — Have you already done some work on Wilhem? If yes, I would very much welcome more information. I also want to try to gather material about his student, Hullah,[1] an Englishman. Today I received a new music publication from Germany, "Music in Contemporary Consciousness", which continues our line, in [Nazi] Party manner — [Friedrich] Mahling[2] is editor — and which shows that the old battle with Schwers[3] is roaring onward. It is very instructive to see that the contradictions remain the same, even in the Total Reich. In my work on the "Humanist Ideas in Music Pedagogy" I shall go into this remarkable fact in metaphorical form. — Your news about Robert Brussel interested me greatly. I did not expect anything different from this man. The "Central Office",[4] however, can go around this dead institute without problem. I now have colleagues in the most important countries who are considerably more worthwhile and more active. But the actual activity in the Central Office will only begin in a few weeks because the resistance of the local German circles must be surmounted first. At any rate, I already have presented a more substantial work program and reported on all foreign possibilities. By 1935, I expect to bring the first Congress here, with Anglo-American help. The government is already in agreement. — Around 10 days ago, my office neighbour in the Wilhelmstraße also showed up here. He had had the intention to go to Holland. Like all people, he also is the same; he seems to have accepted the false conclusion that catastrophes and relationships change us. Despite "The Hostage" [*Der Burgschaft* — ballade by Schiller] and its high-minded moving spirits, I daily experience that great character traits stay con-

---

[1] John Pyke **Hullah** (1812-1884) - English music teacher, conductor, and composer. He popularized musical education.

[2] Friedrich **Mahling** - (1899?-1945?) German musicologist. Immediately after Hitler became chancellor, Mahling, Gustav Havemann, and conductor Heinz Ihlert started the Nazi synchronization (*Gleichschaltung*) of musical activity in Germany. In September 1933 Goebbels took over this organizational body, thereby putting all musical activity under the control of his propaganda ministry. In June of 1935, Goebbels eliminated Mahling from this organization, ostensibly for having allowed an advertisement for the Soviet "Intourist" agency to appear in a newspaper.

[3] Paul **Schwers** - (1874-1939) - German writer on music and editor of the *Berliner Allgemeine Musikkzeitung*. In his publication, in June 1933, after Havemann, Ihlert, and Mahling had begun the process of nazifying music in Germany, Schwers attacked this nazification, writing that it followed "one-sided partisan political lines" and showed "no consideration for the political mentality and views of the members of the [musical] organizations" [AMZ 60, 1933, pg.289]

[4] The "Central Office" was the short, working name for the International Music Educators' Organization, with headquarters in Prague, which Kestenberg was successfully bringing to life.

stant. —

Have you seen Chantavoine recently? When the statutes of the Central Office are certain, I shall contact him officially. He too has agreed kindly to offer his support. And I certainly am counting on his help. Are you also in contact with Lichtenberger? Perhaps next year a couple of Liszt lectures in German could be held in his institute. But that is probably utopian. And, of the German musicians and emigrés, whom do you see? I have just read the "Tragedy" by Bernhard.[1] It is a really superficial book but one that presents the material succinctly.

I am now sad that I delivered to the Berlin State Library [*Berliner Staatsbibliothek*] Busoni's great Liszt collection. It is the only complete [collection] of all the [Liszt] works for piano. I fear that it is no longer possible to reverse, even though the financial settlement has been honoured only in a beggarly manner.

In order to bury for all time our mutual vengeance-feelings, shouldn't we conclude a non-aggression pact committing ourselves to regular letters at one-month intervals? Or, should one of us have no time or be ill, at least a short ersatz message, possibly by postcard?

Warmest regards to you both and Happy New Year

Your old Leo Kestbg

14. KBG to FWB — 1933.12.24

[1] Georg **Bernhard** - (1875-1944) - Jewish Social Democrat. He was the director of the Vossische Newspaper, 1914-1930 and one of the most respected economic journalists of the 1920s. After the Nazis cancelled his citizenship, he took refuge in Paris, where he edited German emigrant newspapers and participated in anti-Nazi, emigrant Front activities. In the same year, he published *The German Tragedy. Suicide of a Republic*. His publisher was Orbis (Prague). He died in New York.

15. 1933.12.27 — Grete and Ruth Kbg to Beidlers

[handwritten]

27 Dec. 33.

My dear old Beidlers — a curse on this bleak mechanism of the world that builds up so many kilometres and so much else that is unbridgeable between people who belong to each other and who like each other so much that they would like best to wake up at close quarters. I am arrogant enough to think that you would like to do this as much as I — damn everything that divides, and thrice blessed be this poor, martyred, oppressed heart, with feelings that go all the way over to you and embraces you and likes so much to linger with you. A small consolation and ultimately also a great joy of the present day. I was moved that you thought of me. I return to you all your good wishes, for the new year <u>must</u> make amends again for so much with which the past one violated the whole world and us.

How are you doing, dear Beidlers? Are your affairs making progress and how are you settling into your new world? Leo gives you detailed reports about us. Tunja has been here since October 1 already and lives in harmony with us at our place. I love and respect him very much and it is good to have him with us. He is studying hard, like Ruth who is hoping to receive her doctorate here this summer. Only our youngest has gotten off track, has left school and has not yet acted on her Palestine plans. Hedwig is still doing well (knock on wood!). Recently she asked, also just now, for your address; it would certainly make her very happy if you would write her sometime: W.30, Rosenheimerstr.23. My sister is also well. Peter is also still charming and is trying everything possible and impossible — naturally without any success up to now. My brother is touching; without him, Ruth could not continue studying at all and Rahel could not go to Palestine. For now, he is providing for both of them.

Grandma, too, is feeling "adaptable" — she is well and alert and cooks for us splendidly. I hope that you find my detailed "weather report" satisfactory.

Farewell my very dear, dearest of all Beidlers. If I'm not mistaken, we spent last December 33 [should be 32] together; let's be optimistic and conjure up a prompt reunion, and, at any rate, a *Prosit* [cheers, Happy New Year] despite everything!

Always your old Grete K.

[Ruth handwriting]

Dear Beidlers, I'm joining in; for I too would like to see you again and to sit with you at night. Hereabouts, we have certain fixed schemata for the prerequisites of conviviality. A very important one is called "Beidlers," lock, stock and barrel. Have you already got a room that is truly Beidlerish? And, in general, are you feeling well? Concerning the curious sphere of interest of your thief you need not distress yourself. I don't do it either. 1 — I had a carbon copy, — I changed my subject somewhat, am making a critical comparison [*collationiere*] at the moment [this and the following partially illegible], a 'short' work on a warm [?] mystical Pr. Joachim manuscript about the Bohemian aristocracy which will now form the core of my doctorate. It is a shame, though, only for the Glossary of Middle Latin of Habel. It is probably also gone? So everything is very very good.

Your Ruth.

PS. I was very happy that you were able to get away and settled somewhere else after the door shut [i.e. to get out of Germany after strict laws shut the door on emigration].

I hope that the present location is only a stage and you will land somewhere near us!

15. KBGs to FWB — 1933.12.27

16. 1934.01.01 — FWB (Paris) to Kbg (Prague) — [typed]

Beidler
Paris (18): 1 January 1934,
Aviation-Hôtel,
27, rue Tholozé.

Dear Comrade Kestenberg, our finalized resolution was not to allow the new year to make its ultimate entrance without first writing to you, regardless of whether news had arrived from you or not. The arrival of your family letter prevents us now from submitting evidence of this assertion. It will not have escaped your notice that the Beidlers confront you in an infinitely more critical manner than in days of yore; but that does not impede us, either in a positive or negative sense, from arguing with the great galvinizer, whereby, once again, a contact will be stipulated, which is, often enough, of a whimsical nature, but always solid and intimate, wherefrom the mentioned but unprovable decision proves itself self-explanatory.

It would be far off the mark to assume that our surprise and joy were less great as a result. But I already see myself being put in a difficult position again. As people who are known for thoroughness, we are used not only to reading every line of a letter with real exactitude, but also even between the lines. And after such a hard-earned familiarization with the content of your letter, the outcome, once again, is naturally that the complete answer would have to fill a very respectable number of pages, in the presence of an undiminished plethora of Leo-nine faces!

For the purpose of solving the problem, I shall bring forward something that will perhaps be of use to you. We are on exceptionally good terms with Lichtenberger and are presently attending his very *soigné* (but kid-glove boring) Wagner lecture. I'll take advantage of the next meeting to give vent to your lecture-plans. What I do not want to hide is the fact that I cannot imagine such a lecture covering more than the travel costs. They are not lavish here, and with honoraria, not at all. If it turns out to be doable, it would have to be combined with other things.

I see that you are pinning great hopes on Chantavoine and I feel duty-bound to say something about that. There is no question that he is charming and that, personally, he is helpful. In the Conservatoire, he organized a reception for us that almost embarrassed us. Whenever I want anything, he receives me immediately, even during exams. There is nothing to be said against him. But I repeatedly notice that he does not appear to be able to do all that much and, strangely enough, actually rarely emerges into view. What I am trying to say with this is that I am not yet at all clear about where the button here is that has to be pressed in order to attain the desired outcome. All the same, I am in continuing, close contact, especially with the whole musicology scene and I already know a considerably sizable cross-section of the tangled network of extremely shrouded relationships, especially the rivalries and open antagonisms ("open" is absolutely mistaken, it just does not exist here), naturally in order to be able to steer clear of them. It seems to me, however, that you can get the most done with Prunières. Perhaps this is so, precisely because he is anything but well liked by the "official" musicology. Only now am I coming into closer contact with him. Every week, in the offices of the "Revue musicale"[1] he regularly holds a sort of musical *cercle*, during which two lectures are usually given. We have only taken him up on his invitation once and want to attend often in future. (This one time was comical enough. We did not know what was on the program. Who should appear and give a lecture on Jewish music? Alice Jacob-Loewenson![2] It would have been better for her not to give it — at least not here!! For many reasons. Here, above all, by God, we do not need matter that arouses even more pronounced *rishes* [Yiddish: anti-Semitic malice]. It was embarrassing, and as much as I like her personally, I can describe her own "compositions" simply as brazen provocations). We want to see what can be realized with Prunières, also along your lines. (You will be aware that he is a "non-Aryan.")

Once again, I feel forced to repeat myself. You relate many positive things about the "Central Office." Unfortunately, it is not concrete enough. Please let me in on it better so that I will be placed in the happy circumstance of being able to put out propaganda about it. International congress for musical pedagogy in 1935? Something similar has already been suggested; I had material circuitously rerouted to the C.I.C.I. some time ago. I have not yet given up all hope of organizing the congress, as I.I.C.I., together with you. At the moment, my involvement is less a problem than the existence of the League [of Nations]. And please enlighten me a bit about your new "colleagues" — in the end, one would like to be acquainted with his successors.

Then: you write laconically "after my trip to Holland"! So Hilversum did happen? We are having remarkable thoughts about your travel route and conclude that nothing came of Zurich? At any rate, it is pleasing, although not astounding, to see you in full work-mode. What is the subject of the article that is due at the beginning of the year and

---

[1] The ***Revue musicale*** was a publication aimed mostly at musicologists, founded in 1920 by Henry Prunières. The Revue treated all aspects of musical performance, including recorded music, and especially contemporary music. Many famous writers contributed articles: Paul Claudel, Jean Cocteau, Colette, André Gide, Emil Ludwig, Maurice Maeterlinck, Romain Rolland, and Paul Valéry, among others. There were nine editions annually. Excellent designs were contributed by the likes of André Derain, Raoul Dufy, and Picasso, among others.

[2] Alice **Jacob-Loewenson** - (1895-1967) - German-born pianist, composer, music teacher, and writer. She studied piano with Kestenberg and Busoni. After fleeing Germany only weeks after Hitler became Chancellor, the Jewish musician and her husband Erwin Loewenson settled temporarily in Paris, moving to Palestine at the beginning of 1934, where she remained active in pedagogical, performance, and archival activities in the developing Jewish musical scene.

where was it published?

In the next days, I shall send you the January edition of the "Sammlung" which will contain my article, "Music in the State of Weimar." At the moment, I am once again very busy with Wagner and am writing an article about Wagner legends for the "Manchester Guardian," which will be the most acerbic but also the best that I have ever written. After its publication, my German citizenship and my Berlin doctorate probably will be invalidated, which I'll care a lot about for sure.

Our stay in Sanary gave us an enduring gift, profound, very warm, joyful and superior contact with Thomas, as with Heinrich Mann, who maintains a very pleasing rapport with Leon Feuchtwanger.[1] As soon as I get to it, I shall try to tell you more about this, although all of it understandably more or less eludes recounting. Not till a few days ago did I again receive a long, completely wonderful letter from Thomas. Schickele, on the other hand, has excluded himself for me after his statement against "Sammlung,"[2] a certain loss, less as a human than as a writer. — I say "certain" because his last work is in no way at all at the highest level. The legacy on the Rhine does not seem to have been very opulent. By the way, it is completely unfathomable to me why he asked you about me. I had only a very loose connection [to him], based on the association defined by my bond with the brothers Mann. How did he justify his question to you? In this context: I recently wrote to Klaus Mann about your once admired Friend Döblin — literally: "If a person could once take D. seriously, there would be nothing left to a person other than to call him a characterless scoundrel." From which you can see that I am more combative and absolute than ever, to which, between ourselves, in view of the "situation," a certain portion of courage is truly required. . . ! Since we are at "friends," what do you actually think about Schünemann? —

I'll stay brief and break here even though only a tenth of the news was written about. Expect a separate letter to Frau Grete and Ruth and Tunja, and write again very soon.

16. FWB to KBG — 1934.01.01

---

[1] Lion **Feuchtwanger** - (1884-1958) - Major German author. He was an early and massive opponent of the Nazis. He fled Germany in 1933 and settled in Sanary-sur-Mer where he stayed until the German invasion of France, at which time he was able to flee to the California where he lived to the end of his life.

[2] **Die Sammlung** - (*The Collection*). An exile publication, in German, founded and edited by Klaus Mann, son of Thomas Mann. The publication, edited in printed by Klaus Mann's Dutch publishing house, Querido, located in Amsterdam, put out 24 editions between 1933 and 1935. Many famous exile authors and others published articles during that time; among them, Thomas Mann, Ernst Bloch, Albert Einstein, Lion Feuchtwanger, André Gide, Ernest Hemingway, Golo Mann, Heinrich Mann, and Joseph Roth, to name only some of the most prominent.

16a. 1934.01.04 — FWB (Paris) to Heinrich Mann

[typed]

Paris (18): 4.I.1934,
Aviation-Hôtel,
27, rue Tholozé.

M. Heinrich Mann,
11, rue du Congrès,
Nice / A.M.

Dear, most venerated Mr. Mann,

great, profound, heartiest, moreover longingly awaited joy in Montmartre [Beidlers lived in the Montmartre area], intensified by pride in the sign of trust in the assignment! Of course, all necessary steps will be taken immediately. A report, and, I hope, also the 500 francs, will follow as soon as possible. (20 percent commission? That is an inducement to usury. Alright, if I were a publisher . . .)

I am extremely astonished that you wrote me such a lovely letter. Actually — how should I put it? — I would expect you to believe me a subhuman. That is because it emerges clearly from your letter that you did not receive a long letter from me, garnished with attachments, written at the end of November and mailed to the address of Félix Bertaux at Sèvres.[1] Compared with you (as is well-known, adversity always strikes the most vulnerable spot) I am apparently the plaything of all devilish letter hamsters. It's already the second case! It is not because I believe that this is about an *opus aere perennius* [Latin: a work more lasting than bronze (Horace)], that today I am sending you the copy, but rather: first, in order to rehabilitate myself with you; second, to display the usefulness of a (rented) typewriter which makes possible a reconstruction from the copies; third, because of the attachments.

We had felt the need, *per se*, to send you our good and hopeful wishes, right at the start of the year. But in the hope that our letter had reached you, we thought rather to try to counter somewhat the impression of scandalous intrusiveness which our behaviour on the Côte d'Azur inevitably must have aroused and therefore made us decide to to rein in all impulse to pass on news.

More or less the following could be added to the November letter: 1) a small packet

---

[1] Félix **Bertaux** - (1881-1948) - A French professor of German literature who taught at the College of Sèvres, where Bertaux had settled in 1923. He was in contact with Heinrich Mann and other important writers.

with the therein mentioned odds and ends will be put on its way posthaste to your address; 2) Herr Kühn has condescended to honour me with this answer:

Dear Mr. Beidler,

I am much obliged to you for your letters of the 20th and 21st of the month [November]. I have sent them, along with your disclaimer and the article referred to by you, and drawn attention to them, with the Berlin authorities so that they are apprised of same.

With greatest respect, I am
Your very devoted,
(signed) Kühn

(On the 21st of November, I had sent him a copy of the disclaimer which I had directed to the "Rempart." At the very minimum: inside of the control-sphere of concentration camps — outside of much obliged and greatest respect! That is what this gang is!

In the meantime, we have read a few essays of yours with great, heartfelt joy, namely, the essay "The Blackmailers" [*Die Erpresser*] in the "Weltbühne" [World Stage]. It is an exhilarating feeling to know that, even if all the others, little by little, become weak and pathetic, à la Döblin and Schickele, one man certainly will never make his peace with the outlaw- and killer-regime: Heinrich Mann. We are determined, in this too, to follow him as paragon.

Guess what, among other things, we are reading for the first time. "Eugénie"! [*Eugénie oder Die Bürgerzeit*, Eugenie or the Bourgeois Period, novel by Heinrich Mann, 1928] In Professor von Heines we believe we recognize, with much enjoyment, the "familiar" traits of [Ernst von? d.1909, dramatist] Wildenbruch. [the novel's character, Prof. von Heines, is based on the lyrical poet, Emanuel Geibel, of Lübeck, where the Manns were born.] It fills hardly a page and is nonetheless for all eternity: the Professor's farewell after the cat's fall from the roof and the hangover-quotation — "razor-sharp"! [razor-sharp — a pun in the original — *katzenjämmerlich* — Katze = cat]

With the most affectionate of greetings and wishes, some of which you will no doubt deliver to Mrs. Kröger,[1] I remain always in great respect and loyalty, your

16a. FWB to Heinrich Mann — 1934.01.01

---

[1] Nelly Mann **Kröger** - (1898-1944) - Heinrich Mann's second wife; they married in Nice, on Sept. 9, 1939.

17. 1934.01.12 — Kbg (Prague) to Beidlers (Paris) 1934.01.12
[handwritten]

Prague XIX - Dejvice č. 1646
12./I.1934

Dear Beidlers! You do promise in your New Year's letter to write again soon, but I prefer not to wait for it and to start by thanking you for this letter. Although, in your new year's prelude — Bach always seems to have begun the church service with "*In Dir ist Freude*" [Joy is in You] — you emphasize the "infinitely more critical" manner, I have not noticed much of this in its implementation. By the way, I cannot imagine at all how you could have become more critical: I have often experienced the critical element in both of you — admittedly also with regard to your own work — as disruptive of freedom from inhibition in the work of production. Basically, however, these are questions of disposition, about which a more critical statement would be idle.

Now to your questions right away. The "Central Office for Musical Pedagogy" intends to start by collecting material about music-pedagogical issues in all cultured countries (hourly rates, methods, comprehensive education of teachers, relationship to the state, interrelation with private music and with choral societies); then compare critically and publish these in a periodical. The goal is naturally to invigorate musical pedagogy, for the time being, through a movement at home in this country; then, however, also in lands that are amenable to this sort of impetus. Through the very energetic co-operation of Minister Krofta, through the young Alois Haba (internationally recognized as quarter-tone composer) and also the professors of the three Czech universities, the position is all but certain — Becking,[1] of the Germans, is keeping aloof, naturally, if not hostile. Admittedly, I do not yet have an office and Grete is the first and only secretary. But I still think that these superficial things should be straightened out by April 1; perhaps even my appointment as director of the Centre. The first commitments to co-operate have arrived from England, France, Switzerland, Holland, and Hungary. Edward Dent[2] suggested that the Anglo-American Congress should be invited by the government here and this is already at an advanced stage. Dent writes that participants from all countries "with the ex-

[1] Gustav Wilhelm **Becking** - (1894-1945) - Musicologist, Professor at the Karl-Ferdinand University in Prague. He was devoted to proving German identity of composers normally viewed as Czech (e.g. Stamitz, Benda, Schobert, among others). He was a notorious proponent of the secessionist Sudeten-Germans in pre-WWII Czechoslovakia. He was executed in Prague one day after WWII ended.

[2] Edward **Dent** - (1876-1957) - British musicologist, teacher, and writer. He was an active promoter of increased international co-operation between composers, musicians, and teachers of music.

ception of the Aryans" will happily come to Prague if they are called and if I draft the program and bring it through to completion. Now, "on behalf" of the Central Office Society, I am going to make contact with interested musical pedagogues or people who seem interested in all countries in order to form the first foundations for statistics. Naturally, I shall receive much more data for these statistics than I need and shall process them further. In that connection, I would like to give you an immediate proposal that has occupied me the whole day today. As I see from a cursory memo, Krill[1] — incidentally, one of the most detestable of the nazified [*gleichgeschaltet*] heroes — has published only a calendar limited to Germany (Hesse-Stern) [publisher] and he is also thinking of repeating only that next year. Could you not find a publisher in Paris or A'dam [Amsterdam] (possibly also Orell-Füßli in Zurich) which would publish a really complete international calendar (optionally without Germany)?

The first thing necessary would be to find out if America has a special reference work, which possibly is still extant. Do you want to know more about the Z.f.M.? [Central Office for Musik]

In Holland — between three lectures and concerts here and in Brno — I gave three lectures at the Society for School Music which were received very well. I hope that I can be invited there again. If it were possible, for instance, in autumn, to give lectures on Liszt at Lichtenberger's, I would be able to combine it with Holland, which could ease the financial question. What you write about Chantavoine is correct. His influence does not reach very far. But, of the French writers on music and politicians whom I know, he is the most serious. Busoni, too, admired him greatly. Prunières, on the other hand, is very superficial, vain, and a French edition of Adolf Weißmann[2] (I don't know at all if you got to know him). But he is still interesting and surely now active along our lines. — Your depiction of Alice Jacob-L.'s [Jacob-Loewenson] lecture was very amusing. — It is astounding to us that she always manages to force her way forward with her music presentations, of which I have a very low opinion.

And what is happening about the proposal to collect material for me about Wilhem or to work on him yourself, which you accepted with such enthusiasm some time ago?

---

[1] Hans **Krill** - (1884-1946) - Kestenberg's description of Krill as an utterly despicable Nazi, is supported by a letter of 1947, in which Alfred Einstein refers to Krill's having committed suicide. "He had good reason to take his life," he writes. According to Einstein, the publication edited by Krill from 1933 to 1942 was just about as perfidious as the *Stürmer* or the *Völkischer Beobachter,* two of the most blood-curdling, official Nazi publications.

[2] Adolf **Weissmann** - (1873-1929) - A German music critic and essayist.

Nourrit,[1] K[?]ainzer and the Englishman Hullah would also have to be disinterred. You know certainly that Kretzschmar[2] first came to his pedagogical work through Hullah. Hullah is a student of Wilhem. — What I've got in mind, for you too, is an extension of muscial organization in international dimensions, about which you are also doubtless thinking. I want to concentrate on musical pedagogy, however, because I see immediate, positive tasks before me. I very much regret that I receive so little news from Germany, from which so little can be gleaned about the disputes between the various tendencies. Today, Connor wrote me that he wants to come here for 2 days. I hope to hear more from him. About "friends"! What should I say about Schünemann? He was always faint-hearted. And since he started playing dead in March, I don't know anything more about him. He seems to have died for me: Requiescat in pace — Or has he somehow acted in unsympathetic ways without my hearing about it? — Germany is a problem that causes me to have worries about the Central Office. About this, as well, I want to confer with Connor. Has Walter Jacob visited you already? I could imagine that you could get along with him well and follow up on plans together. What is doing with the family relationships that you so brilliantly began? [Olliviers] And when is your *Sammlung* article to appear? I am eagerly awaiting your Richard Wagner essay. I am giving 5 lectures about "Active Listening," for which the conniving couple, whose pictures we were so grateful to receive back then — I do truly miss, despite the "more critical" attitude which they threatened. Yesterday the local "Social Democrat" published a very nice review of the first lecture. Come here sometime to do some enlightening! Until then, very affectionate greetings — also from all the other dwellers in our ark

Your old Leo Kbg

[Grete K. in margin] I'm waiting, and send regards! Your G.K.

17. KBG to FWB — 1934.01.12

---

[1] Adolphe **Nourrit** - (1802-1839) - Famous French tenor and educator who specialized in operas by Rossini and Meyerbeer.

[2] Hermann **Kretzschmar** - (1848-1924) - German musicologist, writer, educator, and reformer.

18. 1934.03.20 — FWB (Paris) to Kbg

[typed]

Background:

After months of cultivating contacts in Paris, Beidler could take some satisfaction at how the Wagner and Liszt lineage had opened all doors to him. Still, none of these many, friendly, contacts gave him even the slightest hope of being able to obtain work or earn money in the French capital. In this letter, Beidler expresses his frustration voicing sarcastic opinions about many denizens of the musical world, including several who had been especially kind to him and his wife. By the end of March, 1934, Beidler was all too aware that, although he was treated as something of a sensation in Parisian musical circles, this status was no help to an uprooted emigré with little money. Having worked and lived with Kestenberg since 1927, Beidler also knew that his very open and critical tone might not find the approval of his former boss. Given his difficult situation Beidler, typical for emigrés, doubtless expected Kestenberg to sympathize with his frustration.

There was at least one other matter causing a problem. Kestenberg kept at Beidler, asking him, almost ordering him, as in days past, to do research on the educator Wilhem because he needed material which he could use in preparing a lecture. The following is the extant part of an undated letter from Beidler to Kestenberg (page one is missing), some of which will also have grated on Kestenberg. Beidler's ridicule of Kestenberg's friend, Paul Bekker, will surely have irked Kestenberg.

The extant part of the letter, probably of late January, 1934, is presented here:

Chantavoine again apologized profusely to us for not personally delivering the material to you, but he was really so overburdened that he just was unable to get to it. And since everything here is so peculiarly impenetrable, it doubtless demands a huge amount of work. I'd prefer to put it all together for you. But, more recently, in connection with various plans, I somewhat turned away from music and have tried to refresh the areas that were my specialties in the pre-Kestenberg period. [pre-1927]

This change is also connected, for the time being, with my not continuing to follow up on the lineage: Wilhem, Hullah, Galin Paris,[1] Chevé etc. At any rate, allow me to note that we are decidedly overrating the outcomes of Wilhem's reforms for France. And that is completely apart from their failure to emerge beyond Paris (in France!). Today, if you ask a musician or a musicologist about Wilhem, he first ponders the matter, only to say

[1] Pierre **Galin** (1786-1822) - A French music educator who developed a notational system that became known as the Galin-Paris-Chevé system.

finally, "oh yes, that is the man with the orphéons" [mass choral societies]. By the way, I shall remain skeptical about his achievements of pedagogical reform until I am able to be convinced otherwise. I hope to get to plowing through the material in April, in the Conservatory library, while the National Library has holidays. In any case, at least here, he no longer has any current significance (I do not know how it is in England).

My present scholarly re-orientation (to sociological-statistical problems!) is connected with my not adopting your almanac suggestion as much as it doubtless deserves. In light of the present situation, I do not have the courage to proceed with such a labyrinthine project, one that would long monopolize my work potential, without at least first knowing where we will land in the immediate future and from what we will be able to earn a so-called living. At least, I did speak about the plan with the publisher [Jacques] **Heugel** whose name you know from "Ménestrel."[1] To me, he did not really seem eager to get involved. In principle, by God, I would like to get my own back on the obnoxious Krill. If my plans relating to the Institute were to develop, which I do not expect, the matter would immediately look differently. By the way, in America there is a "Pierre Keys 'Musical Year-Book'" (but which is plenty paltry and bad).

A propos of America. Are you actually aware that your beloved Terramare Office has become the hub for Hitler propaganda in the USA? Apparently with the same personnel! Really! The personnel! Is it not a joy to open up a real German periodical? The complete collection is there, to the extent that they were not sadly but very urgently hindered for organically racist reasons. Knorr[2] as Nazi-brown house-composer, Wunsch reaching the object of his wishes, Schering[3] like "Führer," Lothar Band presents "The Song for the *Volk*" on May 1; then your friend Preetorius …But the most amusing is "The National Association for Choral Singing and Folk Music," business office: Hardenbergstr. 36! But be honest: have we really earned "co-workers" that are at all different?? I don't mean you personally — actually, you would have deserved others; I mean the gentlemen republicans

---

[1] **Le Ménestral**. - The Minstrel - French music journal published weekly, 1833-1940. It was acquired by the music publishers Heugel until it ceased publication at the beginning of World War II.

[2] Ernst-Lothar von **Knorr** - (1896-1973) - German composer, teacher, and Nazi music officer. In 1937 he began teaching music at the State University of Berlin, where he became a professor two years later. He was music advisor to the High Command of the German Army, 1937-1941. Various of his musical compositions, much of them composed for Nazi occasions, were supposedly destroyed in a bombing in 1944. After the war he became music advisor to the Federal Army. He received the Great Federal Awards Cross in 1961.

[3] Arnold **Schering** - (1877-1941) - German musicologist. Active member of various nazified musical organizations. He wrote musical analyses according to racist, Nazi principles.

of the Social Democratic Party, who are now publishing their snivel-paper, "Revolution Against Hitler"....

Let's admit it: we cannot make a state, not any sort of state, by means of "emigration" (with the exception of a couple of greats, such as the Manns, in every respect). We see extremely little of this. What we do see is partly dismal, but, much more, deeply annoying. Recently, I received an invitation to a sort of Art Club — naturally, in a posh hotel. Anything less would be impossible when instigated by Herr Dr. Spiecker.[1] Sensing something unpleasant, I turned it down, just to be on the safe side. Afterwards, I found out who all was in on this. Hugo Simon,[2] Döblin,[3] Grzesinski,[4] Frau Hilferding,[5] Georg Bernhard[6] .... Imagine what would have resulted if I had unwittingly blundered into

---

[1] Carl **Spiecker** - (1888-1953) - Originally, a journalist associated with the Centre Party, after World War I, he became involved in secretive operations on behalf of Germans in Silesia. He worked with a Freikorp unit that was responsible for assassinating many "German traitors" (court case, 1928). In the 1920s he adopted republican views and worked to weaken the Nazis, who had him fired in 1933 and forced his emigration to France. He founded a German Freedom Party and sought to topple the Nazi government.

[2] Hugo **Simon** - (1880-1950) - Jewish-German banker and politician. Simon was a wealthy banker who was an important part of the cultural, artistic, and political scenes. He donated money to institutions such as the National Gallery in Berlin and advised about new purchases. He had a very large and significant collection of paintings. His open house was often the scene of salons attended by the leading writers, painters, theatre people, and publishers. In 1933, he and his wife had to flee Germany. They were able to take only part of their art collection with them. The rest was seized by the Nazis on October 9, 1933. The Simons fled via Switzerland to Paris, where they started a bank. When the Nazis invaded they had to leave quickly and managed to escape to Brazil.

[3] Alfred **Döblin** - (1878-1957) - see note in Introduction.

[4] Albert **Grzesinski** - (1879-1947) - He was Minister of the Interior of Prussia, 1926-1930. Member of the Social Democratic Party. In August 1933 the Nazis cancelled his citizienship and he fled to France, via Switzerland. Together with other German emigrants in Paris, he worked to establish a Front against the Nazis with the long-term goal of restoring democracy. He emigrated to America in 1937 and settled in New York.

[5] Margarete **Hilferding** - (1871-1942) - wife of Rudolf Hilferding (separated 1922). Austrian teacher, medical doctor and adherent of Individual Psychology. Murdered in Treblinka.

[6] Georg **Bernhard** - (1875-1944) - See note in letter 14.

that…! And I shall never again be invited anywhere Breitscheid[1] and Hilferding are; in that vein, I have established a truly energetic and not at all socially acceptable precedent.

But there is one man here who makes up for the whole Emigration [crowd]: Kurt Löwenstein![2] We are extraordinarily happy that he is near us here. We are in constant contact with him. A few days ago, we spent a whole, content-rich night with him and his. Fundamentally, the [horrible] events have caused him to grow — clear and tireless, clean and profoundly insightful. And above all, again: clean!

Once we were with Paul Bekker for a whole evening, alone with him and his (disagreeable) son. You know how, deep inside, I stand up for him, despite that thing he has for opera and voices, etc. But warm to him? That's just not on for me. As we were leaving, he pressed upon us his wish that we get together again. I replied that we really could not expect him to subject himself to more such lost evenings, lost to himself (and to us…). This seemed to please him and he begged us all the more urgently [to return]! He lets you talk and does not say a word, looking all the while like a crocodile lying in the sand in the Egyptian sun, squinting, making highly unauthoritative remarks about things of which he understands nothing nor wants to understand, and feels somehow comfortable with that! Peculiar man! Still, person-to-person, I like him. But, that he is the author of books, of which one made me downright sick and half-crazed, that is something that a person cannot comprehend when looking at him. He protests massively against the impertinent assertion that he is writing a history of music in the Weimar State. "I ask you, what is a person supposed to write about that? In the end, I cannot simply write that the only reasonable deed during that time was the appointment of myself as [Theater] Director. You see, something like this just goes beyond my understanding and my ability to comprehend such things in a man of Paul Bekker's stature … Nonetheless, I like him (which is saying a lot at the present time).

Have you heard anything from Fritz Schönbeck? That would interest us. Then, what did Connor have to tell? What are his plans? What do you say about Susanne Trautwein's sudden death?

---

[1] Rudolf **Breitscheid** - (1874-1944) - a leading Social Democrat. After losing his citizenship in 1933, he emigrated to France. In Paris, he participated in efforts to establish an anti-Nazi Front until he was captured by Vichy officers and handed over to the Gestapo. He died in Buchenwald concentration camp.

[2] Kurt **Löwenstein** - (1885-1939) - Nom de plume: Kerlöw. Jewish Social Democrat. Member of Parliament with a special interest in education. In Paris, he joined the Front movement and continued his work on behalf of education. He died in Paris.

In the Conservatory we were moved and full of reverence when we caught sight of your signature on a Liszt manuscript (from Busoni's collection).

A thousand greetings to everyone, above all Frau Grete and Tunja, about whom we have spoken a lot recently. Does he know where Kurt Neumann has landed? I have re-established a Russian connection and perhaps I can be of help to Kurt. It has to do with an important man.

Always, your old, somewhat caustic

18a. 1934.03.20 — FWB (Paris) to Kbg

[typed]

Paris (18): 20 March 1934,
Aviation-Hôtel,
27, rue Tholozé.

[head of letter:] Oh this Beidler!

Professor Leo KESTENBERG,
Dejvice c. 1646,
Prague CSD

Dear Comrade Kestenberg,

You will gradually understand why, despite so many luminous paragons, I confront all pedagogical "successes" with maximum skepticism, all the while being wholly schopenhauerized, and remarking somewhere that if education could bring something to fruition, then how is it that Seneca's pupil could be a Nero? Precisely in my own "black soul" I keep re-discovering that man is unchangeable and fundamentally incorrigible. Despite the very best and sublimest resolutions at the start of the year, since my last letter around two-and-a-half months have disappeared and, in the meantime, the subject matter has expanded so much that there is no knowing where to begin. But since "Music in Contemporary Consciousness" has officially certified that I used to be "a close friend" of yours, I must, for my part, give a care for the continued existence of this condition.

Being used to talking bluntly (much less so in deed, unfortunately!), I am returning to your plan for lectures in Paris and announce that, for starters, it has been done already by Sauer (quite appropriately, since, in local terms, he is a youth, … a youth!!).[1] He was invited by a private piano school (that of Mme Margherite Long[2] — the less said about her the better — because I have the honour to be acquainted with her opinions). In January, in three evenings for pupils, he gave commentaries on Liszt pieces played by the students and also played a few things himself. Ollivier found it good (but that is not saying much … here, everything is excellent, as long as it is only 80 to 100 years old and has a penetratingly moldy smell.)

In no way should this prevent you from speaking about Liszt in another venue and

[1] Emil von **Sauer** - (1862-1942) - German piano virtuoso, composer, and educator. He embodied a continuation of the tradition of the Franz-Liszt school of piano-interpretation.

[2] Marguerite **Long** - (1874-1966) - French pianist, teacher at the Paris Conservatoire 1906-1940.

from playing things that are not *en vogue*. The only question is just which venue would be right. You were thinking of Lichtenberger's workshop. Possible. I have not spoken with him for a long time (his Wagner lecture was so sleek, so shaped, and so puke-aesthetic that we simply could not go along with it anymore — this as an "aside" and between you and me; because, objectively, it is shameless ingratitude on my part against the old fellow who is lovely to us). Only a few days ago, he celebrated his seventieth birthday (therefore, according to the local view of things, has entered the prime of life), by which, naturally, I enthusiastically congratulated him (and two days later, had a hand-written, magnificent thank you note in my hands — flawless to the....). That being so, I can easily manage to consult him about your plans. Should I? Or do you prefer, because you know him, to write same to him? If it doesn't work out there, I want to keep my ears open for different alternatives. Would you also possibly do it in French (that is, to read it off, like Kurt Sachs, who, as is generally known, having been worthily replaced by Schünemann, is now here near the Trocadéro)? The date would be late autumn, right?

Today, I shall skip your question about the "living" Liszt in Paris, in the hope of writing you in detail, sometime soon, about the musical climate here. Doing so requires taking a few far-flung tangents. But a small story, belonging in the Liszt context, should follow here. Do you know Friedrich Schnapp (of course you know him).[1] It's like this: Daniel Ollivier knows Frau Busoni and asked her, about a year ago if she knew anyone who could give him information about German names and relationships for the notes in his edition of correspondence. She recommended Schnapp and there developed between the two a positively immense correspondence with queries and, from Schnapp, superbly precise answers which must have demanded much work of him. Ollivier found him prodigious and wanted at least to reimburse him his expenses, which Schnapp refused with the explanation that he did everything out of love of Liszt. The German translation had hardly just appeared when an enormously long letter arrived with the most minute criticisms of the translation; the conclusion stated that the translator, Käthe Illch, not only had no clue about music (which, as it happens, is right), but was also scandalously illiterate and had translated miserably. My impression is that the latter, although not false, is somewhat exaggerated. With the help of the French publisher, Schnapp wants to force S.Fischer to put him in charge of translating the second volume. Do you consider him to be qualified for this? For the rest: no doubt that Frau Illch is anything but a good translator and committed a number of super-howlers, which, even in the presence of a minimal intellect and a bit of accuracy, should have revealed themselves as avoidable. But: do you find Schnapp's methods fair? I don't. What kind of person is he really? I would be very grateful for some enlightenment. (Additional remark, solely between you and me: the way that Ollivier is

[1] Friedrich **Schnapp** - (1900-1983) - German musicologist, recording director.

"taking care of" publishing these two volumes of correspondence is beneath contempt and would be absolutely impossible in Germany. At least in the second volume I was able to prevent the worst of the irregular and slipshod things; but plenty of that still remains).

For today, no more about my panoply of plans and negotiations with all sorts of parties; it's all much too up in the air. Probably, in the foreseeable future, we shall go to Switzerland after all. By now, although we are somewhat suspicious (if a German emigrant is not a Jew, then he has to be a Marxist and, in the meantime, the French, indoctrinated by domestic political developments, have implemented this simple mnemonic inscription), still we have meshed into the very top (and naturally the most capitalistic and even partly the most reactionary!!) social stratum. We are constantly invited, get to know everyone, from the director of the Sorbonne to the present minister of external affairs, all the way up to the Rothschilds, who are in the immediate offing.

Truly, it is at least interesting. And, despite our apparent suspiciousness, about which we make no bones, everyone, without exception, is charming to us. Still, I do not see a permanent, or maybe even a real future for me here. More about this another time.

Many sincere thanks for your information about the "Central Office." Pretty much everyone here is writing that you have a major posting in Czechoslovakia; even "Music in Contemporary Consciousness" has confirmed this — in a snivelling way. Your good relations with Krofta especially interested and gladdened me; you will want for nothing there. Chantavoine will have written to you already that he is not in a position to bring together the material you want and that he advises you to approach the I.I.C.I.. There, however, you are going to have to wait a long time!

18a. FWB to KBG — 1934.03.20

19. 1934.05.06 — Kbg (Prague) to Beidlers (Paris)

[typed]

Background:

Kestenberg's "cleansing thunder-storm" of a response to Beidler's letter, a response, as well, to an article the latter had written in *Die Sammlung*, must have been both crushing and annoying to Beidler. Kestenberg continues in the boss-to-employee tone without much apparent empathy for Beidler's difficult situation. When he uses Beidler's own great-grandfather, Franz Liszt, to scold Beidler, Kestenberg really pulls out the stops. When Kestenberg writes, "…I do not understand why Hitler's victory should cause us to alter completely our personal attitude…" he reveals his strength as well, perhaps, a weakness or two. Luckily, for Kestenberg, this attitude had to do with theoretical and political matters; for instance, relations with past members of the Socialist Party. In practical affairs, Kestenberg was both fast and flexible, as witnessed by the speed with which he quit Nazi Germany while so many others lingered. At any rate, like so many other musicians, the Kestenberg of this letter is a man who is guided by the life and works of Franz Liszt, even sanctifying the great pianist and composer for extreme idolization. His urging Beidler to follow in his great-grandfather's footsteps is probably redundant and futile. Especially with regard to the Nazis, Beidler was utterly intolerant, voluble and aggressive. Nothing Kestenberg could say about maintaining cool, Lisztian equilibrium would be able to change that.

Prague XIX - Dejvice č. 1646.
Sunday, May 6, 34.

Dear Comrade Beidler, in a letter to the Countess d'Agoult, your great-grandfather [Liszt] writes that he does not presume to make judgments about other people. This tolerance is no symptom of old age but rather seems to me of vital importance for the essence of Liszt. As you know, I have an infinite reverence for this essence and that precisely this statement of Liszt's reaches me profoundly. Supported by this buttress, I could have overlooked things that mortified me in your last letter and also in the article you published in "Sammlung."[1] Since I do not want to equate tolerance with convenience, I view it as more correct to grapple with you on these questions rather than evade them.

---

[1] Beidler had published an article in *Die Sammlung*, an emigré publication edited by Klaus Mann, the son of Thomas Mann. In the article, Beidler took to task various members of the Social Democratic Party for their failures during the Weimar Republic.

As a matter of course, everyone is free to condemn the past and to make individual personalities responsible for any sins. To me, however, it seems at the very least unfair to belie a bond, which outwardly, at any rate, was kept alive until recently through membership of a party. It was only our lack of strength and energy that was to blame for our failure to steer the party in the direction that seemed right to us. Related to this, I remember that not so long ago, you yourself took a very "democratic" position in discussions and had understanding, if not approval, for the approach of Sollmann, Heine, Landsberg and consorts.[1] Today, after our catastrophic defeat, for which we all must feel jointly responsible, it seems to me a lukewarm amusement to berate former party members and to strike attitudes today with an easily constructible, haughty, and ironic stance. As you know, I was more than dissatisfied with the state of many objective and personal matters in the party and that I did not miss any opportunity to bring to the attention of the men who seemed decisive to me, the severe psychological mistakes that, in my opinion, had their origin in the time before the war. But I do not understand why Hitler's victory should cause us to alter completely our personal attitude to these men and to use insults in place of discussion and striving to reach a new standpoint. The efforts towards new programs also seem feeble and the idea that the same men as before again lay claim to leadership roles is risible. But precisely because I know that we are in agreement in this respect, I am requesting a word of clarification from you about your position, which, for the time being, remains incomprehensible to me. This applies to your article in "Sammlung," which contains a whole quantity of apparent historical mistakes, the origin of which I cannot explain. I also do not know what moved you to conceal so coyly and consistently the name of the musician who was to be appointed as head of the department. [i.e. Kestenberg] By the way, the history of the founding of the department is depicted with complete inaccuracy. At the moment, I do not have your article at hand so that I can criticize it only from memory. In any case, it is inconceivable to me, who could have conveyed to you, in this form, the history of the plan for a department of national arts education. I first developed this plan in great detail in 1921. It was the first impulse for the music department of the Central Institute. But at least your article can form an impetus for long overdue description of all these events, to which I may come in the course of the next year.

At the moment, I am actively engaged in work for our "Society for Musical Educa-

---

[1] Friedrich Wilhelm **Sollmann** - (1881-1951) - German social-democratic politician and writer. After the Nazi takeover in 1933, he emigrated to the UK and then to the USA.
Fritz Heine - (1904-2002) - German social-democratic politician. He fled to Prague in 1933. After the Nazi occupation of Czechoslovakia, he fled to Paris, then on to Marseille, where, after the Nazi invasion, he helped many Jews to flee. In 1941 he fled to the UK.
Otto Landsberg - (1869-1957) - Member of the German Social Democratic Party from 1890 on. In 1933, he fled to Czechoslovakia and then to Holland.

tion." Four weeks ago, within the framework of the Music Festival of the International Society for New Music, I gave a lecture in Florence which gave me the opportunity to expand on our plans before the delegates. It seems now that the work is secure. The statutes have been officially approved, the board of directors, which, for the moment consists only of Czechs, has been elected and the first public General Meeting should take place on June 11. I hope that the absolutely necessary financial means will, by then, have been mustered and that we can then begin with the work of the "Central Office". Thank you very much for your kind support. The article by Malherbe[1] was very useful to me. At the moment, France is represented the least in our correspondence. My personal connections are inadequate to obtain material from official bodies there. Chantavoine's skeptical remarks as well as your comments have, up to now, convinced me that it is not advisable to contact the I.I.C.I. directly. I want to wait until I can approach this especially rigid-appearing fortress with the ordnance of the diplomatic corps. I shall make use of the help of either the French ambassador here or the Czech ambassador in Paris. Who is actually the present director of the I.I.C.I.? Is André Coeuroy still employed there? And who is still delegated from Germany? In any case, you know that Miss (Dr.) Rotbart and Dr. Picht used to be representatives there for German arts and science.

I regret that you have no time to occupy yourself more closely with Wilhem. Nowadays it goes completely without saying that nobody knows him. But it would be very interesting to me to learn of literature about him, particularly about his reform of school music, in the vanguard of which was the introduction of obligatory voice lessons in the elementary schools of Paris in the year 1835 and the connection of this singing instruction with the male choral societies. Perhaps, after all, you could make the effort sometime to have a look at the bibliography about Wilhem and possibly make a copy of it. Otherwise, it seems completely natural to me that you now should return to your old sociological-statistical specialty and devote less interest to musical "issues."

I welcomed with gratitude your reference to possible prospects for Liszt evenings in Paris, but these plans are no longer of such serious interest as they used to be because I am so absorbed in the "Central Office" and in my suggestions for a program for the Czechoslovakian area, from Bach to Busoni which I must prepare. The antipathy to Liszt in this land is diminishing only gradually. Lately, in an orchestra concert in the German Theatre here "Mazeppa" was booed as if it was a matter of a premiere a hundred years ago. — What you write me about Friedrich Schnapp does not surprise me. I know Schnapp from Busoni's last years. He did a lot of work on the musical works of

---

[1] Henry **Malherbe** - (1887-?) - French writer, winner of the Prix Goncourt in 1917. Malherbe wrote for Le Temps.

E.Th.Hoffmann and was also supposed to edit Busoni's correspondence. He is exceptionally dependable and conscientious and his attitude in the question of the Liszt letters corresponds to his disposition, which I know. His interference in this affair is admittedly tasteless. Your description of the visit with Paul Bekker is very amusing. Just a few days ago, he sent me a few chapters from his new book, for which he has not found a publisher. I read this part of the manuscript with the most lively intensity.

Rahel is in Palestine and writes with great humour and contentment. She is in an agrarian school there. Ruth and Tunja are doing well. Ruth wants to take her doctor's exam in the autumn. She is working with great intensity now on her dissertation. Tunja is studying philosophy and also works in the library service. Grete is feeling quite well again. She has now connected somewhat more affectionately with Prague. My mother is still very fresh and lusting for life.

When you last wrote to me — it was on April 8 [not preserved] — little woman [Ellen Beidler] had just had her birthday. Even four weeks too late, we all want to express our congratulations, all the more affectionately. The bonds of our cohesion and solidarity stretch to one another, above and beyond all the difficulties, misunderstandings, and disagreements of this time. And despite certain doubts, I still believe that we shall continue to understand and feel connected to each other. My long letter is meant to be a document of the fact that, by all means, I should like to keep alive the relationship with you both and even to strengthen it. Now I'm awaiting the echo, which, after this cleansing little thunder storm, one hopes will not be long in coming. With the most affectionate regards to you both

Your old

Leo Kestenberg

[Grete K., handwritten:]

Dear Beidlers!

I have already written to you three times. However I did not mail the letters, because I always started talking about politics, and if I talk about politics I become "mean." For that reason, I am now doing nothing other than, like K. Löwenstein, "spiritize."

I think of you very often and once a month especially often for several days (this is also the case now); i.e. when I use a handkerchief with the initials "F.W.B." on it. Write to me occasionally sometimes so that I could then pull myself together and answer you.

All the best

Tunja and Ruth and very affectionately. [Ruth's handwriting] Tunja and I have concluded from your letter that you are now a "comrade." Is that right? I find, at least partially, that Papa is right with reference to the past, to the extent that you, in a word, had to mention that you too belonged with these gentlemen. If you do not anymore, *tant mieux* [so much the better]; I congratulate you and am joyful. And you have [illegible] the right of clan inheritance [?-illegible] with [illegible] this historical note in my opinion also.

19. KBG to FWB — 1934.05.06

20. 1934.11.25 — FWB (Zurich) to Kbg

[typed]

Zurich: 25 November 1934,
30, Bolleystrasse.

[head of letter:] FRANZ W. BEIDLER-WAGNER

Dear Comrade KESTENBERG,

it would contradict all tradition but also my inner feelings towards you if I wanted to let the 27th of November pass by without expressly saying to you that we are thinking of you with affection as in days of old.

It happened. In line with the accustomed candor of our dealings (that must be said), we left your last letter - dated May 6th of this year - unanswered until now, and not without reason and intention. An immediate answer could not have been sent without a certain acrimony. It would have entailed disputes about things that now hold not only no reality but also no longer even the slightest importance. Should we, too, prove to each other that we — so truly in the manner of emigrants — had learned nothing from the events and had wanted not to learn anything?

I want to hone in on the point in which I am completely at one with you: we all share the guilt for what happened in Germany. But each according to the degree of responsibility imposed on him. Neither you nor I bears political responsibility.

Isn't it finally time for us to admit that people like us were never taken seriously in the political framework in which we chatted ourselves up as "movers and shakers" — at times more, at times less? And that — seen historically — was completely right. We intellectuals never were integral parts of the organizational complex, into which the calamitous development of the German situation forced itself, half unconsciously, half inescapably. In an organization which was there to represent, quite exclusively and with certain legitimacy, the day-to-day interests of trade-unions within the given societal framework, we were never anything other than superfluous outsiders, who were allowed to decorate the external facade, each according to his "name," or, if "oppositional," to be perceived as mere nuisances. Eternally refusing, at all cost, to admit this fact, emphasized as it was, sometimes with thousands of really well-grounded reasons, was our — or at least my — share of the guilt — and it was a gigantic inanity.

The year 1933, I think, taught us forever that our best motives were also **wrong**. For my part, this has led me to draw radical consequences. One reason to keep up human bonds existed less to the extent that they had never existed before. In addition, certain events, of which you may have no knowledge, have erected a dividing wall which is final. I only have to remind you of the foreign trips of Messrs Herz, Stampfer, Kirschmann etc.,[1] which were carried out on behalf of Mr. Goering to give you an approximate intimation of what I mean. Incidentally, such details from the "inner life" of "our" party have only become known since Hitler's seizure of power — and not until then, so that it would be well-nigh a scandal not to distance oneself with utmost severity from the players and "insiders." If we had known these things back then, they would have made an immediate break with the party simply unavoidable. But we were, in fact, all and sundry pitiful outsiders and the others had every reason to smile constantly at our approach. How anyone can **now** talk of solidarity, is incomprehensible to me.

What astounded and wounded me much more was your assumption that, in one of my scribblings from back then, I had "coyly" concealed your name. Actually, I was of the opinion that I had given you no reason for **that**, and felt very strongly reminded of **Busoni** ....

With that, I have already arrived at Zurich, where, as you see, we have pitched "our tents." And this since August. We did not leave Paris lighheartedly. Precisely in the last months of our stay there, all doors had opened to us. But building a new life in the "homeland" [Switzerland] seemed easier and more secure. That does not prevent us from orienting ourselves on Paris and to preserve the continuing connection. As a farewell, I gave a lecture there on "Music and musical life in Germany since the war," on the premises of the I.I.C.I., under the *présidence* of **Chantavoine**, with whom deep ties of friendship have been established and to whom I owe many debts of gratitude. All in all, I can say that, during our months in Paris, we experienced more warmth of human relationships than during our whole lives in Germany, which has already become so alien to me,

---

[1] Carl **Herz** - (1877-1951) - Jewish-German Social Democratic politician. He was the local Mayor of Berlin-Kreuzberg 1926-1933. Physically thrown out of his office in March 1933, he eventually fled to England. His youngest son was murdered in Auschwitz. In 1946, he moved to Palestine.

Friedrich **Stampfer** - (1874-1957) - Jewish-German Social-Democratic politician and journalist. Editor-in-Chief of *Vorwärts*, 1916-1933. Member of parliament, 1920-1933. Stampfer had travelled to Moscow to urge co-operation between the German Communists and Social Democrats. Perhaps Goering was already thinking of reaching the agreement with the Soviets which later was signed.

Emil **Kirschmann** - (1888-1948) - German Social Democratic politician. Member of parliament 1924-1933. Fled to France where he helped others to flee Germany.

as if it had never had anything to do with me. But we also do not have the slightest cause to complain about Switzerland. People here have been, quite generally and right up to the highest levels, extraordinarily obliging and helpful to us and give us the feeling at every opportunity that we are definitely viewed as belonging here. Our re-established and very close contact to Thomas Mann and family contributes much to our good mood at the deepest level.

How are you and yours doing? What we recently heard from Vladimir Vogel[1] does not at all satisfy inquisitiveness. Despite long interruption in our contact, we are still interested in everything that has to do with you, Mrs. Grete, Ruth, Rahel and Tunja, whereby the beloved Grandma should not be forgotten. Has Ruth completed her doctorate? How does Rahel like it in the "homeland?" And how are your projects coming and your artistic activities? (No doubt, you have withdrawn from the politics-of-the-day as much as we have.). With all of these questions is attached just as many good wishes

Your old

20. FWB to KBG — 1934.11.25

[1] Vladimir Rudolfovitz **Vogel** - (1896-1984) - Swiss composer of German-Russian origin. He studied with Ferruccio Busoni in Berlin. As son of a Jewish mother, he fled Germany in 1933 - to France, Belgium, London, and, Switzerland.

21. 1934.12.19 — Kbg (Prague) to Beidlers (Zurich)

[handwritten]

Velvarská 59
Prague XIX - Dejvice
19 December 34

My dear friends!

Your birthday letters and wishes gave me all the more joy because, half melancholy, half wrathful, I had almost given up all hope of ever receiving an answer to my last letter. Now I wholeheartedly join you in your view of the absolute sterility of such discussions. You know for sure that my whole temperament compels me always to live for "tomorrow." The older I become, the less also my interest in yesterday, which mostly seems to me an eternal yesterday. As valuable as much in the epoch that lies behind us seems, I nonetheless think essentially about the missions that lie ahead of me and on the so limitlessly increased responsibility and the obligations which presently arise for us all out of the experiences of the last decade. After this double bar therefore, first of all, sincere thanks for your good and faithful remembrance, for your unchanged high-mindedness.

I heard on the grapevine of your new whereabouts in Switzerland, also about your lecture in the I.I.C.I. And to that, the tenor of my first request is already tuned. Do you still possess the manuscript of this lecture or a plan that you might possibly put at my disposal, on loan? It would be extraordinarily interesting for me to get to know your remarks. Specifically, there is a possibility of my giving 1 or 2 lectures here about a similar theme, wherein I certainly shall go more or less explicitly into the current situation. My aim is to show the complete lack of instinct of the present rulers, who, in virtually incomprehensible ignorance, reject youthful commitment and jostling collective forces and increasingly devote themselves to the liberalistic-individualistic style. Fundamentally, this is only consistent and a triumph of Schacht's, in this area too.[1]

And my second request concerns your general experiences in Paris. I have not really succeeded in finding a personality who could report to me with reasonable clarity and detail about musical-pedagogical conditions there. Even if I must also assume that there is not much to report, the short indications of Chantavoine seem much too resigned and

[1] Hjalmar **Schacht** - (1877-1970) - German banker and politician. President of the Central Bank of Germany 1923-1930 and 1933-1939. Federal Finance Minister 1934-1937. Full name: Horace Greeley Hjalmar Schacht.

pessimistic. Do you now Masson[1] of the Sorbonne? The latter, on prompting from Dent, recently wrote me and gave me the addresses of the official inspectors of music. In this, there would be obvious foreign-affairs reasons for an especially brisk relationship with France to be especially welcome.

And now I already come to my own work. For a few weeks now, our Společnost pro hudební výchovu, in German "Gesellschaft für Musikerziehung" [Society for Musical Education], has been located in very beautiful offices in the courtyard of the Tuscan Palace on the castle square. Minister Krofta, the deputy of Minister of External Affairs Beneš, is our Praeses [Lat. patron] and bestows on us not only the nimbus of his position and his name but he also works with us with a joyfulness and endurance that I find completely unusual for ministers. His secretary, Jindra,[2] is young and intelligent. From the very first moment, he seemed devotedly friendly to me; he is also our assistant and my closest colleague. Beside the collection of materials from all lands, with which we are constantly pre-occupied, we are now preparing for an international congress, which, following the Karlsbad Music Festival of the I.S.N.M, should take place in Prague from 6-10 September. Don't you feel like participating as you did back then?

By the way, in Paris did you track down any traces of Robert Brussel and the somewhat curious Association d'echange artistique etc.? [Association of Artistic Exchange] My repeated inquiries remained unanswered so that I received the impression that there, too, a certain Hitler-amenability must have seeped in.

And now, a further request which actually claims pride of place before all others. In the last few months, I have been giving private lectures on the history of music and this has led me to the sociology of music. Naturally, for this I need all possible material that can be found, especially pictures. Grete tells me that, in the turbulent days of the house move and the partial liquidation of the library, she had handed over to you to store for me, approximately 60-70 parts of "Handbook of Musicology," which Bücken publishes in the Athenaion Publishing House in Potsdam. Do you perhaps remember this arrangement - and if yes, could you tell me anything about where these now extremely important works are located - which would make me very happy - and to have them sent to me, possibly at my expense? I admit that I fear Grete either has made a mistake or that you long ago gave the volumes away or had them put to some other use. At any rate, I would very

[1] Paul-Marie **Masson** - (1882-1954) - French musicologist, educator, composer. Specialist in the works of Jean-Philippe Rameau. He taught at the Sorbonne 1931-1952. He founded the Institute of Musicology at the Sorbonne in 1951.

[2] Jaroslav **Jindra** - (1890-1970) - He was Kestenberg's deputy in Prague.

much welcome receiving news about them very promptly.

If you should encounter musical recordings that are of historical interest, I would be very grateful for information. For this reason, I wrote to Prof. Sachs in Paris a few days ago but I am constantly searching for suitable material.

By the way, would you occasionally like to write a Wagner article or anything else of music-history for the *Neue Weltbühne* [New World Stage]. I spoke to the publisher, Buzilawsi about you and he would be very pleased to receive a contribution of this sort from you.

Your warm words about Thomas Mann also made me very happy, and even happier that you have such a close personal relationship with him. A few weeks ago, I sent him a small novel in manuscript, since then published as a book, which he read immediately and then promptly rated as exceedingly favourable. The young author from Prague is completely happy and proud about this and this truly princely and human trait confirmed to me once again the greatness of this effulgent person. I am endlessly joyful at the prospect of seeing him again at the end of January during his promised visit to Prague. Please give him my regards with expressions of my profound reverence.

Tunja has already written to you, and Grete and Ruth inform you about all further family and personal news. Rahel seems to be standing up for herself in Palestine with courage and confidence. I often have terrible, almost physically perceptible yearning for the child.

And now, write to me again very very soon, above all what you are up to in Zurich and if you are well. Also whatever you hear from Berlin. How good it would be if you could visit us. Unfortunately, at the moment I do not have any opportunity to travel. Only 8 days ago I was expatriated and without a passport. I shall probably receive the Czechoslovakian [passport] after a few weeks; and second, I lack a "productive" pretext since this year the Dutch have not invited me again. So, most affectionate regards to you both
Your old

Leo Kestbg

21. KBG to FWB — 1934.12.19

22. 1935.01.04 — Kbg (Prague) to Beidlers (Zurich)

[typed]

Prague XIX, Velvarská 59

4.1.35.

Dear friends, first of all, kindest thanks for your letter and most lovely New Year's wishes to you as well. Your description of conditions in the I.I.C.I. is extraordinarily interesting and important to me. I share entirely your characterization of the former German personnel. I often have heard of Henry **Bonnet** without knowing at the moment in what context I encountered the name; ostensibly, however, as a bigwig at the I.I.C.I., since this was where I always aspired to seek orientation. I should very much like to arrange for the chairman of the Společnost pro hudební výchovu [now shortened to S.H.V.], Minister Dr. **Krofta** (incidentally, a well-known historian, who is on leave from the university at the moment), to inform Bonnet directly about the functions and aims of the S.H.V. and to draw his attention to the congress in Prague. If, on the other hand, you should view it as more practical that I take care of the introduction to the S.H.V., I could also write to Bonnet. But I have the impression that it would be more effective if Krofta, who is, as you know, the deputy of external affairs minister, Beneš, would venture the first step. I must ask you, please write me as precisely as possible what position Bonnet occupies and how important is he, personally. Perhaps you can already draw Bonnet's attention to these things now, also to signal that it would be tremendously important for us to enter close contact with the I.I.C.I. and that it would be urgently necessary, for general political reasons, that the international basis of the S.H.V. emanate from the Czechoslovakian-French entente. For the present, the connection to England is the strongest plus in our international relations, as a result of the extremely active Prof. Dent, who, during the past days was in Prague. Dent is also going to have a propaganda office of his own opened in England on behalf of the congress and ostensibly also arrange to have an English children's choir travel here. But it would be more natural if the connection with France could be effected as of first priority. After the very skeptical remarks of Chantavoine, which I have gotten used to over a span of years, I admittedly do doubt if the problem will be taken at all seriously in France. In the name of our Board of Directors, I have asked Ch. to give a paper about the situation of the teaching of music in France, and I am curious if he will accept.

Admittedly, I should very much like to know now how the teaching of music is handled in French kindergarten, elementary school, secondary school, and the various other categories of school. Masson gave me a few names and addresses which I shall want to contact in the immediate future. It would be ideal if the I.I.C.I. would call on the S.H.V.

to conduct a formal investigation into all of these questions. In this way we would have official bona fides in hand, including for France, with which to gain access to exhaustive information. The responses coming from other lands are more definitive and clearer than those coming from France. Perhaps, because of that, it might one day be necessary to intervene personally. All the same, it could still be conceivable that you might be successful in scouting out something or other about this.

I would have liked to get to know your lecture but please, do not, under any circumstances, put yourself to any effort to try and reconstruct it. I can pretty much imagine what you said.

Your remarks about Fellerer are very valuable for me and I ask you to respond with kindest greetings. Please ask him if there are good gramophone recordings of Gregorian examples available. I have only the quite tepid ones in the German collection of Sachs.

I can most likely find the works you mentioned about the French school system in the local French Institute. If you would be so good as to give me an indication, I shall try to find my way around. I am including a general questionnaire. It is, admittedly, only a primitive document but is still adequate for securing a certain uniformity.

For the time being, Music Director Sam. Fisch, at Stein am Rhein, is reporting for Switzerland. He seems to be playing a leading role in the musical youth movement. This Swiss musical movement makes a very lively impression. It may also be strongly inspired by Jöde who, for a long time, has been organizing very successful courses in all cities of the German area. I regularly receive the Swiss music-pedagogical papers and see from them that the little canton-spirit in these associations seems to be more important than anything else. If you want and can help me with these tasks, I, of course, would be incredibly grateful, since the authenticity of your reports is still unrivaled!

With regard to Bücken,[1] I immediately wrote to **Seidels**. I am curious whether I receive it. Have you dealt with Mr. **Katz** personally about the missing shipments? The work is to the present day still not complete, as I see in the press, and, in the past, releases also did not take place in order, one after the other, so that it would be possible that the ones that were missing at that time belonged to those that had not yet appeared.

I definitely hope that we will now maintain a brisk correspondence and that you will be so good as to keep me informed immediately after your talk with Bonnet. Between you and me, I could also arrange for a leading French musicologist or teacher, to give lectures

---

[1] Ernst **Bücken** (1884-1949) - see note Letter 1.

for the local French Institute and for radio. Wouldn't you like to come to Prague sometime? We would very much like to see you both again. Maybe it would also be possible to arrange for a lecture. Farewell and most affectionate greetings from

Your old Leo Kestenberg

[Grete handwriting]
The "questionnaire" will follow in the next few days.
I am waiting in anticipation for the letter which you promised.

All best regards!

The loveliest "secretary."

22. KBG to FWB — 1935.01.04

23. 1935.01.23 — Kbg (Prague) to Beidlers (Zurich)
[typed]

[letterhead]

Ministerial Council, retired
Prof.Leo Kestenberg

Prague XIX-Dejvice,
Velvarská 59
23.1.35.

Dear Comrade Beidler,

I felt that your reminder card was very pleasurable evidence of your firm intention to keep up a regular and uninterrupted correspondence. I would have thanked you long ago for your handwritten news if I had not hoped to be able to give you clear and definite information by now about the I.I.C.I. But the way business is done here is even much more cumbersome and is taken much more seriously than in the Prussia of blessed memory! Two days ago, I finally reported the essential points in your letter to Minister Krofta. As our chairman, he urgently beseeched me to make contact here first with Professor Šusta, the Czechoslovakian representative in the I.I.C.I. and to begin by conferring on this question with him. I am convinced that co-operation with the I.I.C.I. will materialize but the goal seems reachable only via detours. If you already prepare and loosen the ground through talks with Henri Bonnet, it will be all the easier for the young little plant that is our S.H.V. to get settled in the I.I.C.I. As soon as the conference with Prof. Šusta takes place, I shall again immediately keep you informed. I have registered your personal remarks about Bonnet's predecessor and also about the present personnel with lively satisfaction because I had similar impressions during my visit there, which did not allow me to hazard an opinion at that time. If your future hopes with the I.I.C.I. were to be realized, naturally that would be especially pleasing.

About 2: In a charming letter which arrived yesterday, Chantavoine basically agreed to attend the congress. His misgivings can be very easily dispelled so that I am counting with absolute certainty on his coming. I am endlessly grateful to you for this intervention too. I also believe that Chantavoine will enjoy giving a paper in the framework of this congress and to renew his acquaintance with Prague.

About 3: The S.H.V. will acquire the works you cited by Lavignac and Chevais.[1] For further international work, they seem indispensable to me. Here in Czechoslovakia a publication similar to the yearbook is now being prepared and of which our yearbook is godparent. A young musicologist, whom the municipal library has hired for three years, has been entrusted with this work.

About 4: I shall not send out invitations to Prague of the leading music teachers until after the congress. I would like to complete this dress rehearsal well and await its success before I make suggestions of a similar nature.

About 5: Fisch, who continually sends me reports from Switzerland, appears to like placing his personal work in the limelight. He participated in two courses in Berlin and that is why I know him well personally. He makes the typical Schwitzer nature-boy impression and must still have good relations with Jöde and his circle. For our undertaking he is not unimportant since he seems to be in the closest of contact with the youth movement.

About 6: Walli Seidel wrote to us about Bücken that she remembers with certainty that she received only a part of the shipments from you, whereas another is supposed to still be with your former landlords in Ruhleben. I cannot understand this procedure. Walli Seidel asks you to supply the names of your former landlords and possibly also your present address, since she wants to pick up the notebooks there.

About 7: With regard to the Beidler trip to Prague, I am not yet able to set out certain prospects. But in this case, as well, I do not doubt that reaching this goal will succeed.

And now I shall emancipate myself from your exemplary point system to tell you right off that yesterday we visited Thomas Mann and his wife in the hotel and that the subject Beidler activated a very warm atmosphere of mutual fondness and congeniality. All the Manns are celebrating triumphs here. With her "Pfeffermühle," Erika, too, has had a resounding and very genuine success.[2] What seems odd to me, though, is that

---

[1] Albert **Lavignac** - (1846-1916) - French musicologist and educator. His principal work was *La Musique et les Musiciens*, 1895. He was a principal collaborator in the large project of the *Encyclopédie de la Musique*, five volumes, 3,395 pages, 1913-1922. He also wrote *Le voyage artistique à Bayreuth*, 1897, with which Beidler would have been familiar.
Maurice **Chevais** - (1880-1943) - As inspector of music education in Parisian schools, 1919-1940, he was an indefatigable advocate of reform in the field of musical education.

[2] The ***Pfeffermühle***, The Pepper Mill, was a brilliant satirical cabaret founded in January 1933 by Thomas Mann's children, Erika and Klaus. Their initial success ended in flight from Germany because of the Nazi takeover. The group moved to Switzerland and toured widely in Europe. By 1936, when the group disbanded, it had given 1,034 performances.

Thomas Mann does not know <u>your</u> Wagner work, about which Dr. Einstein wrote with extraordinary praise. If you still have a copy, I would be much obliged to receive it! - Thomas Mann's Wagner lecture captivated me once again for its form and inspired me to great admiration. Too bad, however, that Mann did not concern himself with Liszt and seems never to make the attempt to confront the Wagner-problem with the universalism of Liszt.

By all means, I shall attempt to make the acquaintance of your friend Lévy-Bruhl.[1] I take it that you have supplied him with our address (telephone: 70697) and that he will get in touch with us.

For everything, many thousand thanks and affectionate regards, also for Mme Colibri and "specially" from Grete, but also from Grossmama, Ruth and Tunja.

Always your

LeoKbg

I am very eager for your first reports of your attendance at classes of French schools. I have not been able to reach this stage yet here!

23. KBG to FWB — 1935.01.23

[1] Lucien **Lévi-Bruhl** - (1857-1939) - French philosopher who drew associations with sociology and ethnology, especially in his investigations of the mentality of primitives (*How Natives Think*, 1910, 1926).

24. 1935.02.06 — Kbg (Prague) to Beidlers (Zurich)

[handwritten]

Prague XIX, Velvarská 59

5.II.35

Dear friend Beidler!

Despite the outcry over my lack of judgement, your letter of the 1st of the month is very valuable to me, and, as you see, I am rushing to answer it immediately.

Well...: Your interest in the finances of our S.H.V. is really moving and, in general, this concern would also be very legitimate. But because our treasurer is, in his main profession, the director of the big local municipal library and works very energetically on the expansion of this conjoined music division, it is at least conceivable that he would buy the Lavignac for his institute and put it at our disposal. I shall, however, ascertain beforehand if it might be present in the university library or in the French institute. You made it clear enough in your letter of the 8th of January [not present] that it is not actually worth acquiring. Given the francophile attitude of the local offices, it will doubtless cause no problems to scare up the work, even though it be as covered in dust as can be.

By the way, has no later year than 1929 of the "Annuaire artistique" [Artistic Annual] appeared, since you cite only this one? But please do not strike me dead again because of this droll question. There are once even supposed to have been some stuck-away yearbooks somehwere.

Your information about the association "Musique pour Tous" [Music for All] and about Mr. Weisweiller[1] is very stimulating. That seems a counterpart to the Londoner Robert Meyer, who looked me up in Berlin years ago on the recommendation of Artur Schnabel[2] and whose youth and school concerts in England also enjoy great popularity.

We are going to give this chapter a big place in the context of our congress, in as much as the Czech Toscanini, <u>Vaclav Talich</u>, whose name you may know, has put on such youth concerts here with his orchestra.[3] Talich is the second chairman in our S.H.V. In

---

[1] Mr. **Weisweiller** - [??]

[2] Artur **Schnabel** - (1882-1951) - Great Austro-German concert pianist of Jewish origin.

[3] Arturo **Toscanini** - (1867-1957) - Great international conductor.
Václav **Talich** - (1883-1961) - Czech conductor, violinist, educator - the Czech Toscanini. Charles **Mackerras** and Karel **Ančerl** were among his pupils. Widely known as "the Czech Toscanini."

America, Ernst Schelling[1] has been active for years with great success in this area. (Very lovely, somewhat kitschy but dramatically arranged programs).

It would be very kind if you could obtain for me 10-20 copies of the enclosed questionnaire of "La Musique pour Tous". If it should cause you any inconvenience, I'd be very happy to write directly to them, which, at any rate, would be advisable, at some point, don't you think?

Unfortunately, the meeting with the representative of the I.I.C.I., Prof. Šusta,[2] could not take place yet. Have you informed Bonnet about the aims and mission of our S.H.V.? I find it grandiose that you have received official permission to visit music classes in public schools. I have not yet attended to this here. But after the congress I shall probably have to dig into conditions in this country, although an overly precise knowledge of specific results tends to lead to confusion more than clarity. I avidly await your description of your impressions.

You do seem to want to stay in Paris. But, with the exception of music-pedagogical matters, you remain silent. Is there a deeper reason for this?

Yesterday, I received a very illuminating private letter from music director Fisch of Stein am Rhein. It is about the way music is being taught in Germany. It leaves nothing to the imagination and shows its writer to be completely trustworthy in our sense of the word. It is amusing to see how that set which was most eagerly in standby for the coming of the Third Reich is not totally out of favour. — In the near future, Kleiber is going to conduct the "Holländer" here.[3] A protest campaign by the local German Social Democrats against this guest performance got all bogged down in the initial stages because Kl. was depicted as a martyr with heroic convictions. I have neither time nor inclination to bother with this eternally repeated baloney.

---

[1] Ernest **Schelling** - (1876-1939) - American pianist, composer, and conductor. He was the first conductor of the Young People's Concerts of the New York Philharmonic, starting in 1924.

[2] Josef **Šusta** - (1874-1945) - Czech historian, writer and politician.

[3] Erich **Kleiber** - (1890-1956) - Eminent Austrian conductor and father of Carlos Kleiber. In 1923 he became musical director of the Berlin State Opera. He left Germany because of the Nazis and conducted in Buenos Aires 1936-1949. He was highly respected for his interpretations both of the classics and modern works. "Holländer" — Wagner's Flying Dutchman.

Today we received a despairing letter from Dr. Walter.[1] I know, you could never stand him. Nonetheless, he is a splendid fellow whom we absolutely must help to get a grip on himself again, as they say here. If only he could be helped to obtain a passport. By the way, W. writes that Döscher is seriously ill in Eisenach.

Your social engagements in Paris remind me of the breakfast and tea politicians of our old Wilhelm Street.[2] It sounds a bit like "I come here from radiance and joy." [Lohengrin to Elsa, Act 3, sc.2] and poor Elsa (whose dimensions accord completely with the local stand-in for the sister of the Berlin Konetzny)[3] will feel extremely jealous in the process. But that is surmountable and capable of being admired without envy. In this respect, we here are provincials, somber but amusing and with a whole company of "Merry Wives of Prague." - Happy about our active correspondence, the warmest of greetings are sent you both by

your "loyal-to-homeland" ancient

LeoKbg

[Grete:]
Kisses to both of you!
"Gretchen."

24. KBG to FWB — 1935.02.05

[1] Arnold **Walter** - (1902-1973) - Czch-Canadian music teacher, administrator, writer, and composer. After fleeing Germany in 1933, he first lived on Mallorca, then England, and, finally, in Canada, where he became a driving force in the creation of opera and instrumental studies at the Toronto Conservatory of Music. He founded the music faculty at the University of Toronto and was active in international music organizations.

[2] In Kestenberg's time, the **Wilhelmstrasse** was the centre of government in Berlin. K. had his offices there. The German department of external affairs was often referred to in English as "the Wilhelmstrasse."

[3] **Konetzny** - two sisters, Anny and Hilde who each made impressive operatic careers, especially in Wagnerian rôles.
Anny **Konetzny** - (1902-1968) - K.'s Berlin Konetzny - she sang 1931-1934 at the Berlin State Oper (Unter den Linden)
Hilde **Konetzni** - (1905-1980) - She sang in Prague 1932-1938.

25. 1935.03.16 — Kbg (Prague) to Beidlers (Zurich) - *[typed]*

SPOLEČNOST PRO HUDEBNÍ VÝCHOVU
SOCIÉTÉ D'ÉDUCATION MUSICALE
SHV
SOCIETY FOR MUSICAL EDUCATION
GESELLSCHAFT FÜR MUSIK-ERZIEHUNG

PRAHA
IV. TOSKÁNSKÝ PALÁC.
16.3.35.

[letterhead of SHV]
16.3.35

Dear Comrade **Beidler**,

after your letters of January 8 and February 1, both rich in content [not extant], and your assurance that you were happy about our active correspondence, I felt secure in assuming that this regularity would continue. I feel painfully disappointed that my letter of February 5 has remained unanswered until now and, once again, I cannot find any explanation for your long silence. Please - write me, at least a card, from which I will be able to see if you are still in Paris and if you both are in good health.

The plan to bind our "Společnost" more closely to the I.I.C.I. has received further attention in the meantime. Professor **Šusta** has received a report, signed by Minister **Krofta**, informing him in-depth about the basis of the S.H.V. and its functions and aims. Since he is the highest representative of Czechoslovakia to the I.I.C.I., we must first await his agreement before we can take further steps. I hope that Prof. Šusta will give his agreement for us to approach M. **Bonnet** directly. In your letters, you implied that you would inform M. Bonnet about the S.H.V. and apprise him of our intentions. Since Minister Krofta is to give three lectures at the Sorbonne in Paris at the beginning of April, it would be conceivable that the two men could have a conversation about these questions. Toward this end, however, I would have to give Minister Krofta some points of information and I would therefore be very obliged to you if I could receive news from you as rapidly as possible about whether B., in fact, has received information from you about the S.H.V.

Everything else is alright with us - with the exception that we are so concerned about your silence. Put this state of affairs to a rapid end and, really, write immediately.

With the best regards from us all, especially from my wife,

Your

Leo Kestenberg

26. 1935.03.20 — FWB (Zurich) to Kbg – [typed]

Zurich: 7: 20. March 1935,
134, Klosbachstrasse,
Tel.: 28.214

[head of letter:] Dr. FRANZ W.BEIDLER-WAGNER

Dear Comrade Kestenberg,

to our greatest joy, we just now received your kind letter of the 16th of the month, forwarded from Paris, and I am sitting down to give answer, as ordered and wished. You are right to be unhappy. But we beg that you be so good as to take into account that the recent past in Paris was quite mad and that we were left all but no "private" time for ourselves. Additionally, I did not have a typewriter at hand and, with my bureaucrat's script, even the shortest letter took hours to write.

We have only been back here a few days and actually only yesterday finished with "furnishing" our new home. It is charming here: two small but very nice rooms in a villa, high above the city and the lake, in the midst of a beautiful garden, completely undisturbed (we have the whole ground floor with our own entrance and hall for ourselves) with genteel fellow-countrymen of Italian origin (not anti-Semitic! Sadly, you have to watch out for this here too, to some extent. It is the German soul that, every now and then, extends this far). In this environment, we can get back to real work and, above all, resume our interrupted contact with you, stauncher than ever.

That's what I thought from the start: that the connection with the I.I.C.I. would have to be made by way of Prof. Šusta (who, in passing, like your Minister, is also an historian, right?). It is as follows: as I believe I wrote to you, I spoke with **Bonnet** in detail about the SHV and also - with no obligation and purely as private preliminary information - held out to him the possibility of an invitation to the congress in autumn. He did not yet know if he would be free, said, however, that in case he could not come, he would send **Coeuroy** (from whom, ostensibly, you certainly would not gain much, given the proverbial lethargy of the otherwise very nice C.). Thus Šusta would have to see that Bonnet comes in person. If you want more information about the I.I.C.I., I am at your disposal and consider myself extremely competent, since I am in continuous contact with it and, in addition, can find out more or less everything that goes on there.

About my impressions of the Parisian primary schools, I want to write an article. In the next days, I shall be speaking with the editor of the "Schweizerischen Musikzeitung." [Swiss Musical News] As soon as the article has appeared, I shall send it to you and will be able at that time to add the more confidential marginal notes, which are only meant for "in-house use" and, naturally, cannot be uttered to the generality. I view this as the simplest and least time-consuming *modus procedendi* [Lat. method of proceeding]. Agreed? (I have seen a lot more and visited at least 20 schools in Paris and suburbs). Only one thing: please do not get too involved with M. Weisweiller of the "Musique pour tous." This organization made the only consistently bad impression on me and I am of the opinion that we are dealing with a fraudulent enterprise, presumably attuned to financial takings by the clever businessman Mr. W. whose project, as pedagogy, is, at best, of negative interest. The public authorities are, by the way, absolutely against the venture. I am in the know about how Mr. W. manages to get into certain schools (not at all into all!) with his things. To explain this would be too much of a diversion today.

I shall be travelling soon through the whole of Switzerland: to Bern, Basel, Solothurn, Lausanne, Geneva, Fribourg, etc. (Among other things, I shall visit Paderewski[1] who lives in Lausanne). If you have got any errands you would like me to do for you in these areas, please tell me soon. - Grete **Rothbarth** intends to go to Palestine during her holidays this year and asks to have Rahel's address! Write to her directly; it will make her happy, for sure. She seems to like all of you. She had very nice things to say about the house of Kestenberg. (By the way, she lost her father recently and could not attend the burial because she is not permitted to set foot in the country of Kultur!) Speaking of which, we spent quite some time with Picht (at Sautreaus).[2] Mr. Hilferding[3] puts on grand teas, like a sovereign on his throne .... !!! There is not much at all left of "socialism" with this man; he's relinquished that to Hitler ..... You see, that's what is called dying beautiful. I am asked to send you regards, especially from Lotte **Leonard** and her husband; we are very good friends! - Since 1929, no new volumes of the "Annuaire artistique" have appeared. No mistake please: parts of **Lavignac** are excellent!!! If the SHV has enough money all the better; the acquisition is very worthwhile! - I shall write again soon! In the meantime, a thousand most affectionate greetings, above all, naturally, to Frau Grete!

26. FWB to KBG — 1935.03.20

---

[1] Ignacy Jan **Paderewski** - (1860-1941) - Polish concert pianist, composer, third Prime Minister of the Republic of Poland (1919), and California vintner.

[2] **Sautreaus** – Dagny Sautreau - (1876-1974) - née Dagny Bjørnson, daughter of Bjørnstjerne Martinius Bjørnson (1832-1910), Norwegian writer, winner of the 1903 Nobel Prize for Literature. Dagny Sautreau was an author in her own right.

[3] Rudolf **Hilferding** - (1877-1941) -Jewish, Austrian-born Marxist economist, socialist theorist, Social-Democratic politician, and physician. He was Minister of Finance in Germany 1923 and 1928-1929. In 1933, he fled to Zurich (1933-1938), then Paris, where he died in 1941 at the hands of the Gestapo. His wife died in Auschwitz in 1943.

27. 1935.03.26 — FWB (Zurich) to Kbg

[typed]

Zurich: 7: 26 March 1935,
134, Klosbachstrasse.

[head of letter:] Dr. FRANZ W.BEIDLER-WAGNER

Dear Comrade Kestenberg,

since you so amiably expressed a wish to hear about our plans for the future, today I shall present you with a section out of our broadly sliced picture of projects which preoccupy us at the moment. Primarily, I want to attempt to create a position for myself in domestic broadcasting, not only as a reporter or associate from outside but rather from inside, as organizer! There would be artistic and educational things to do and initiate on a national level. For this reason I am travelling on Thursday to Bern for a meeting with the most important man in this area.

In connection with these intentions, a "founding idea" has been occupying me for a long time. In a foreseeable period of time, I would like to be far enough along to be able to suggest to the responsible authorities the establishment of a special institute for broadcasting at the (famously excellent) Swiss Technical University [*Eidgenössische Technische Hochschule*]. What I've got vaguely in mind as a model is the "Experimental Radio Centre" which, back then, you created in Berlin at the University.[1] Vaguely: because I am not at all clear about either its internal organization and technical design or about its actual functions. I am not adequately up-to-date on the state of technical and acoustical research to be able to fixedly define the technical starting point of the planned institute, and I naturally would seek only to secure for myself work on the artistic, aesthetic, and pedagogical side. Of course, the technicians here at the ETH are present and of the first quality. I envision the job of the institute as the experimental collaboration of both these elements of broadcasting. I take it that this was also your main idea in founding the Berlin Centre. If and how this works today, is beyond my knowledge. It likely cannot be much more than it was, despite Mr. Schünemann.

You are — outside of my wife-and-co-worker, of course (you are very well aware of this indissoluble unity) — the first to whom I have spoken of this plan. This has completely self-centred motives: I am dependent, to the highest degree, on your advice and your expert opinion and therefore am determined this very day to get the first preliminary discussion with you moving, which should mean: I would be extraordinarily grateful to

---

[1] As early as 1926, K. had begun to work on creating a program of radio studies in the relationship between the new medium of radio and the art of music-making, drama, and education. Schünemann seems to have worked to gain increasing bureaucratic control of this intitution without furthering its artistic goals to any significant extent.

you if you could, when opportune, as far as you might find the time, express your opinion and also perhaps tell me what concrete intentions you wanted to realize with the Berlin Centre (I believe, incidentally, to remember that you were not at all in agreement with the set-up in which the experimental radio centre then actually worked). Here, in many influential quarters, I've come across a strong willingness to be responsive to proposals, so that I am quite convinced that, in an urgent situation, I could find financing for such an institute. Admittedly, that presupposes a well-balanced organizational plan that is worked through to the last detail and various additional things, especially including extensive on-the-job training on my part. But I believe that it could be worthwhile, in every respect, to force out a well-grounded project outline. Do you want to help me in this (naturally, it must not cost you too much time and effort, that is understood!)?

I was happy to hear that Einstein wrote nice words to you about one of my articles. So that you can form an opinion for yourself, I am including a copy of the original text in German, which, in the English translation, unfortunately lost all of its character and very much of its abysmal venom. A good piece of "art sociology" from the past century is sketched out in it and I am working at fleshing out and expanding these studies. But that requires time (especially in my case!!) because nobody anywhere went farther than the very first beginnings, basically including your friend Wiesengrund-Adorno[1] as well. I fancy myself now already to be somewhat farther! Are you not amazed that, in my old age, I am beginning to become conceited? I can vividly imagine how happily you will smile at that. .... (Good old Honigsheim[2] is weighed down by the idea of writing a musical sociology .... because he is a descendant of [Max] Weber .... oh God! This between you and me; because, basically, I am on good terms with him). - Today, for the first time in a long while, I again heard Rachmaninoff play, in a rehearsal. I am a regular patron of the orchestra rehearsals, in order to stiffen my "specialized knowledge," in which you always placed little trust. Zurich is very spoiled, above all by its many guest soloists: Horowitz, Menuhin, Milstein, Morini, Cortot (according to his convictions – a pig...!), Huberman ...... You will admit, that people here are **not** anti-Semitic!!

27. FWB to KBG — 1935.03.26

[1] Theodor W. **Adorno** - (1903-1969) - born Theodor Ludwig Wiesengrund. German philosopher, sociologist, and musicologist.

[2] Paul **Honigsheim** - (1885-1963) - German sociologist. He was a student and friend of Max Weber's. In 1933, he emigrated to France, then to Panama, and to the USA where he taught at Michigan State University.

28. 1935.03.27 — Kbg (Prague) to Beidlers (Zurich)

[typed]

[letterhead of SHV]

27.3.35

Dear Comrade **Beidler**,

Your letter of the 20th gave me great joy. So much security and confidence rings out from it. Even if I do not have a clue from where you are drawing these enviable qualities, I am nonetheless happy that you possess them. Everything is going as wished with us. A few days ago we even became Czechoslovakian citizens and I took the oath for this Masaryk[1] state with enthusiasm. — To begin with, I want to answer your question about Einstein's address. As Einstein wrote me, until the end of this month, he is at Prof. **Kurth**,[2] **Spiez** "Haus Waldrand," and will then move into a villa in Mezzomonte which his wife is readying at the moment. It is anticipated that he will stay the next two years in M. near Florence and then perhaps return to England. I do not know the exact address in M. but think that I should receive it in the next few days. It is certainly to be assumed that letters to Dr. E. will be forwarded by Prof. Kurth.

In early April, Minister **Krofta** will give a few historical lectures at the Sorbonne. I have arranged for **Bonnet** and **Chantavoine** to be invited to the social events which will certainly take place on the occasion of the presence of Minister Krofta in Paris. I do hope that these men will get acquainted with each other. Given the fussiness of the bureacratic apparatuses, I am skeptical, however, about whether this meeting will take place. Doubtless, it would make the whole situation easier and expedite all the matters I have been pursuing. I shall also make a special request to Minister Krofta that he personally invite Bonnet to the congress. Perhaps you could be so obliging as to prepare Bonnet already for the possibility of a reception and also write to him that he is associated with the S.H.V. and with me. In a conversation, the significance of the congress can be described better than in the most detailed of letters.

I am very curious about your article in the Swiss music paper. Lovely that you are sending it to me right away and that you also want to make a few personal marginal notes

---

[1] Tomáš **Masaryk** - (1850-1937) - Austro-Hungarian and Slovakian politician who became the founding president of Czechoslovakia. Masaryk was the most revered figure of his country; K. was right in calling Czechoslovakia "this Masaryk state." He meant it as high praise for the country and for Masaryk, a man of extraordinary achievement, character, and humanism.

[2] Ernst **Kurth** - (1886-1946) - a Swiss-Austrian musician and musicologist specializing in theory and psychology of music. Important books: Romantic Harmony and its Crisis in Wagner's "Tristan" (1923).

for internal use. Since, in the official world of musical pedagogy, French stock does not presently rate highly, it interests me quite particularly to learn your impressions. I shall take your warning about M. **Weismüller** to heart and, in line with your intimations, shall distance myself accordingly. -- I shall write to Grete **Rothbarth** very soon. Your remarks about **Hilferding** did not in the slightest surprise me. He and his wife especially never comprehended what personal responsibility means.

Tomorrow, we are travelling for the Společnost to Schönbach and Graslitz. These are the two villages of instrument makers who, until the Hitler regime, were in closest contact with Mark-Neukirchen but now, naturally, are completely separated. We want to visit the instrument technical schools there and also to listen to the youth orchestras (string and wind orchestras). There is plenty of work for the S.H.V. The preparation for the congress making demands on all our people. Since I additionally am teaching three courses on music history and a course for music teachers about musical education, the days are more than full. — If interesting, new literature on music history should come your way, I would be very grateful to you for every reference. — During your circuit trip around Switzerland, will you be through Stein am Rhein? Music Director **Fisch** lives there, as I already wrote you. He has given me excellent reports about the musical youth movement and about all modern endeavours in musical pedagogy. He also publishes a lot and seems to have a certain significance in the whole world of Swiss musical pedagogy. — I am very curious about your "personal letter." And it is really of the uppermost interest finally to learn what you are primarily engaged in. — Dr. **Walter** is unfortunately still doing **very** badly. Sadly, his first attempt with Prague was declined. Could you not get works of his placed in Swiss newspapers? After all, he writes excellently and on all imaginable subjects. By the way, **Reinking**[1] is supposed to have behaved very very badly. He has become a denouncing super-Nazi who has intrigued especially badly against **Ebert**[2] and **Busch**.[3]

---

[1] Wilhelm **Reinking** - (1896-1985) - German scenic designer, stage director, and writer. He was a progressive stage designer. When Carl Ebert took over as director of the Opera in Darmstadt in 1927, he gave Reinking his first big breakthrough as stage designer. Reinking's career was established by Ebert during the Weimar Republic.

[2] Carl **Ebert** - (1887-1980) - German opera director, actor and administrator. In 1933, he fled Germany for England where he, together with Fritz Busch, founded the Gyndebourne Festival. He was director of opera at the University of Souther California, 1948-1954 and Director of the Deutsche Opera, Berlin, 1954-1961.

[3] Fritz **Busch** - (1890-1951) - Great German conductor: directing conductor Stuttgart 1918-1922, Dresden 1922-1933, Bayreuth 1924-1925, New York, London. In 1933, he infuriated the Nazis by refusing to eliminate Jewish musicians in Dresden. Busch left Germany for England, where he and Carl Ebert founded the Glyndeborne Festival. Artistic director, the Met, New York, 1945-1950.

The description of furnishing your new home is incredibly agitating and, at the same time, heart-warming. If any opportunity at all should arise to give lectures in Switzerland, I would very much like to take advantage of such an occasion to visit you. But those are dreams that are hardly likely to be realizable.

Write to me again very soon; and for you and Frau Ellen our most affectionate greetings from your

Leo Kestenberg

Have you already seen Thomas Mann again?
Grete sends both of you regards and longing.

28. KBG to FWB — 1935.03.27

29. 1935.04.03 — Kbg (Prague) to Beidlers (Zurich)
[typed]

[letterhead of SHV]

3.4.35

Dear Comrade **Beidler**, I actually wanted to answer your letter of March 26th immediately because I am joyfully surprised, even thoroughly excited. If you prevail in entering into any sort of relationship with Swiss radio, I would consider that an extraordinary success and I do not doubt that you will end up sitting in the saddle once you have put even a single foot into the stirrups! Although I hardly need say it, I should like to give you my utmost help in this. Apart from the personal reasons, there are wholly cogent, objective reasons that persuade me to put my modest experience at your service, in every way.

My proposal for the experimental radio centre, which, at the time was happily spirited away by Schünemann, emerged from the realization that radio really had not yet ever brought the influence of its technical miracle to bear on music. The attempt has hardly ever been made to use radio to turn into reality the utopian portrayals of visions in sound such as are to be found among the Romantics, especially E.T.A. Hoffmann,[1] despite many passages reading as if they foresaw radio. We often spoke with Busoni about Aeolian harps[2] and the music of the spheres long before anyone talked about radios.

These ideas of a music specific to broadcasting brought me to the conviction that the university would have the obligation to confront these problems, artistically and scientifically, from the point of view of sound and acoustics. As you quite correctly write, the experimental broadcasting centre, sadly, went off on another path. Although support for electro-acoustic instruments also emanated from this centre, the focus was placed in singing and speaking in front of the microphone. It did happen that this and that was accomplished that was reminiscent of the origins, and, at every opportunity, I emphasized the ideas of creating a music that is specific to radio. The programs of the radio congresses in Göttingen and Munich were also imbued with these foundations and a few compositions were brought to performance within this setting. But it is only natural that a satisfactory solution still was not found. — The whole development of this question then got trapped

---

[1] Ernst Theodor Amadeus **Hoffmann** - (1776-1822) - German writer, composer, conductor, music critic, and caricaturist.

[2] Aeolian harp (wind harp) is a musical instrument which is driven by wind blowing through strings stretched across two bridges over a box with a sounding board. It is the only stringed instrument which plays only harmonic frequencies.

in a dead end since the broadcasting people — the directors as well as the technicians and the musicians — declared that there is no such thing as a music specific to broadcasting and no such thing should be permitted, and that the only important thing is to broadcast any sort of music with such technical flawlessness that it would no longer be possible to hear a difference between the original and the broadcast. I consider this standpoint wrong and I am pleased to find reinforcement of this outlook in several articles that I just received from Paul **Bekker**. Writing in the "New Yorker Staatszeitung," B. has just commented about these problems, very much in the same vein. It is a polemic against **Stokowski**[1] and, essentially, a recapitulation of his thesis about the educational power of music in society, which, of course, is not refuted by radio. It is, however, a profound falsification to make use of operas and oratorios, cantatas and masses with radio technology and thereby to divest these completely of their own original spheres. With symphonies and quartettes, this is also basically the case. The whole slacking-off of our musical life, its societal absurdity, becomes all the more obvious.

For your practical operations, it would probably depend on your making contacts with progressive Swiss musicians, which you should not find difficult to do. I do not know at all if **Schöck**[2] has any understanding of these problems. In Switzerland, there are various personalities, also from the former Busoni circle, who, with absolute certainty, would be interested in such questions. [Beidler marginal note: Honegger[3]] I'm thinking of **Blanchet**[4] in Lausanne and also **Balmer**.[5] There are also a few seminal articles on these

---

[1] Leopold Anthony **Stokowski** - (1882-1977) - British conductor who conducted without baton and drew sumptuous sound from the mostly American orchestras which he led. He was a pathfinder in self-promotion, including using special lighting effects to focus attention on himself during performances. He also was exceptionally free in altering orchestrations in many different pieces to achieve special effects and wrote quite a number of transcriptions for orchestra of works meant for keyboard or instruments. He made his first recording (with the Philadelphia Orchestra) in 1917 and continued to make numerous recordings and radio broadcasts after that.

[2] Othmar **Schoeck** - (1886-1957) - Swiss composer and conductor centred in Zurich. He befriended Busoni in 1916 after the latter had moved to Zurich to escape wartime Berlin. In 1918 Schoeck composed Das Wandbild to a libretto by Busoni.

[3] Arthur **Honegger** - (1892-1955) - Swiss composer, born in France, a member of Les Six.

[4] Emile-Robert **Blanchet** - (1877-1943) - Swiss composer and pianist. He studied with Busoni in Berlin 1898 and was a concert pianist 1902 to 1904. He was the director of the Lausanne Conservatory 1905-1908, dedicating himself after that to composing. He was more famous as an Alpine climber than as a composer. He reached all the Swiss summits over 4,000 metres.

[5] Luc **Balmer** - (1898-1996) - Swiss conductor, pianist, and composer. He studied with Busoni in Berlin 1919-1921.

problems in the book about "Art and Technology," [*Kunst und Technik*] which I brought out as editor back then with People's Book Club Publishing [*Volksverbandverlag*].

Switzerland would be brilliantly appropriate as a focal point for all matters having to do with experimental broadcasting. Advancement of these intentions is in the air. Just when your letter arrived, the founding general assembly of a Czech Society for Sound Technology was taking place. I am on its board; the top man is the professor for acoustics at the Czech University, Prof. **Teige**.[1] As you see, here, too, much is stirring in this direction, even if the official radio management has refused to co-operate in any way for the time being. It would be splendid, however, if you could succeed in Switzerland to convince the leadership of official broadcasting of the importance of these questions.

If you should wish it, I am more than prepared to give you further, more practical hints. Today, I only wanted to give you a short, general salutation for your plan. I am also very happy to know at last what you, personally, are occupied with and I am really pleased that you have chosen an area that is so infinitely important, so lively, and so rich in future possibilities.

With the most affectionate regards for you both from **all** of us here, also from Grandmama, naturally!

Your old

Leo Kestenberg

29. KBG to FWB — 1935.04.03

[1] possibly Karel **Teige** - (1900-1951) - Czech avant-gardist, multi-media pioneer.

30. 1935.04.07 — FWB (Zurich) to Kbg

[typed]

Zurich: 7: 7 April 1935,
134, Klosbachstrasse.

[head of letter:] DIE BEIDLERS

Dear Comrade Kestenberg,

Your letter of the 3rd of mth. was for us one of the very rare great and pure joys! Additionally, it again gave a strong reminder of how much I owe you intellectually and how very much I am your student! It is truly a special infamy of Mr. Hitler & Co. that they have so torn us apart! On the other hand, what has been proven to me precisely in this separation is that I have for you such a strong feeling of intellectual kinship - yes, I'd like to say: a unique feeling of absolutely co-aligned, intellectual unanimity. What we [Beidlers] both really are missing is the opulence of daily stimuli that we received from you. But even a letter, as this very latest one, contains a respectable number of such - yes, indeed, it certainly does! For this, the greatest of thanks!

Today I am sending you the German original text of my contribution to the "*Enquête sur la radiodiffusion et l'éducation du grand public*" [Inquiry into Broadcasting and Public Education] in manuscript form (the volume should be out one of these days but I do not yet have a sample copy). From this, I think you will be able to gather a full confirmation of the claims that are laid out in indent 1 of this piece of writing. Still, I ask you for a word of criticism. Further, I am including a report on the work I cited by Honegger-Larronde,[1] which will interest you (with request of eventual return because I only have this one review). I know Honegger and spoke with him at length in Paris about radio problems. At any rate, I definitely could be sure of his active co-operation in our presumptive centre. Many thanks for the special note about **Blanchet** and Lucas **Balmer**; I shall make use of it as soon as I feel strong enough to be able to get the project rolling.

That is now the main point for me and, as the so-called "scholars" tend to do, I am beginning to become interested about what has been written and said about the questions at hand. Back then, you sent me "Art and Technology." I'll have it forwarded to me now.

Now, please forgive me for asking a couple of subordinate questions: did a printed program appear for the **Göttingen** radio congress? (I was not along in Göttingen and

---

[1] Carlos **Larronde** - (1888-1940) - A French intellectual active in early radio. He had great influence as a critic and radio reporter. He was a leader in creating radio meant specifically for radio. A book about him by Christopher Todd calls him a "poet of the waves."

have little idea of what was said there). I am asking because I was unable to discover such a publication in the official book catalogues. The information on Radio in **Munich**, if I remember correctly, was contained in the general report of the 7th German School Music Week (where have you vanished to, ye wondrous days of old?!). As far as I can remember, what was submitted there, especially by **Westerman**, was not very significant (my fury at Pfitzner at the time had strongly reduced my receptivity). I shall obtain the article by Paul **Bekker** - thank you for pointing it out. Then: of the "Publications of the Experimental Radio Centre of the State Academic University for Music in Berlin," edited by Georg Schünemann, there was, as far as I know, only one volume published ("Electric Music" by Friedrich Trautwein[1]) - neither the pompous title [of the series] nor its most estimable and renowned editor had more in them [than one volume].

I saw Maurice **Rambert**[2] in Bern, spiritual leader [spiritus rector] of the "Swiss Broadcast Society," and, at the same time, with the "International Broadcasting Union" [Union Internationale de Radiodiffusion] in Geneva, to whom I was recommended favourably. In general terms, I put to him my wish to enter broadcasting as a co-designer, without immediately broaching, during our first contact, the complex things occupying us here. He asked me to send my inquiry-article quickly, just as soon as it appears in print. At any rate, I do have there immediate access anytime and shall stay in contact.

May I draw your attention to the fact that - according to the Bulletin of the abovementioned International Broadcasting Union - the "Advisory Committee For Czechoslovakian Broadcasting," in Czechoslovakia, at its meeting of September 19, 1934, enacted a more effective supervision of light music. Where would it be possible to learn more about this? Do you have any contact to the musicians who sit on said committee?

What have you heard from Paris? Did the meeting of Krofta and Bonnet take place? I was especially pleased that you had Chantavoine invited; he is a really splendid person and a good, loyal friend. (Recently, in Nice, he spoke about Paganini's influence on Liszt, but I am not familiar with what he said.) - A few days ago, we had a long talk with Carl **Ebert** and his wife; he's tricky but also a really magnificent fellow, and one of the few courageous ones. He fully confirmed what you wrote about Reinking.

From the bottom of my heart, I congratulate you on the highly respectable citizen-

---

[1] Friedrich **Trautwein** - (1888-1956) - German musician considered a pioneer in electronic music. He invented the trautonium, a forerunner of the musical synthesizer. A later version of this instrument was used in Alfred Hitchcock's film, The Birds.

[2] Maurice **Rambert** - Director General of the SRG (Swiss Broadcast Society, Schweizerische Rundspruchgesellschaft) 1931-1936.

ship, into possession of which you have now entered! Have you accomplished relinquishment of the German? I am nursing the thought of doing without my still extant German add-on nationality, since nobody has given me the joy of repudiating it, something that I have been waiting for the whole time!

We just heard the symphony "Mathis der Maler" by Hindemith. In part, very beautiful and proper, if not without concessions to those wound backwards (asses'-) ears and to the "German soul." Especially clean, clear in structure, poised and profoundly genuine the third (last) "movement" (technically very difficult for the orchestra!!). Poor Ebert came here for the - "Witches' Song" !!! Wüllner[1] had cancelled (out of fear of police informers !!!!)

The mysterious death of Dora Fabian[2] especially (whom we both knew very well) affects us very much! Suicide seems extremely unlikely! The English are simply pigs!!

30. FWB to KBG — 1935.04.07

[1] Ludwig **Wüllner** - (1858-1938) - German singer and actor.

[2] Dora **Fabian** - On April 4, 1935, Dora Fabian, 33, a writer and journalist on political and economic subjects had been found dead with Mathilde Wurm, 60, also a journalist and, until 1933, a Social Democratic member of the Reichstag — in their flat in Great Omond Street, London. Both were refugees from Germany. Drugs, including morphine, and a broken hypodermic syringe were found in the flat. The papers presented the matter as a probable suicide pact.

31. 1935.04.15 — Kbg (Prague) to Beidlers (Zurich) –

[typed - no letterhead]

Prague XIX- Dejvice, 15.4.35.

Dear Comrade **Beidler**,

in the midst of the preparations for our congress, it gives me great joy once again to be brought together, through you, with the important problems concerning broadcasting. Your article for the "Inquiry into radio, etc. etc." brings a whole wealth of insights and clarifications. Your ground-breaking analysis of the audience is incredibly fruitful for the whole essay. Only, I might have wished that you would have treated your "Entry of radio into musical life" somewhat more expansively.

To me, it seems somewhat abrupt, all the moreso (as so often in historical treatment) since these first, tentative steps were immensely enlightening and characteristic of further developments. As far as I remember, in its initial stage, radio was not taken seriously and only a few sensed the great future of this new force. Precisely in these first years, experimentation was also much more in favour than today where radio already seems burdened - despite its youth - with all the sins of tradition and routine. — Your remarks are excellent about the significance of popular music and about the necessity, admittedly not intensively treated by you, to create this so-called "light music" in an artistic way. During our last years in Germany, attempts were repeatedly made along these lines (by **Hindemith**, for instance), without a satisfactory result being reached.

In the last few days, I again have felt the absolute need to proceed productively in this area. While visiting the exceedingly interesting villages, **Graslitz** and **Schönbach**, where instruments are built, I heard youth bands that propagated monstrous rubbish. At any rate, I am extraordinarily grateful to you for your work. I have learned a great deal from it. — Your Wagner article is comparable, although I must admit candidly that I cannot persuade myself to see Wagner in the light which you have designed! I am convinced that he, too, would have gone to Hitler, with all flags flying. The Kaiser March [by Wagner] and the whole *Patronatsverein* business [Association of Patrons] speak loud and clear - despite Parsifal and all the essays in the 10th volume [of Wagner's Collected

Writings].[1]

But wouldn't you like to write an article sometime for the "New World Stage?" [*Neue Weltbühne*] You have such an enviably clear and logical way with words that, in any case, you should weigh in on a current theme. Just yesterday, I read an article in the "Weltbühne" by Hermann **Reichenbach**,[2] who now lives in Moscow ("United Front in Music"), which was no less than clear and convincing. The only thing of interest in it was the announcement of a musical olympiade in Strassburg, of which I had heard completely by chance at a lecture evening in Reichenberg. Could you obtain for me brochures or other printed matter about this musical olympiade? I would be very grateful to you.

Now, write to me againery soon how your plan is continuing. As you can imagine, every phase is of very lively interest to me and if you really should get serious with your ideas about proceeding with a sociology of music, you can depend on my readiness to cooperate at any time. You know, of course, that this is a question that incessantly keeps me in fervent occupation. **Wiesengrund's** [Ardono] works are all much too marked as quirky and tendentious and **Honigsheim** is so superficial that it cannot seriously be put

---

[1] Kestenberg is saying that Wagner would have gone over to Hitler the same way he bowed to the Hohenzollern in 1871 after they made war on and defeated France, after which Wilhelm of Prussia had himself crowned in Versailles as Emperor Wilhelm I, all of which disgusted Kestenberg who was a pacifist and a strong advocate of democracy. As demonstration of his enthusiasm for the successful war and ostensible loyalty to the new German Emperor, the former revolutionary of 1848, Wagner, composed a 10-minute *Kaisermarsch* to honor his new hero and his victorious soldiers. Unfortunately, the Empress disliked the piece and Bismarck was also not keen. It really is quite repetitive and uninspired, sounding in many places like some of the embarrassing music composed by Wagner's son Siegfried.

The Society of Patrons referred to by Kestenberg was one of the first large-scale fundraising efforts by subscription in history. By paying 300 Talers to gain membership in the Society, rich people could gain tickets for the best seats in the Bayreuth Festival Theatre. They also imagined - falsely - that they could influence programming and casting. Kestenberg saw this as a betrayal of Wagner's original democratic and even socialistic ideas — theatre for the people as inspired by ancient Greece. Perhaps Kestenberg had in mind Hitler's announced subscription plan by which ordinary people could pay into a fund in order to receive a Volkswagen or Peoples' Car. once they accumulated 990 Reichsmarks.

[2] Hermann **Reichenbach** - (1891-1953) - Physicist, philosopher, and logician.

on the scales, at least not from the musical point of view. — Ever since Rachmaninoff[1] stated here that all modern music seems to him like Chinese, and he has absolutely no intention of learning Chinese, he exists for me only as a welcome negative example of a musician of our times.

Best and warmest regards, also from my ladies and also to yours! Heartily, as of old,

Your Leo Kestenberg

31. KBG to FWB — 1935.04.15

[1] Sergei Vasilievich **Rachmaninoff** - (1873-1943) - Russian composer, concert pianist, and conductor. His composition style was late romantic, very lyrical, expansive, with lush orchestration. Unlike contemporaries such as Schönberg, Rachmaninoff was firmly dedicated to tonality in composition. Modernists like K. and Adorno, were withering in their criticism of Rachmaninoff's music. From 1932 to 1939, Rachmaninoff spent summers composing in the Villa Senar on Lake Lucerne.

32. 1935.07.13 — FWB (Zurich) to Kbg – *[typed]*

Background:

Beidler apologizes to Kestenberg for being so very categorical, in this case about the Nazis. The subject comes up when Beidler very colourfully relates a chance meeting he had with H.J.Moser, a German musicologist whom the Beidlers regarded as a semi-Nazified careerist and fellow-traveller. As we have noted, Beidler was not like his Wagner relatives in Bayreuth. Just around the time Beidler was writing his bitingly sarcastic comments about Moser as Nazi-enabler, his relatives were basking in the happiest of fascist days. On the 9th, for instance, only four days before Beidler wrote his letter to Kestenberg, Winifred wrote to a friend that Hitler intended to give her son Wieland a nice gift, a magnificent, custom-made Mercedes convertible. And only two days after Beidler wrote to Kestenberg, who should turn up completely unexpectedly for dinner in Wahnfried? Adolf Hitler himself. As usual, the Wagners and their employees were absolutely in heaven. Winifred's secretary Liselotte wrote to her parents: "… I must really say, for such an event I would gladly give up ten years of my life."

Zurich: 7: 13 July 1935,

134, Klosbachstrasse.

[head of letter:] BEIDLER

Dear Comrade **KESTENBERG**,

this time it is not a "relapse." "Ur-revolutionary upheavals" are to blame. Would you ever have thought it possible that your former colleague could throw all his habits overboard, and, for weeks now, wake up daily at just after 6:00am? Yes, and that he even is becoming a morning type and correspondingly optimistic? All true. Why? Because, since the end of May, I have been employed at the "Office of Statistics of the Canton Zurich), temporarily, for a half year to begin with, and with advance crisis-payment. (Thus, here too, again, public administration. It seems to me to be predestined. Apparently "governmental" from birth…). Only after a few days there, I was promoted to department head (retail market statistics) and have command over 8 men, including even a doctor! The radical readjustment and the pressure for quickest possible job-reorientation left me with not one minute of time - you will understand that. Both have gone well. My first homeland-reference will be excellent and I have a strong impression that I can succeed here, in a relatively short time, to attain a large, fine, fulfilling position which will then develop a wide-ranging international reach, especially to France. By hook or by crook, I want to succeed in this, energetically put aside everything "private," rigorously rationalize time and labour, and work eleven hours a day.

For today, this is all the factual news that I have to "report." The radio plans, naturally left unpromoted during the last weeks, of course will be sustained. Added to that, many other things (lectures in autumn and winter, probably even on - your **Liszt** ....). Mr. Beidler is becoming versatile and is confident he can do it.

With that, the era of "emigrantitude" would then be conclusively surmounted. From one of the attached items, you will see that we - in an impolite nutshell - have drawn the consequences of this. Without even the slightest regret. I, above all (my dear wife was - oh racial theory! - always "more German" than I and therefore follows developments more slowly), have "de-Germanized" myself over the last two years. I can not anymore. I do not want to anymore. Everything that comes from there nauseates me, no, not even that any longer, it only amuses me. It is truly just too dumb.

One time more was it able to produce an "emotion" in me, however. But in-depth. **Hans Joachim** [Moser], pure-of-race, spoke here at the "Bach Festival." Not that I went to hear him. But I saw him right in front of me at a concert. That is: I looked away. He, however, approached me with the question whether we no longer knew each other. You understand: in the Third Reich, he has been placed on quicksand (and how!!) and he does not want to have any enemies here. At the Wagner celebration in Hardenberg Street on February 13, 1933, he ostentatiously cut me dead. Now I said: *accipio confessa* [I accept what the confession.] For the rest, I am more indifferent to everything personal than ever before. And then, without the slightest mercy, he heard the following: nationalism is the breeding ground in which the pestilence of our age has thrived. People like him bear the intrinsic responsibility that in Germany the yeast, the cesspool, the latrine, the manure came to power - he had no right at all to complain because, right from the start, he most unhesitatingly participated over there and still would be doing it today if the others allowed him to. He, personally, also had collected much experience about what it is like if a whole people is systematically bestialized, and it is extraordinarily healthy, precisely for the "intellectuals." Nor did I forget to remind him that, in 1931, I, very much on my own, went to the utmost imaginable trouble to hang a disciplinary action around his neck, that could have led to his dismissal, unfortunately in vain, and because of him, you and I almost went our separate ways. .... His only response was that we were not speaking Esperanto [*Volapük*] or Latin, which caused my dear wife to interrupt and opine, that might be preferable. .... Fundamentally, exactly like you, I have a certain affinity for his agility and slickness, the affinity for intelligence in an ocean of inanity, and mortified, downright indescribably mortified as he was, he almost made me feel sorry for him .... The extraordinarily dynamic scene was, in its dramatic onesidedness, doubtless something new and not exactly pleasant for him, and, later, I had to laugh a lot. As you see, I am more "categorical" than ever. This part of my character is not something that you admire, but I had to tell you about this nonetheless.

Further "attachments": documents for the olympiade in Strassburg, about which you wanted to hear. Was my request successful? I, myself, did not want to participate. After my experiences with Germany, I "no longer know any parties." [quote of Kaiser Wilhelm II on Aug. 4, 1914]. …. I did not sign the resolution. Actually, I wanted to justify this in detail; but then I told myself that it was not worth the effort. Hymns of praise to Russia, I relinquish without envy to Mr. Kurt Hiller[1] in the "Weltbühne" and make do for the time being with taking note, with regret, of a not very joyful reality but with optimism for a future that is relatively near. Otherwise, as well, the resolution is based on a false analysis, anachronistic, childish. Admittedly, the idea of the event as a whole excellent, but, sadly, I am not informed about its effective realization.

How is your congress doing? How are you actually, personally and objectively? We take great joy in hearing news about you all (Tunja included, of course) and beg you not to seek an eye for an eye. With us, the interruption was an exception (in virtue of an "act of God") and will stay that way.

In old, always identical, affectionate, even tender bonds

Your

We are asked to send regards to you from poor Schönlank,[2] who occasionally has a very frugal meal with us.

Additionally, very great thanks for the criticism of my piece about the Inquiry into the Parisian institutes. Like everything that comes from you, it was of high value and contains, as ever, excellent suggestions.

32. FWB to KBG — 1935.07.13

---

[1] Kurt **Hiller** - (1885-1972) - pseudonyms Keith Lurr and Klirr. German-Jewish essayist and pacifist journalist noted for his originality of expressionist style. He was a leftist and a proponent of gay rights. He spent most of 1933 and 1934 in concentration camps, fleeing to Prague in 1934, then London in 1938.

[2] Bruno **Schönlank** - (1891-1965) - German lyricist, playwright, novelist and author of radio plays. He left Germany for Zurich in 1933. He wrote several works in "Sprechchor" form (oratorios mostly in spoken form).

33. 1935.12.27 — Kbg (Prague) to Beidlers (Zurich)

[typed - letterhead of S.H.V.]

27. XII. 35.

My dear Beidlers,

Today, you will not yet receive a thank you and a response for your dear, wonderful birthday letter. [not extant] Taking care of this private correspondence must wait for a more tranquil time, although I can hardly know whether a break can be squeezed in somewhere before our congress, which we definitely expect you both to attend.

But your trip to Paris comes so opportunely for me that I cannot deny myself asking you, in the usual old way, for a couple of favours. If only one or the other of these can be attended to during the short duration of your stay there, I would be extraordinarily happy and grateful, since a few of the personalities whom I am asking you to call on cannot be induced in any way to answer letters. And with that, I am already in the midst of my official subject.

1.) After Ruth paid a visit to Mr. **Chantavoine** in October, he once again confirmed, very briefly, his willingness to give a paper at the congress. He also sent us his picture, which we had requested, but despite my repeated requests and letters, I have not succeeded in finding out the subject which he has in mind for his talk. I suggested that he talk about the boundaries of musical education of professionals and amateurs, since he, as general secretary of the oldest music academy in the world, would be able most easily to dissipate the misguided prejudices which are directed against our efforts by professionals of the whole world. It was only here that I first saw that **Schwers** and consorts can be found in many other countries, often with the same buzz words, and almost always afflicted with a similar narrow-mindedness. I believe that Chantavoine, of all people, would be the right personality to handle these problems with the necessary stature. Please, pay him a visit, either in his place of residence (Val de grace) or in the Conservatoire and do not leave him before he has formulated a specific subject.

But, whilst dictating, it crosses my mind that you yourself are a completely unreliable letter writer and that, with my inquiry, I am betaking myself from the frying pan into the fire!! Nonetheless, I shall defy this danger and am counting on a miracle - not only with you but also with Chantavoine.

I have been experiencing very good results with all other Parisians. **Roger-Ducasse**[1] always responds posthaste and has mentioned you to me, as well, Dr. Beidler, in the most enthusiastic terms. He will be giving a paper about music education in Paris and I hope that he will have been informed by the official invitation of the city of Paris which was sent out some weeks ago, from here, via the Czech embassy in Paris. We mentioned Roger-Ducasse in this invitation. The same applies to Chantavoine, except that he is thought of as the representative of the French government. **Coeuroy** and Prof. **Sachs** will also come here from Paris - the first as representative of the I.I.C.I., with which, thanks to your past efforts, we have good relations. The details of cooperation between the I.I.C.I. and the S.H.V. will be talked over on the occasion of the visits to Prague. I hope that you can take part in this in person.

33. KBG to FWB — 1935.12.27

[1] Jean Jules Amable Roger-**Ducasse** (1873-1954) - French composer, protegé and friend of Fauré. Professor of composition and orchestration at the Paris Conservatoire.

34. 1936.01.06 — Kbg (Prague) to Beidlers (Zurich)

[typed]

Prague XIX- Dejvice, Velvarská 59

6. I. 36.

My very dear Beidlers, your kind cards from Paris [not extant] were refreshing to me, given my pessimism with regard to your writing habits. In this respect, you have trained me so well that every sign [of life] from you seems like a miracle without precedent! I have taken to heart your hint about Chantavoine's subject and I shall write to him again to ask that he choose a subject from the entire territory of musical listening, and, at the same time, intimate that I also understand this as including the historical development of the concept of audience in the nineteenth century. I believe that the boundaries have now been drawn so widely, that it cannot be difficult for him to find a subject that really appeals to him.

I have to thank you sincerely again for all your good wishes. You cannot imagine how happy your loyalty and your unchanged attitude make both of us. As pleasant as the atmosphere of Prague is, and as secure as I do believe to have found solid new starting-points for my work, it still seems as if we were fated never to form new friendships [here]. We cannot complain about a lack of truly good and sweet-natured acquaintances, and I would be unappreciative if I refused to recognize that I have found magnificent co-workers here - but still, I feel as if such dependable, dear, and good friends as in Berlin would never again be possible to find.

Adieu and write again soon, especially about how you both are doing. And once again, a thousand thanks for your tenderness and affection, which I - as you know - reciprocate from the bottom of my heart.

Always yours Leo Kestenberg

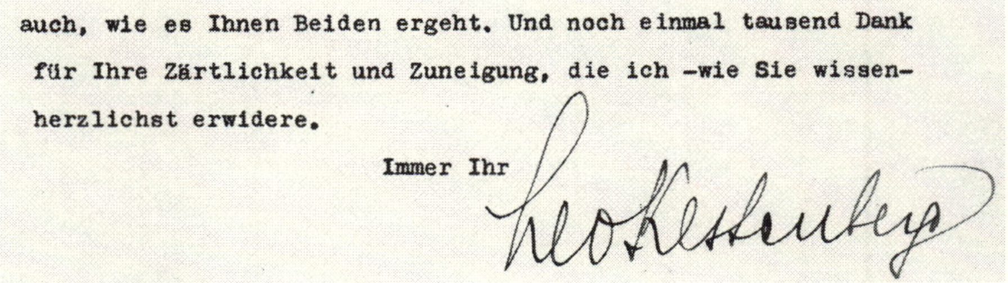
auch, wie es Ihnen Beiden ergeht. Und noch einmal tausend Dank für Ihre Zärtlichkeit und Zuneigung, die ich -wie Sie wissen- herzlichst erwidere.

Immer Ihr

Leo Kestenberg

34. KBG to FWB — 1936.01.06

35. 1936.04.13 — FWB (Zurich) to Kbg
[typed]

Background:

Once again, Beidler must apologize to Kestenberg, this time for being unable to attend Kestenberg's great accomplishment, the International Congress of the *Spolecnost por Hudební vychovu* (Society for Musical Pedagogy). It opened on April 4, 1936 in the Hall of Mirrors of the University Library, under the patronage of the Czech President, Edvard Beneš. Kestenberg's son-in-law Tunja Gladstein had set up a large exhibit describing teaching practices in various countries. There were, for instance, large diagrams showing the hourly rates earned by teachers internationally. At the time, Rumania was in first place. There were more than 700 delegates and participants from 21 or more countries with choirs from Hungary, the Netherlands, Switzerland, and Yugoslavia, all dressed in their national costumes. Nineteen governments were officially represented. Among the prominent speakers were Edward Dent, Ernst Křenek, Olga Samaroff-Stokowski (wife of conductor Leopold Stokowski), Hector Villa-Lobos and Émile Jaques-Dalcroze, who gave an eight-day course in rhythmic gymnastics after the Congress. Kestenberg closed the Congress with a speech emphasizing the importance of international, organized and co-operative musical education.

BEIDLER

Zürich 7: 13. April 1936
134, Klosbachstrasse.

Dear, dear Comrade **Kestenberg**,

please do not believe that we do not take it as a special perfidy, perpetrated by our "fate" that, of all things, we had to be absent from the first great materialization of your new intellectual reality. For two reasons it just was not possible:

1) I am doing an official publication here which just now has gone to the printer and which requires me to be here;

2) the financing of the trip also did not succeed as we had thought it would, because several newspapers which I had approached either sent their own people, or, as with the

Berner "Bund," had "no interest."[1]

Both points, together and connected with our still quite unstable general situation, caused us to drop our travel plans at the last moment. For the congress, it was no loss; on the contrary, objectively seen, it was much more valuable that the "Neue Zürcher Zeitung" [Switzerland's leading newspaper] sent **Willi Schuh**,[2] (in every respect exceptional, tremendously erudite, and certainly very open to your thoughts in particular). The Basler Nationalzeitung [National Newspaper, Basel] sent an editor from its own music section. I am an outsider in the musical-educational life of this country, and therefore lacking in intimate familiarity with things, that I could not have been capable of featuring the connections that doubtless will now arise.

What remains is the "private-and-personal" and that is bitter. But for all that, it is certainly just a postponement and our deeper contact with you is greater, more intensive, and more tender than ever. I am waiting for the reports with great interest. There can be no doubt that everything had the greatest success. Above all however: profound thanks for the amassed invitations, of which Ruth's last one moved us especially. I am inserting a page for her.

We consoled ourselves with Scherchen[3] who did Alban Berg's *Five Pieces for Orchestra* from "Lulu" and who gave us a great deal in the rehearsals, which we attended from the very first. We were with him a lot. I tried to counteract his rabid feelings against you, among other things (unfortunately, he lumps you together with the whole of Weimar) and to appeal to his deeper rational faculties, without much evident success, for the time being. But I am all too well aware that whatever you tell him has a strong after-effect, that it gets to him somehow. Add to this the strong inner isolation which makes him more receptive. With all his "robustness" and refreshing, undeviating wholeness, I find him more mature and deliberate than before. For us, he represents the prototype of the "class of the future," [proletariate, working class] which will look something like this, and that is not bad — on the contrary.

Everything is progressing for us. My slow-motion tempo with my own work — you

---

[1] **Berner "Bund"** - Swiss daily newspaper published in Bern, the capital of Switzerland.

[2] Willi **Schuh** - (1900-1986) - Swiss musicologist, writer, and journalist. Schuh was an authority on the life and music of Richard Strauss as well as that of the Swiss composer, Othmar Schoeck.

[3] Hermann **Scherchen** - (1891-1966) - Prominent German conductor. He was the principal conductor of the city orchestra of Winterthur (near Zurich) 1922 to 1950. He conducted many premieres of new works by modern composers. He was a creative conductor who made many recordings.

know it well ... — admittedly eats up an unbelievable amount of time, since, of course, the "official" occupation is also thoroughly demanding and since we, regrettably, can no longer live so reclusively as we wanted and all too often must all-but "entertain" again. But that is unavoidable. Moreover, people are so unimaginably good to us here, as — with the exception of Leo and Grete KBG — nobody in Germany ever was to us.

A little while ago, my dear wife said: "Write short and right away rather than long and not at all!" The advice has been obeyed and the result is meagre. Put up with it for the time being. It goes without saying that, for now, all those "tidying-up operations" will prevent you from responding. I shall send you whatever I find in the newspapers and duplicates are also worth something.

A thousand profound greetings, naturally also to Frau Grete and with distance, to Grandma.

Always your old

(the ex-pair of intriguers)

P.S. Yesterday we had a long talk about you with Marie **Buelow**[1], who did not have the slightest clue about your "true character" and was more than a little surprised. ... She is almost 80, and what vitality... — At the moment, I am writing what is (for me) the most beautiful chapter of my book. It is called "Antisemitism" and will be a sublime, unassailable settlement of accounts with Bayreuthianism. I flatter myself that it will have the impact of a bomb. (Confidentially: this is the actual meaning for me of the whole book - but don't pass this on any further ...)

35. FWB to KBG — 1936.04.13

[1] Marie von **Bülow** - (1857-1941) - née Schanzer. She was Viennese, beginning her career as an actress in Basel, Switzerland. After marrying Hans von Bülow, the first husband of Cosima Wagner, Marie gave up her acting career. She lived in Berlin.

37. 1936.07.08 — Kbg (Prague) to Beidlers (Zurich)

[typed]

[letter head of SHV]

8 July 1936

Dr. F.W. Beidler-Wagner
Klosbachstrasse 134
Zurich.

Dear Beidlers,

You have once again expired into your renowned mass-grave-rigor mortis [condition] and I only hope to awake you by means of the question: who lies above, who below. Out of these two possibilities, I hope that you will choose the third and at last write to me. But, in order to amass further burning coals on your sinning heads, I am sending you a further product of my diligence, an offprint from the "Auftakt" that just appeared.

Best regards

Your old: Leo Kestbg

37. KBG to FWB — 1936.07.08

38. 1936.09.26 — Kbg (Prague) to Beidlers (Zurich)

[hand-written; no letterhead]

Prag XIX, Velvarská 59
26.IX. 36

My dear friends!

Despite the way I bristle at sentimentality, today, on the Day of Atonement [Yom Kippur], a whole horde of childhood memories are storming about all around me.

Almost physically, they are taking possession of me and I hope only to escape them by turning to an entirely opposite existential circle: your essay about Cosima Wagner, which you recently sent me and for which I am genuinely grateful.

Above all, I admire the brilliant, polished shaping of your thoughts. Please allow me to say this: your talent for composition has made truly surprising progress. Your close connection to Thomas Mann is of perceptible and original benefit. Only someone who knows you both, understands what it implies when you write a sentence like: "It just was some talk about her diary," in this context. You now have attained a beautiful, tranquil, free style which seems matter-of-fact and makes your work a joy to read.

As far as content is concerned, as an increasingly reluctant Wagnerian, I have little to say. Richard and Cosima - I always see, experience, judge them only from Liszt outward, and Cosima, in particular, especially from her mother,[1] for whom, at last, a vindication would be desirable as against Lizst's later period and as against Carolyne [Sayn-Wittgenstein].[2] In the same number in which your article is published, there is an

---

[1] Marie **d'Agoult** - (1805-1876) - Marie Catherine Sophie, Comtesse d'Agoult. Pseudonym as author: Daniel Stern. Born Vicomtesse de Flavigny. Her mother was Maria Bethmann (1772-1847), of the Bethmann banking family of Frankfurt. She had a storied affair with Franz Liszt, 1835-1839. The liason resulted in three children, Blandine (1835-1862), Cosima (1837-1930), and Daniel (1839-1859). She wrote several estimable history books and a well-known novel, *Nélida* (1846) of which the title stems from her pen name, Daniel.

[2] Carolyne zu **Sayn-Wittgenstein** - (1819-1887) - Polish aristocrat, married in 1836. After meeting Franz Liszt in 1847, she became Liszt's mistress, moving to Weimar with him in 1848. The Vatican refused to annul her marriage so that she could marry Liszt. They both remained close. She was an enthusiastic writer, probably including much of Liszt's literary output. She had a long correspondence with Berlioz as well as with other figures in the musical world of the time.

article about Wotan by C.G.Jung,[1] which occupied me very actively. All the improbability that is playing itself out today in the lives of nations, the repulsively cheap buffoonery that unrolls on the international stage, with Hitler and Mussolini at the summit, all this seems, on a very much higher level, to have been, at one time, the prerogative of gifted individuals. This non-bourgeois element in the life of the artist, inimical to the normal, existential sequence, as with Beethoven's legacy to the 19th century, rises to the surface in Liszt's circle and is also perceptible as procreative, primordial matter in Cosima's essence, despite all her yearning for legitimacy and restoration. There is in noble-mindedness a profound responsibility to [strive for] self-perfection which I find to be stronger in Liszt and Cosima than in Wagner, in whom, despite all his genius and immensely powerful achievement, I detect too strongly the German man of violence ever to be able to warm to him fully.

Your portrayal shed much light for me. The contrasting of both natures is immensely effective and convincing, the material you cite, very illustrative and exhaustive. At any rate, the article arouses great hopes for a large, comprehensive work on Wagner by you and I hope that you finally will realize your plans.

Since we are now already at "hope," I am planning a trip to Paris, since, in the course of next summer, we want to hold an international seminar there, for which there soon will have to be preliminary, on-the-spot consultations. Naturally, I would then travel via Zurich, where, however, I would very much like to give a lecture, in an appropriate setting, about our society. Or, should visiting you be the exclusive goal? Please get in touch with Mme Prof. Stadler, on our recommendation, in Zurich, Russenweg 8. We have told Mme Prof. a lot about you and I would be happy if you received the same favourable impression as we did.

Are you in contact with Dr Arnold Walter, who has finally landed in London or do you wish to be?

There is not much else to report about us. Rahel[2] very comfortably passed the entrance exam for the local Oktavon (Oberprima) [final year of high school/grammar school] and is once again a darling schoolgirl. Ruth will soon send you a work about Hus-

---

[1] Carl Gustav **Jung** - (1875-1961) - Swiss psychiatrist and psychotherapist; founder of analytical psychology. He developed concepts used in his writing, including on mythology and Wagner's operatic works: the archetype, the collective unconscious, the complex, synchronicity.

[2] **Rahel** had returned from Palestine at the beginning of 1936. In the space of months, she very diligently not only completed the school years she had missed by leaving for Palestine but also graduated from secondary school with the so-called "*Abitur*," the certificate prerequisite for university entry.

sites and Jews. Tunja is working on his "doctor" and we are striving not to fall too much behind the young generation. Beside building up the organization of the "Society," playing the piano - the eternal, unhappy love - makes ever greater demands on me: just now the Hammerklavier Sonata [Beethoven, Op.106], which actually already includes every conceivable problem in the world of sound, if only it is correctly understood. But with that, I am once again at youthful memories, at the "long" day, at "our" world and the hour with you and your glorious ancestors is at an end. A pity, but to a rapid re-thinking and re-guiding [a pun on farewell -auf Wiedersehen, which Kbg replaces with auf wieder-denken and auf wieder-führen]

Most affectionate regards to you both

Your Leo Kbg

[Grete K. handwriting]

The letter must be sent, but not without love from me. The old God is vexing the Jews - it is raining here, pitifully - unfortunately, he is always with Hitler. To a victorious Spain! Your Grete.

38. Kbg to FWB — 1936.09.26

39. 1936.10.06 — Kbg (Prague) to Beidlers (Zurich) – *[typed]*

[letterhead of SHV]

SPOLEČNOST PRO HUDEBNÍ VÝCHOVU
SOCIÉTÉ D'ÉDUCATION MUSICALE
SHV
SOCIETY FOR MUSICAL EDUCATION
GESELLSCHAFT FÜR MUSIK-ERZIEHUNG

PRAHA
IV. TOSKÁNSKÝ PALÁC.

6.Oktober 1936

Herrn Dr. F.W. Beidler-Wagner
Klosbachstrasse 134
Zürich.

My dear Beidlers,

You reward me with a virtual torrent of surprises. This activity is almost alarming and I can only hope that the personalities whom you have imposed on, strike a somewhat more plodding tempo. From among those [personalities], as a friend of Busoni's I have known and genuinely admired Dr. Schuh for a long time. I also would not have any idea, at the moment, how I could get away for a trip during the next weeks since I am very actively preoccupied now. However, if a definitive commitment by both instances takes place, I certainly shall find time to travel to you and then to Paris.

Incidentally, in re-reading your letter, I stumbled over your remark that it would hurt me if you had to utter a bad word about Franz Liszt. If the biography is anywhere near as good as the preliminary study, then decidedly I advise you to drop everything else and work on the biography alone.

Despite the quantitatively rich materials that the Liszt-year has brought, it seems to me as if what is still lacking is a depiction of the whole [Liszt] circle which has truly superior writing and captures the historical relationships and the whole *Zeitgeist* of the era. During his last visit to Prague, I also talked to Thomas Mann, admittedly in a very short conversation, and upbraided him mildly for making an unending mass of pronouncements about Wagner without ever even mentioning Liszt. And still, I believe that the image of Liszt, precisely because of its complex of problems and its almost incomprehensible inner contradictions is more interesting, on a human level, than Wagner's.

And here we are now at the "bad word": the same Liszt who, in the Vienna of 1848, is supposed to have treated workers on the barricades to cigars, but, in the same instant, becomes a raging reactionary when these same workers murder his friend, Prince Lichnowsky. There are a thousand details in this life which seem completely contradictory and which cannot be made sense of, if the whole personality is not understood and affirmed.

I am endlessly anxious to become acquainted with your portrayal of the relationship [of Wagner] to the Countess d'Agoult and to Liszt and Cosima. Your hints give me a right to assume that, beyond the somewhat meagre biographical material, you will know how to illuminate the background, which, stands in a virtually dialectical opposition to the facts being played out in the foreground. With that, we perhaps come to the most interesting consideration: the romantic era favours, and almost obligates these artistic beings to a fantastical individuality. What appears bizarre and illegitimate today, as perhaps in the life of George Sand[1], is, for this first and greatest bohemian, a necessity and an indispensable correlate in the permanently overheated production-boiler. This is exactly the opposite of today, to this era in which Stravinsky searches for and finds the ideal of the creative musician in the engineer type. Wagner retained the beret and the velvet jerkin from this era to the very end.

Let us hope that we'll soon be able to talk in person and at length about this subject.

In the last few days, I have received a brochure about the book by H.Kayser[2] and a review from the Bund of Bern. In any case, I shall try to obtain the book.

By the way, how has Fellerer[3] been behaving? The last news was quite catastrophic.

Once again, sincere thanks and best regards,

Your

Leo Kestenberg

39. KBG to FWB — 1936.10.06

[1] George **Sand** - (1804-1876) - Amantine Lucile Aurore Dupin - French novelist. She was a colourful and rebellious figure in her day, having multiple extra-marital relationships, including one long one with Frédéric Chopin. She went about in public dressed in men's clothing and smoked big cigars.

[2] Hans **Kayser** - (1891-1964) - A German theoretician of art and music, writer, and musician. He revived interest in the so-called music of the spheres by returning to the work of Pythagoras and developing a new system of harmonic ideas from there.

[3] Karl Gustav **Fellerer** - (1902-1984) - German musicologist - close friend of Beidler's. The latter called Fellerer "Kare".

40. 1936.10.25 — FWB (Zurich) to Kbg

[typed]

BEIDLER

Zurich 7: 25 October 1936,
134 Klosbachstrasse.

Dear Comrade Kestenberg,

today, in response to your last letter, I am sending you the first chapter of "Cosima," with a much lighter heart than would have been possible before. It has shown me - more between the lines than expressly — that we both basically are in complete agreement about the stature of Liszt. "We both" is, for my part — although I could bring "blood" into the weighing — …. a certain insolence, since you — even if only in virtue of the piano world, but also for reasons that put a Plus on your side and a clear Minus on mine, and show you as standing much closer to Liszt than I do. Anyway: I have the feeling, after seriously battling for "truth," that I am right - but no more than that. You will doubtless be disappointed and, I hope, will criticize me fiercely.

Because: candidly speaking, I am not yet happy with the first chapter. It does not yet have its final form. There will be corrections in many places and there are still even some small errors in it (for instance, Cosima was born in Como, not in Bellagio, which I have only known a few days via birth certificate, and which is basically damned dull and only fun because there is not a single "official" publication that does not indicate Bellagio). The wording is also not yet satisfactory in many spots.

But it is precisely because of this that I am sending it to you, since you are the only one who can really judge it. To the extent that I have been able to follow the publications, the Liszt year has not enabled a single voice to sound that even remotely could compare with your Liszt lecture.

You are correct in writing that, up to the present day, there has not yet been a superior portrayal of the connections of *Zeitgeist* and history. I do not flatter myself that I can achieve this, although the next chapter of my book, with which I am presently wrestling, should actually include this if it is to reach its goal. But I cannot hide it from myself that I simply am not adequate, and everyday I become more conscious of just how much of a brazen, reckless, daredevil venture it was on my part to throw myself into this book. But there is no way back now and I must see to it that I emerge from this as respectably as possible. At the moment, I feel especially close to you because I have to describe the **Al-**

tenburg[1] (in its objective significance simultaneously with it subjective importance for Cosima as a pre-school for "Bayreuth"!) and I continually tell myself that you would be the only one that could really write this! Naturally, as soon as this chapter is finished, I shall send it to you.

An additional short preliminary note: please do not view the statement of contents before the first chapter as in any way binding in its wording. It simply gives approximate points of reference for what will be examined. Recently, I sketched the actual meaning of the book for an interested person (a writer of the communist persuasion), as follows:

1) It is not a music book but rather a study of a special case in the problem "art and social order," conceived in the form of a biography of the person in whom the polarity that was characteristic of the 19th century – restoration-evolution – is personalized vis-à-vis Wagner. What is to be understood under this antithesis, which in no way is only "political," but rather much more comprehensive, can be found, as suggested on page 680 of the preliminary study in the "Neuen Schweizer Rundschau."

2) It is also not a Wagner book in the usual sense, at most a post-Wagner book, or better, a book about the mass impact of the Wagnerian art. It will show the interaction of personal and societal factors presupposed by the "success" of Wagners' work (by no means only in Germany). It will analyze the meaning for society of the continuing force of this success into the present.

Among the personal factors, the one that takes first place as the driving force: Cosima Wagner with her staff and circle of allies in various countries. It is important, above all, to reveal the gimmicks of the pre-1848 leftist, anti-middle-class opposition aspect, which dominates the ideology of all of Wagner's work, seemingly retained, but then reinterpreted into that aristocratic, rightwing, anti-middle-class opposition, the last mass offshoot of which is National Socialism! That this was at all possible is due, above all, to the ambiguity and complexity which constitute the essence of great art.

Well now, enough of me! (Although, at bottom, I do not play any **rôle** here, but rather serve in an all-important cause!). I am attaching the negative response of

---

[1] The **Altenburg** is a large villa built 1810-1811 on the outskirts of Weimar. Starting in 1848, Franz Liszt and Carolyne zu Sayn-Wittgenstein and her daughter lived there – for over a decade. Students and followers of Liszt also lived there and studied with their master. People often mentioned "the Altenburg" in the way they later did "Wahnfried" or "Buckingham Palace", each encompassing a tight-knit structure of power or dogma from which radiated influence over a large swath of human thought and activity centred around one person and an immediate inner circle of dedicated adherents.

Dr.Spühler[1] - one does not see from the Swiss-cool-official writing that, in reality, we are on good terms. I talked with him again afterwards and determined that a lecture would be easy to reach in the long term (the Social Democrats here are at least just the same civil servants and bureaucrats as formerly in Germany! Of these, I do not know even a single "prominent" one, outside of Spühler, who is very bright and young and wrote an excellent work about Saint Simonianism.)

Willi Schuh called me immediately, seemed very obliging, but also pointed out that the winter program of the music-pedagogical association was ready and promised further that he wanted to "scout about." I think that something could come of this, if you would only first give me precise dates and perhaps also the subject that you would want to talk about. At any rate, we would be out of our minds with joy to see you again!

And now something more: you do know **Golo Mann**[2] (Thomas Mann's second son)? He has become a Czech and is now already in Prague. Without a shadow of a doubt, he is the only gifted one among the children of Mann — but therefore very gifted, mentally adroit, idiosyncratic, and cantankerous. We hold him in very high regard. His attitude to me is quite problematic: some diabolical natural law or other drives him to hate me, although a bit of empathy is also mixed in. Think of certain "anti-aryan" feelings that a certain Leo Kestenberg had to feel for me for long years and you will understand Golo just as well as I understand him. He sees in me — the devil knows how groundless it is — a Sunday's child, the "loved one," the "charmer," the one who lives on the sunny side of life and all sorts of whatever, along these lines (just as if the smoke of my victims rose vertically towards heaven!). He cannot do otherwise and constantly behaves himself so impolitely and so impossibly to me that I can do nothing other than give up my wooing of him; which at least follows a forthright line. But I still consider him a power, if also with strong psychopathic traits of character, and I believe that he should be looked after, especially because of his immensely depressive vulnerability. I could imagine that Tunja would get along with him famously. But he would also be of interest to you. On the other hand, I

---

[1] Willy **Spühler** - (1902-1990) - Swiss Social Democratic politician from Kanton Zurich. He obtained his doctorate in 1925 with a thesis about Saint-Simon. He became a municipal councillor in Zurich in 1928 and was a national councillor 1938-1959. He was President of the Confederation in 1963 and 1968.

[2] Golo **Mann** - (1909-1994) - He was an historian, the third child of Thomas and Katia Mann. After the Nazi takeover in 1933, he helped Monika, Elisabeth and Michael, his three younger siblings to leave Germany with his parents' savings. In 1936, when the Nazis revoked the German citizenship of the Mann family, they were able to gain Czech papers. Golo was in Prague for a time, only to join his family in the USA, where he joined the American war effort as a translator and radio commentator.

would deem your influence excellent, especially as a highly effective remedy for the damned "little Moritz atmosphere" of his paternal house, which is very detrimental for him! Do you have time and inclination to give him some attention?

When it comes to you, my heart and brain are so overfull that I am sure to forget a thousand things that I wanted to say. But this formless monster of a letter should not swell up any further. And now — a quick finale! Otherwise this will become a love letter, for which there is a steadily growing danger if I write to you.

Much love and a thousand tender regards!

Mme Grete, Grandmama, Ruth, Tunja, and Rahel are always included!

PS 1) "Catastrophic news" about **Fellerer** ?? Puzzling to me! He has behaved the same to me since 1933, tremendously decent, open and honest. He is so little nazified [*gleichgeschaltet*] as the editor of a publication appearing in the Third Reich can be, at all — according to everything I know. Since we are in very regular contact (and he tells me a lot of confidential things), I am very interested to learn what those catastrophic communications are! (By the way, he has continually and very conspicuously pulled back from "official" anti-Semitism; e.g. in bringing works for his series in Fribourg, at least half of the authors of which are "non-aryans." As I hear it, he is supposed to be quite under suspicion and with no career prospects.)

[marginal note] You should read what he hears from me from time to time!! And not a single protest has ever come from him.

On the subject: have you read **Preussner's** book (the middle-class music culture)? I do not want to. But naturally, it is very interesting to me. This must probably be the result of the Kestenberg-incubation-period???! Where else is it supposed to have come from otherwise???

"Monday" (Karl Tschuppik,[1] editor) wanted from me, on the basis of a biting note of mine in the Neuen Zürcher, my "biography" with a picture .... (I include the letter with the request that you return it, since I will probably have to answer at some point!) What kind of paper is that?

Thanks and once again sincerest regards!

40. FWB to KBG – 1936.10.25

[1] Karl **Tschuppik** - (1876-1937) - Austrian journalist, author, and editor. He worked for the Prager Tagblatt (Prague Daily) 1898-1917 as editor and publisher and wrote for several left-oriented papers in Vienna and Berlin. Tschuppik was on the initial black list of banned authors published by the Nazis in 1933.

Walter **Tschuppik** - (1889-1955) - younger brother of Karl Tscuppik, editor of the Prager Tagblatt 1914-1926 and editor-in-chief of the Süddeutsche Sonntagspost 1926-1933. He was an oponent of the Nazis and a proponent of German-Czech friendship. In 1933, he spent four months in German captivity. After that, he lived in Prague, where he published the papers, Der Montag (Monday) and Prager illustrierter Montag (Prague illustrated Monday). He fled to England, by way of Switzerland, because of the Nazi invasion of Czechoslovakia.

41. 1936.11.09 — Kbg (Prague) to Beidlers (Zurich)

[typed]

Prof.Leo Kestenberg
Prag-Dejvice 1646
Prague, 9 November 1936.

Dr. F. W. Beidler
Klosbachstrasse 134
Zurich 7.

Dear Friends,

I devoured your Chapter 1 with a certain feverish excitement. Previously, I inwardly resisted paying attention to the dark shadows which cast darkness upon the personal life of Liszt from his [first] encounter with the Princess onward. Your portrayal of Liszt as tyrannical father showed me unambiguously and for the first time that it would be feeble to retouch these shadows out of the portrait. The only way out remaining to me is to accept that it was Liszt's destiny, as so often, to act against his own better self, and that he also never had the opportunity to learn the difficult art of being a father. At any rate, your chapter made a really strong impression on me and I congratulate you for this achievement as a writer.

One thing that stood out for me, however, was that the outline of this chapter shows a certain unevenness: I especially miss a detailed portrayal of Liszt's relationship with the Countess d'Agoult during the Geneva years. The characterization of the Countess is brilliant and, it seems to me, the first presentation worthy of this magnificent personage. If it were not presumptuous, I would really say that I am personally grateful to you for this presentation. What I do miss here, however, all the more sadly, is a characterization of the colossal youth, the revolutionary élan which must so mark Liszt as unique, at the time he conceived of the *Album d'un Voyageur* [1837-38]. It is too little if you take as your starting point the poor child prodigy who is forced to earn money from early on. I believe that you would need to treat precisely this period of young love somewhat more in detail, perhaps more dithyrambically, in order to portray correctly the extravagance of both these devil-may-care adventurers. I am firmly convinced that this era was not just favourable, as you write, to "brilliant amorous feats," but rather the artist of that time, actually felt almost obligated to live a life that was not bourgeois, that the artist, as romantic apex of creation, had the right to shove all conventions to one side. Well then: it seems to me that the depiction of the essential significance of the time during which Cosima was conceived comes up somewhat too short and the union of the two, in my opinion, is treated too superficially and cursorily. Only after the years 33-37 are interpreted from the positive side can the detailed portrayal of later events be brought into a proper equilibrium. I also believe that it would be beneficial, in this context, to say something about the musical atmosphere in which Cosima spent her youth. You do not write one word about Daniel's education, despite this appearing to me to be indispensable for the whole picture. What also disturbs me, finally, is also the plethora of French quotes, as interesting and new as they may be. They interrupt the flow of the account much too much and it would be more advisable, perhaps, to interpret them within the text and then offer them, in extenso, in an addendum.

You also should not forget that you are not writing the book for a narrow circle of connoisseurs of the Liszt and Wagner literature. As you yourself say, it is not a music book, but a study of a special case within the problem, art and societal order, encased in the biography of that person in whom the polarity characteristic of the 19th century — restoration-revolution, is personalized with relation to Wagner. Further, you speak of the all-embracing antithesis that is understood under this [polarity]. For this reason, it might be desirable to describe the milieu so as to make comprehensible to laymen the area that stands to be discussed.

These are but very slight objections, in view of the whole achievement, which I judge to be the best I have read up to now about Liszt and his circle.

Please allow me to keep the carbon copy for a few more weeks. I should like to quote a few things in a Liszt lecture which I am to give in December, if you allow me to make reference to the coming book.

Too bad that you did not immediately respond to "Monday". If this paper has not earth-shaking importance, nonetheless it is well-read and, at any rate, it would not hurt to answer such an inquiry. Admittedly, it would be better if you made contact with the Prague daily or with the Prague press. If you want, I can sound out the editors of these papers.

I would be especially happy to see about Golo Mann if I could get his address. I am in touch here with a lot of young people and I believe that he would feel well in the circle to which Ruth and Rahel also belong. Please write to me immediately, where I can find him.

I found your remark about Fellerer to be most kind. I shall write to him soon, also about our Society [SHV]. Please give me his exact address.

Have you read anything about Mersmann's[1] lecture in Basel? You know that M. is still behaving excellently [with the Nazi regime] and accordingly must suffer terribly.

Naturally, Preussner's book, that I obtained by circuitous routes, was begun in **our** era. I read it with pleasure and profit. It very cleverly sidesteps every compromising position.

I should love to come to Zurich. But precisely at this moment, to my great joy, I have such a great deal of work in the Society for Musical Education that I cannot even think of a trip. A few days ago, we had the Society's first performance. It will be followed by a whole series in other social institutions. Outside of that, we are already preparing our international working conference in Paris, which already is beginning to take on precise forms. We also are going to hold interstate conferences that will address the subjects of pre-school music education on the one hand; on the other, cultivation of the folk song and its artistic and pedagogical importance. These conferences are supposed to take place in Brno and Bratislava. Further, we are thinking of a governmental regulation of private musical instruction such as we carried out in Prussia in 1925. We also want to work toward setting up a state recordings library.

You can see that I really have my hands full with things to do, in addition to my playing the piano very much. On December 12, I am playing "Lyon", the motto of which is "Vivre en travail ou mourir en combattant." [live working or die fighting] It occurs to me here that you must have a look at this composition because it is significant for the relationship between Liszt and the Countess d'Agoult. Admittedly, it is characteristic that Liszt cut "Lyon" from the second version of *Année de Pélerinage*.

In November I am giving a lecture on musical education and my past organizational work in Germany, during which I naturally shall make appropriate remarks about our "Yearbook."

And now [I] ask for further prompt packages, especially a second chapter and news just as extensive as the latest.

With the best of wishes from all of us

Your old:

LKbg

41. KBG to FWB — 1936.11.09

[1] Hans **Mersmann** - (1891-1971) - German musicologist. See note, Letter 13.

42. 1936.11.25 — FWB (Zurich) to Kbg

[typed]

THE BEIDLERS

Zurich 7: 25 November 1936,
134 Klosbachstrasse.
Dear Comrade Kestenberg,

the Nobel Prize for Ossietzky[1] - "under the prevailing circumstances" is this still the best birthday gift, not even for pretensions that are too modest. This "so insolent challenge and insult to the new Germany" shows one thing: that the Germans — despite manifold middle-class sympathies — under Hitler's command, have earned a net worth, throughout the whole world, in hate and contempt, against which what accumulated before 1914, also not small, amounted to no more than a reserve penny. Woe if that should go off! For a time, it looked as if, with respect to England, they were operating very deftly, even intelligently. In the meantime, not surprising for those in the know, the Indian-story roots of their "foreign policy" made an ever-more obvious appearance. They had luck long enough, brazen luck. Recently, the typically German adolescent behaviours, a really incomprehensible immaturity, have brought reversals of the worst sort (the much vaunted Poland policy!), and after the world has finally understood that it is all bluff, even a good part of the military build-up, and that they [the Germans] can take a chance on the "cataclysm" even less than Wilhelm (which, however, cannot mean that they would not do it again!), then it is high time to call out, once again, "Germany awaken!" It will be an evil awakening.

You cannot imagine how calming it is for me, what a feeling of security I gain by being able to put before you and discuss with you what I write! Everything that you say about the first chapter, on the whole and in detail, is spot on and gives me what I miss — a firm support! Let me say the following, so to say, "just this once," and with the 27th of November coming: except for you, I do not have **any** person, who would be superior to me, of one mind, one conviction, one belief. Even the relationship with Thomas Mann, which, after all, is the next closest, cannot be compared in any way, for many reasons. In

---

[1] Carl von **Ossietzky** - (1889-1938) - German journalist, writer, and pacifist. He accomplished his most important writing for the significant leftist publication, Weltbühne (World Stage). After the Nazi takeover in 1933, Ossietzky was subjected to brutal treatment in concentration camps. It was said that he was injected with TB bacilli. He did, in fact, come down with TB. In 1936, through the work of Willly Brandt in Norway, Ossietzky was awarded the Nobel peace prize for 1935. After trying to pressure him not to accept the prize, the Nazis prevented him from accepting it in person. Hitler soon passed a law to prevent any German from accepting a foreign prize in future.

particular, in the case of this book, he can give me little. That may sound strange but it is so. I saw that after the first chapter. He is very positively disposed but the content was so new to him, he limited himself to commenting on the formal and technical aspects. It is very curious: his Wagner essay is without a doubt the pinnacle of the "ideological" Wagner literature. With more emotional proximity [to the essay], however, one notices that it has grown purely out of the artistic affinity, out of the intuitive comprehension of the personality [of Wagner] and its origins, not out of the knowledge and penetration of the objective facts nor of "history." In conversation, it continually recurs that you are astonished at how completely skewed the look and the judgement is, and that unessential statements are raised to [the level of] decisive significance. And as you very rightly remark: he has never noticed even a hint of the Liszt world, just as he is utterly unmusical (God forgive me the sin!), in that deeper sense in which the "Wagnerian" is unmusical and has been felt as such by "genuine" musicians of all eras. His judgement about new music, for example, is downright alarming, his enthusiasms often no less (not consistently natural: he came home from Salzburg Fidelio-drenched and spoke only about that months later, that this was the work of the German liberation from Hitlerism). It is shameful of me and ungrateful, because I have never been so pampered and so lovingly treated as by him (the addressee is permanently excepted), but I must speak out to you (and **only** to you) about this relationship. After a long tale of woe, the essays under the rubric (which he did not want) "Achtung Europa" have appeared [in print]. They are written as if from out of our own hearts, the same with you certainly and we did not rest and constantly nagged until he finally published them, in German language and on a large scale (in Spring, 1935 they started out as a contribution to a discussion of the Coopération in Nice about "the creation of modern man," [*La formation de l'homme moderne*] in which he then did **not** participate but still had his contribution read in French). But they [the essays] can also be understood as **very** reactionary! It is the "ignominious ambiguity" of everything German which, – completely undesired by him, of course! – always and again breaks out and of which you, in reading my book further will hear more than enough. It is as if a calamitous historical law wanted to prevent this most noble and greatest personage of a sinking middle class from finding his way into a new, "unidimensional" world. And the support which I so urgently need along this way - it can't be found with him.

Back to your (all too mild) "critique": Daniel's upbringing and personality, the musical atmosphere into which Cosima made her entry – all that does not appear until the second chapter. This in explanation. In Paris, the atmosphere in which the children grew up was, without any doubt, unmusical, despite all external relationships, despite playing piano and Berlioz concerts. Are you of a different opinion? (I suggest the unmusicality of the upbringing with Liszt's splendid letter about the Weber sonata - on page 26 of the carbon copy, which I ask you to please retain.) It is absolutely correct that the "romanticism," the dithyrambic ebullience emerges insufficiently. I shall try, however, to capture it. But first — I'm not good at describing it; second, right from the first line, my aim was to eliminate brutally the Wahnfried style at the same time as the style of Pourtalès[1] and Kapp,[2] and naturally went much too far doing it.

[in margin: I am very conscious of the aggressive intolerance, one-sidedness and injustice that this contains.]

Imagine, **Scherchen** absolutely wants the book for his publishing house! From time to time, he has attacks (very congenial and boyish) of affection-madness and then wants to have one around him all the time. It is very funny. Last week, we were together a lot and talked about everything under the sun. All the while, I was seldom so convinced as in his case that I cannot give or mean anything whatsoever to him – and that he will also find that out. I have a high regard for him and like him very, very much, but what divides us — forgive me the seeming presumption — is the same thing as divides you from him. (Is it perhaps the same thing that separates Thomas Mann from the "linear world"?? That would be bad for us!). I hear that, in January, you are organizing a representative performance as introduction to "Music viva" and I was happy about the relations that have been resumed. He seems to have given up his ultra-intransigent stance completely, which is a very positive development. He is now systematically retrieving his former German circle around himself, including the turncoats such as Werner Egk.[3] From my own recent experience with young German musicians, I know how good and how necessary that is; it is simply impossible to form any accurate idea of the (outward) instability of these people in the Third Reich. One of them recently answered me (he is completely "unpolitical"), when I spoke to him about my horror about how the Jews of Germany, themselves, already are affirming their intellectual ghetto and live in airless rooms like phantoms: but that is the way it is with all of us (he is a devout Christian) [*Urchrist*].

But I see a great danger in Scherchen: the fragmentation and, as a result or cause,

---

[1] Guy de **Pourtalès** - (1881-1941) - Swiss writer born in Germany. He wrote many books including lyrical biographies of Liszt, Chopin, Ludwig II of Bavaria, Nietzsche, Wagner, and Berlioz. In 1920, his translation of Shakespeare"s Measure for Measure into French was performed at Geneva and Lausanne with music by Honegger.

[2] Julius **Kapp** - (1883-1962) - German author, much interested in all things Wagnerian. In addition he wrote books on Berlioz, Liszt, von Weber, and Meyerbeer. One of his Wagner books, Richard Wagner und die Frauen. Eine erotische Biographie (Wagner and Women. An Erotic Biography), although widely read, gave him a well-deserved reputation for superficiality.

[3] Werner **Egk** - (1901-1983) - German neoclassical composer. He composed many Nazi-coloured celebratory pieces during the Third Reich.

damned dilettantism. Beaming like a schoolboy, he tells me that, in the next issues of "Musica viva" several articles would be coming that prove "within a whisker" that, actually, the whole of history (not perhaps music history!) must be written all over again. Why is it that precisely the best musicians again and again get snagged in the thickets of areas about which they cannot have the slightest comprehension? What, for instance, did Bülow, whose musical writings were always solid, put out in the way of ghastly nonsense about God-only-knows what non-musical matters! And Wagner?? And Liszt?? (The latter – to his credit, it must be said – relatively the least!). I do not want to say that Scherchen is a "jack-of-all-trades," which would go too far. It would also go astray. But he is overreaching. Not even he can unite ten professions, although, time and again, it is still astounding what he can bring about.

This book is too much of a serious matter to allow of experiments. I therefore cannot give it to him. Are you of the same opinion? Admittedly, I do fear annoying him and want to do it in the friendliest way — but a new man in a new publishing house with a book containing blasting powder (finely dispersed) — it is impossible. And then there is his unreliability, which he really cannot be blamed for because he overburdens himself so badly. About his little Chinese tea-plaything, whom you probably know, another time.[1]

Through him, I made the acquaintance (at a students' concert in Winterthur with new music only) of Karl Amadeus **Hartmann**,[2] the young Munich [3 lines of text on this carbon copy illegible because of being typed twice on the same lines]

At that, he answered me so neatly, that you should also hear it:

I went to the Munich Academy and studied there with Prof. Haas.

It is horrifying how little can be learned there. To be honest, I have to admit that I learned <u>nothing</u> with Haas. I could take to nothing in his fraudulent musical style and, on a human level, he means nothing to me. The three years passed and shortly before the state exam, Haas informed me that I was unmusical and, with that, I was driven out of the Academy.

The years 1928-33 followed, in which I had to support myself. I worked a great deal. Then I came under the spell of Hermann Scherchen. I learned from him everything that

---

[1] **Teepuppe** - Hermann Scherchen's wife was Chinese composer, Hsia Shu-sien (1905-1991).

[2] Karl Amadeus **Hartmann** - (1905-1963) - German composer, most significantly of symphonies. Having idealistic, leftist convictions, he refused to allow performance of his works in Nazi Germany, even though he lived there. He was a protégé of Hermann Scherchen.

an artist can learn. It is to him, alone, that I owe my professional advancement as an artist up to now. And it was he alone who recognized my talent. I am firmly of the opinion that no composer is too great to be incapable of learning something more from Scherchen.

What a document! In how many directions!

But now an end to this overflowing letter and only a couple of questions:

Is there a chance of reading the Liszt lecture that you will be giving (in December) or are you presenting it, in good old custom, extemporaneously, with only keywords?

Of what sort are the criticisms that should be made of **Fellerer**? I should like to see things very clearly there and have no inhibitions at all in getting tough and taking him on. (His address, with "titles," is: Prof. Dr.Karl G. Fellerer, Dean of the Faculty of Arts of the University, 15 Avenue de Pérolles, Fribourg, Switzerland).

How is **Becking** behaving himself?

Have you heard about the trouble **Seelig**[1] has gotten into in Paris and he was sentenced to be jailed?

Golo Mann will have contacted you in the meantime. Here, just the same, is his address (which I only obtained a few days ago): Pension Ada, 17, Plzenska, Prague XIX (thus not far?).

We knew nothing about Mersmann and heard only after he had spoken here (and in Basel) that he is giving an excellent account of himself and was also removed from the Techn.University. Iniquitously, we did not attend his lecture.

You know my sentiments, feelings, wishes. In all simplicity, I may say: I congratulate myself and wish for a reunion in [my] new year of life. And a thousand greetings to all the Kestenbergish people and "newcomers," to express it in the style of my homeland.

Always your old

42. FWB to KBG — 1936.11.25

[1] Eric **Seelig** - (1909-1984) - Boxer. In 1933, the Nazis stripped the Jewish middleweight/light-heavyweight boxing champion of his titles and warned him never to try to fight again in Germany. He left Germany for France where he competed for two years. After that he moved to the USA, where he was able to fight, reaching the number six ranking for his weight class in 1938.

43. 1936.12.16 — FWB (Zurich) to Kbg –

[typed]

Zurich 7: 16 December 1936,
134 Klosbachstrasse.

Dear Comrade Kestenberg,

I am misusing the birthday of Mrs. Grete in order to ambush her with a wish: does Baron Christian Ehrenfels[1] ring a bell with you? If he is still alive, he is Pofessor (of history of literature, I believe) at the German University in Prague.

Why do I ask this? Ehrenfels belonged to House Wahnfried's circle of friends (old Wagnerians). I, myself, cannot remember having known him. But my mother, mostly when as a girl, was good friends with him and later always told me about "Christel E."

I therefore intend to ask him about correspondence material and various other things. Naturally, I can only do this if I know in advance that he is no Hitlerite or otherwise an aggressively anti-Semitic Teuton. As far as I know, he is not a ritualistic Wagnerian Bayreuther. I also remember an essay of his in "Anbruch" (ca. 1931), which put forward anything but Bayreuth ideology.

Would it be possible for you - without your having difficulties doing it - to get a clarification for me along the suggested lines?

At my request, Fellerer sent me Preussner's "little book" and added: "Nothing special. Conglomeration of really nice facts, but the inner connection? The significance of the concert for general music education completely missing etc." I can only confirm this; in fact, if I were to adjudicate, quite a few nuances harsher. The author stops exactly at the point where it begins to become significant. Often, he is only two steps away from the decisive problem, only then to turn around and start somewhere else! Not a trace of Leipzig, Gewandhaus, Mendelssohn! And this calls itself "Middle-class Music-culture." I do not comprehend how a person can come up with the idea to publish a quantity of lovely, preliminary and individual studies under such an ambitious title! I would not have the courage to do so. I do not find that Preussner has undergone any development. Many an earlier essay by him was more mature, better, and also stylistically more acceptable. But in the Reich, writing German is being unlearned at express speed. It is indescribable what

---

[1] Christian Freiherr von **Ehrenfels** (1859-1932) - Austrian philosopher, one of the pathfinders of Gestalt theory. He was Professor of Philosophy at the German University, Prague, 1896-1929. His wife Emma was a friend of "Wahnfried", including Beidler's mother, Isolde.

they are getting to read there now. Admittedly, in comparison with the Nazi style, Preussner's is minted gold.

Do you know the newly published book by Robert **Bory**[1] (otherwise a lazy head, sloppy and kitschy): "The Life of Franz Liszt in Pictures." You see, there are moments when I get angry at not having money. Otherwise, that would really be a beautiful Christmas gift for you. It is earmarked for this purpose at any rate. Do you know that there are no less than two photographs in it that bear a positively fascinating likeness to you! (Except that Liszt appears much older than you have done up to now and will still not do for a long time.) If you have the opportunity to borrow the book from a library, turn to the following pages: 182 and 186.

Curse at me with confidence as an idiotic "idealist," I still say: it is the spirit that builds the body. (Nowadays, risibly, that is a revolutionary concept!)

Allow me, in contrast, to ask you for a Christmas gift: a proper photograph which can be set up or hung on the wall! I do have one of you, a larger one with a very complimentary dedication, but – you are much too young on it and therefore I have not hung it. (It is the one with a cigarette in your right hand, seated, head turned to the right for a frontal view.) Outside of that, out of all of Kestenberg, I have only one, very comfortable postcard with the glass from Marienbad (there is too much background on it, public not wished) and a photograph of the **Kokoschka** portrait. I like that much better today than back then (development? my dear wife, on the contrary, finds it just as abominable), but to hang it — no, that is not possible.

Can you imagine how I am burning to find out what you have 1212to say about "my" Altenburg! I hope to have this (damned!) chapter finished by Christmas and will send it to you, ostensibly for New Year's. It will be incomparably better than the first chapter.

I have moved closer to you as well, through Hanslick's[2] Memoires, which, as is generally known, begin in Prague. I have to read it again, specifically now. Therefore, I close with Ambros' "Nationalities-Equalization-Gruntsound":

---

[1] Robert **Bory** - (1891-1960) - Swiss lawyer interested in music. He published a pictorial biography of Franz Liszt in 1936 and other such books about Wagner, Mozart, Chopin and Beethoven. Part of his collection was acquired in 1956 by the Netherlands Music Institute in the Hague.

[2] Eduard **Hanslick** - (1825-1904) - Austrian music critic, one of the most renowned of his time. The figure of Beckmesser in Wagner's Die Meistersinger was meant to satirize Hanslick's narowness of mind.

Emme-lem-elem !

[hand-written: Attachment in writing re: Theodor Lessing's[1] *Reminiscences*]

43. FWB to KBG — 1936.12.16

[1] Theodor **Lessing** - (1872-1933) - Jewish-German writer of socialist convictions. Born in Marienbad, the in Austria-Hungary - Czech). Writing, from 1923 on, in the *Prager Tagblatt* and the *Dortmunder Generalanzeiger,* he became one of the best known political writers of the time. He gained prominence by opposing the presidency of Hindenburg ("Hidden behind a zero, there always waits a Nero.") His book, Der jüdische Selbsthass (1930) [Jewish Self-Hatred] aroused much controversy, especially among European Jewry. In 1933, after he fled Germany to Marienbad in Czechoslovakia, Nazi assassins shot him to death in his home.

44. 1936.12.22 — Kbg (Prague) to Beidlers (Zurich)

[typed]

[letterhead of SHV]

22 December 1936.

Dr. W. Beidler [sic]
Klosbachstrasse 34 [sic]
Zurich 7.

Dear Friends,

It is an event of rare character, to be able to answer two letters from you at the same time. Actually, I should savour this elation slowly, but since I have undertaken to liquidate all debts of correspondence in the old year, and since I do hope, with certainty, that the allegro tempo of our correspondence will be maintained now, I shall respond immediately to both of your letters.

Please excuse the harsh word, but I slurped down your comment about Thomas Mann with unbelievable gratification. I was extremely agitated when I received the article "**Achtung Europe**," brought me by Mrs. Busoni returning from Vienna because I could not make sense of the monumental superiority of the 3rd Joseph volume[1] against the truly reactionary position expressed here [in *Achtung Europa*]. The extraordinarily clear and three-dimensional portrayal of your relationship with Thomas Mann and the characterization of his essay dispersed my doubts and brought both my admiration and my lack of understanding for Thomas Mann once again into a proper balance. By the way, I was also helped in this by Golo Mann, a magnificent, unusually valuable person, a real human being, who also thinks highly of you.

I give unqualified support to your decision to refuse Scherchen's offer. I am very skeptical of all these plans for publishing companies and I urgently recommend you, to make contact only with a solid publisher which is as renowned as possible. I am already bent on [receiving] your Altenburg chapter.

Old Professor Ehrenfels, about whom there are still many myths and sagas making the rounds here, died around three or four years ago. His son, Ralph Omar (address: Lichtenau Castle, near Krems on the Danube). I made his acquaintance through Kokoschka. He is a pleasant, cultivated, somewhat degenerate man who, because of his Muslim convictions, seems a tad unconventional. It seems that he also has good connections to India and Islam there. (Incidentally, a few days ago we received a letter from Lahore, to where we had written on his instigation. Much to my surprise, on the letterhead was a

---

[1] Thomas Mann, ***Joseph in Egypt***, volume three (1936) of Joseph and His Brothers.

picture of the mosque which we know so well in the Berlinerstrasse in Wilmersdorf. In the letter, we are recommended to contact Rabindranath Tagore.)[1]

The widow of Professor Ehrenfels still lives in Prague. She is supposed to be an especially fine and interesting personality. Perhaps you could gain access to the material you wish through the son's intercession.

I have a less harsh opinion of Preussner's book than you and Fellerer. But, in that, we do come back to an old difference, which I do not wish to continue now.

I shall try to obtain Robert Bory's book. Some time ago, I received a huge tome, *Liszt*, by Sacheverel Sitwell,[2] which you will also know. From what I have seen so far, it is a curious potpourri of completely subjective impressions. The Busoni chapter still awaits me.

I am simply unable to read Theodor Lessing. Access to this literature is closed. We non-aryans seem more sensitive than **you** in being against specifically Jewish [literature]. In a completely different and much more explicit sense, such a being as Anton Kuh[3] is also abominable to me.

I shall select a picture in the next few days. Would you not rather wait until a very proper bust of me is ready, which the very gifted Dr. Vogl is fashioning right at present?

My inability to do dictation is making itself evident again in this letter, in exponential form. Perhaps I shall soon get to telling you, in handwritten form, what I still want to tell you, as befits a proper letter. My secretary has just now told me that my attitude is ridiculous and old-fashioned, but the leopard cannot simply change its spots. Incidentally, Prague is much more pleasant with respect to secretarial affairs than Rosendorf in Berlin.

Best regards to both of you from all of us.
Your old
LeoKestenberg

44. KBG to FWB — 1936.12.22

---

[1] Rabindranath **Tagore** - (1861-1941) - Bengali writer, the first non-European to win the Nobel Prize in Literature (1913). He introduced Indian culture to the West.

[2] Sir Sacheverell **Sitwell** - (1897-1988) - English writer, art critic. He wrote Liszt, 1934, 417 pages.

[3] Anton **Kuh** - (1890-1941) - Jewish Austrian journalist, satirist, and orator. In the 1920s he warned against the rising rightwing wave and its consequences for the future. He had to leave his home in Berlin in 1933. Five years later he had to flee Austria for the same reason, this time to the USA.

45. 1937.02.10 — FWB (Zurich) to Kbg - [typed]

BEIDLER
Zurich 7: 10 February 1937,
134 Klosbachstrasse.

Dear Comrade Kestenberg,

with the same post, I am sending you the "Altenburg" as registered printed matter — "finally," say we. For the whole thing is fundamentally nothing other than a highly private discussion with you, word for word and line for line!

Lately, with reference to Preussner, I spoke of the "Kestenberg incubation period." Very well: this whole section could **not** have been written without you, without the years of profound contacts, including in human relationship! Now you should decide whether, to some extent, it reaches "the pitch of the Kestenberg times."

Towards the conclusion, you will even re-encounter verbatim formulations which you coined. Nothing better can be found. For that reason, I simply worked them in and, in this way, adorned myself, outwardly as well, with Leoish plumes. Since there is a forward, I am doing without source references through notes, because it would be absurd to refer to a "source" for a detail, **with** which **and against** which everything took form (I believe: more **with** …). At any rate, (attention, here comes something nasty!), my — let us say, hmm: — "scientific conscience" would rather not again draw to it the reproach of having "shamefully concealed" something …. (Base fellow, this Beidler!)

For me, it is as if I were never closer to you during the whole dozen past years than now. We are afire to know if you feel this. But, in various respects, I expect you to have a tough go at me.

You are – curse it – not the first to receive this piece. We are living in an age of capitalism, and since I need credit, I've had to come to terms with giving readings to small groups. The original is with Thomas Mann who is supposed to open a road to a publisher. Outside of the copy, which you are receiving, I have no copy. Since the original must soon go to a publisher (probably Bermann-Fischer, brrr! - but at any rate not Scherchen, who is pestering me all the time and now is deeply aggrieved …), I'd be very grateful if you could send back the copy in the not too distant future (perhaps with a crushing verdict?). But since we are awaiting your echo with utmost impatience — next to this, precisely with this piece, nothing else counts for anything — we ask you urgently, at least to set down your first impression as soon as possible on a slip of paper and send "same" back to us.

From the whole of our grateful hearts and with much tenderness

more than ever your

46. 1937.02.18 — Kbg (Prague) to Beidlers (Zurich)

[typed]

Prof. Leo Kestenberg
Prague XIX, Velvarská 59.
Prague, 18 February 1937.

Dr. Beidler-Wagner
134 Klosbachstrasse 7.
Zurich 7.

Dear Beidlers,

It does not come easy for me to speak about your second chapter, perhaps because, "in itself" it left a strong, enduring impression on me. Your characterization of Liszt seems to me to be veritably unsurpassable, as is Bülow's, three-dimensional and faultless. But, nonetheless, what I miss is connection to the beginning. The rationale for the detailed depiction of these personages and events, Cosima, is only mentioned once, and, sadly, the description of her road from Paris to the Altenburg is missing. I know that it is almost presumptuous to express such criticism with reference to such thorough and fastidious work, but you have loaded me down with so much responsibility, that I feel myself obligated to this degree of candidness. Everything that you write actually should be drawn with a few strokes as background, before which the figure of Cosima comes forward. The reader also expects this, especially since the chapter has as title: "Hans von Bülow's comrade," without anything being said about the comrade, something I looked for in vain in the second half of the chapter. No matter the importance of the milieu, of the period, and the personal conditions, the reader will not comprehend why the personality, to whom the book is dedicated, is completely cut off. Perhaps you can explain this to me with a few words so that this objection is rebutted.

I should like to note a couple more details, which, however, are hardly worth the effort: on page 69 you speak of the revolutionizing of the "musical province." I would deem it right if you were then to stay within this province and bring the "industrialization" in connection with the music publishing business, with music criticism, and the genesis of the "masses" in respect of the concert-going public. Another deficiency, for me, is too little emphasis of the unusual musicality of Bülow, which, in spite of all its undoubted objectivity, must have had something captivating about it.

But these remarks should not in any way weaken the impression that I had, in all essentials, and which I have already tried to outline. I shall send the manuscript back to you in the next few days so that you can put it to use in the way you desire. Now I am even more curious about the next chapter, especially since Daniel is supposed to turn up in it.

It is somewhat discomforting to have to preach this sermon to you. At present, I am even more hounded than usual and could only read your work piece by piece. Perhaps the lack of unity rests more with the reader than with the author. I would be genuinely grateful to you if you would let me know that you are not angry at me because of this. — I've never had in hand the book you mentioned, "My Musical Life," by Walter Damrosch.[1] It would please me very much if I could have the book for a few days, since we just now want to contact Damrosch.

Things are once again better with us after mother and Grete recovered from severe bouts of head colds. Today we received the shattering news of the death of Roesi, whom you doubtless still remember. She died 8 days after the death of her second child. Right up to the end, she seems to have approximated the image that we make for ourselves of a German madonna in all its attributes.

With the greatest of affection your old

LeoKbg

46. KBG to FWB — 1937.02.18

[1] Walter Johannes **Damrosch** - (1862-1950) - German-born, American conductor and composer. Damrosch popularized Richard Wagner in America, trailblazing the performance of music on radio.

47. 1937.02.22 — FWB (Zurich) to Kbg

[typed]

BEIDLER
Zurich 7: 22 February 1937,
134 Klosbachstrasse.

Dear Comrade Kestenberg,

that is a horrible piece of news! The poor child. We still remember Roesi wholly as a childlike, babyish being. Beyond that, we see in this end a tragedy of the will to be "down-to-earth" at all costs. Dreadful.

What you have of the second chapter is nothing other than the "Prologue in Heaven," namely 18 pages out of a total of 50. Therefore not yet half. The other, larger half naturally contains everything which you found lacking, and much more. It goes up to the year 1864. The segment that you have reaches only up to 1855; that is, the year of Cosima's uprooting to Germany, which is treated immediately thereafter.

Out of 50 pages it is quite alright to spend 20 portraying the environment which Cosima gets uprooted into, all the more so, since father and first husband must get their due at the same time. I was not prepared for the criticism, from **you**, that I had treated Liszt too **expansively**. Bayreuth always treated him as a minor character, which he was on no account. In the further continuation of the second chapter, as well, he still appears very often. The relationship of his daughter to him, in particular, which is extraordinarily crucial, will be put up for still more extensive discussion.

In order to explain your letter to myself, I see (this time not just two, but:) three possibilities:

1) it was written in a phase of work-related over-exhaustion or "general listlessness,"

2) for whatever reason, you are annoyed with us (more correctly: with me),

3) you are alienated by my portrayal of things, find them loveless, coldly analytical, "corrosive", an icy breath blows at you from a world that you find uncongenial. In short, expressed boyishly, "the whole tendency" ["*die janze Richtung*"] doesn't suit you.

With this last possibility, I have assumed the worst of all cases. From your letter, however, it is not apparent if it applies, which, to tell the truth, would distress me enormously. At any rate, I have the impression of a general, deep-seated unease on your part, which, perhaps does not allow of being put into words so fast, and about the content of which you, yourself, are perhaps not yet clear.

If I may ask one thing, assuming that possibility no. 3 prevails, — that you take the trouble to make your discontent concrete and tell me openly what you find horrible, etc. (The problem is not with the level or with the style, because you would have told me so without further ado.) Please, without mercy! I am only "angry" — (were such a word and the idea that belongs with it capable of finding any sort of place in our relations) — if, as with your letter which arrived today, you were to entrench yourself behind a facade which looks almost like a fading interest because it is supposed to serve to prevent secret thoughts to be spoken. Is that nasty or unjust of me?

One of the fundamental facts for understanding all later events [in the book] is what I have couched in the conceptual antithesis between Weimar [Liszt] and Leipzig [Wagner] and which I clearly label as a **social** antithesis. This is bold (and not yet ever ventured in any portrayal). If that can be shaken, a keystone of my whole analysis of later, societally determined events is detonated away. That is why it is of really crucial importance for me to learn your view about this (also as a professional musician).

Bülow's really almost unequalled musicality likewise comes later into the correct light (here he is no older than 25 years).What is it that you have for **Daniel** [Liszt]? He was absolutely no Hyperion, but rather a sorry, intellectually overstuffed and, most probably, inwardly empty young person who, later, was apotheosized by the surviving sister into a godly youth. There are enough documents in support of this which, however, in my portrayal, will be more touched upon than explicitly expressed.

May I also say that I was especially surprised that the first chapter, which I no longer like at all, seemed so good to you, while I find the part of the second chapter that you have to be incomparably better in every respect?

In a few days, I shall send you Damrosch's book of Memoirs; at the moment I have a borrowed copy. In my last letter to Damrosch, by the way, I spoke a lot about you.

Klaus Pringsheim[1] recently wrote me, quite amiably. Are you in contact with him? In any case, I gave him your diverse addresses and note his new one: 14 Kaga-Cho, l-chome, Ushigome-Ku, Tokyo.

47. FWB to KBG — 1937.02.22

---

[1] Klaus **Pringsheim**, Sr. - (1883-1972) - German-born composer, conductor, teacher. His twin sister, Katia married Thomas Mann in 1905. He exerted great influence on Japanese approaches to western, classical music.

48. 1937.03.02 — Kbg (Prague) to Beidlers (Zurich)

[typed]

Prof. Leo Kestenberg
Prague XIX, Velvarská 59.
Prague, 2 March 1937.

Dr. Beidler-Wagner
Klosbachstrasse 134
Zurich.

Dear Friends,

I must answer your letter of February 22 as briefly and quickly as possible to the effect that all three of the possibilities that you mention do not apply, the third one least of all, since I really did like your Liszt-characterization very well and I consider it completely new, original and, in an elevated sense, exhaustive. After your explanations about the architecture of the second chapter, I can also completely retract my objections. The only thing I would ask is that you send me, as soon as possible, the still missing part of the second chapter.

Please do not be angry with me that I am so short, but it means a lot to me, infinitely so, to clear up these misunderstandings. Next time, I shall write in detail.

Best regards from all of us to both of you

Your:

LeoKestenberg

48. KBG to FWB — 1937.03.02

49. 1937.04.28 — Kbg (Prague) to Beidlers (Zurich)
[typed]

[SHV letterhead]

Prof. Leo Kestenberg

Prague XIX, Velvarská 59.
28 April 1937.

Dr. F.W.Beidler-Wagner
Klosbachstrasse 134.
Zurich.

Dear Friend,

Despite my being unable to get rid of the mortifying feeling that you are still angry at me, because of urgency, I should like to direct two questions to you, which you can perhaps answer by return mail.

We are intending to put on an international working conference in Switzerland next year and have already been in contact with our most important opposite numbers and colleagues there. In the circle of our directors it was suggested to hold this working conference in Bern, where the federal government has its headquarters. Our Swiss friends have more or less openly stated misgivings about the choice of this place without there being a clearly visible reason for this position.

You surely now have so much local Swiss knowledge that, in this case, you can presumably give me advice: Zurich or Basel is repeatedly recommended to us from people in Switzerland. Those of our offices that work together with the ministry of external affairs want to stick with Bern, or, if this is not acceptable, suggest Geneva. But the lack of interest in our problems by French Switzerland speaks against Geneva, as does the fact that this year from 28th to 30th June, we are holding a working conference in Paris, so that putting on a another conference in a French area seems unjustifiable. In addition, we want to convince the German-speaking Swiss especially, who were oppositional at our congress in Prague, that their assumption that Prague violates democratic customs in affairs of congress is groundless.

And now the second question: the Thomas-Mann fund has the intention — assuming that 300 committed subscribers can be won — to choose 4 book manuscripts and to publish these in association with well-known publishers. The prospect that 300 subscribers can be found is favourable. Would your Cosima Wagner book come in question for this promotion? If yes, I would immediately inform you of all the details. Your agreement to this plan would doubtless find an enthusiastic reaction here.

Personally, I cannot report much pleasant news. Grete and Rahel are still ill and I am also not exactly in brilliant form.

As evidence that you are no longer angry at me, send me very soon the continuation of the second chapter, which I have been waiting for so long.

With the very best of regards to you both,

Your old:

LeoKestenberg

49. KBG to FWB — 1937.04.28

50. 1937.05.02 —FWB (Zurich) to Kbg

[typed]

BEIDLER

Zurich 7: 2 May 1937,
134 Klosbachstrasse.

Dear Comrade Kestenberg,

I angry with you?? First, there is no reason for that. Second — even if there were one, I would never be "angry" at you, but rather say with complete candidness, what is on my mind. Third, you are still the person to whom, far and away, I feel attached the closest, most related, most deeply — in short: wholly, completely and without reserve, and, in all certainty, will ever be. Would you like to give me the joy of finally acknowledging this? And do the same as I in this, strike for all eternity from the scale of our "relational values" the possibility of "being angry"?

You know, I am a friend of precision. For this reason, your dear letter puts me into a certain embarrassment (which could almost be called "locally usual"); for, at least at the moment, I cannot answer your two questions unambiguously.

Zurich just counts as the "intellectual capital of the country," as our "Minister of Education," Federal Councillor Dr. **Etter**[1], himself, once told me. If you were to ask him, he would refer you to Carl **Vogler**,[2] whom you know (I do not know him, cannot stand his type of person). He is the liaison officer for music of the federal government … And, naturally, out of convenience and local ambition, he would say to you: only Zurich can come into consideration. This, most likely, could also be seen as the point of view of the federal government. I make the point because, behind the wish of your official authorities to choose the federal capital, I presume that they do not want to create a precedent in any country, enabling conferences to be held in "provincial cities."

---

[1] Philipp **Etter** - (1891-1977) - Swiss politician, member of the Catholic Conservative Party. After 1933, he was disparaged for his failure to criticize the crimes of the Nazi regime in Germany. He was Federal President in 1939, 1942, 1947, and 1953. He repeatedly spoke out, publicly, for more authoritarian leadership and interference by parliament and the parties.

[2] Carl **Vogler** - (1874-1951) - Swiss musician, teacher, composer. He founded and participated in several organizations for musicians and teachers. As director of the Zurich Conservatory, he followed traditionalist points of view.

In Geneva, there is, at least, Henri **Gagnebin**[1], director of the conservatory, with whom I am on very good terms. He certainly would go all the way for the working conference. But whether the atmosphere is favourable, is something that I also doubt, without being able to evaluate it completely (incidentally, the Geneva government has been taking an extraordinarily reactionary course for the last while — liquidation of the "red era" Nicolle[2] by means of deceitful and brutal methods — that is perhaps also something to keep in mind).

I can not cast any sort of judgement about Bern. I do not know even one of the local musical giants. **Kurth** is at the university but is probably not well suited to this sort of conference. I do not know his assistant, **Zulauf**. At any rate, I shall draw on some more investigations. Please consider "today's drift" as preliminary.

Purely from sentiment, I actually would be for **Basel**. Main reason: The local musical omnipotent is Hans **Münch**.[3] By God, no progressive extremist, but fresh, young, venturesome, happy to experiment, not senile, original musician by nature, smart, self-confident (that amounts to: he is from Alsace, i.e. not Swiss by birth!). I am on excellent terms with him (we are related through his wife) and I personally should also be able to spur his interest in the conference. A second, not unimportant reason: socialist minister of education, likewise venturesome and eclectic (name: Government Councillor Karl **Hauser**). Despite all my aversion to Social Democrats, of which you are well aware, this fact is relatively worthy of consideration. The citizenry of Basel is not very enchanting, but where is it different?

For today, this is actually all that I can say about it — damned little it is. I should like to add that, a few days ago (on April 25) the general assembly of the "Swiss Music-Pedagogical Society" took place (ignoring Othmar Schoeck's being made an honorary member … You must know that he just fulfilled the dream of the Swiss also to have an

---

[1] Henri **Gagnebin** - (1886-1977) - Belgian-born Swiss composer. He was director of the Conservatory of Geneva 1925-1957. He had close friendships with Mstislav Rostropovich, Arthur Rubinstein, Ernest Ansermet, Andrés Segovia, and Frank Martin.

[2] "Red era" **Nicolle** - The name of the fiery leader of the socialists in Geneva of the early 1930s was Léon Nicole. The conservatives blamed him for the Swiss army firing on a demonstration by workers on November 9, 1932 in which thirteen demonstrators lost their lives. The demonstration was partially against a growing fascist movement in Geneva. As a result of the unwarranted killings, Nicole won the next election; he formed the first leftist majority government in Switzerland.

[3] Hans **Münch** - (1893-1983) - Alsatian-born Swiss musician, conductor, teacher, and composer. Active in Basel, he was director of the Basel Music School and Conservatory 1935-1947.

opera of their own…), at which Miss Linda **Bach** from Winterthur gave a paper "on the present state of private music education." The press clipping which I have before me, continues: "The convocation of a conference to clarify questions of musical education was deemed necessary." Incidentally, the association has got 1200 members. I intend to take an interest in the paper and the discussion as well, and perhaps more later.

Now a couple of questions in return: with whom are you mainly in "business contact" here? With **Schuh**, above all, I presume, then probably with **Vogler**. Then: what purpose is the working conference supposed to have? After I have a clearer idea about this, I shall be delighted to wrack my brain about what more can be done. In general: dispose of me as if I were your **secret** envoy. Since I have "libre accès" [free access] more or less everywhere, perhaps I can be of use with this or that and help with preparations — even if today's meagre result does not look that way.

Now to your question regarding my "Cosima." For that, as is my duty, I bring the following to your notice:

I am not a "German emigrant" (although "expatriated" in 1935, the German citizenship being just an appendage), but rather a member of the "Swiss Writers' Association," which gave my book an advance of 1,000 Francs, even though I had only been a member for a few weeks;

I am just now beginning negotiations with Bermann-Fischer (Vienna) about settling on a publisher for the book and am unable to go over his head for the simple reason that Thomas Mann and his wife have already had preliminary negotiations with Dr. Bermann. Out of that there have emerged questions and consequences which I do not want to broach today, because point 1) probably suffices on its own to prohibit the book from coming into consideration for the "Thomas-Mann-Fund."

If, however, something were to come of it, it would please me greatly and, on any account, I thank you very much for thinking of me in this connection.

As far as the book itself is concerned, I, myself, am gradually coming to believe that it will be good. I held several readings from it, privately, for "invited circles," and the success was very encouraging — especially, as well, with younger people who have not even the slightest connection to the world of Wagner and Liszt. The leftists do have, indeed, an immediate, instinctive feeling that this somehow belongs to them, but the rightists are so dazzled by the "objective-scientific" form that they go along with it — at least for the time being, since it gradually gets more dense. On Mai 31 I'll read it to the – "posh" – Lyceum Club.

Tomorrow, I'm sending you, as a down-payment and proof of my bad conscience, the part adjoining "Weimar." I ask you urgently, however, to observe that this is not yet the end of the infamous second chapter. That has become a grotesque finale — you will receive it soon! We recently read Busoni's letters to his wife. Of course, the first look was at the index: the name Kestenberg not noted at all! Great disappointment, which, moreover, leaves room for the most diverse possible interpretations. But also otherwise: what value do these sorts of collections of correspondence have if everything that is really essential, all profound judgements, everything really central, is eliminated and scrupulously expunged? Somewhat embarrassed, you ask yourself, why, out of all of these sad fragments, only precisely those parts were allowed to remain in which recognitions or often even highly private tendernesses to the lady recipient are included? ... I could not say that the personage Busoni, which I know only through you and, I almost would have to say: because of you (although it is a shame, as my inadequate total knowledge of his works belongs to my worst blemishes), has come any closer through this cadaver-carved correspondence. And then the preface! Before this, I had a favourable opinion of Schuh; but he wrote this with clogs on! Not a breath of atmosphere! And downright off-putting this miserable, filthy, suffocating local patriotism which does not even notice (or wants to notice) how much Busoni made fun of the Swiss! But I find utterly scurrilous the portrayal of Busoni in his last years as if he had been allowed to wither away, unappreciated, unfathomed and unhonoured!! That is truly a shameless falsification of history, and I only ask myself, who would have an interest, or who informed Mr. Schuh to that effect or expected him to portray things this way. (As for the passage about my parents, it would interest me to know what, precisely, was omitted - do you believe that it could be found out from Mrs. Busoni?). When, down the road, I publish **your** letters, that will be a different book! Let it be said by your leave: in this comparison, Busoni does not come off well.

We are very worried that your health apparently is not doing as well as it should. How are Mrs. Grete and Rahel doing? And how about you? And how are Ruth-Tunja-Golo (united front?) doing? Klaus Pringsheim writes me that Milka is "most intimate" with your house. I am making a question mark.

Now you cannot complain: a letter so long that you will have neither time nor desire to read it right to the end, and promptly! The most beautiful and best is that we shall be seeing you in June, before <u>and</u> after the Paris working conference! Superb! For lodgings, if you want, i.e. if you are not greatly particular, it's all arranged here.

Yet another thing about the "Thomas-Mann-Fund," but confidential: I have the impression that the matter is organized in a dilettantish way and is represented by personell, the brilliance of which is not exactly consistent. As it happens, I wrote to Burschell[1] about this, four weeks ago, quite explicitly and gave him certain suggestions relating to the difficult territory of Switzerland.

Do you know the following "sweet little book" [*Büchelchen*]: Hans E. Wind: "The Terminal Crisis of Bourgeois Music and the Role of Arnold Schönberg" (Vienna 1935)?[2] If yes, is it worth reading?

A thousand profound regards from us both:

In old love and with very much tenderness always your

Please be so kind as to send back, before May 31, the copy that I'll send you tomorrow; I must give a reading from it.

You did receive Damrosch's book?

50. FWB to KBG — 1937.05.02

[1] Friedrich **Burschell** - (1889-1970) - a German writer, friend of Ernst Bloch. During the Weimar Republic, he lived in Munich and Berlin. When Hitler came to power, he fled to France and Spain, and, in 1934, to Prague, where he wrote for the Neue Weltbühne and the Prager Tagblatt, and founded and ran the Thomas-Mann-Fund to help emigrant writers. In 1938 he fled the Nazis to England, where he worked for the BBC. He published books about, among others, Friedrich Schiller and Jean Paul.

[2] Hans E. **Wind** - pseudonym of Kurt Blaukopf - (1914-1999) - Jewish-Austrian sociologist of music, musicologist, critic. In 1938 he fled the Nazis to Paris and lived in Jerusalem 1940-1947. After that, he returned to Vienna.

51. 1937.05.10 — Kbg (Prague) to Beidlers (Zurich)

[typed - dictated]

[SHV letterhead]

Prof. Leo Kestenberg
Prague XIX, Velvarská 59.
10 May 1937.

Dr. F.W. Beidler-Wagner
134 Klosbachstrasse,
Zurich.

Dear Dr. Beidler,

We are exceedingly grateful for your amiable offer to help us with preparations for the Swiss conference by engaging in personal conversations, if they should be needed. However, before you take any steps at all, I ask you to familiarize yourself with the decisive relationships that exist between our Society and the Swiss groups that are linked to us.

Last year, at our congress, to our joy and surprise, many more Swiss turned out than we had expected originally. At first, we were in contact only with Director of Music, Sam. Fisch, whom I had known from the international courses at the Central Institute [Berlin]. Under the auspices of the congress, Mr. Fisch also gave a lecture about the youth music movement in Switzerland, which received brisk applause. He is known as an editor and writer of good and useful articles which are published by HUG and he seems, in general, to be a very active man. He now lives in Kreuzlingen. His main professional activity is not completely clear to me. Only today he wrote to us that, concerning the Festival of Swiss Musicians and the conference of Swiss music teachers, he will make every effort to find out what the best place and time would be for the planned conference.

The senior member of the Swiss delegation at our congress was Director Vogler, whom you also mentioned. Buttoned-down and demonstratively naïve as he seemed, he gave me the impression of being a conservative, a school-potentate with a touch of papistry, one who strives to oppose anything new. His report on our congress in the Swiss music-pedagogical papers began with the implication that the founding of our Society actually should be traced back to my emigration [from Germany]. That is not exactly very generous and gave us an unpleasant surprise.

That the Swiss delegation voted against the proposal to have the 2nd international congress on music education in Prague once again, can probably be traced back to his [Vogler's] initiative. (N.B. The working conferences in Paris and in Switzerland in 1938 count as intermezzi). It is even more astonishing that he has not responded in any way to all the extremely polite letters and questions that we sent him after the congress. I would be very grateful to you if, with diplomatic formality and adroitness, you could prowl up closer to him to find out whether he really is against us or if it is more just an unintentional matter of passive resistance. He actually does seem to be THE authority for the old-established music pedagogy in Switzerland, while all the younger people more or less stand opposed to him.

I count Miss Mimi Scheiblauer[1] (Zurich, Biberlinstrasse 14), as among these younger people. She also seems not to have been completely in agreement with the results of our congress, but is exerting herself, if, in a somewhat demure way, to promote the conference in Switzerland. Apparently, she is an authority in the area of musical therapeutic pedagogy. But she continually recommends to us the all-purpose prophet Hanselmann,[2] known to me from his writings, who appears to beguile all old spinsters in the renowned Pied-Piper manner. But, as you know, I do have a weakness for such phenomena. [in margin in FWB hand: good! Prof. f. therapeutic pedagogy]

Now for further, younger music teachers who were here: to start with, the very spirited Mr. Huber[3] [FWB in margin: Walter Simon Huber] from Basel, who was the spokesperson of the Swiss during the debate, whereas Vogler, as the official delegate of the government, spoke at the opening. The radio man and director of the Bern boys' choir, Hugo Keller,[4] who, in speaking about the next congress, at least officially, avoided associating himself with the Swiss. And Mrs. Biedermann, leader of the girls' group, who participated successfully in the congress.

This information should be enough to give you an approximate picture of the Schwyzer men and women with whom we remain in contact. I do not want to leave un-

---

[1] Marie-Elisabeth (Mimi) **Scheiblauer** - (1891-1968) - Swiss. She was an early proponent of using rhythm as an educational tool in remedial teaching. She studied with Emile Jaques-Dalcroze in Geneva and Dresden. In 1926 she founded the Seminar for Musical-rhythmic Education as an independent department in the Zurich Conservatory. There, she trained rhythmic teachers. In her chosen specialty — as teacher, writer, and publisher — she was a powerhouse working for the benefit of disabled people.

[2] Heinrich **Hanselmann** - (1885-1960) - Swiss teacher. In 1931 he was named the first Professor of Remedial Teaching at the University of Zurich. A follower of Heinrich Pestalozzi, Hanselmann was the leading Swiss expert on Remedial Teaching.

[3] Walter Simon **Huber** - (1898-1978) - Swiss organist, composer, conductor, teacher.

[4] Hugo **Keller** - (1887- ?) - Choral Director, composer, teacher. He founded the Bern Boys' Choir (Berner Singbuben) in 1922.

mentioned that our attention was drawn, in confidence, to some Swiss people, who, during the trip back home from Prague, made some rather derogatory remarks about our congress.

The plan is for next year's Swiss conference to clear the atmosphere for the 2nd International Congress in Prague.

It will be of interest to you that, today, two different sources already have passed on news to us of a conference in the Ministry of Propaganda, Berlin, laying down standard procedures for the German visitors to the Paris world exposition, whereby pride of place is occupied by the [German] boycott of the Paris congress being headed up by the Czechoslovakian music pedagogue, Kbg. I am very proud of the attention that is still being dedicated to me by the 3rd Reich.

Additionally, to our great joy, we are able to inform you that Walter Damrosch cabled us yesterday to say that his participation in our Paris conference is definite. His lecture in the framework of this conference will take place on June 29. Is that not a convincing reason for you to come to Paris too?

Presumably, I shall leave for Paris already on the 18th or 19th of June and, of course, I shall skip at least one train [connection] in Zurich.

With best greetings,

Your:

Leo Kestenberg

[Notes in FWB hand:]

Fritz Hug, Wattenweylweg 21, Bern
Teachers' Association: Schoch
Fritz
Sektion Schweiz der IGF. IV Erz, Gottfried Kuhn, Zurich 7
3 Directors of Education . Zurich, Bern, Basel
3 Cities: School Federations

51. KBG to FWB — 1937.05.10

52. 1937.05.11 — Kbg (Prague) to Beidlers (Zurich)

[typed]

[SHV letterhead]

11 May 1937.

Dr. F.W. Beidler-Wagner
134 Klosbachstrasse,
Zurich.

Dear Friend,

Just after sending off the detailed letter to you, we received a letter from Dir. Vogler, a copy of which is attached. The unfriendly position is clear from the contents of the letter. Mr. Vogler was, of course, present when the 1st International Congress for Music Education , on April 9, 1936 adopted the resolution that the next congress would once again be held in Prague. With the exception of the Swiss, everyone voted for this resolution. Since around 20 governmental representatives from various countries were present, the overwhelming majority with which this resolution was adopted is completely obvious.

We shall write at once to Miss Scheiblauer, Music Director Fisch and Mr. Keller and inform them of what the Swiss Musicians' Association has said. For us, there are now three alternatives: 1. convince the Musicians' Association to change its position, 2. mount the working conference while bypassing the Musicians' Association, since it deals with subjects, which, in any case, would not require participation of the professional as a decisive factor (it is the old confrontation between music and the professional musicians), 3. hold the conference in another country in 1938.

I would be very obliged to you if you would make your statement on the whole matter public as soon as possible.

With best wishes
Your:

LeoKestenberg

52. KBG to Beidlers — 1937.05.11

52a. 1937.05.09 — C. Vogler (Zurich) to Kbg (Prague)

[typed]

Swiss Musicians' Association
Zurich 7, 9 May 1937.

Dr. Leo Kestenberg

Spolecnost por Hudební vychovu
C.S.R. Prague
Toskánsky palác.

Dear Dr.,

The directors of the Swiss Musicians' Association has considered your letter of April 13 and mandated me to communicate to you that we do not consider the subject "Relations between Musical Education and public instruction" alone to be sufficiently interesting to be fruitful for an international congress. Nor would joining this with a treatment of questions concerning therapeutic pedagogy be anywhere near enough to attract interested people from far away. Now that a congress has been held, in the interest of the matter, we view it as dangerous to insert a half-measure. Whether you call this a "congress" or only a "working group" changes nought in the fact that an uninteresting and inadequately attended event would put the reputation of the whole cause in jeopardy.

We consequently come herewith to advise you not to hold this event in Bern.

It would be another matter if, in the year 1939, on the occasion of the Swiss National Exhibition in Zurich, a specifically international congress were to be held. From our standpoint, this question would then be amenable to serious discussion.

Sincerely,
Swiss Musicians' Association
The President

signed C. Vogler

52a. Vogler to KBG — 1937.05.09

53. 1937.05.27 — FWB (Zurich) to Kbg

[typed]

Zurich 7: 27 May 1937,
134 Klosbachstrasse.

Prof. Leo Kestenberg,
Spolecnost pro hudebni vychovu,
Toskánsky Palác,
Praha IV.

Most respected, dear Professor Kestenberg,

Information, which, in the meantime, I have gathered from various competent parties, allows me, today, to give a manner of policy statement with regard to the questions touched upon in your letters of the 10th and 11th of the month. But first, allow me to express special thanks for your messages. You are all too well aware of my interest in everything relating to all the work connected to your efforts, for me to have to emphasize it once again.

A picture is gradually beginning to come together for me of the possibilities and limits of your plan to hold a working conference in our land with the subject "Relationship between Music Education and Public Education." The friendly shades of colour in that picture easily predominate. I, personally, would therefore opt without question for the second of the three alternatives, pointed to in your letter of the 11th of the month: holding the working conference **without** the Musicians' Association.

Concerning the question of location, it seems to me that the Gordian knot can be cut very easily by holding the conference simultaneously (much more: one after the other) in several cities. Because of the limited dimensions of our country, this does not present even the slightest problem and has been done just recently (congress of art historians, e.g.) and with success. Our national railway routes will take special joy in putting light-rail cars at the disposal of the conference. The choice of locales seems to me to depend on which places sent positive responses; and, with that, I come to the circle of possible hosts (outside of the SHV, obviously).

The way I see things, SHV very officially approaches the following bodies or organizations with invitations to co-host the working conference:

1) to the departments of education (or administrations) of the cantons of Zurich, Bern, Basel and, possibly, Geneva,

2) to the school boards of the cities of Zurich, Bern, Basel and, possibly, Geneva,

3) to the "Swiss Association for Music Education,"

4) to the "Swiss Teachers' Federation"

5) to the Swiss section of the "International Society for New Education"

6) to the conservatories of the cities Zurich, Bern, Basel and, possibly, Geneva,

7) to the entities — adapting myself to the syle of these circles, I take care not to speak of "organizations!" — and facilities of the vocal, instrumental, and remaining musical youth movement,

8) to a scientific pedagogical society still to be determined.

Allow me to emphasize that this is only a preliminary "catalogue" and probably should be expanded, since, in my opinion, the group of hosts cannot be large enough, if only to impede certain personal resentments from coming into play.

re: 1) In our federal state, with the exception of certain federal measures, facilities, and institutions, the educational system and cultural policy, in the broader sense, come under the competence of the cantons. For this reason, it is an obvious given that the SHV make contact with the canton governments as the instances with preeminent jurisdiction.

As far as Zurich is concerned, a positive response seems not improbable, at minimum. Some strings would have to be pulled, the ones that exist between the Teachers' Association and the canton government. From what I hear, Bern is supposed to be lively and happy to try out new things; for the time being, however, I am unable to assess things over there. I already wrote to you in private about Basel, and that modern trends in the educational system prevail there. I consider it a sure thing that Karl **Hauser**, the responsible member of the governing council, will have a positive approach, providing perhaps, that you write him, not only an official letter but also a "semi-official" one which draws his attention to how important this is; otherwise, there is always the danger that the very busy governmental heads refer "musical things" to the Musicians' Association. I would therefore ask you to notify me a certain amount of time before sending off your official letter, in every case (not just in the case of the canton governments) because — e.g. in the case of Zurich and Basel — I, myself, can drop a hint or find ways and means to have it done. If at first only two canton governments give their assent, the third or fourth can always still be obtained.

As far as Geneva is concerned, I would consider it very desirable that the French-speaking part of our country be included, if only as a matter of principle. At any rate, it seems advisable to me, before taking any official steps with the government, to bring things to Henri Gagnebin, Director of the Conservatory, for preliminary consultations. If you wish, I would be happy to introduce the subject first, completely in confidence, since I am — I would almost say : on especially good terms with Gagnebin. In any case, he is extraordinarily approachable about our efforts.

re: 2) The support of the local school authorities really seems especially important to me. Basel and the canton government have a unified workforce, unless I am mistaken (excuse me for my lack of learning, but, at the moment I really do not know — we have 22 cantons and half-cantons and all of them are organized differently!). I am unable to assess Bern; nor Geneva, for which the same applies as what I wrote above about its government. In Zurich, the school chairman, Dr. Briner's[1] unofficial "music advisor" is the primary school teacher, Rudolf **Schoch**,[2] whom I should like to take this opportunity to commend to you with special warmth. More about him later. Under these circumstances, a positive response from Zurich is as good as certain.

re: 3) Well-informed persons have drawn my attention to the fact that, for some time now, relations between music teachers and the "musicians" could pretty much be characterized by the way the music pedagogues take part with special joy in things that the musicians reject.... At any rate, I am told that people are quite confident of and counting on a positive response from the music pedagogues. This is, of course, decisively important, since the thing would probably not be possible with a complete absence of the professional music association.

I am able to shed some light on the personal makeup of this association. The president, after the death of Georges Humbert-Droz[3] (formerly director of the Conservatory in Neuchâtel), is the former vice-president, Emil **Braun**[4] (Basel). He is described to me as one of the "silent ones in the land," who, for a time, clung tightly to Mr. Carl Vogler's coat-tails; lately, however, he has been marching with the stronger battalions. But these

---

[1] Robert **Briner** - (1885-1960) - Swiss politician, chairman of the Democratic Party for many years; member of the governing council for Canton Zurich 1935-1951.

[2] Rudolf **Schoch** - (1896-1982)

[3] Georges **Humbert-Droz** - (1870-1936) - Founder of the Neuchâtel Conservatory in 1918; director to 1936. President of the Swiss Musical-Pedagogical Association 1932-1936.

[4] Emil **Braun** - (1870- ?) - Cellist, teacher at Basel Conservatory. President of the Swiss Music Teachers' Association 1936-1938.

should be commanded in our interest now, primarily by Kurt **Joss**[1] (Bern), the board member who is supposed to have great influence and, more especially to possess the confidence of the younger, more progressive members. It seems very important to me to come into direct contact with this man and I am fiddling about with this. A very close, personal friend of Carl Vogler has a seat on the board: Mr. E.A. **Hoffmann**[2] (Aarau), who, however, in recent times has begun to reorient himself so that he likely will be limiting himself to passing on information to Mr. Vogler about proceedings of the board. Dr. **Schuh** is not showing much backbone, which is easily explained by his only beginning to occupy himself with building up a position for himself without wanting to provoke any opposition. I am at least on good enough terms with him that I could discuss everything with him if you wish. But decisive action can hardly be expected of him. I do not want to conceal from you that, at the last general assembly in Lucerne, the younger element of the association was not yet able to carry its point in a desirable way — possibly owing to the *genius loci* [protective spirit of the place] of Lucerne. In this connection, I do not want to leave unmentioned that from the parties which traditionally have been Germany-oriented, and which, like Othmar Schoeck, still enjoy being endlessly fêted in the Third Reich, oppositional movements cannot, at the very least, be excluded. Without a doubt, this sort of consideration is behind Mr. Vogler's stance, which, in this country, some people occasionally like to call: "neutrality."

re: 4 and 5) As a middle-man, I recommend Rudolf **Schoch** (126 Scheuchzerstrasse, Zurich 6), the primary school teacher whom I already mentioned, who wants to smooth out the terrain of both organizations. By the way, he has already been indirectly in touch with you, by way of Fritz **Hug**, the editor of the workers' and singers' newspaper in Bern.

re: 6) As far as the administration of the Zurich Conservatory is concerned, I allow myself to present the following comparison (admittedly with only relative units of measurement!) in order to make everything clear to you right away:

Volkmar Andreae[3] : Carl Vogler = Schreker : Schünemann

Still, I do ask you not to neglect to send the letter to the Conservatory under any circumstances. The majority of the teaching staff is disposed completely differently from

---

[1] Kurt **Joss** - (1898- ?)

[2] Emil Adolf **Hoffmann** - (1879-1963)

[3] Volkmar **Andreae** - (1879-1962) - Swiss conductor, composer, teacher, administrator. He was the leader of the Tonhalle Symphony Concerts in Zurich 1906-1949. Director of the Zurich Conservatory 1914-1939.

Mr. Vogler so that he might very well experience a surprise from his own colleagues! I shall take on Hans **Münch** in Basel completely on my own. It might be worth giving serious consideration to inviting the conservatories of **Neuchâtel** and **Lausanne**. Please tell me if I should collect information on them. At any rate, I am planning to go over everything we have again, and recheck it systematically so that nothing can be accidentally ignored.

re: 7) On the subject of these entities, you are more knowledgeable than I and Mr. Fisch is surely the best authority. He will probably also have put you in touch with Mr. **Stern** who is very active here in Zurich. I have a special reason to have asked you to write an official letter to Mr. **Schoch**, whom I have mentioned several times, in his capacity as President of the "Public Piano School, Zurich." He has on his board Mr. – Carl Vogler and he assures me, it would be a very big, exquisite delight to him to have an "eye-to-eye" conversation [about it] with Mr. Vogler inside the board! Do it for him (and me)!

re: 8) As for the scientific pedagogical society, I ask that you consent to somewhat more time for me. It seems desirable to me to make contact with Dr. **Fritz Medicus**,[1] Professor of Philosophy and Pedagogy at the Federal Technical University, who plays a pivotal role within scientific pedagogy and is especially important because, through his person, as it were, we get the federal government to participate directly in our cause (the Technical University is a facility of the federal government). I do not know Medicus personally, but it would not be difficult to meet him and explain everything to him, naturally only if this is alright with you, and about which I ask you to inform me.

I would like to put the question up for discussion as to the extent to which private music schools should also be invited to participate. I would not fail to do this in the case of the "Music Academy Zurich," the director of which, Hans **Lavater**,[2] I know well as an especially sophisticated musician in our city.

I should not like to leave unmentioned that I have been assured that many good, interesting, and serious things could be had from the relationship Scheiblauer-Hanselmann (who is a university professor). They seem to have a different point of view. As for everything having to do with therapeutic pedagogy, I declare myself, to an especially high degree, incompetent.

---

[1] Fritz Georg Adolf **Medicus** - (1876-1956) - German-Swiss philosopher, author. Professor at the Swiss Technical University Zurich 1911-1946.

[2] Hans **Lavater** (1885-1969) - Swiss composer, conductor, teacher. He was the director of the Musikakademie Zurich 1923-1959.

May I repeat that I would be very obliged if, in all cases, you would notify me not too short a time before sending off official letters? For instance, in the case of the **City** of Zurich, I can mobilize significant leverage beforehand.

As for technical things: if you should not be sure about exact addresses etc., I shall have fun supplying them to you with the exactness that you know.

Finally: if you believe that I can be useful in any way, please dispose of me however you like — it would give me wholly extraordinary joy to be able to contribute something toward the success of the working conference.

53. FWB to KBG — 1937.05.27

54. 1937.06.02 — Kestenberg (Prague) to Beidlers (Zurich)

[typed]

[SHV letterhead]

2 June 1937.

Dr. F.W. Beidler-Wagner
Klosbachstrasse 134.
Zurich.

Dear Dr. Beidler,

Thank you sincerely for your detailed letter and its wealth of exhaustive information. I assume that we shall have the opportunity to discuss all questions during my stopover in Zurich.

To my surprise, Mr. Hug in Bern, the editor of the Swiss worker-singer newspaper, has gone over completely to the views of Dir. Vogler. On the other hand, Mr. Keller, director of the Bern Boys' Choir [*Singbuben*] and music radio in Bern, has taken up our point of view, but is very careful in talking about it. At the next opportunity, we shall write to primary teacher Rudolf Schoch in the sense that you indicated. But I hope, through my visits in Zurich, in the synthetic manner that I always love, to be able to lead everything to a satisfactory conclusion.

Whether my wife will come to Zurich and Paris has again come into question during the last hours. Presumably, I shall arrive in Zurich on Sunday, the 20th of June after 8pm.

With all best wishes to you both

Ihr:

LeoKestenberg

54. KBG to FWB — 1937.06.02

55. 1937.08.06 — Kbg (Prague) to Beidlers (Zurich)
[typed]

Background:

On the 20th of June, Kestenberg had finally been reunited with the Beidlers on his way to Paris for the second International Congress of the Society for Music Education. The theme of the congress was the education of young musicians, under the motto that only the best is good enough for young students of music. Special emphasis was given to the role of youth concerts. A French youth orchestra was part of the program. There were also solo concerts. The Paris World Exposition of 1937 provided a sensational background the the Second Congress. Kestenberg later saw this Congress as the point of origin for what later became the Jeunesse Musicale, just as Kestenberg's international organization established the foundations upon which the International Society for Music Education (ISME) was built.

[SHV letterhead]

6 August 1937.

Dr. Beidler-Wagner
Klosbachstrasse 134.
Zurich.

Dear Friends,

To start with, we thank you again, most deeply, for the innumerable demonstrations of your friendship which almost smothered us. As large as our circle of friends is, we can only speak of a few genuine and dependable friends and it is a great stroke of luck and an inexpressible joy for us that we can count you among these friends.

Immediately after my return I energetically began to eat away at the mountain of work that had piled up during my absence. In Switzerland as well as in France and Holland, during the many meetings, I gained the impression that the prerequisites for our work are right and that the concept of our Society [SHV] is capable of being happily realized if conditions over the next years allow further work in tranquility. The direct and also material support that is allotted us from other countries will be of decisive importance. Above all, my impressions in Paris make me believe that we must do everything in order to attain closer relations with France. Without a doubt, French music pedagogy is essentially conservative today. But all the same, impulses for musical education, as we see it, will be able to count on fertile soil here and there. In any case, it will be necessary to be clear about a basic stumbling block in all of the Latinate lands: I view the French as fundamentally incapable of being organized, despite all apparent contrary signs. Although I also take personal pleasure in the way everyone there possesses a strong shot of individuality, this does set up a certain barrier against our efforts. Mind you, I believe that government agencies under the influence of the *Front Populaire* will be easier to win over than they used to be. We must only locate the right pathways to these government agencies. In Paris, I was assured from all sides that the "salon" was still the unavoidable passport, by which alone access to the decisive authorities can be found. The ladies mentioned by you, Mme Chocarne[1], Mme Malaterre-Sellier[2] and Mme Brunsvicqu[3] probably are in the best position to help us and build a bridge between Prague and Paris over the waters of music education. Please write to me about how we should introduce ourselves to these ladies; if we can write with reference to you or if you would like directly to undertake introducing them to our Society. The goal would be to found a local group of the Society for Musical Education in Paris with an appropriate honorary committee and with an Action Committee and a financial contribution — within reasonable limits, intended quasi as a recognition fee — to our head office in Prague.

Perhaps our previous Paris friends, foremost among them André Coeuroy and Jean Chantavoine, might be of help in this. Admittedly, in recent years, Chantavoine has shown only a moderate interest in our projects. And if something can also seem to be done through the representatives of the workers, especially the Communists, for national musical education — for which a certain evidence was supplied at the May congress of the *Fédération Musicale Populaire* [Federation for Music of the People] and for which Charles

---

[1] Suzanne **Chocarne** - (1873-1955) - Chocarne was vice-president of the Federation of Public School Pupils.

[2] Germaine **Malaterre-Sellier** - (1889-1967) - During WWI, she was decorated for attending to wounded soldiers under fire, and while wounded herself. After the war, she presided over women's groups working toward international peace. She campaigned to have women vote and fought for causes such as widening education for all classes of people.

[3] Cécile **Brunschvicg** - (1877-1946) - née Kahn, of a Jewish-Alsatian family. In 1899, she married the feminist philosopher Léon Brunschvicg. Over the years, she exerted herself on behalf of women, including the suffrage movement and reforms in the education system to help underprivileged students. In 1936, she was made under-secretary of state for national education in the government of Léon Blum. Because of her Jewish ancestry, when the Nazis invaded, she and her husband had to flee and go undercover, separately.

Koechlin[1] seems to be at the forefront — nonetheless, I do not have the impression that in France there exists even one personality who has an overview of the whole complex of the movement or who can make it his own. We are still searching for just such a capacity. And I ask you, as well, to stay on the lookout, along these lines.

We are now writing to all the Swiss people with whom I came into closer contact during my trip in order to finally and definitively determine whether the conference plan for September 1938 can be realized. In spite of Hugo Keller of Bern assuring me in Paris that he would immediately straighten out the matter of Vogler, which could be traced back to him, I still have received no news. Presumably, the matter will not be able to be sorted out until after the holidays.

Yesterday, I had the opportunity to speak with Lecturer Dr. Nettl,[2] an advisor to the German radio (i.e. the German broadcast in the Czechoslovakian Radio). He seemed to have a great interest in you and told me that, on an appropriate occasion, such as the 100th birthday of Frau Cosima, he would like to arrange for you to give a Urania lecture in Prague. Apart from the overwhelming joy we would have if you could visit us, I would view it as very appropriate that you introduce your book from here. Perhaps a Czech edition of the book could be encouraged at the same time.

But the main thing now is that you send us the manuscript of the next chapter soon. We are waiting for it on pins and needles. I hope that, in the meantime, the question of a publisher has made good progress.

I also spoke with Dr. Nettl about Hellmut Chr. Wolff.[3] He is quite prepared to broadcast a performance of a chamber music composition by him, if the instrumentation and length are suitable and, of course, if the skills correspond to the requirements, about

---

[1] Charles Louis Eugène **Koechlin** - (1867-1950) - French composer, theorist, teacher, and author. He studied with Massenet and Fauré, among othes. In addition to his large oeuvre, he wrote the first biography of Fauré as well as authoritative treatises on harmony, music theory, and orchestration. His most prominent pupil was Poulenc, although his friend Milhaud also viewed him as a teacher. He gave seminars at the University of California 1918, 1928, 1929, and 1937. His fascination with the cinema led to at least one large work. While writing for large orchestra, he was also fascinated by 12-tone music and modern instruments such as the saxophone and the Ondes Martenot.

[2] Paul **Nettl** - (1889-1972) - Jewish-Austrian Director of Music for German Radio in Prague 1933-1939. He emigrated to the USA in 1939, teaching at Princeton University. Professor of Musicology at the University of Indiana at Bloomington in 1946. He wrote over 30 books and many articles.

[3] Hellmuth Christian **Wolff** - (1906-1988) - German (born in Zurich) composer and musicologist.

which, after your remarks, I have no doubt.

Thousand regards from us both

in old sincere friendship

Your:

LeoKestenberg

55. KBG to FWB — 1937.08.06

56. 1937.08.21 — Kestenberg (Prague) to Beidlers (Zurich)

[typed]

[SHV letterhead]

SPOLEČNOST PRO HUDEBNÍ VÝCHOVU SOCIÉTÉ D'ÉDUCATION MUSICALE **SHV** SOCIETY FOR MUSICAL EDUCATION GESELLSCHAFT FÜR MUSIK-ERZIEHUNG

PRAHA
IV. TOSKÁNSKÝ PALÁC.

CG 21.August 1937.

21 August 1937.

CG

Dr. Beidler-Wagner
Klosbachstrasse 134.
Zurich.

Dear Friends,

please do not interpret today's letter as a subtle hint meant to cause you to reply to my letter of the 7th of this month. It only seems absolutely necessary that I inform you of our further progress with reference to the preparation of the international working conference in Switzerland.

On the 18th of the month, we received a very friendly letter from Miss Scheiblauer, in which she communicated her final agreement to the holding of this conference and also named the personages whom we should contact about this. We are already in the process of writing to Councillor Briener, Prof. Hanselmann, Rektor Enderlin[1] and Governing Council Member Hafner[2] and shall also write to Dr. Schuh and Teacher Schoch in Zurich, Hugo Keller (Bern), Councillor Hauser and Seminar Music Teacher Huber in Basel.

Perhaps you can also personally motivate Schoch and Dr. Spüler [Spühler] to shed some light for Councillor Briner on my dark but all the more copious appearance. Miss

---

[1] Fritz **Enderlin** - (1883-1971) - Teacher and Politician, especially for educational matters in all of Switzerland. He wrote several books, including several for use by students.

[2] Karl **Hafner** - (1878-1947) - Member of the governing council, Zurich 1929-1943. President of the Education Council.

Scheiblauer is presently giving a course in which Prof. Pfeffer[1] and Mrs. Feudel[2] are participating. I take it that you know and think well of one of the ladies. If yes, it would be good if you could contact her.

Everything is as best as can be and we hope it is the same for you and send sincerest regards.

Your

Leo Kestenberg

56. KBG to FWB — 1937.08.21

[1] Charlotte **Pfeffer** - (1881-1970) - Jewish-German specialist in the use of rhythm for therapeutic treatment and education. She studied with Jaques-Dalcroze. In 1933, she fled to Italy, where she worked with mentally handicapped children in Naples and Rome. After war, she returned to Germany and worked in Berlin, later Freiburg/Breisgau.

[2] Elfriede **Antonie Feudel** - (1881-1966) - German pioneer in the use of rhythm for therapeutic treatment and education. She studied with Jaques-Dalcroze at Hellerau. From 1927-1945, she directed Rhythm education in Dortmund, Essen, and Leipzig,

57. 1937.09.27 — Beidler (Zurich) to Kestenberg -

[typed]

The Beidlers

Zurich 7: 27 September 1937,
134 Klosbachstrasse.

Very beloved Kestenberg friends,

after Grete's call from the heart an answer must be forthcoming! But you must excuse me: I have a cold, my head is therefore dopey and this letter will be the same.

Now then: we are doing well. Nothing has happened. Our not writing was pure egoism: all out-time since our last meeting was supposed to be, and really has been dedicated to the book. Result: it has made a lot of progress - but it is not yet finished. Why: because it has unexpectedly turned into a large-scale, incredibly caustic settling of accounts with the whole of post-Wagnerianism, also with reference to the artistic side and is undertaking to destroy the whole false mystique from the ground up. We believe that it has all gone very well, much better than what you have already come to know and, above all: razor-sharp! At the moment, we are negotiating with the Oxford University Press. If this publisher publishes it, which does not seem hopeless, we no longer will have to worry about anything.

A Czech edition? That would be fine and would be welcomed in these parts, in the highest quarters! Many whole-hearted thanks for your so successful intervention with Dr. Nettl – it will bear fruit.

It is getting to be high time that I respond to your letter. Meanwhile, listen, completely privately, to what I have thought up with reference to France. To begin with, for my part, at the beginning of October, I shall put out "Salon"-feelers to the women named by you. Mme Chocarne and Mme Brunsvicq seem quite good prospects to me. As for the competent personage, who would be capable of taking the whole matter in hand there, in a realistic way, I have fallen upon our friend **André Schaeffner**[1]. He is an ethnologist

---

[1] André **Schaeffner** - (1895-1980) - French ethnomusicologist, a significant figure in French musicology. After studies with Vincent d'Indy, among others, he became interested in modern musical developments. Stravinsky's Rite of Spring fascinated him. His interest in "primitive" music and Afro-American jazz grew. In 1929 he founded a department of ethnomusicoloy in the Trocadero Ethnographic Museum. After a long field trip to Africa in 1932, he set up in this museum a phonothèque which grew rapidly. While writing and publishing many books, Schaeffner continued his phonographic field trips, this in a concentrated way after World War II.

and musicologist, still young for France (forty something), works at the Musée Ethnographique du Trocadéro (where [Curt] Sachs also was and who naturally knows Schaeffner very well) and made a name for himself with a brilliant book about Stravinsky. He is of first-class quality. Whether he indeed is agile enough and whether he might be interested at all — both are questionable. At any rate, you would have in him a full-fledged and high-class personality, who, however, because of the experiences during several expeditions in darkest Africa, views our European "culture" with the greatest skepticism. Should I write him an "information only" letter sometime? Or does it have to be a music pedagogue?

To be quite open, in the meantime I have not concerned myself further about the Swiss things (except for a wink to Dr Spühler for Councillor Briner), because you seem to have prepared everything so well that my intervention could be of no additional help. All the same, I shall call Mr. Schoch tomorrow to gather information about how things stand. Meanwhile Miss Eva Stadler was at our place and took some material for Prof. Hanselmann (She is very congenial! Smart and sensible without being arrogant! For us, too, valuable on a human level!) She will certainly be very successful in carrying out her mission with him. On the other hand, contrary to your suggestion, I did not attend Miss Scheiblauer's course, because I do not know Miss Pfeffer at all and Miss Feudel only superficially — but above all because of lack of time.

Very special thanks to you as well for making yourself available on behalf of Hellmut Chr. Wolff, from Halle. I want to write to him this week.

I am burning to send you at least the third large chapter of Cosima — but, idiotically, I do not have a copy at home, because of the publisher. Just as soon as I have one, you will receive it, of course, in our own, most immediate, interest.

A chance question (probably sounding quite strange to you): do you have knowledge that the Belgian musician Franz Servais was supposed to have been a son of Liszt and Princess Wittgenstein (or possibly of Agnes Street)? Have you read or heard anything about this anywhere? It is a shadowy story. Today I shall not reveal anything more in order not to influence your memory in any way.

Every day in China hundreds of poor members of the civil population, far from the line of battle, are being slaughtered. And the "world of culture" watches it all in tranquility as if it were a natural event! If this swinish culture is not overripe for extinction, then I really do not know if anything in history was! (Great respect, by the way, for your Minister Krofta. Yesterday I read a "Cooperation"-article by him which was a masterpiece of political brilliance!)

You, Grete, Grandmama, Ruth, Rahel and Tunja — all of you are to be hugged and kissed by us!

Always your

57. FWB to KBG — 1937.09.27

58. 1937.09.29 — Beidler (Zurich) to Kestenberg

[typed]

Beidler
Zurich 7: 29 September 1937,
134 Klosbachstrasse.

Dear Boss-of-Old

(famously, this has nothing to do with "old" but is the Swiss expression for the French "ancien"), this is actually supposed to be an official letter in French to the Toskan-Palais. The only thing is that what I have to report or suggest today is not important enough for that. Next time!

I would not find it amiss to try to have the *Neue Helvetische Gesellschaft* [New Helvetian Society] participate in the conference that you are going to put on next year. It is an eclectic, "non-partisan," and "patriotic" organization, although in this country these epithets do not carry the penetratingly repugnant and hardline reactionary sense that they do in Germany. On the contrary, the Society discusses things with a frankness that is often astounding, although naturally also thoroughly "bourgeois." Since it always tries to move on a scientific level that can be taken seriously, it would be possible, in certain circumstances, to take up with it, especially since it traditionally is regarded with respect and functions on an inter-kantonal level. (+ *expat Swiss* ! [pencilled-in by FWB])

I include some conference minutes. Dr. Schohaus[1] is an important man — a kind of school reformer and apparently solid. Maybe it might be possible to find common ground with the catchwords "leisure activities."

Mr. Schoch told me yesterday that the Zurich school administration had made a positive decision [in favour of the congress]. I imagine that you are now also in possession of other positive responses. Nor do I want to miss this opportunity to say that Schoch is somewhat disappointed that, in his opinion, the conference is too limited by its concentration on the "pathological." It seems that he said the same to Rektor Enderlin but is, of course, in a positive frame of mind. As much as I understand and also approve of the motives that have animated you to constrain fields of topics as sharply as possible, I would still be for pursuing the "normal" and "healthy." In other words: interpret the term "healing power" as broadly as possible. That is also the reason for my small suggestion about the New Helvetian Society.

---

[1] Willy **Schohaus** - Swiss school reformer, recognized through Switzerland for his years of achievement 1928-1962. He edited several collections of works about Pestalozzi.

In the meantime, I made the personal acquaintance of Professor Fritz **Medicus**,[1] the advocate for philosophy and pedagogy at the local university, on the occasion of an (abominable) lecture in a private setting, about Nietzsche. Great disappointment! The man is the very caricature of a "professor," hideous mixture of pastor and senior school teacher, with the obligatory north German falsetto voice. Really horrible. He enjoys such a great reputation here because of a circumstance which, sadly, in such a small country as ours, hits you in the face at every turn. To put it in a nutshell: provincial! The university, in contrast to the Technical University, has thoroughly provincial standards in the humanities, something confirmed enormously by my recent experience. At any rate, I have free access to Medicus at any time. Make use of this if you find it useful.

(Medicus = Spranger[2] minus 85%)

I just received a letter from Golo's mother, from Locarno, with the following truly refreshing sentences:

"At the moment, everything is being dwarfed by the gargantuan, universally historical happening of one cutthroat visiting another. [Hitler and Mussolini] The art of swelling up, itself, likely has never yet celebrated such orgies as with these gentlemen. And that the two gigantic pigs come together only to save the peace, while the war unleashed by them in China and Spain rages and the peace-loving powers, primed and ready (and how long still?) to prevent the worst, is still an enormity that must bring the coolest to the boiling point."

This, above all, for Grete! For the rest, let us remember how, in his first years, Louis Napoléon stepped from success to success and, from time to time, seemed to be master of "world politics"!

Profoundest greetings from the heart!

Backround Note:
The visit of Mussolini to Germany at the end of September, 1937 was a sickening event for Beidler but a glorious one for his Wahnfried relatives. As Beidler's Aunt Daniela reported on October 3, "...We heard the Duce's magnificent speech with the greatest of

[1] Fritz Georg Adolf **Medicus** - (1876-1956) - German-Swiss philosopher. Professor at the Swiss Technical University in Zurich 1911-1946.

[2] Eduard **Spranger** - (1882-1963) - German philosopher and psychologist, student of Wilhelm Dilthey.

inner elation; he was not in B.[Bayreuth] but all those days W. [Winifred] was the Führer's guest in Munich as in Berlin. The mightiest woman in Germany!!"[1]

58. FWB to KBG — 1937.09.29

[1] Daniela Thode to M. Coudenhove - RWA Hs43.

59. 1937.11.23 — Kbg (Prague) to FWB (Zurich)

[typed]

[SHV letterhead]

23 November 1937.

K/G

Dr. Franz W. Beidler
Zurich 7, Klosbachstr. 134.

Dear Dr. Beidler,

best of thanks to you for the friendly and valuable tip-offs in your private letters of the 27th and 29th of September, as also of the 14th of this month [not extant]. We would be much obliged to you if, at some point, you could draw the attention of Mr. Schoch and your other friends to the fact that we decided on the theme of music education and therapeutic pedagogy only after long hesitation and that the organizational problems that surfaced in the Spring, caused us to keep the framework as narrow as possible. With this limitation, we believe that we can avoid misunderstandings and antagonisms. But it is not only these negative reasons that determined our choice of this field of themes. More to the point, we believe that this conference, contrary to other congress-parades can yield completely new and surprising results. We are assuming the fact that the question of hearing music only very seldom has been the subject of scientific studies in the pedagogical and psychological literature. The works presented up to now demonstrate the necessity of thorough research, and I believe that clarification of the various forms of musical perception processes in individuals who are neither physically nor intellectually normal, will bring light into this darkness. In these children, certain stimuli and associations which confuse and broaden the hearing process of normal individuals, are absent from the outset. Without doubt, the hearing process in all of us is an almost incalculable, all but chaotic conglomeration of sensual impressions, emotional and motor reactions, of associations of the most diverse nature, and only seldom a structural-intellectual comprehension and understanding in the sense of the work and of its creator. At the same time, we must also remain conscious that many works — especially those of the romantic period — require of the listener a different calibration of the hearing process, for which many works of our great masters, Liszt and Wagner, are fully valid proofs. If we succeed in precisely analyzing the processes of hearing and perception in deaf and dumb, blind, intellectually and emotionally disabled children, which, in these children are, naturally, easier than in normal ones, then we shall have made substantial gains by avoiding many sources of error. The Swiss conference can provide completely new and important factual material for these experiments. It is only a matter of making the importance of these problems clear to the serious music pedagogues. We further believe that this conference will be attended by a circle of interested people and professionals that is small but qualitatively all the higher in stature and that further important opportunities for work will materialize out of the initial meetings of the music teachers within therapeutic pedagogy. Through the addition of talks about the cultivation of music in penal institutions and through visiting the Goetheanums[1] in Dornach, the tendency of our whole social and generally humanistic activity will be formed for tangibility and comprehensibility.

Since our project is often still subjected to misinterpretations, especially now in Switzerland, for which, once again, the unambiguous evidence is the criticism of our anthology volume by the editor of the "Swiss Music Newspaper," by Mr. Dv. (David?), we view it as a necessity to underline our character by means of the program of the conference.

With the same post, we are sending you the anthology volume, edited by us and recently published, "*L'education musical - trait d'union entre les peuples.*" [Music-Education - the hyphen joining peoples]. The preface offers a basic portrayal of our essence and the sense of our efforts. The articles largely go back to the talks that were given at the 1st International Congress for Music Education 1936 in Prague. These are supplemented by reports from other countries, which were not represented at the congress or from those which had representatives but had not sent speakers. As far as we know, ours contains the first publications that offer a quite comprehensive international overview of modern trends in musical education in individual countries.

Even if you are now buried in the midst of your Cosima Wagner work, we still hope that you will have a chance to have a look at the volume, with which I especially ask you to read the preface.

Your efforts in pointing out the Paris salons with which you are acquainted, on behalf of our challenges and project, are always extraordinarily desirable but not always urgent. Perhaps, during your next visit to Paris, you could accomplish this or that for us. We would be very happy if we could obtain, in return for our international activity, whether from Switzerland or from France, a recognition fee. This sort of contribution, of which the amount would be relatively inconsequential, would give support to morale in our own country. If you could also be of help to us along these lines, we would be very grateful.

It will interest you to learn that Dr.Hermann Reichenbach and his family have left the USSR and are now in London and trying to start a new life there. Dr.Arnold Walter

---

[1] **Goetheanum** - Rudolf Steiner (1861-1925) designed the imposing, monumental Goetheanum in Dornach near Basel as a centre of anthroposophy and for the Anthroposophic Society.

has had a happy landing in Toronto and seems to feel very well there.[1] The former publisher Kurt Wolff,[2] who settled down near Florence, was in Prague a few days ago and brought me regards from Mrs. Dispeker, who is still "living" in Berlin. We received an SOS call from London for the flautist, Nico Draber, from his aunt Susanne Friedburg. Until recently, young Draber, who worked for the SU [Soviet Union?], had to leave it suddenly while leaving his wife and child behind. He would be happy at the moment to find a job as flautist. He is supposed to be an excellent musician; perhaps you could give him some attention. His address is: Zurich, Schanzengraben 27, bei Bordollo.

The only fully legal offspring of Angelo Neumann[3] lives here, his daughter, Dr. Gottlieb. Just yesterday, I spoke with her and told her about your interest in Angelo Neumann. She would like to know if Neumann's "Memories of Richard Wagner" are still recommended and distributed in Bayreuth.

Your suggestion to arrange for "Pierrot lunaire"[4] with Dr.Stiedry[5] in Prague would have to be forwarded to an efficient concert society. I do not have much hope that enough paying customers could be found to permit such a project.

---

[1] Arnold **Walter**'s landing in Toronto turned out to be happy for him, and even more so for the people who loved music in that city. He was a force in founding the Canadian Opera Company, in bringing good teachers to the Conservatory, in establishing a music school at the University of Toronto and an Opera School. Through his reforms and expansion of music in the city, he played a key role in producing singers such as Jon Vickers and Teresa Stratas, to name only two of the best.

[2] Kurt **Wolff** - (1887-1963) - German publisher, editor, writer, and journalist. He was the first publisher to promote and publish Kafka and Werfel and several writers in Prague, such as Max Brod and Felix Weltsch. He and his wife fled Nazi Germany for Florence, then the USA where he founded Pantheon Books.

[3] Angelo **Neumann** - (1838-1910) - German theatre director in Prague. Although Jewish, he was the most loyal and enthusiastic theatrical adherent and promoter of Wagner. In 1882 and 1883, he took a Wagnerian touring company all over Europe, including England, giving 135 performances of the Ring des Nibelungen and 50 Wagner concerts. The English satirical magazine, Punch, called the London performances *"succès de steam,"* a witty reference to the use of live steam onstage to present the ever-present Nibelung and Vallhall mists.

[4] **Pierrot Lunaire** - Piece by Arnold Schoenberg (1874-1951), premiered in Berlin in 1912. Many expressionistic elements, including Sprechstimme, made the work a first of its kind.

[5] Fritz **Stiedry** - (1883-1968) - Austrian conductor and composer. He fled Germany in 1933 and became principal conductor of the Leningrad Philharmonic Orchestra 1933-1937. He moved to the USA, where, after the war, he conducted at the Lyric Oper of Chicago and the Metropolitan Opera. He co-founded the Hunter College Opera Workshop.

The attached newspaper clippings about the "New Helvetian Society" and your "Wagneriana" are very interesting for us and we thank you very much.

With reference to your suggestion to take in the New Helvetian Society as a co-host of our planned working conference, we can inform you that the Swiss Music-Pedagogical Association has declared its readiness to give the conference every moral support and also to put its name at its disposal, so that we likely do not need any further oath-helpers [a pun on confederacy, *Eidgenossen*, oath-helpers, i.e. Switzerland, therefore meaning "no further Swiss helpers"].

With best regards,

most humbly

LeoKestenberg

59. KBG to FWB — 1937.11.23

59a. 1937.11.23 — Kbg (Prague) to FWB (Zurich)

[typed]

Prof.Leo Kestenberg
Prague XIX. Velvarská 59
Prague, 23 November 1937.

Dear friends and comrades,

dear Beidlers and young bosses,

the colleague in our German section, Comrade Greull, reminds me that I was supposed to add a personal word to the official letter. I am following up on this suggestion all the more eagerly since, we were so especially happy about your last report, which implied that your manuscript is nearing completion.

Happily, we have only good news to report about ourselves. Grandmother, mother, and children are enjoying general cheerfulness, as far as is permissible in these tempestuous times. In addition to my day-to-day work, I have three big articles to write and many lectures to prepare, of which the next is supposed to happen on the 30th of November in the "Union for Justice and Freedom" about the theme "Democractic and Fascistic Methods of Education." Latterly, I spoke at a morning function put on by the "Bodenbach Public Choir." Bodenbach is located right at the German border and it is hard to describe how courageously and staunchly the comrades there stand at their posts. Otherwise, I felt myself sent back to earlier days there because all the preconditions that were decisive for our undertaking our worker-singer unions could be revisited here, right up to the last props. — Uplifting and ghostly memories from which, once again, the law can be derived that certain facilities seem a necessity of nature.

Write again soon and accept the hearty regards of all of us,
most of all from me,

Your

LeoKbg

59a. KBG to FWB — 1937.11.23

60. 1938.01.22 — Kbg (Prague) to Beidlers (Zurich)

[typed]

[SHV stationery]

K/G

Dr. F.W. Beidler-Wagner,
Zurich, Klosbachstrasse 134.

My dear Beidlers,

Many thanks for all that you sent us. We are rejoicing fervently over the progress of your work and hope soon to receive the news of its final completion.

Today, we would like to inform you that a program for our Swiss working conference is finally available. We shall be sending you the first draft in the next days. Zurich, Bern and Basel — each of these three cities is forming an honorary and a working committee. Beyond that, there will be a Swiss committee to represent the common interests to foreign countries. This somewhat cumbersome machinery seems to work well, however, because Miss Scheiblauer continues to be the soul of the project. We are in the midst of negotiations with good prospects with various interesting foreign speakers; presumably, Henry Wallon[1] will participate with a psychological lecture. If Dr.Medikus is to be considered seriously, he will have to be recommended to us by Swiss people.

Otherwise, we are now actively occupied with preparations for our 2nd International Congress for Music Education, which will be held in Prague from 1st to 6th of April 1939. In order to manage the wide-ranging material more practicably this time, we shall work in four sections — 1. Music education in the school, 2. in youth associations and institutions for public education, 3. in the private educational system for music and 4. in radio. We repeat most urgently our invitation to this event about which we shall have the opportunity to have intensive talks in connection with the Swiss conference, at the latest.

Recently, we have received very optimistic news from France. With the help of our old friends, with André Coeuroy at the forefront, there will probably be an official recognition of our work and also a financial membership contribution. One of the next issues his of the "Revue musicale" will be dedicated to music education in Czechoslovakia and

---

[1] Henri **Wallon** - (1879-1962) - French philosopher, psychologist (social psychology), teacher, and politician. He joined the socialist party in 1931. In 1942, he joined the communist party. He was a distinguished academic and practitioner, specializing in childhood psychology. The influence of his ideas extended well beyond the borders of France.

also our international activity.

It astounded us somewhat that Thomas Mann did not send us even a word of confirmation of receipt of our letter and also our anthology volume, "L'éducation musicale - trait d'union entre les peuples." The only sign that the volume must have arrived was the notice in the books column of [Thomas Mann's exile newspaper] *Mass und Wert* [Mass and Value].

Soon I shall write to you privately,
With best regards,
Your heartfelt and humble,

LeoKestenberg

60. KBG to FWB — 1938.01.22

61. 1938.01.26 — FWB (Zurich) to Kbg -

[typed]

Beidler

Zurich 7: 26 January 1938,
134, Klosbachstrasse.

Dear Comrade Kestenberg,

may I count on your leniency today if I reply rapidly and totally privately to your well-structured, formally perfect, semi-official letter — because I lack material that is "officially useful"?

This is already almost worth getting jealous about: everything is going so well without my participation, let alone assistance? My goodness, let us rejoice for the sake of the cause. As you know, I am on standby for you, just in case.

You should not be "astounded" that the poor, much-vexed Thomas M. [Mann] did not immediately send you fervent thanks for the anthology volume. During the last months, he has been a bit under the weather and very overburdened. Both of them are now in Arosa, and Katia just wrote me that they are unable to recuperate because of so much correspondence.

Meanwhile, when I saw that the anthology volume had been advertized in *Mass und Wert*, I immediateley told Golo Mann that it was important to me that it should receive a proper review, he should make sure of that. At that, he asked me if I would take that on, and I, in the interest of the cause, bellowed Yes. Now, for the paper, things are like this: Dr. Lion[1] has the editing in his grip and, apparently allows of no interference, especially not from Golo. I heard nothing more about the matter, and when I asked Golo after a while how things actually stood with the review, he only cursed terribly about Lion. I have my reasons for not offering to help Mr. Lion, just as I have maintained a thoroughly reserved stance towards his unbelievably boring and leathery publication. Consecrating a chapter of my book is likely something that I shall have to make sense of after Thomas,

---

[1] Ferdinand **Lion** - (1883-1968) - Swiss journalist and writer. Friend of Thomas Mann and Alfred Döblin. After World War I, he was a reader at Ullstein publishing in Berlin. He worked as editor of "Mass und Wert" 1937-1938. He wrote libretti: Der Golem, Eugen d'Albert, 1926, and Cardillac, Hindemith, 1926.

almost in anger, said to me at Christmas, in the presence of the Bermanns,[1] that he would prefer not to have to ask and remind me again. It is not as if I am taking sides against Dr. Lion, who, by all that is holy, I do not envy for his job of having to edit a publication in partnership with the whole family Mann and camp followers (this only between us, please!). But it cannot be denied that, from issue to issue, the publication is becoming more insipid, drier, more indigestible, more hanseatic, and, at the same time more snobbish. A crying shame: the print run of the first issue was 6,000. What an immense opportunity is being willfully put to waste.

Mr. David (= Dv.) of the "Swiss Music News" is half a Frontist (=Nazi), despite his deceptive name. The publication is correspondingly miserable. I know him, and since he kowtows before me, I am certainly in a position to tell him what I think. At any rate, we want to talk this question over, before the working conference, with Schuh (with whom I am closer every day and who is becoming bolder every day!)

Nicolo **Draber**, Miss Friedburgs nephew has been with us several times. I have tried to bring him in contact with people who can be of help to him, and this by all possible means. Whether this was or can be a success, I cannot say at the moment. What is constraining and complicating is that, from March on, he will be without valid identity papers. The cases are piling up from day to day! And there is almost nothing that can be done — depressing enough. At present, the case of Bella Amster's sister worries me. Next to several dozen others!

I am sending the following today (with a request for a speedy, informal return):

1) a short report by Paul Stefan[2] in the Viennese "Stunde" (the whole thing occurred without my advance knowledge or even my wish — you know how little I can stand this

---

[1] The **Bermanns** - Gottfried Bermann Fischer (1897-1995), born Gottfried Bermann, and Brigitte Bermann Fischer, born Fischer (1905-1991). When they married in 1925, Gottfried took over direction of the Fischer publishing house founded by his father-in-law, Samuel Fischer. Fischer was Thomas Mann's publisher. In 1936, Bermann, who was Jewish, moved part of Fischer publications to Vienna. While the Berlin operation was meant to continue publication of autors acceptable to the Nazis, the Viennese part would publish unacceptable authors such as Mann, Hermann Hesse, Carl Zuckmayer, and others. When the Nazis occupied Austria, the Bermanns fled to Switzerland, thereafter to Sweden and, finally, to the USA. Only in 1950, could they return to Germany and resume business as the S.Fischer publishing house.

[2] Paul **Stefan** - (1879-1944) - born Paul Stefan Grünfeld. Austrian musicologist, writer and critic. After the Nazi occupation of Austria, as Jew and opponent of the Nazis, he had to flee Vienna to Winterthur, then to France, and on to Lisbon, and, finally to the USA (1941). He wrote many books, mostly on musical subjects relating to Vienna and Austria.

sort of personal promotion). But the words about you pleased me — it is the reflection of my talks with Stefan. You see, indirectly, from this how I grumble about you.

2) a correspondence with **Fellerer**, to show you that I can take friends to task, rigorously when necessary. He tries to squirm free in the Bavarian way [*auf bajuwarisch*] but a slightly bitter taste remains (the guy actually writes of Schoenberg: "asphalt-artistic" and "corrosive tendency"![1] [a Nazi phrase with anti-Semitic intent]. After my intervention with the New Zurich Newspaper, his new little book will **not** get reviewed.

A request: could you send me as soon as possible Alfred Einstein's address - via the SHV?

To all Kestenbergish people, closer friends, and those marrying into the family, a thousand greetings in love and loyalty of old!

61. FWB to KBG — 1938.01.26

[1] Arnold **Schoenberg** - (1874-1951) - Jewish-Austrian, expressionist and atonal, 12-tone (serial) composer, teacher, and painter. In 1933, Schoenberg emigrated to the USA after having reaffirmed his adherence to the Jewish religion (he had converted to Lutheranism 1898). With Kestenberg's assistance, Schoenberg was appointed Ferruccio Busoni's successor as Director of the Master Class in Composition at the Prussian Academy of Arts in Berlin. He took up this position in 1926, leaving it only in 1933.

62. 1938.03.25 — Kbg (Prague) to Beidlers (Zurich)

[typed]

Background:

Kestenberg is obviously agitated and worried in this letter. February and March had been terrible months. Hitler had drummed up complaints that the Austrians were mistreating German minorities. On February 12, he had summoned the Austrian Chancellor Schuschnigg to his Führer redoubt, the Berghof, at Berchtesgaden, near Salzburg. There, Hitler forced Schuschnigg to accept the Nazi, Seyss-Inquart as Minister of the Interior in the Austrian cabinet. When, on March 9, Schuschnigg announced his intention to hold a referendum on the subject of the continuing independence of Austria from Germany, Hitler ordered the Austrian Nazis to begin taking over the country. German troops crossed the border on March 12 and Austria was rapidly annexed by Germany. Kestenberg already saw that Czechoslovakia was in similarly great danger. Hitler's minorities argument would be much stronger applied to the Sudeten Germans than they had been in Austria. By the end of March, Hitler had begun organizing Nazi Sudeten Germans to undermine Czechoslovakia and so to enable his annexation of the country by October 1.

In Germany, the anti-Semitic racist measures had evolved over five years. In Austria, they came into effect in the space of three days, causing horror and misery. Typically, Kestenberg sought outside help in aiding the Jews such as the writer Paul Stefan to escape the Nazis. He also let out a cry to Beidler to stay in constant contact, as stalwarts and friends. While recognizing that there was now "minimal" cause for optimism, Kestenberg nonetheless continued to express his belief in optimism as a spiritual priority.

PROF.LEO KESTENBERG,
Prag XIX.,Velvarská 59.

Dear Friends,

it is incomprehensible that we have gone for such an infinitely long time without any news from you. Precisely now is the time when each of us feels the need to gather the few stalwarts around, and, at any rate, to stay in constant contact with our friends.

Prof. Dr. Paul Stefan of Vienna has urgently asked if he can be active in any way possible in Switzerland in the preparation for the international working conference of the SHV in order to legitimate his stay there. I am giving him your address, among others, so that, if need be, he can get in touch with you.

Otherwise, we are as optimistic as the matters do minimally allow. Above all, we ask that you send news as promptly as possible, even if short.

With best regards Your

LKbg

Dr. Franz Wagner-Beidler
134,Klosbachstrasse 134. Zurich 7.

62. KBG to FWB — 1938.03.25

63. 1938.04.03 — FWB (Zurich) to Kbg -

[typed]

Background:

The brutal annexation of Austria and the immediate pogrom against the Jews of Austria inspired Beidler to a profound conviction that he must do everything possible to fight the scourge of Naziism even though he was convinced that things would get much worse before they could get better.

Obviously, and as usual, his relatives in Bayreuth did not share his sentiments in any way. They experienced veritable orgies of joy over Hitler's territorial expansion and at the speeches of self-glorification by such as Göring and the other government thugs. Writing to her Viennese friend, Marietta Coudenhove, Eva Chamberlain, Beidler's aunt, gloried in a radio broadcast of Goering thanking Hitler for his awesomeness.[1] The speech, she wrote, "was distinguished by the stamp of truth and clarity. We enthusiastically identified with Göring's thanks to the Führer." There was, however, one sad factor. Eva's half-sister, Daniela Thode was in great sorrow that the Jewish conductor, Bruno Walter was forced to leave Austria. "She treasured his artistic achievements greatly, and these cannot be made up for by either Knappertsbusch or Elmendorf, or Reichwein." On this subject, Eva cited a letter by her husband Houston Stewart Chamberlain, in which he said that the individual is "a sacred mystery of creation and therefore holy and therefore immune to generalized theoretical decrees." Her father had, after all, allowed the Jew Levi to conduct *Parsifal*. "However," she continued, "there can be no doubt that the pestilence of Jewish theatres, department stores, newspapers, doctors, pharmacists, lawyers etc. etc. must be destroyed [*vernichtet*]. Whether **this** cleansing can actually succeed? We are confronted here with the severest of problems." Significantly, she is ripping a page, the last one, out of her father's anti-Jewish screed in the 1869 version of *Judaism in Music*.while wishing violent destruction of all Jews rather than merely self-deportation of Jews and spontaneous self-destruction of their religion, as her father had advocated. All the Wagners, including Beidler's mother, Isolde, had been raised to believe that Jews were a pestilence. All the more staggering that Franz W. Beidler swam against the racist family current. His relatives viewed him as nothing less than a turncoat.

Writing to Daniela Thode from Paris on Oct 10, 1938, Friedelind Wagner, who had recently been in Switzerland, reported that what she called "Beidler's anti-Wagner essays" were becoming "the mode" among the Swiss.

---

[1] Eva Chamberlain to Marietta Coudenhove, 1938,03.19, RWA, Hs43.

> I cannot express just how greatly this behaviour by a relative nauseates me! I try to excuse it by explaining it as a matter of earning money.... And doing it under the rubric "grandson", a priority tool in establishing that he is important! He **should be ashamed of himself!** His book against grandmama is supposed to be coming out before Christmas, a blessed gift... for **her** birthday! What I have to say is: both Grandpapa and Grandmama can withstand the criticism of a grandson; they endured plenty and only became greater!![1]

How interesting that Friedelind, conversing with her aunt, took it as self-evident that Beidler was a grandson of Richard Wagner, and therefore that Isolde had been the composer's natural daughter. It was only in public that the Wagners continued to marginalize Beidler as some sort of interloper from outer space. Soon enough, Friedelind, like Beidler, turned on her family and opposed Hitler. Be that as it may, the whirlpool of Nazi and Wagnerian racism almost drowned the other Wagners in their own filth as they cheered their Führer for his love of Wagner and for his pogroms and for his final solution.

FWB

Zurich 7: 3 April1938,
134, Klosbachstrasse.

Very beloved friends,

heartfelt thanks for the sign of life! It was much-desired and long-awaited. For the time being, it is not for us to give such things. On the other hand: is our silence really so "incomprehensible"? Is it not much more self-evident that we are restrained by a whole succession of very serious worries, which we cannot bring to paper? May we ask questions that you yourselves, perhaps, cannot answer yet at this moment, despite their pushing in on you?

Or should we affirm that we are in no way crushed by the "force of facts" (which admittedly, in face of all the circumstances, would require the resistance of a buffalo)? Or should we actually say, explicitly, that we are willing less than ever to make peace with the momentarily decisive powers? The events (by God not "unexpected") — which nonetheless brought enough of surprises, in "detail" — in a very acute sense, admittedly have

---

[1] Friedelind **Wagner** (Paris) to Daniela Thode, 1938.10.10 (Daniela born 1860.10.12), RWA, Hs 27.

posed the question, in what form, if at all, men of our way of thinking can hold our ground in Europe, during the forthcoming period of time, whereby "hold" is still meant to imply a minimum of activity. We are determined to try to do so to the utmost limits. It is impossible to say more at the moment. The trough, down into which we have blundered, is deeper than could have been fairly predicted. It seems that the deepest point will not be reached for a long time. Apparently also not that of the intellectual disorientation in "our camp." All the more stubbornly do we hold true to the "old creed" and are more convinced than ever that it is **right**.

"The" book is growing, slowly but steadily. We are working on it in tranquility and with the quiet cheerfulness of those who are intermittently put off course. This is no less good for the contents, as for the form: everything is getting better, more comprehensive, clearer than we had hoped. The last three weeks admittedly have brought many disincentives. One of these, Paul Stefan (not an "easy" case … As unsuited as possible to "striving towards new shores," because - too "rooted"…).

Soon we shall see each other! The program, which — "full-fat and solid" is what my little wife likes to call what is being created here — has impressed us. Less the – idiotic – advance item about your article. The main thing: it has appeared in print.

With us, for the time being, what is changing is — prospectively and nonbindingly ! — nothing. We come into question only as news recipients; secondarily as answerers of questions. But we make an urgent plea for situation reports, as far as they can be given.

To all of you, the most profound greetings!

63. FWB to KBG — 1938.04.03

64. 1938.05.08 — FWB (Zurich) to Kbg

[typed]

The old Beidlers

Zurich 7: 8 May 1938,
134, Klosbachstrasse.

Dear, respected boss, friend, and comrade-in-belief,

putting aside all inhibitions of bad conscience (which both of us could have!), I am sending you along with this, a letter to Angelo Neumann's daughter, Dr. Gottlieb, of whose existence, but not her address, you informed me. Would you be so kind as to forward it onward as soon as possible? Since you will soon be with us, the postage bill can be taken care of at our place.

Sincere thanks for your latest essay. I must admit that I have not yet studied it adequately simply because I did not get to it yet. That means that I shall be "fructified" by my fatherland for the purposes of tourism, as you can gather from the attached festival pamphlet. Beside that, I am to give a big, programmatic lecture in the city theatre at the beginning of the Festival: "Zurich Wagner Tradition and Festival Idea." You know us well enough to know that it will be clear-cut. But that is precisely what costs time and effort.

When are you coming? We ask that you notify us in good time! At any rate, we now tend to judge the situation more optimistically. (But that you inform Martha John better about your intentions than us … alright, let's forget it. By the way: I believe I have helped you a bit concerning the difficult paper problem, through establishing a connection. Next Thursday, she is reciting for a group [line or lines missing after this in cut-off margin p.1 of letter] … are "present" … It all also has an indomitably comical side and this exactly is lucky).

Are you possibly able to say where Dr. **Nestriepke**[1] is residing and what his address is? Many thanks in advance.

What we should do for Isabella Amster's sister, whom you probably see here and there, is not completely clear. Conditions have changed in France so much that my sway to get her entry has waned, at least for the moment. I will not manage to write to her now, immediately. Would you please tell her, when you see her, that she will not be forgotten?

---

[1] Siegfried **Nestriepke** - (1885-1963) - Social Democrat, journalist, theatre director. In 1933, he was made jobless and, for a time, was banned from writing. He eventually obtained some work with a film company.

For the moment, for better or worse, she must hold out where she is, and we do not see a really acute danger in this at the present time.

Hindemith is here now. We see him here and there. Wouldn't you like to come already for "Mathis"? I believe it would be worth it. (The last performance is already on June 16th, however, and your course begins only on the 23rd.)

Heartfelt greetings to you all, you dears! And stay well for us! We vice versa too.

Your old

64. FWB to KBG — 1938.05.08

65. 1938.06.13 — Kbg (Prague) to Beidlers (Zurich)

[typed]

Background:

By this time, things looked very bad for Czechoslovakia and therefore extremely unstable for the Kestenbergs. Increasingly, after the annexation of Austria, Hitler had been drumming up a crisis in Czechoslovkia. On May 20, the Czechs began a partial mobilization in order to prepare themselves for an expected German invasion. Despite the shaky political and military situation, Kestenberg continued to bring his Swiss working conference to fruition and completion.

[SHV letterhead]

K/V

Prague, 13 June 1938.

Dr. Franz W.Beidler-Wagner
Klosbachstrasse 134
Zurich 7.

Dear Dr. Beidler,

we have the honour to present, for your esteemed wife and for you, 2 press passes, included here, for our International Working Conference for Music Education and Therapeutic Pedagogy.

We allow ourselves to assume that you will have the occasion to report about this event, perhaps already with an announcement drawing attention to the significance of the conference.

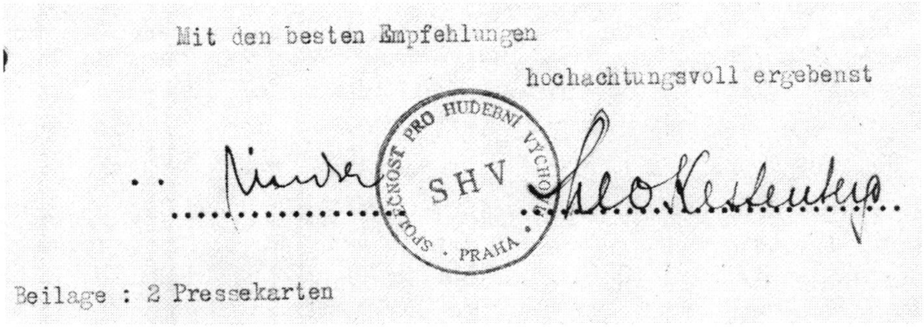

Mit den besten Empfehlungen

hochachtungsvoll ergebenst

Beilage : 2 Pressekarten

With best regards,

respectfully yours

Leo Kestenberg [and an additional signature]

[Additional handwritten, personal note]

Dear Friends!

Your copious package of printed matter overjoyed me and I thank you very much! I am happy that I shall soon have the opportunity to see you and to discuss everything personally. I do not know yet when I'll be leaving but, of course, I shall call you immediately after my arrival. Please send me your telephone number, by airmail, to the S.H.V.

Whole-heartedly your old

L.

65. KBG to FWB — 1938.06.13

66. 1938.06.15 — FWB (Zurich) to Kbg -

[typed]

Zurich 7: 15 June 1938,
134, Klosbachstrasse,
Tel. : 28'214

Dear, highly esteemed friend Kestenberg,

sincerest thanks for your lines which just arrived and for both press passes. You were not so very wrong in your assumption: I shall be writing for the "Neue Zürcher Zeitung" not only a welcoming article but also a reportage about Zurich (Bern and Basel fare worse because I shall not be able to travel there with you, for financial reasons, and, more especially, lack of time). Please do not expect too much of the welcoming article: originally, I was allotted 160 lines for this purpose. But I made a point of having a narrower "expert" write something (I do not have a foggy notion about therapeutic pedagogy). Actually, Mimi Scheiblauer was supposed to do this. It seems, however, that she had no time to do so and recommended Mr. **Ferand** to me. On my instigation, he will, in turn, write in our newspaper about the theme of our working conference. In return, admittedly, I had to abandon the largest part of the space which had been allotted to me, so that only 60-70 lines remain for me. You see, we do what we can.

The main thing is and remains — that we'll be seeing each other again! About everything else: in person. If it is still possible for you to tell me your time of arrival (airport?), I'd be very happy: because I would like so very much "to take delivery" of you.

Is Grete coming with you?? To all of you, the very sincerest of greetings and to a happy reunion!

66. FWB to KBG — 1938.06.15

67. 1938.07.19 — Kbg (Prague) to FWB (Zurich)

[typed]

Background:

From June 23-28, Kestenberg's organization, in co-operation with the "Société Pédagogique Suisse de Musique" and the "Seminaire de l'Université Zurich pour la Pédagogie des Déficients", held the last of the organization's three great meetings, the International Working Conference for Music Education and Therapeutic Pedagogy. This event took place in Zurich, Bern, and Basel, as Beidler had suggested. The conference dealt with how music could be used to treat children who had been born deaf and who, without therapy, had been regarded as hopeless cases. This was Kestenberg's third successful international conference, all brought to life and organized during his five-and-a-half years in Prague.

During his time in Zurich, Kestenberg had been the Beidlers' houseguest. At last they had had time to talk in detail, person-to-person, as in the days of the Weimar Republic. Kestenberg had had the opportunity to read parts of Beidler's Cosima manuscript and was much impressed. No doubt they also discussed what Kestenberg would do if worse came to worst (Sudentenland crisis and the increasingly likely invasion of Czechoslovakia by Hitler's armies).

Prague XIX. Velvarská 59

19 VII 38

My dear, good friends! After a completely wonderful, indescribably quiet flight — if you didn't look out, you would have thought that you were not moving — I arrived, a quarter of an hour earlier than in the flight plan and greeted with jubilation by my Grete. This whole trip already seems to me like a fable, full of wonders and exhilarating events. But I owe you both the way it was rounded off, its human and heartfelt high point. Its most important benefit, of a personal nature, was perhaps the confirmation, renewal, strengthening and deepening of our friendship. In the airplane, I had a welcome time to reflect. Inevitably, your opus pushed its way into the foreground. Half-dreamlike, the ghostly figures of your drama danced around me. Just how strong your depiction of the events and persons takes hold became completely clear to me only in retrospect, since the protean-natures of the leading figures step out of the previous, artificially constructed darkness into the light of your, of our, truth. What you have achieved there is a masterpiece of writing, which goes beyond description and narration of objective events, and in every sentence of which the heartbeat of the creator can be felt. I am convinced of the epoch-making significance of this book, and it is from out of this conviction that the urgently serious plea becomes a commandment: spare no effort to complete this work as quickly as possible and avoid all diversions and events that seem so exceedingly important.

I, too, together with our conference, view myself, in relation to you, as an undesirable interruption. Admittedly, I am confronted by the problem of how else I might have come to this attitude, which, in my relation to you is not unusual. I may grant myself extenuating circumstances, but ask you otherwise to proceed with all severity.

Now then, again, sincere thanks for everything; it was so lovely in Klosbachstrasse and I am happy that, in the end, I learned "mutual understanding."

Most sincere greetings,

Your old LeoKestenberg

67. KBG to FWB — 1938.07.19

68. 1938.07.20 — Kbg (Prague) to Beidlers (Zurich)

[typed]

[SHV letterhead]

K/G

Prague, 20 July 1938.

Dr. F.W.Beidler
Klosbachstrasse 134
Zurich .

Very esteemed, gracious woman,

and dear Dr.Beidler,

having returned home, it is a pleasant duty to thank you enthusiastically for the efforts that you bestowed on our international Working Conference for Music Education and Therapeutic Pedagogy. We are especially deeply obliged to you for the incredibly understanding presentations in the *Neue Züricher Zeitung*.

Through the exposure of the actual, original idea, which led to the constituting of our conference, the public was informed in a far more visible place about the sense and essence of the event. Both your welcoming article as well as your presentation about the discussions and demonstrations in Zurich distinguish themselves through your particular clear and lively style and through the objectivity and sophistication of your language. We also ask you to accept a heartfelt thank you for the personal charm which you showed all of our colleagues.

In the certain hope of further good work together and with the wish of being able to welcome you to our 2nd International Congress in Prague

best greetings to both of you

Your

LeoKestenberg

68. KBG to FWB — 1938.07.20

69. 1938.07.31 — Kbg (Prague) to Beidlers (Zurich)

[handwritten]

Background:

How shocking it is to read Kestenberg's letter and realize that 700,000 German soldiers were at that very moment massing on the Czechoslovakian border. The die was already cast for the snuffing out of the country harboring Kestenberg. For the first time in this correspondence, he now engages in an almost panicky parade of intellectual ruminations about Wagner as a sort of prototype Nazi. Either he was in denial, which is highly unlikely, or he was sending up some warning signals to Beidler about his state of mind. Kestenberg also began at this time to show new interest in America. Clearly he was looking at the United States as a possible refuge from the coming annexationist Hitler-hordes.

Sunday, 3 July 38

My dear friends!

After the lively, varied weeks of congress and travel, I now have returned home again to the bottoming-out that is more suited to me, of a regular inner tranquility, which is emphasized by the summer vacations of my mother, Ruth and Rachel as well as of a part of the office staff. Through Tunja, our Philomen-and-Baucis comfort and harmony are more supported than disturbed.

I am reading and learning a lot, but am essentially busy drafting an essay meant for America, which I think of as an outline for a book on a theory of music education. Hardly finished breaking ground, I already stumbled upon a conflict which was necessary to fight in the Weimar period, against over-intellectualism, which now has been getting into a suspicious neighbourhood. It is, however, unavoidable that we accept everything that seems genuine and true to our limited perception, even if it now stands as a poisonous flower in the garden of the Anti-Christ. We spoke hastily about this problem that keeps getting closer to me, which also commands an increasing priority in literature. Negation must not be permitted to drive us into the arms of the reaction, unless we actually feel at home there. (That does not apply to Th.M., who has long been aware of this danger and has distanced himself from it with the most brilliant clarity.)

In this discussion, a decisive significance will pass to your Cosima book. Yesterday and today I have been reading the first issue of the "Journal for Free German Research"

(July 1938), published by Science & Literature, 21, rue Cerjas Paris V^{e}, which is excellent in its basic approach, but less successful in execution. [*Zeitschrift für freie deutsche Forschung*] It is what I have longed for since 1930, a platform for a serious, scholarly debate with our enemy, without these ridiculous, sterile tirades-of-the-day in most of the emigrant papers. In almost all of the articles, Wagneriasm turns up more or less obviously as the birthplace and promotional shrine of Hitlerism (e.g. Siegfried Marck[1] in his essay, "Zur Philosophie des N.S." [*On the Philosophy of National Socialism*] In the end, everything is consolidated into a vulgar Wagneriasm and every good German must feel goose bumps running up the back at the vision of the radiant god [i.e. Hitler], in accord with the scene of Lohengrin's arrival. But, of course, it is the deified features of Wagneriasm, those that no longer have anything to do with Nietzsche, which lead to that resurrection. There, where Wagner unites the most refined technique with use of themes that are essentially sentimental and, in a bad sense, folkloric, there, admittedly he must signify the ideal of National Socialism.

This is a disfigured Wagner, who no longer has anything to do with the great line of musical culture to which he belongs. The intelligence of the complete history of mankind can be put in opposition to such a Wagner, against whom, in "Mein Kampf," Hitler "hurled the enraged thunderbolts of an Oriental despot." .... Page 5a ff.

And Johann L. Schmidt,[2] who seems to be the *spiritus rector* of this publication and of the Free University in Paris (a shame - had I known this earlier, I certainly would have paid him a visit), in his programmatic article, "Functions of Free German Research" [*Aufgaben der freien deutschen Forschung*], urgently demands a battle against the National Socialists' practice of appropriating all of the great men of history for themselves and violating them for their own purposes. "Even in the works of Nietzsche .... views can be found that not only do not correspond to the national socialist theories and terminology but which boldly contradict them. The same applies to Richard Wagner, who, just as much as Nietzsche, is made use of by the National Socialists."

But completely opposite to this propounded demand, an excerpt is presented in the

---

[1] Siegfried **Marck** - (1889-1957) - Jewish-German philosopher and liberal Social Democrat. In 1933, after being banned from his previous university positions, he fled Germany, settling in France until the invasion by the Nazis. He then was able to flee to the USA.

[2] Johann Lorenz **Schmidt** - pseudonym for Laszlo Radvanyi. He was a Hungarian sociologist and economist, and the husband of Anna Seghers. In November 1935, he and others opened a Free German University in Paris for German emigrants. He was also instrumental in publishing the Zeitschrift für Freie Deutsche Forschung. See Jean Michel Palmier, Weimar in Exile: The Antifascist Emigration in Europe and America. (Verso, London, 2006).

same issue, from a book yet to be published, by Dr. Wolfgang Hallgarten:[1] "Alienness Complex and Supernationalism," [*Fremdheitskomplex und Übernationalismus*] contributions to the social history of the German ideology of racism, which goes into the reasons for Wagner's being that way in a somewhat superficial but very detailed way (pages 82-108). I urgently request that you obtain this issue, which is dirt cheap (Sw.Frcs. 2-). I am writing at such length because, for me, Hallgarten's work represents a danger for your book. After having you ignite my interest in this witches' cauldron, I would be deeply saddened if your original and convincing researches, findings, and formulations were to come too late for the actual controversy. I have quoted all this in order to show how topical these problems now are perceived, by the opposing side too, as some are stalking closer from the social and epistemological side, without sensing the essence. Hallgarten also pays tribute to the correspondence with King Ludwig II and gets to speak about the political role of Wagner. But since the context is missing, he arrives at false conclusions. All the same, the point of departure is fairly close to yours and therefore I am once again urging you to hurry.

Tomorrow, a long report on the SHV and its pre-history will be sent to Herbert Peyser.[2] I am having this transcribed for you and request urgently — as I also relate in this letter - that you write a lot to Mr. Peyser about our work in Berlin, especially about the Central Institute and the Music Division and its director and his co-workers. I did ask P. to be very careful and delicate about my function back then; on the other hand, for the reasons I mentioned, it would not be unwelcome to me if, an objective, unhyperbolic characterization could appear, especially in the New York Times, of the school music reform in Prussia and also the [illegible] courses of the Z.I. (Central Institute), of the German School Music Weeks [*Reichs-Schulmusikwochen*], the publications issued by me, Kroll, University etc. The only ones who can present P. with the proper context and with the necessary accentuation are you two! But, in the same instant, it occurs to me that this immediately will represent an enormous "job" for you, with collecting of material and the most precise of source research, whereas I am thinking of a sketch originating totally from an impression, for an American daily newspaper that stresses the news of today and also does not shrink from being personal, in tone or in judgement. Only like this, as a brisk and quick and unobjectionable, typed souvenir picture, could I think of it as amus-

[1] George Wolfgang Felix **Hallgarten** - (1901-1975) - German historian of Jewish background. Forced to leave Germany in 1933, he moved to Paris, where he helped found the Free German University. He then left for the USA by way of England. During the war, he worked for the American army in the radio department.

[2] Herbert **Peyser** - (1886-1953) - American music critic and foreign correspondent. Friend of FWB.

ing and active, and only if you declare yourselves in agreement with this form, would I not have a bad conscience for this new burden. But I fear that you will not decide for this facileness which, in your eyes, is not far from frivolousness. And without your cooperation, P. probably will have to stop. Please write me what you think about this.-

I have to close this letter suddenly because an unexpected visitor has come over. By the way, Mr. Jindra has been ill for a few days. It is to be hoped that he nonetheless will be able to accept the very kind invitation of Mrs. D. [one illegibile word] to give a lecture at her place about the SHV, at which you doubtless also would be present. Then Greull would also come with. Mrs. D.I. lavishes fantastic kindnesses upon him.

By the way: I forgot the admired black, polished house shoes in the magnificent upper apartment. Have they come to light? Incidentally: to find ad vocem [?]: the last issue of Maß und Wert is very excellent!

Most sincerely, Your LeoKbg

Monday 1 August

P.S. Unfortunately, Jindra's condition has become worse and we are all very worried. The recent political agitations are certainly partly responsible for his fever. — Despite all our personal optimism, the general situation must still be judged as very serious. That is also the reason for my request that you write to Peyser and give him a report under the not explicit but nonetheless recognizable title, "Who is Kbg?" It is not yet necessary to send out the SOS signals. But it seems right to me to keep an eye on all situations and to decide on preparations now. Despite our being taken by surprise 24 years ago [1914], as on 20th July 32 and on the 30th January 33, it now seems to me especially urgent to anticipate all eventualities.

Grete sends you her very best wishes. In about 10-12 days, a very worthy man, Dr. Epler, will presumably contact you. I ask you to receive him with your usual amiability. He is a piano student whom I have befriended, who, however, has never gotten beyond the very first of beginners' steps, but all the more movingly exerts himself. I always say about him that the teacher's art first reveals its quality when faced with an ungifted student. Admittedly, to date, I have shown nothing.

With all best regards,

Your Leo

69. KBG to FWB — 1938.07.31

70. 1938.08.21 — FWB (Zurich) to Kbg -

[typed]

The Beidlers
Zurich 7: 21 August 1938,
134, Klosbachstrasse.

Dear, very esteemed Professor,

once again you have put us to shame with your diligence, with which we cannot compete. And beyond that, you have sent us many kind and important letters! Most sincere thanks. I was again ill. But things are getting better now and you should at least receive a few lines right away.

May the student allow himself a word of criticism? Your essay for Herbert Peyser is magnificent. It has only one mistake — that he will not read it. Newspaper people do not have time for such things. But that does not matter: I will be seeing him here in Zurich in a few days and shall "actuate whatever is necessary." He wrote favourably about me and my lecture, beyond all expectations, as if it were a manifesto of secular significance! I point that out only in order to show you just how much he can be relied upon.

I shall reply "officially" with reference to the review of the report on the Congress of 1936 in "*Mass und Wert*" as soon as I have the report.

Dr. Epler paid us a visit and made a good impression, at least on me (Frauchen is more critical).[1] I gave it some effort to be as nice as possible because he is your student. Nevertheless, what I find questionable is the commendatory, smug, even admiring way that Jews today often talk about the current Germany! For a contrast, you should hear the Viennese correspondent for one of our largest newspapers! It does you good and would not be unhealthy for you either: for I begin to shake my head when I hear from you about a "battle against over-intellectualism." Only one thing is needed today: new enlightenment, rationalism. And if this does not harmonize with "artistic issues," (which I energetically dispute), the whole of Art should just go to hell for a certain amount of time! By the way, I believe that, in my book review of "Wagner the Revolutionary" [*Der revolutionäre Wagner*], I demonstrated how "the suspicious neighbourhood" can be unmasked and brought back to what it is and to its origins! The effect is excellent and courage is known to produce more courage. (On the other hand, I also shall take the Hallgartens and consorts in hand soon!)

---

[1] Beidler often used the affectionate term "Frauchen", little wife, for Ellen.

It goes without saying that we are following with great anxiety the situation in and around Czechoslovakia. Admittedly what game is being played can only be suspected. In particular, we are not at all able to judge how the situation is developing for you personally. Alright — we shall also speak about this in detail with Herbert Peyser.

Greull is here again. Unfortunately, I am unable to be of help to him in any way.

Please give our best regards to Mr. Jindra. Congratulate him on his recovery and thank him for the photograph — a gracious attentiveness that gave us much joy.

The beautiful house-and-bed-shoes! Imagine, they did not turn up here! Could it be that you did not pack them? It is virtually impossible that they could have gone lost here in the house.

Please give me a sign if you think that I can do anything concrete for you having to do with the chapter "preparations for the eventual case." As indicated, I shall deal with Peyser. Otherwise, at the moment, my hands are tied, as are yours, most likely, as well. Still, it can "start" any day. But sitting-on-the-powder-keg has become a habit so much that there seems no harm in it any longer. And if it gets serious, you do know where you are expected, right off.

To all of you, regards, kisses and tender hugs!

70. FWB to KBG — 1938.08.21

71. 1938.10.05 — Kbg (Prague) to Beidlers (Zurich)

[handwritten]

Background:

This letter, coming only five days after the shameful signing of the Munich Agreement, is full of worry and even panic. As Kestenberg knew only too well, as did the Czechs around him, their country was finished, betrayed by the Western Powers and about to be cannibalized by the surrounding countries, especially Germany. As Kestenberg described it, "In so many words, I was informed that I should leave the country as swiftly as possible. A small sum of money was handed to me in order to make the transition into a renewed exile as easy as possible."[1] One of his few hopes at the moment was Beidler. Whether Beidler could get Kestenberg permission to enter the USA as a refugee was much in doubt.

5. X. 38

My dear friends! "I shout to you out of the depths of distress!"[2]

---

[1] Kestenberg, *Bewegte Zeiten*, 94.

[2] Aus tiefer Not schrei ich zu Dir – Luther chorale, 1524 – Psalm 130 – set to music by J.S.Bach, Mendelssohn, Max Reger.

This word is engraved on every visage in our Czechoslovakia and directed at all "humans" beyond our puddle-borders. — Our board has resolved that the international activity of our SHV, which, up to now has been so generously enabled by our land alone, will be moved as soon as possible to the U.S.A. I am therefore forced to commence the necessary immediate steps there to acquire an affidavit or a different form of entry and to find a basis for a livelihood for Grete and me and also for a continuation of our work. Could you help me in this? The first thing would probably be an urgent appeal to Herb. F. Peyser, who absolutely would have to write something now, and who could use his connections to the maximum on our behalf and with all decisiveness. And the second would be an immediate letter that you should write to Thomas and Katja Mann. I assume with certainty that they are in touch with official and artistically-minded authorities, who can place a high value on the continuation of our work. It would be of special value right now to the U.S.A. in particular. — Please write me immediately to say if you have undertaken anything!

With all best greetings Your LeoKbg

71. KBG to FWB — 1938.10.05

72. 1938.10.06 — FWB (Zurich) to Kbg -

[typed]

The Beidlers
Zurich 7: 6 October 1938,
134, Klosbachstrasse.

Beloved Friends,

before and instead of all other remarks, only the declaration that we have experienced and suffered every phase of these disgraceful days and weeks the same as you.

So it is now here, the expected letter which merely draws the self-evident conclusions. We rejoice that it speaks with the same will that we have and hold: to stand our ground, no matter what! Even if, in the near future, things should get grievously bitter for all of us and if perhaps, in Europe, things are made completely impossible at times. At times! Let us think of Lafayette and Mirabeau!

To the point: I shall write immediately to

Herbert F. Peyser
Thomas [Mann]
Damrosch.

Peyser wanted to wait for a newsworthy reason to write something. Now he has one!

I think it is not necessary to say that you absolutely must contact both Mrs. Samaroff-Stokowska [Olga] and Mr. [Leopold Stokowski], who attended the Prague congress as representative of the New York Times. Both have been described by Peyser as especially important and influential.

I am enclosing the *Neue Zürcher* [newspaper] so that you can see how at least the prestigious Swiss organs are calling a spade a spade (no, I shall send it separately as printed matter so that you will receive this letter, come what may). Cold comfort, and, seen from here, more a "national justification."

a thousand profound greetings!

72. FWB to KBG — 1938.10.06

72a. 1938.10.12 — FWB (Zurich) to Peyser

[typed]

Franz W. Beidler
Zurich 7: 12 October 1938,
134, Klosbachstrasse.

Dear Mr. Peyser,

Without a doubt, during the last weeks, you and Mr. Hayes have had so exactly the same feelings as we have, that I need not waste many words on it. Suffice to say that we old pacifists have come so far as no longer to be able to hear the word "peace" without puking, so reversed and lied into its opposite the word has become. This "peace" will bring us to the point where people with our cast of mind will soon not be able to keep going any longer in Europe because the new "Holy Alliance" of the bourgeoisie is suffocating and gagging us, if not something worse. We would never have dreamed that we one day would become one with the opinions of the die-hards. But in this squalid old "continent" everything has become perverted!

Outside of saying hello and letting off steam, the purpose of this letter and its content is to utter a cry for help! Not for us (not **yet**!), but for our mutual and like-minded friend, **Kestenberg**. There is not the slightest need for me to tell you what the consequences of the Czech "realignment" are for his work and existence: he will, of course, be slaughtered and thrown to the Germans as a victim. Yes, things have gone so far that he can no longer hold his ground in Prague and already, in the next days, will be coming to Paris with his delightful, magnificent, and valiant wife. (His address: 102, rue de Grenelle, VIIe, chez M. et Mme Hugo Simon).

It would be a crying shame if his work, begun with so much hope in the arena of democratic, humanitarian music education, could not be continued. Admittedly, I no longer see even the slightest possibility of this in Europe. What remains! Your enviable, immense country, which is becoming more and more cherishable, from everything that I hear and read (as far as that is possible, since my fellow-feeling was always very great).

Conclusion: is it possible to help "transfer" our friend to the USA? Would it, for instance, be possible, to make use of the current events and draw attention to the fact that among the sad consequences of the Czech catastrophe in the cultural area, is the impossibility of continuing the work of that Prague Society of which, in every respect, Leo Kestenberg was the *spiritus rector*?

In the case of many an immigrant to the USA, I inwardly ask myself if they will be of value for your land and come – alas! – often enough to a negative conclusion. Kestenberg is an enormous exception. This highly cultivated man, whose wealth of ideas is virtually inexhaustible, personifies the entire spirit of a European musical culture which already no longer exists. Without a doubt, it will be possible to put his great experience, especially in the area of organization, to good use in the reforms in public education which apparently are being carried out in the USA in the most broadminded way. And although he was Busoni's student, thank goodness that he did not share Busoni's arrogant attitude to America, which particularly disgusted me in his "Letters to his Wife."

But I have already written much too much; for you know all this at least as much as I do, if not much better. And I know, in any case, that you are certain to to everything that is within your power.

There is not much to tell about us. We are working very hard, dedicating all available time to the book which is slowly growing and will be very malicious.[1] At the end of the week, we are going to spend a few days in the mountains, in an effort to recover a bit from the atrocities of the recent past. In the meantime, what have you undertaken and gotten to know?

with the most sincere greetings to you both,

from your old

72a. FWB to Peyser — 1938.10.12

[1] In the event, the parts of the book which were completed were in no way malicious. The overwhelming impression left by Beidler's writing is of a granite-solid work, fair and objective, and therefore also fair but critical.

72b. 1938.10.13 — FWB (Zurich) to Katia Mann -

[typed]

Youngsters

Zurich 7: 13 October 1938,
134, Klosbachstrasse.

Dear, most highly esteemed Frau Katia,

to you, I need not waste many words about our present and recent "mood." It would seem that the guessable providence will spare us nothing at all: the most dangerous possibility, propagated for years by Benito, with his splendiferous Four-Power Pact, could now be realized: the Holy Alliance of the European upper and feudal classes, reinforced by the German and Italian mastiff, which, may be let loose, as needed, on recalcitrants. The perspectives for the immediate future are therefore not rosy. The pressure is increasing from day to day. The German press has already assaulted Switzerland, screaming that it is the "paradise for warmongers in the heart of Europe" (!) — simply because the Swiss newspapers permitted themselves to find that the "peace" that we received was not necessarily of a sort that must be applauded. It is not hard to predict that the courage of a small country will not last over the long term: from within and without, they will see to it that people gradually will famously come back down to earth and — shut up, seemingly the most comfortable way of self-adaptation. And that means that we shall soon be completely gagged in our noble continent.Then, it will be time to follow certain examples — not to appear to be too arrogant, that of Lafayette or Mirabeau, with the intention and even the certainty: to come back at the given hour.

This letter is a cry for help. For now, not for us. But for a victim of the "peace": **Kestenberg**. Let me briefly recapitulate facts: on his initiative a "Society for Music Education" was founded in Prague with the goal of encouraging international co-operation in this cultural area in the spirit of democracy and humanism. In a short time, much was achieved, precisely through the active participation of anglo-saxon circles, among others. The outcome of the goals set by the Society is the fate of this Society and, along with it, the personal fate of Kestenberg. He has already been sacrificed to the Czech "realignment"; in other words, "slaughtered" for the Germans. Apparently, things already have gone so far that he can no longer even survive in Prague: at any rate, he is already on the way to Paris with his magnificent wife.

I see no possibility of his continuing his work anywhere in Europe. There is only one: to the USA! With many immigrants to this beloved land the question unfortunately often arises, whether they will be an asset, and often enough recently, inwardly, I have come to a negative conclusion. With Kestenberg, thank goodness, this is different. In fact, I am convinced that his great experience, combined with his almost inexhaustible wealth of ideas, can be put to use (excuse this "materialistic" word) in the service of assigned functions which the USA presently is undertaking in the area of art and public education. And despite being a student of Busoni's, he sensibly does not share, in any way, the former's arrogance with respect to everything American. I should think that, if there is room for a Hallgarten or even a little Kurt Rosenfeld,[1] that must also be the case of a man who, in his field, virtually personifies the best intellectual traditions of the now shattered Europe.

Now the big plea: do you see a possibility of approaching a crucial authority on behalf of your fellow-countryman? We read about a "Committee to Save Czechoslovakia." Since there is absolutely no longer anything more to save there, could it not perhaps change its goal to saving valuable people who are now or otherwise condemned to destruction? But you know about all this much better and anyway, I know of you that you will do everything that is within your power. The main thing is that entry be made possible for him. This resourceful and extraordinarily adroit brain will take care of everything else, on its own. If he could first have a chance to present his intentions to official authorities, then he will have won the game — this is the way it always was. A thousand profound thanks in advance.

In these weeks we had a curious kind of consolation: we said to each other, perhaps this new shock will lead us again, as half a year ago, to "diary skimming" [*Tagebuchblättern*], and if that should be the case, then we would like to endure everything that was and that is yet to come. Apart from that, we are very diligent and let all the wrath and poison of the "sublime grandmother" stand us in good stead. What luck that your dear mother will never set eyes on the book! Must it be said, that we miss you? I believe: no. Because now as ever, belonging to your household and personal effects

the [youngsters]

72b. FWB to Katia Mann — 1938.10.13

---

[1] Kurt **Rosenfeld** - (1877-1943) - Socialist politician and lawyer. He was a member of the Reichstag (parliament) 1920-1932. In 1931, he defended Carl von Ossietzky in the *Weltbühne* case. When the Nazis came to power, he fled to Paris where he founded an anti-fascist news agency. He then emigrated to the USA where he led German anti-Hitler groups.

73. 1938.10.23 — Kbg (Paris) to Beidlers (Zurich)

[handwritten]

Background:

Kestenberg and his wife departed Prague by plane on October 15, leaving his daughters, son-in-law, and mother behind. On the way, their plane had a problem that almost caused them to have to land in Germany. Fortunately, they made it to Strassburg, from where they continued on to Paris. Like Beidler, Kestenberg met with immediate success when he suggested continuing the work of his international organization, this time in France. Unfortunately, of all the enthusiastic Parisians with whom talked, not one mentioned how Kestenberg might be remunerated. Once again, like Beidler, Kestenberg had to eliminate France as a place of exile and work.

Another possibility had begun to open for Kestenberg in August. In 1936, the great violinist, Bronislaw Huberman had formed a Palestine Orchestra made up of leading Jewish musicians from all over Europe who had lost their jobs because of anti-Semitic persecution. The man who had been manager of the orchestra from its inception, Dr. Heinrich Simon, wrote Kestenberg on August 21, to inform him that he had to leave Palestine and asking if Kestenberg might be interested in taking over as his successor with the orchestra. On August 26, Kestenberg had answered that he wanted to remain loyal to his organization and to the Czechs who had taken him in after the Nazi takeover in Germany.

The Munich catastrophe changed everything. On October 12, Huberman wrote to Kestenberg inviting him to his home on Lake Geneva for further discussions. These talks led to Kestenberg agreeing to travel to Palestine to get to know the land and its orchestra.

Huberman's achievement is one of the signal accomplishments of Judaism during the time of the Third Reich. With astounding foresight, Huberman determined that the whole of the Jewish population of Europe was threatened by the crescendo of Nazi fanaticism. He watched in anguish as Jewish musicians were dismissed from their orchestras. Partially as a way of helping the best of these musicians, partially to show that Jews could fight back against international depravity, Huberman put his concert career on hold and began auditioning musicians for an orchestra that he would bring together in Palestine. It became known as the Palestine Symphony Orchestra.

The first conductor of the orchestra was Arturo Toscanini, who led the orchestra during its first season, from December 26, 1936 into January, 1937. The inaugural concert in Tel Aviv was attended by 3,000 entusiasts, including the British High Commissione Arthur Wauchope, Chaim Weizmann, David Ben Gurion, and Golda Meir. The concert was broadcast throughout the world and, under Toscanini's leadership, made a strong statement about the strength of Jews to retain their culture despite the attempts of the The Third Reich to snuff them out.

It was not lost on people throughout the world that Toscanini, who had cancelled his contract to perform at the Bayreuth Festival in 1933, meant his appearance in Palestine as a strong gesture of support for Jews everywhere and a gesture of defiance against fascism. Fascists took notice in early 1936 when the Maestro's plan to travel to Palestine was announced. Beidler's aunt Daniela Thode wrote to a friend on March 7, 1936: "I hope that [Toscanini's] trip to Palestine is just a poisonous newspaper hoax. I wish it for the sake of the dignity of his beloved name."[1] Reacting to Toscanini's success in Palestine, Daniela wrote to on January 29, 1937:

> Sadly, through his headstrong eccentricity, He [Toscanini] has done himself great harm in the eyes of favourably-disposed people. I am frequently asked if he is a Jew!! But, caught in the snares of the Jews, he allowed himself to be dragged into this dismal affair, making music with Jews for Jews at the very moment when Jewish Bolshevism is terrorizing the whole world, in the land where they crucified the Saviour!! I have suffered for Him. And you know how sincerely well-disposed I am to noble and good Jews and that I deeply deplore the unjust naz. soc. [Nazi] action against them![2]

Daniela's comments show once again that Richard Wagner and his family (including Daniela) were able to tolerate the existence of Jewish friends on a limited, individual basis. For the rest of the Jews as a mass, Daniela saw the Jewish mission in life as self-destruction (or liquidation by other means).[3]

Huberman managed to save a thousand Jews, musicians and non-musicians from being gassed and incinerated. The orchestra he founded continued as a monument to Jews' refusal to self-destroy, as an ethical reminder to people like Daniela Thode that their intolerance was rejected by ethical paragons like Arturo Toscanini. Daniela was a good

---

[1] RWA

[2] RWA

[3] cf. Wagner's message to the Jewish people at the end of *Judaism in Music* (1869): "But keep in mind, only one thing can be your redemption for the curse which weighs upon you: Ahasverus' redemption — extinction." (*Das Judenthum in der Musik*, vol.5, p.85)
cf. Wagner's reaction, as reported by Cosima, to a theatre fire. TCW II, p.852, Dec. 17, 1881: "That 416 Israelites perished in the fire does not increase R.'s sympathy for the accident. … Dec.18, 1881: "He says, joking ferociously, all the Jews should be incinerated in a performance of Nathan." [Lessing's play *Nathan der Weise* which centres on a Jew]

woman who had suffered the ethical misfortune of growing up in the house of Richard Wagner. Obviously, Huberman's orchestra and its first conductor tweaked her conscience. That Leo Kestenberg became part of this great institution was yet another milestone in his life's voyage, one that was difficult for him but one with which he made a significant contribution to the survival and development of his people.

23. X. 38

My dearest friends! Our departure from Prague by airplane was relatively well-managed. Half contented and half in desperation, we left behind Ruth and Tunja, Grandma, and Rahel and everything having to do with the SHV. Our first days in Paris have been filled with many discussions. All of these are about securing employment and are shaping up well. We were invited to Peyser's for tea, with many other people. The main thing, however, is the invitation (to a discussion) with Huberman[1] in Vevey, which presumably will take place on Wednesday or Thursday, the 27th of the month. And if it is at all possible, I want to go from Vevey to Geneva, to Jaques-Dalcroze and to Zurich to you, to go to Miss Scheiblauer and to the other Zurich friends. But since the Paris matters must now be pursued with high pressure, there unfortunately is little time for these complex plans. I am giving you notice of all this so that you will not be surprised if I show up during the next days. Essentially, right now, understandably, I fervently long for you and I would be pleased if you could welcome me at the Zurich train station. Grete, who, after all the turmoil has become afflicted by a painful case of shingles on her leg, is jealous that I can see you again so soon and she would urgently wish that you come to Paris before the further changes that may be imminent for us. But I hope to discuss all of that with you, face-to-face.

Profoundest greetings and to a good reunion,

Your

Leo

73. KBG to FWB — 1938.10.23

---

[1] Bronislaw **Huberman** - (1882-1947) - Jewish Pole, violin virtuoso. He was one of the most celebrated violinists of his time. In 1937, a year before the Nazi invasion of Austria, he moved from Vienna to Switzerland. In 1936, Huberman had founded the Palestine Philharmonic Orchestra, which was inaugurated in December of that year by Arturo Toscanini. Huberman and this orchestra proved to be the miracle which saved Kestenberg and his family from the Nazi pogrom against all of Jewry.

74. 1938.11.03 — Kbgs (Paris) to Beidlers (Zurich) — [handwritten]

Paris VII, 31 rue Vaneau Hotel de Suède

Mailing Address: 102 rue de Grenelle ℅ Hugo Simon

3 November 38

My beloved friends! The few hours that I recently spent with you and at your place still warm me now with the fervor of your spirits, which, in this cold world, is doubly deserving of thanks. I have talked about you a lot here and you will soon come to feel the effect of these enthusiastic vibrations, which applied especially to your book embryo, when Annette Kolb[1] and Hugo Simon visit Zurich. My efforts to continue my work in Paris continue indefatigably, despite the fact that I am supposed to travel to Palestine on the 22nd of this month on the "Patria." No responses have arrived from our colleagues in the U.S.A. And I have not yet been able to effect an appointment, despite my having phoned him repeatedly. Please write to Director Scheffner of the *Musée de l'homme*! I want to visit his co-worker, Mlle Claude Marcell-Dubois[2] shortly, who knows me and has also worked with Prof. Curt Sachs. Very best

unfortunately at the moment rushed greetings from your

LKbg

[Grete Kestenbderg to Beidlers]

My dear friends,

everything is so eventful that the days just trickle away — I remain constantly behind schedule, otherwise you would have heard a word or two from me and received my thanks for so many beautiful Swiss chocolates, you tempters! Leo came home so delighted by you. I hope that the day soon will come when I too can see you again for once. For the time being, however, it looks as if the winds will be blowing us far away from each other. And if only it were only the winds! But my heart, you know it, always remains near you and beats with yours – today more than ever. Farewell and you are embraced and kissed by your old Grete K.

74. KBG+Grete to FWB — 1938.11.03

---

[1] Annette **Kolb** - (1870-1987) - Anna Mathilde Kolb was a German writer. Her father was an illegitimate offspring of a Wittelsbacher; Kolb included aristocrats and high-society in many of her novels. In 1933, she emigrated to France; in 1936, she became a French citizen. In 1941, she fled to New York. After the war, she lived in Paris, Munich, and Badenweiler.

[2] Claudie **Marcel-Dubois** - (1913-1989) - After studying music, ethnology, and Asian archaeology, she joined the staff of the Trocadero Ethnology Museum (Musée de l'Homme) in 1934. She became the soul of the phonothèque and other departments 1937-1981.

75. 1938.11.08 — Kestenbergs (Paris) to Beidlers (Zurich)
[telegram]

Paris 11-8-08,35

Zch 08 XI 38 10 08

beidler 134
klosbachstrasse zurich

visit bonnet tomorrow write him immediately

kessenberg [sic]

75. Kestenbergs (Paris) to Beidlers — 1938.11.03

75a. 1938.11.08 — FWB (Zurich) to Henri Bonnet
[typed in French]

Zurich 7^{e} : 8 November 1938,
134, Klosbachstrasse.

Monsieur
Henri Bonnet,
Director of the I.I.C.I.
2, rue de Pontpensier,
Palais Royal
Paris 1^{e}

Dear Sir,

permit me, after an interval of silence that was too long, to address you and to draw your attention to the fact that my former director, **Kestenberg**, is presently residing in Paris and will certainly not fail to present himself to you. From 1933 on, he succeeded in creating an organization for international cooperation in the area of musical education, an organization with permanent headquarters in Prague. As a result of the tragic and disastrous events of last September, this weakened capital has ceased completely from constituting a centre favourable to an action integrally based on collective ideas of humanism and democracy. As a result, Mr. Kestenberg, whose inexhaustible activity I admire, is seeking to find new headquarters. Would it be possible for you to procure for him your precious advice? If it were possible on this occasion to coordinate the action corresponding to the special area of the general organization for intellectual cooperation, the advantages which could result seem evident.

Spreading cognizance of certain works and effort of the I.I.C.I. in our Zurich newspaper is something that ranks among my projects for the immediate future. It might occur that I might once again take the liberty of inconveniencing you in order to obtain more directly some information which, perhaps, is not sufficiently published, and I offer you my apology in advance.

With the most exquisite memory alive in me of the illustrious director of the I.I.C.I., I beg you, Monsieur, to believe in my inalterable sentiments and to accept the assurances of my perfect and unending attachment.

75a. FWB to Bonnet — 1938.11.08

76. 1938.11.08 — Beidler (Zurich) to Kestenberg – *[typed]*

The old Beidlers
Zurich 7: 8 November 1938,
134, Klosbachstrasse.

Beloved Friends,

Leo's telegram arrived at 10:45, at 11 Ellen called Franz at the office, at 2pm a posh-perfect French letter was on its way by airmail. These rotten times discipline one to un-beidlerish promptness, but not just that: if it were not about Leo and Grete, who knows if B's would function in this way?

Henri Bonnet is always very much for propaganda. *En passant*, I held out the prospect of reporting soon in the *Neue Zürcher* about some works and efforts of his institute. I hope that this will not fail to have its effect. Whether the letter has arrived in time, that is before your meeting, I can, of course, not guarantee.

On the other hand, I have simply not yet gotten to writing to Schaeffner, because now, of all times, I have been having damned harried days. But tomorrow, despite everything, I want to send off the letter. Friday or Saturday, Madame Dietz will be on the order paper: she is probably not yet *à la campagne*.

As far as you can find time, we are naturally happy to hear about all progress and success (about which we here do not harbour even the shadow of a doubt). But better still, always first use "*tachles*" [yiddish: straight talk] and only then start reporting. So: we shall be patient, no doubt. But: a thousand sincere thanks for your kind, kind letters since our reunion — as such, they did a world of good.

Thursday, we shall see and hear Annette Kolb. Hugo Simons' extraordinarily friendly letter caused me some embarrassment for reasons of nationality and neutrality. But together we shall find a way out. The objection that the Swiss also belong to the BND does not carry much weight in the face of names such as Abegg and Emil Ludwig. And I am not enthralled at the prospect of supplying to our indigenous Nazis weapons that are all too cheap. But, as I say, we shall see what can be arranged. Would you be so kind as to make my excuses to H. Simon for not yet replying?

Our thoughts are always with you, which at the same time means: with Ruth and Tunja, Rahel and Grandma. As soon as we have "done" something, and therefore are permitted to write, please repeat today's procedure which succeeded well! Always yours:

76. FWB (Zurich) to KBG (Paris) — 1938.11.08

77. 1938.11.09 — Kbg (Paris) to Beidlers (Zurich)

[typed]

XI. 38.

My dear friends,

early yesterday I telegraphed you and asked you to write to Henri Bonnet, whom I visited this morning. When I was with him, he had not yet received your letter; he did tell me, however, that he had heard a lot about me through you. B. was very charming. But, like all French people, he assured me that there was hardly any possibility of finding financial resources for the continuation of our work. B. will have the plan officially raised in the I.I.C.I. Coeuroy will make the presentation, since he has known and valued my work for a long time.

Equally interesting is, however, an answer to a very modest and polite letter that I sent to Chantavoine after my discussion with you. Since C. still writes in Minstrel [*Ménestrel*, a French music publication], I should not like to annoy him in any way and answer rudeness with rudeness. But you should consider if it might possibly be advisable for you, to comment on this letter in your usual genteel manner. But perhaps the right thing is to leave it completely ignored.

Every day I pursue my affairs further with a success that varies from day to day. In the end, I do hope that my optimism will also prevail in Paris.

I ask you again to write to Scheffner. A thousand profound thanks, also from Grete,

Your
LeoKbg

1 enclosure.

77. KBG (Paris) to FWB (Zurich) — 1938.11.09

77a. 1938.11.07 — Leon Chantavoine (Mussy) to KBG (Paris)

[typed]

Copy

Mussy -sur- Seine
(Aube)

7.XI.38

Dear Professor!

Returned from a short trip, your valued letter came to my attention only today.

I am truly sorry to hear that, once again, you had to emigrate. In my opinion, however, you should not permit yourself to think of settling in Paris: first, Paris is a quite thankless place for your project; second, the massive immigration by foreign Israelites in the last years has already caused a developing anti-Semitism, which is growing from day to day and which one must count on if people in France want to avoid German or Italian conditions. Perhaps you can best find your fortune in Palestine or America. In the hope of still being able to greet you in Paris at the next opportunity (but when?….), I am, highly esteemed Professor, with best regards

most respectfully yours

signed Leon Chantavoin.

77a. Chantavoine to KBG — 1938.11.07

78. 1938.11.16 — Beidler (Zurich) to Kestenberg (Paris) -
[typed]

Beidlers

Zurich 7: 16 November 1938,
134, Klosbachstrasse.

Dear, dear Leo[1],

the following can be said in the case of Chantavoine: he was always ultra-reactionary. It seems that because of that he has had the bad luck of being pensioned off early (French pensions are slim; as Chantavoine himself told us, he cannot live in Paris from his pension but only in the country). Who to blame for this? The government of the Front populaire [a leftist coalition]. So, he has become a fascist, ever more openly and clearly. And since Protestant through and through and therefore already more easily amenable to anti-Semitism, he forgets that he himself was largely "made" and advanced by Jews and has joined the ranks of the bitter and cantankerous. A completely natural process, albeit sad, ugly and small, but unchangeable. I have long let relations with him go dormant; there would be no purpose to challenge him now. On the other hand, I did mention this to Schaeffner, to whom I finally sent a long letter yesterday heralding your visit.

We are keeping track of the situation in France but, generally, with great apprehension and pessimism. You see this brutal program of social reaction that Reynaud[2] has now presented! And there are also other very ugly signs of Fascism advancing. Add to this the enormous position of Jews in the economy and science, which, is continuously referred to by the Germans with diabolical precision and systematic method. All things considered, we increasingly tend <u>not</u> to view France as an appropriate base for you plans of reconstruction; rather, we are thinking much more strongly of a combination of Palestine and the USA. — Of course, you will be able to judge this better on-site, but we did not want to keep silent about our concerns. In addition, in the artistic area, France is so little open-minded to the sort of ideas that you represent, that obstructions would have to arise at every turn.

You will know and share our frame of mind in these days. Apart from the general

---

[1] By now, Beidler and Kestenberg were on a first-name basis. [*Duzfreunde* in German]

[2] Paul **Reynaud** - (1878-1966) - He was a French politican of the Centre-Right Party and was the next-to-last Prime Minister in the Third Republic. He was strong in his opposition to Nazi Germany but had a laissez-faire attitude to business and deregulation (he wanted to eliminate the 40-hour week.)

situation, we are worried and uninformed about several members of Ellen's [Frauchens] family. It will be the same for you. And what in the world can anyone say about that? There is a constant feeling of suffocation. Nonetheless, I have a feeling that tells me: enough will soon be more than enough! But then come the reprobates who stand behind the "Times" and destroy all the vague hopes. And the visit of Mr. Pirow[1] .... But for all that, the wave of horror, contempt, and disgust which has now gone through the whole world, is of inestimable value and will have an horrendous impact at the moment of truth, of this we are certain!

Would you be so kind as to inform Mr. Simon that Dr. Oprecht[2] recently tried in vain to reach him in Paris. Oprecht asks him to call, in the event that he comes to Zurich.

When does your crossing start? On Nov.27 will you already have a land address or will it be necessary to send [birthday] congratulations to the ship?

As I promptly informed you, I wrote in detail to Bonnet. Support for your plan by his institute should not be scorned even if France, as such, is judged so unfavourably at the moment, for instance by us.

To you both, greetings, kisses, and hugs!

78. FWB (Zurich) to KBG (Paris) — 1938.11.16

---

[1] Oswald **Pirow** - (1890-1959) - South African lawyer and rightwing politician, Minister of Justice and Minister of Defence after that. He toured Europe in 1938, making clear his great admiration for Hitler and Mussolini. He wanted to make South Africa into a one-party state dictatorship, no doubt with himself as a Hitler clone.

[2] Emil **Oprecht** - (1895-1952) - Swiss bookseller and publisher. During WWII, Oprecht turned his home into a resource centre for emigrants. He was very generous in his support of persecuted artists from both Germany and Italy. He published many authors-in-exile, such as Ernst Bloch, Heinrich Mann, Golo Mann, and Bernard von Brentano, among others.

79. 1938.11.25 — FWB (Zurich) to Kbg - *[typed]*

The Beidlers
Zurich 7: 25 November 1938,
134, Klosbachstrasse.

Dear, dear Leo,

the problems of the day do not encourage the writing of "beautiful" letters. On the contrary, I think, all of us will be forced to become more sparing of words, but precisely therefore more to the point perhaps, and "more hardened." One thing essential, above all: sticking together, more than ever, and single-mindedly in persevering with what we hold to be right, just, human, and good, come what will. A time in which everything is remorselessly weighed has one thing in its favour: one day it will and must be proved on which side substance is. We draw upon this conviction daily for a renewed feeling of fortitude, despite all the absurd abominations that assail us every day, and we know that it is and must be exactly the same with you! Let us enter your new year of life with you, full of good and determined confidence and profound greetings to you!

We are — collective work as ever [Ellen and Franz] — in the midst of a work about Marie d'Agoult and probably will be finished right on the 27th of November. So we will feel "objectively" twice as close, as well. As soon as it appears (*Neue Zürcher Zeitung*), we shall send it to you, of course (where to?). And yet another "birthday" matter: you are aware of my great reservations about Liszt. A few days ago, however, I again heard the E flat major concerto (as you know, it belongs to my very earliest musical impressions, because my father was crazy about it like a child and had revolutionized the Leipzig Conservatory with it, about which he had a lifelong, no less childish, pride), played by Robert Casadesus, who belongs among my ideal musicians and can turn me into a piano enthusiast, which is a demanding task. In a nutshell: I was completely carried away and found it gorgeous, grand, noble and powerful! Does that please you? And similarly, on Sunday morning, just as if it had to be that way, we heard Liszt again, for the very first time, the "Via crucis."

A thousand greetings in unending affinity
from the old
[Beidlers]

Schaeffner wrote about you and your visit exactly as I had expected — and as also was appropriate…!

79. FWB (Zurich) to KBG — 1938.11.25

80. 1939.01.08 — Kbg (Tel-Aviv) to Beidlers (Zurich)

[typed]

***Background*:**

Kestenberg boarded the Providence at Marseilles on December 7, 1938, arriving early on December 12 at Tel-Aviv. (The date of this letter indicates a discrepancy between the letter and the dates in Kestenberg's book. The letter is probably more accurate.) In his autobiography, Kestenberg recalled his feelings: "Although I had never been a Zionist, I was immediately taken with the atmosphere of the old-new land. From the very first, the work that awaited me put me in a hopeful mood." Kestenberg heard the orchestra play Beethoven's 9th and was impressed with the choir, the string section and the acoustics of the concert hall. After signing the contract on December 18, he immediately telegraphed his wife, who had remained in Paris and asked her to travel to Palestine as soon as possible (she arrived at the end of January, 1939).

The present letter shows that, right from the beginning, Kestenberg saw his removal to Palestine not as an exile but as a reawakening. He felt that he had returned to his roots, to his father, and to the Jewish literature that his father had loved. For years, and most recently, he had felt that his Judaism had been an impediment. Only six weeks previously, Chantavoine had presented this impediment to Kestenberg in the most impudent terms. Much worse was come as Hitler and his Nazis tightened the pogrom juggernaut with ever greater constriction and brutality. In Palestine, Kestenberg felt free of all this at last.

[letterhead of the Palestine Orchestra]

THE PALESTINE ORCHESTRA — התזמורת הארץ־ישראלית

DIRECTOR — מנהל
PROF. LEO KESTENBERG — פרופ' ליאו קסטנברג

TEL-AVIV, 8.I. 1939. — תל-אביב.
P.O.B. 4047 — ת. ד. 4047

8.I. 1939.

Dr. Franz and Ellen Beidler
Zurich VII.Huberman

Klosbach Str. 134

My dearest friends!

You must be among the first to whom I want to give the happy news that I have again found a foundation upon which to build my work.

When I came to you, after my visit to Huberman, I did not yet suspect what the proposal signified which Huberman made to me at the time, for he naturally spoke about his favourite problem child, the Palestine Orchestra and he mentioned nothing at all about the miracle and magic of the country. It may be that I had to become so old in order to be able to discover my love for what the land signifies.

Here, for the first time, my own childhood is coming back to life; the great Jewish literature, which my father always recommended so warmly to me, is alive; and on this foundation, my work gains a great and new meaning.

The realization is shocking to me that the vision of music education that has pursued me for decades is hardly realizable any place other than precisely here. I had difficulty to control my feelings when a young farmer from the settlement of Beth Alpha, who had come to the Huberman concert in the main settlement Ein Charod, like hundreds of other young fellows from the local *Kvuzoths*, despite Arab terrorist gangs, and told me the following: music only makes sense for him if he can bring its essence to mind again while working with his tractor or plough, if it then can help him.

This remark encompasses everything, from Plato to St. Augustine, Komensky, to Goethe. This is finally the accomplished education of humanity through music. And this farmer is no exception. It is the rule among these people who, teeming with musical activity, only have to be brought to the hearing and listening intrinsic to them in order to experience as a compelling truth the coherence between the ethics of a Beethoven symphony and that of their own old law.

I believe that what I can attain here is just that which time and again moved me over the last years: overcoming of the aesthetic category despite, or through, recognition of the original, sensual source in all things musical.

In addition to this, admittedly, for me, decisive aspect, is that the land and the people make a very great impression on me. It is exhilarating that here, I no longer need to ponder if it is opportune to relate my name to my work or if it must remain anonymous, that heads can be held high and proud, that, everywhere here, I meet old acquaintances and friends and that here my name generally also sounds good — all that is united here in making me joyful and jubilant. Once Grete is finally here, which I anticipate for the 25th of January, a new chapter in our book of life will begin, for the shaping of which, I am already preparing myself inwardly.

With that, I come now to your book and to the anxious question of how far you two finally are now. I have told all possible people about it — many know and value you and all are anxiously awaiting the ultimate result of your bee-like assiduity.

Now for a couple of requests. As you might expect, with my ministerial experience I am instituting a reorganization of the office here and I am also building up a card index meant to encompass all Jewish music and musicians, but effective modern works by Christian composers are also welcome.

I had to initiate my activity with a battle against the works of your elsewhere, rightfully celebrated Grandpapa. Many German Jews here did not want to do without their "Meistersinger," despite next to Hans Sachs, Streicher[1] also relates to Nuremberg.

If something crosses your path that seems as if it might be interesting to me, I ask you to send me a small note with clippings, addresses, everything, in short, that seems useful to our setup.

We now have Szenkar[2] here, then performances of the 9th Symphony will come — partially also for the union members who are especially in our good books here. (You

---

[1] Julius **Streicher** - (1885-1946) - He was the Gauleiter of Franconia, including Nuremberg and the founding publisher of the rabidly anti-Semitic agitprop hate-sheet, Der Stürmer. On October 16, 1946, Streicher was hung in Nuremberg.

[2] Eugen **Szenkar** - (1891-1977) - Hungarian conductor. Until 1933, he had enjoyed a thriving career as opera conductor in Germany. In 1933, he had to flee Germany for Vienna. In 1934, he moved to Moscow to conduct the state orchestra and at the Bolshoi. He was the conductor of the Palestine Orchestra 1937-1938. After that he moved to Brazil, returning to Germany (Cologne) in 1949.

should not think of Leiphart[1] in this connection.)

Then we make a tour to Egypt and later concerts with Dobrowen,[2] Sargent[3] and, we hope, Rosenstock[4] too, who just cabled me from Tokyo, basically accepting my invitation.

You see, I am once again in fullest operation, completely on my former heights and zealously facing each morning. Since mid-October, I have hardly read a newspaper and therefore have learned nothing of the disturbances which are supposed to be raging here in this land and which make themselves noticeable to me through strong contingents of English and Jewish troops.

The girls and Tunia want to go to America. Rahel has received a scholarship for the girls' division of Harvard University and is, of course, happy about that.

If you know of personalities, to whom I could turn to gain financial support or membership in the Society of Friends of our orchestra, please inform me immediately. I am writing to Damrosch but perhaps you also know of other benefactors, or those who would like to become such.

---

[1] Theodor **Leipart** - (1867-=1947) - A leading German union leader. He worked his way up to being the top man in the main umbrella organization for unions in Germany. In 1932, Leipart was the leader of 3.5 million unionists. After the Nazis came to power, Leipart pandered to the Nazis in an effort to make gains through cooperation. On April 1, 1933, the Nazi occupation of the union headquarters in Hannover should have shown Leipart the folly of his toadying. He nonetheless declared his organization neutral and called on members to participate in the Nazis-created "National Labour Day Celebration," on May 1. On May 2, union headquarters were attacked by SA thugs, union possessions robbed and unionists beaten up. In Duisburg four union secretaries were brutally murdered.

[2] Issay **Dobrowen** - (1891-1953) - born Itschok Zorachovitch Barabeitchik, he was a Jewish-Russian-Norwegian conductor, pianist, and composer. He left the USSR in 1922 and gained Norwegian citizenship in 1929.

[3] Sir Harold Malcolm Watts **Sargent** - (1895-1967) - English conductor, organist, and composer. He was co-founder of the London Philharmonic and was important in saving the Royal Philharmonic Orchestra from termination in the 1960s. Sargent was supposed to have come under fire in an ambush while in Palestine, to which Sir Thomas Beecham commented: "I had no idea that the Arabs are so musical."

[4] Joseph **Rosenstock** - (1895-1985) - Polish-Jewish conductor. He was conductor of the Berlin Jewish Cultural Alliance (Jüdischer Kulturbund), conducting the German premiere of Verdi's Nabucco, with an all-Jewish cast, in 1935. He was the conductor of the NHK Symphony Orchestra in Tokyo 1938-1946. He conducted in New York (at NY City Opera and the Met) 1948-1969.

Write soon and with the best regards

from your

happy old Leo

P.S. Please excuse the typing mistakes. Outside of the office, I employ a private secretary who is not completely perfect. She seems to have come up against big problems with our "Du" [familiar you] and "Ihr" [formal or plural you]. Next time, I shall write you an "official" letter for Peyser!

80. KBG to FWB — 1939.01.08

81. 1939.01.08 — Kbg (Tel-Aviv) to FWB (Zurich)
[typed]

[letterhead of the Palestine Orchestra]

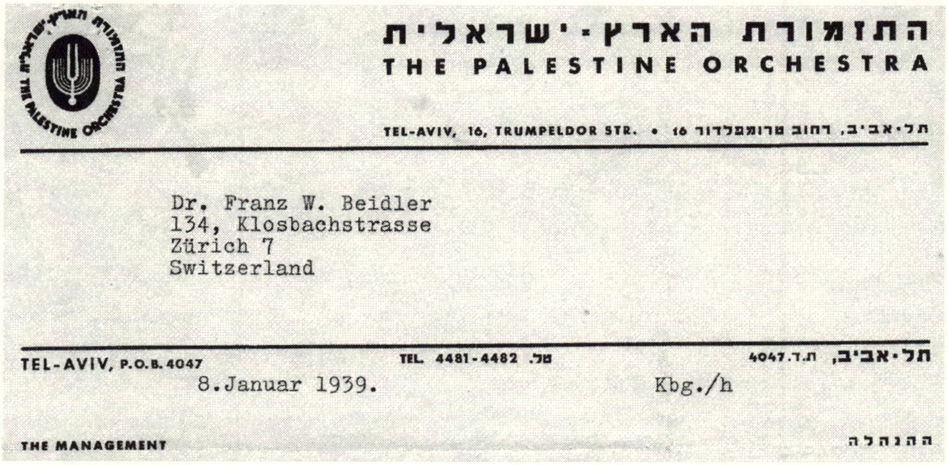

התזמורת הארץ·ישראלית
THE PALESTINE ORCHESTRA

TEL-AVIV, 16, TRUMPELDOR STR. • תל·אביב, רחוב טרומפלדור 16

Dr. Franz W. Beidler
134, Klosbachstrasse
Zürich 7
Switzerland

TEL-AVIV, P.O.B. 4047 TEL. 4481-4482 .טל תל·אביב, ת.ד. 4047

8.Januar 1939. Kbg./h

THE MANAGEMENT ההנהלה

Dr. Franz and Ellen Beidler
134, Klosbachstrasse
Zurich 7
Switzerland

8 January 1939.

My dearest friends!

As I already indicated in my last letter, we are now planning a large-scale propaganda campaign in the U.S.A. for our orchestra. We have there a very active committee, the Palestine Orchestra Fund, the treasurer of which is Mr. Sidney Matz[1] (423 Atlantic Avenue, Brooklyn, New York), and which is extraordinarily alive to the interests of our orchestra.

I would be much obliged if it would be possible for an article about our orchestra, and, more particularly, about my appointment as director of this institution to appear in

---

[1] Sidney **Matz** - (1899-1946) - Owner of the Ex-Lax Co. in America, Matz was a generous supporter of many Jewish causes, including the Palestine Orchestra. Although he died in an airplane crash in 1946 and his last testament left money to several Jewish causes, including the Palestine Orchestra, the probate was still not resolved as late as 1958.

the New York Times. For this purpose, I am also approaching Mr. Peyser to ask him to support our plan with his editor. I would be much obliged to you if you would be so very kind as to recommend to Peyser that he support our good cause. As friendly as Peyser was to me personally in Paris, in fact he has not done anything, which is not meant as a reproof, since a specific reason to write about my affairs had not yet arisen. Now, as well, he can only give us indirect help, since he is the correspondent for France and Switzerland only; Palestine is handled by a correspondent who resides here. But all the same, I believe that his recommendation would be of great value.

I am having a couple of program books sent to you so that you can form an idea of the artistic framework of our orchestra up to now.

This morning, I visited a municipal kindergarten for the first time and I cannot tell you just how happy I am at having actually found here a most musically receptive and active youth; in addition to that, despite the workers' district, all sorts of well-nourished, well-dressed and perfectly clean children; and something that should not be said out loud in order not to lessen the generosity of world Jewry: here, every kindergarten has a piano, something that, up to now, has been reported to me by no other country in the world. That is a record which makes me especially happy. The inspector, Mrs. Fayenne Glück, is an excellent teacher trained in psychology, incidentally also well-acquainted with Minni Scheiblauer, whom she visited only a couple of weeks ago.

With the warmest greetings

Your Leo Kestenberg

81. KBG to FWB — 1939.01.08

82. 1939.07.26 — Kbg (Tel-Aviv) to FWB (Zurich)
[typed]

[letterhead of the Palestine Orchestra]

26 July 1939

Dr. Franz W. Beidler
134, Klosbachstrasse
Zurich VII
Switzerland.

Dear friends!

You have not written for such a shamelessly long time that I am seriously concerned, so that I must once again urgently request that you confirm, at least with a postcard that you are, at a minimum, physically well.

I do not dare to ask about the book anymore. Only your work from time to time in the Zurich newspaper indicates that you are still there and still very keen on Wagner.

We have various things to report. Before I tell you about my work, I only want to say quickly that Tunja fled illegally to his parents in Lodz but did not receive a residence permit there and therefore is floating in danger of being sent back. We are going to great lengths here, with every means at our disposal, to obtain a study-certificate, which, however, naturally comes up against difficulties for a 34-year old; nonetheless, we hope to hold sway. Ruth is spending the holidays with us. She just has come through an appendix operation well and she feels very well here, apart from her yearning for Tunja; she is working here quite happily. Grete is very much preoccupied with household matters. A pity that you cannot see us here, how we have installed our reduced Barstrasse. And I hope finally to be able to have my mother here by August. Rahel writes reasonably amused but unreasonably interesting letters from America. With that, the register of personal news is exhausted.

I believe, in the last months, that I finally have found for myself the sense and aim of my activity here. To begin with, it seems to me that the most important prerequisite is an increasingly intimate knowledge of the land and its particular idiosyncrasies and conditions. And then, I shall become aware of the unique significance that is a given through my bond with this remarkable orchestral entity. The organizational basis which Huberman gave the orchestra seems to be copied from the best American and English models. It offers broad freedoms, without foregoing a tight structure. Through the necessity of gaining financial support from all over the world, an ever more vital flow of contacts is indispensable and this is guaranteed by the international basis within world Jewry. I should like to indicate with this that the orchestra, as well as the whole musical life that it generates, has escaped the danger of remaining a subordinate, local matter, and that we are automatically forced to reckon ourselves as decisive musical and political factors, without wanting to be self-important. Naturally, we are stuck in the conventions of customary, big-city orchestral enterprises. But I am preparing, inwardly at first, an organic transformation and development, which, naturally, must mature very carefully and slowly before it can reveal itself openly.

If, on your various nocturnal study trips, you happen upon orchestral organizations that are of interest to you and seem unusual, please notify me. I think that I already wrote to you that, from the orchestra, ways can be paved in all directions and that, initially, the road that leads to music education seems capable of expansion. My first attempts along these lines have already been made, although, admittedly, I cannot conceal that, apparently, among us Jews, personal complications that are more annoying than elsewhere must be overcome.

By the way, could you help me, without great effort, to obtain exact details about the reform of musical pedagogy that Anton Rubinstein[1] started in the 60s of the previous century, under the patronage of Grand Duchess Helene?[2] Back then, at the Petersburg Music Academy, something like a music high-school must have been established. According to the not very reliable reports of former students who live here, the students received school classes between 12 and 4, but seemingly only in elementary subjects. All the same, to Huberman the facility of that time seems to have been significant and he asked me to obtain material about it for him. I am happy that he is so actively interested in my plan for a music high school that he first wants to inform himself, with me, in order to avoid every detour.

Incidentally, do you know that, last year, an art high school was started in Frankfurt

---

[1] Anton Grigorevich **Rubinstein** - (1829-1894) - Russian-Jewish piano virtuoso, composer, conductor, and teacher. He founded the St.Petersburg Conservatory in 1862. Nikolai (1835-1881), Anton's brother, founded the Moscow Conservatory in 1866.

[2] Grand Duchess Elena **Pavlovna** of Russia - (1807-1873) - She was an enlightened reformer, progressive thinker in politics, the arts, and sciences. As a patroness of the arts, she laid great emphasis on further musicians and musical education in Russia, supporting the founding of the Conservatories of St. Petersburg and Moscow.

a.M. with special concentration on musical subjects? Perhaps Meyer-Leonhardt[1] and Bieder had a finger in the pie?

Only yesterday I received a letter from Thomas Mann which seemed so significant to me that I am including a copy for you.

The most interesting event of the last months was the visit of Hermann Scherchen, who gave 20 concerts here with unusually interesting programs. Outside of a profoundly direct rendering of Bach's Mass in B-minor, especially lasting impressions were left by Bruckner's Fourth, Schönberg's Pelleas and Melisande, but also Bach's Art of the Fugue and Beethoven's Ninth.

I am now, once again, communicating with Schönberg by letter. I am planning at some point for a Schönberg Festival with the Gurre-Lieder as the centrepiece. This contact with the world by post is a matter of personal, fierce necessity. But it is also objectively indispensable in giving our work the resonance that it must have. And with that, we come full circle; I am again at the start of my letter, which should be nothing other than a short exhortation.

With all best greetings, also from Grete and Ruth,

Your old

Leo Kbg

Encl.

82. KBG to FWB — 1939.07.26

[1] possibly Ernst **Majer-Leonhard** - (1889-1966) - German teacher, active in Frankfurt a.M. He was made director of the Lessing High School in Frankfurt in 1926, the first native Frankfurter to fill this post. While he was director, the school became one of the first in Frankfurt to admit girls as students. He was removed from his post in 1933 because he refused to go along with its nazification, continued to be friendly to Jews, and allowed a school opera by Paul Hindemith to be performed. He was forcibly retired in 1937.

83. 1939.09.18 — Kbg (Tel-Aviv) to FWB (Zurich) – *[typed]*

[letterhead of the Palestine Orchestra]

18 September 1939

Dr. Franz W. Beidler
134, Klosbachstrasse
Zurich VII
Switzerland.

Dear friends!

Despite not knowing if my letter of July 26 reached you, since I was not honoured with a reply either to that or to my earlier letters, I must impose on you in the following, vitally important matter.

My mother, who will have her 83rd birthday[1] in two days, is in possession of the official certificate issued by the English government office, the rail and ship tickets and all other documents necessary for the exit to Palestine. The recent events [beginning of World War II], however, have prevented this voyage, which she last noted in a card of August 18. Since then, we are completely without news from her and I therefore ask you urgently to write to her immediately to Prague (XII (Weinberge), Koruni 13) and to ask how she is. Otherwise, as well, I would naturally be happy to have news, through you, about her further intentions.

Tunia has been here several weeks and is already also married to Ruth. I shall write to you about everything else again only after I know that you are still there for me, if at all.

Best regards,

Your

LeoKestenberg

83. KBG to FWB — 1939.09.18

[1] Kestenberg seems to be saying that his mother's birthday was September 20, 1856. It has appeared elsewhere as Sept. 21, 1860.

84. 1939.11.28 — FWB (Zurich) to Kbg (Tel-Aviv)

[typed]

The Beidlers
Zurich 7: 28 November 1939,
134, Klosbachstrasse.

Dear Leo,

this is, I believe, the first time since we met, and it should remain the only time, that you have been left without a greeting from us on the 27th of November! As a writer who increasingly strives for anti-romantic objectivity, I find writing always something of a matter of mood, at least writing to you. To put it more generally, it is a matter of mood in writing to people with whom one is connected, not only through objective relationships but rather through a thousand imponderables, through experiences and sufferings-in-common and through the sometimes weighty tradition of certain cultural circles. As can never be avoided, the last days were days of ill humour, which did not go deep but, still the same, were enough to prevent the Leo-diapason from being adequately found. Still, we were with you yesterday more intensively than usual, and additionally, as if it was meant to be, I met Hermann Scherchen, whom I otherwise rarely see. Our talk, insofar as I was not a purely passive partner in it, centred, naturally enough, around you.

On the whole, it might be said on this birthday that you remain to me, you all remain to us what you have always been to me, you all to us. My grandfather may be frowned upon at the moment, and for me, too, he is difficult to endure. But for the "enduring value" of our relationship he did find the right, unadorned wording and, remarkably enough, put it in the mouth of a woman, Miss Pogner [Eva-Meistersinger]: "through you I conceived, such a spirit." Today as well, it remains so that everything – how should I say it? -– "is measured according to Leo," naturally also our own so-called development, and much speaks for it remaining so.

Since you want to be told, here are a few words about us. Ellen has already told you about my new military function. Beginning in January, at the latest, I must again be mustered, if the situation remains as it is now. This is, of course, not beneficial for the book, but it nonetheless is getting ever closer to its conclusion, which according to the contract with Knopf, New York, is to occur on July 1st, 1940. Apart from that, breadwinning (an official publication by me has just appeared: "Industry in Canton Zurich"; in a few days, in an assistant capacity, I shall take over the editing of a stock-exchange publication; Ellen is now completing a bibliographic work of her own about the problem of older workers and unemployed, which will also receive official publication — you see, we have remained the old Offiziosi [bureaucrats], apparently an inbred, unremovable role, since, ultimately, "the" book also raises its claim to be "official," albeit in a new sense). Finally: very many studies of a sociological and generally socioscientific nature. Only sporadic contact with music, more or less passively in an Ansermet[1] concert, actively in a discussion about the Berlioz book by Pourtalès, about which I must write and shall send you.

The feeling of sitting on fields of mines has become such a daily matter that it now makes no impression at all anymore. Truly, it is positively an alarming question if, after what is happening now has passed, people will not be too deadened to achieve anything at all positive or to help with really creative things. Despite everything, I am full of optimism, more than ever, a condition apparently connected inextricably with my well known, characteristic affinity for the superficial and one that seems firmly anchored in my "static spherical nature," as dear Ellen calls it.

Now to a question to which I have not reacted for far too long: Anton Rubinstein's music reform in the Petrograd of the 60s. I was unable to get a hold of any detailed material about this, above all because extraterritorial library traffic has been forbidden since the "war." Up to now I have not consulted Rubinstein's Memoirs which appeared in German in 1892. It seems best to me if you make direct contact with the competent authorities in the USSR, who, nowadays are so "tradition-conscious" that, without a doubt, they will give information with the greatest of pleasure and pride.

According to everything that we hear (but, since everything is propaganda, everywhere, what should and can actually be believed??), the "war" in Palestine has had a calming effect. That seems highly important for you and your tasks, for the preparation of future, larger things. The necessity of "living dangerously" just does not mix much with productive work and inner growth — we notice this with distress every day. Hence, a report about you, your works and plans and, naturally, about Grete and the happily united young married couple (how Swiss-bourgeois that sounds!) would be very welcome. "Grandmama" distresses us. Ellen wrote to her but received no answer. At present all hell is loose there. But it seems almost even worse in Poland! Ellen received her card to Tunia's sister, returned after fourteen days with the annotation: postal service discontinued. That was at the end of October! There is only one way of receiving news, perhaps, at least: the Red Cross. Therefore, Tunia should, himself, please write to the Red Cross in Geneva, because we fear that we are not sufficiently authorized to receive information. Speaking of

[1] Ernest **Ansermet** - (1883-1969) - Swiss conductor who founded the Orchestre de la Suisse Romande in 1918.

which: Winifred's[1] youngest son Wolfgang was badly wounded in Poland in mid-September but seems to be on the way to recovery. ....

Has the Schönberg Festival been postponed for the time being? How are things going financially? Is Mr. Matz still functioning well? Can we be of help, through propaganda or by naming "wealthy fellow Germans"? [*Volksgenosse* - a Nazi term] Those would be a couple of questions for which we would like to have answers.

All good wishes and warm embraces in addition!

84. FWB to KBG — 1939.11.28

[1] Winifred **Wagner** - (1897-1980) - Wife of Richard Wagner's son, Siegfried. She was an intimate of Hitler's. Nonetheless, FWB continued to like and respect her on a personal level while detesting her political allegiance to and participation in the Nazi Party and its ideology.

Wolgang **Wagner** - (1919-2010) - Winifred Wagner's younger son. He was wounded in the Nazi aggression invasion of Poland but survived. Later, after the death of his brother Wieland in 1966, Wolfgang became sole director of the Bayreuth Festival - eventually, for life.

85. 1943.09.28 – FWB (Zurich) to Kbg (Tel-Aviv)

[typed]

Zurich 7: 1943 September 28,
Schlösslistrasse 40.

Dear Leo,

as if by a stroke of magic, all at once the opportunity opens up for us to write to you once again, with the certainty that the letter will reach you! And during all those years of communications blackout, hardly a day has gone by in which we did not think of you, as a rule with great confidence - albeit with some occasional worries, such as when the Germans pushed through to Crete and Egypt, but above all with the same, unchangeable love and gratitude. During talks with you, the "eternal" is never silenced, now that the iron curtain is rising, we stand there, completely dumb and almost mute and hardly know where to begin.

So let us reach for trusted old methods do ut des [Lat.: I give so that you give] and talk briefly about us: as improbable as it sounds, we are doing well. Our small land, miraculously spared and unscathed, stands more solid and self-aware than ever as an island of peace, freedom and humanity in the midst of the hellish frenzy of madness, terror, and destruction — it is impossible to be grateful enough for this. Our small "family" has become one head larger. In April of last year, "little Ellen" - who would have thought her capable? — brought into the world a daughter, who already is making considerable demands on life. Her name is Dagny (after our friend Dagny Sautreau, the youngest daughter of Björnson).[1] "Cosima" is – not yet finished, although very advanced, of course, since the unforgettable days of your all too mild criticism. It has a period of grace up to the end of the war and, with luck and a big push, can be brought to an end soon. Half a year ago, to my great joy and satisfaction, I was elected to be Secretary of the "Swiss Writers' Association," to which I have belonged for many years. I think that you will be happy to rediscover in me a middle man between a cultural and trade union secretary. It is only now that what I learned with you and from you are bearing fruit. In the scope of my functions there is more than one parallel insofar as music is replaced by literature (which is not to say that I have become disloyal to music – on the contrary!).

I have this new function to thank for being able to write to you, through privileged means. And this is how that happened: among the most pronounced advantages of my

---

[1] Bjørnstjerne Martinius **Bjørnson** - (1832-1910) - One of Norway's great writers, winner of the 1903 Nobel Prize in Literature and author of the text of the Norwegian national anthem. His youngest daughter, Dagny, lived 1876-1974 and was a close friend of the Beidlers.

position is very close contact to Mr. Max **Altorfer**,[1] associate in the Swiss Department of Internal Affairs (translated into our terminology back then: Deputy Assistant Under-Secretary and Head of Division for Literature in the Federal Ministry of Education). In our expansive talks, Mr. Altorfer drives me from surprise to surprise because, although not much more than half as old as we are, he is at home in all regions, latitudes, and camps. Recently, we came to Barlach,[2] and it turned out that Mr. Altorfer has the most lively interest, especially for his poetic works and follows all traces that lead to this. That led us to you and to this letter, to which Mr. Altorfer apparently will attach a few lines with more precise questions. Who could know more and better than you?

You can imagine how, during this talk, I had the Barstrasse before my eyes with all the Barlachs around! May Barlach help us to hear and learn from you, that is, to put it with complete accuracy: from you, Grete, Ruth, Tunja, Rahel, Grossmama, the Palestine Orchestra, your other works and all the other proposals that you no less extravagantly disseminate as before, your co-workers and finally, from the land itself — as far as your time and patience permit, and, we hope, only good things! Last year, we made a hard and fast resolution that the celebration of your 60th birthday would have to be made up for because we were only able to celebrate it unilaterally, and now it actually seems as if the date for this could be set for some time in the foreseeable future!

A thousand greetings to you all! In old love and loyalty, as always:

Franz

85. FWB to KBG — 1943.09.28

---

[1] Max **Altorfer** - (1915-1997) - He entered the Department of the Interior in 1941 with growing cultural responsibilities. He was director of the Federal Culture Office 1975-1980.

[2] Ernst **Barlach** - (1870-1938) - German expressionist sculptor, poet, and artist. Before he became widely recognized, he was given a fixed salary by the art dealer Paul Cassirer, a friend of Kestenberg's. Much of Barlach's work presented anti-war themes, something that the Nazis took as adequate reason to persecute him. See mention and note in Introduction.

86. 1945.07.11 — Kbg (Tel-Aviv) to FWB (Zurich)

[handwritten]

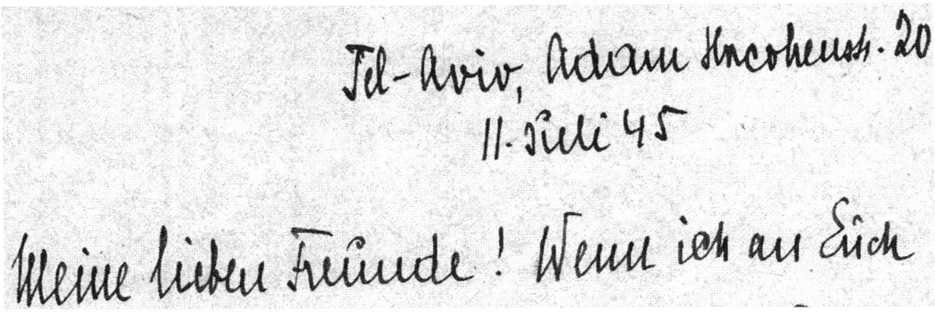

Tel-Aviv, Adam Hacohenstr. 20
11. Juli 45

Meine lieben Freunde! Wenn ich an Euch

11 July 45

Dear friends! When I think of you, I am once again in the magic circle of Wagner and at this moment, I am feeling tense about whether my questioning call will receive an answer. After the miracle of our rescue, and the miracle here in the country, I have become such a believer in miracles that I also believe in the miracle of receiving a reply from you. I hardly need to say how much we would rejoice in receiving some sort of sign or other from you. Precisely at our age and in our situation, we are especially inwardly united with our old friends and we would be very happy if we could receive news from you soon. — At the beginning of this year I resigned from the Palestine Orchestra, because I no longer felt fulfilled by the administrative activity. Now I am again very happy as the leader of a seminar for music teachers and as a private piano teacher. Gretchen is already a full Palestinian, Ruth is expecting a baby in the next weeks, Tunia is working wonderfully at a very effective training centre for apprentices and Rahel has married and has been in Sao Paolo (Brazil) for 3 months. — But the main thing is for us to learn how you are both doing and what you did during all that time. What is doing with the Cosima book? Write immediately With our warmest regards

Leon and Grete Kestenberg

86. KBG to FWB — 1945.07.11

87. 1946.01.20 — FWB (Zurich) to Kbg (Tel-Aviv)

[typed]

Zurich 7: 20 January 1946,
Klosbachstrasse 106.

Dear Grete, dear Leo, all you dears, unique, sorely missed,

finally, finally I find the strength to write to you. Could you imagine me without my little Ellen? I, myself, cannot, and that is why, since her death, I am broken, hardly a shadow of my self.

After it happened, I sent you, without comment, but expressive enough, an obituary notice. Now you want to know how it came about. Starting with a dental problem, Ellen had a festering and spreading jaw inflammation and frontal sinusitis. Despite treatment and – it goes without saying – general medical supervision, this inflammation transmuted out of the blue and, at first, incomprehensibly into an *Encephelatis acuta haemorrhagica*, which, despite all medication (penicillin, among others) in less than three days, led, like a thunderbolt, to her death. The autopsy then brought the explanation of the inexplicable: what we all, including her doctors, had no suspicion of, was that Ellen was suffering from a thyroid cancer which, in relatively short time (about 6 months) would have led to a terribly tormented end. Because of this carcinoma, her body's defence mechanisms were already so paralyzed that it was possible for an essentially harmless infection to lead to death. All the doctors, in unison, call it a merciful stroke of fate; for Ellen was not conscious of her end and did not have to suffer much. Everyone wants to find consolation in that. I cannot. You know best what I have lost: my better me, my memory, my conscience, the bravest, truest, best of all friends.

With our almost unique cohesion in spirit and views, almost a super-human amount of overcoming would be necessary for me — to continue on in this already deeply disappointing world. I confess to you with complete openness, that I could not if it were not for our child, for whom I absolutely must be there. It is really as if my little Ellen who always foresaw and pre-intuited everything, wanted to give me an anchor above and beyond her life, for, suddenly, she wanted a child and that is how our Dagny came into the world in April 1942. I shall include a little photo of her. May she become like her mother, only happier and healthier! Fortunately, she is of an age at which there is not yet any full accounting for what happened, and, outwardly at least, seems reconciled to the fact. At present, she is in a children's home very near me and is thriving just fine. I dedicate to her every free minute, as it were. More importantly: a very close friend of mine, half Swiss, half Czech has taken on the child in the most moving, selfless way. She has the necessary maternal warmth and she is surely much more needed than the bumbling and desperate love of a father who is too old. For the summer, I am seeking a solution that will allow me to have the child with me again, all the time. Once she has reached kindergarten age, everything will be much easier. It will be only months until then. One thing is certain — that, without the child, I would fall, a hopeless victim of grief. Perhaps it will work with her, insofar as I am still nowhere near finding a new, resigned equilibrium.

But why should I trouble you with my, perhaps, all too private lament, doubly unjust in a time that knows nothing but lamentation and misery. So I constantly wrestle with Manfred and forgetfulness, oblivion, self-oblivion, and it is Manfred's world in which I live, much more than the world of Wagner. [ie. *Manfred* by Lord Byron]

It is not little what the whole Hitler thing has done to us, and now, with the reopening of relations to the world, it is horrifying to see how many friends and acquaintances are no long there. After everything that has transpired, life is poisoned and it will never again be possible to be happy. But the worst was the separation from you! Through all those years, we had a continual, bitter homesickness for you and there was, literally, not a single day on which we did not think of you, in old, always newer, actually in increased love, admiration and feelings of profoundest unity. At the end of 1943, by the way, we wrote you a long letter, which, however, probably never reached you. [see 1943.09.28] A clever young civil servant in our Interior Department (back then we would have said: Head of Division in the Ministry of Culture) was devoted to Barlach and, naturally, I spoke to him of you, dear Leo. We then got him to include, with a letter by him, one from us to you which would reach you by way of diplomatic mail, but apparently it did not work. All the greater, then, when your letter of 11 July 1945 arrived at the end of September, only a few days before Ellen's fatal illness and I am thankful and happy that she was able to read it. It was the final, very great joy that she was to experience. You, dear Leo, you have not only remained my great ideal, you actually have continued to intensify as such. And if there is anything at all that I still strive towards, it is always to become more like you, as much as I know how, despite my never being able to reach your level, for the simple reason that I lack any sort of artistic productivity. My greatest wish would be for life again to bring us together, even if that seems so improbable at the moment. Nothing is more important to me than the closest possible contact with you, now more than ever! That is the only thing that makes it at all endurable to go on living.

Now the report you wished in all brevity: after three years of exceedingly stressful, worrisome work for war economy authorities of our land, in March 1943 I was elected Secretary of the Swiss Writers' Association and since then a middle man between a trade union and cultural organization secretary. Presently, I have been temporarily granted an 8-month partial leave of absence in order to finish writing the Cosima book. Ellen was so happy at the prospect of our working together on the completion of the book – and just when we were supposed to begin, she had to leave me and the work! You will be able to judge just how horribly difficult it is to work on without her. But it must be, now more than ever, after Friedelind, Winifred's seemingly renegade daughter, put into the world such cheap kitsch in the form of a book. Poor Wagner — despite everything, he did not deserve such progeny.

Writing to you like this, it occurs to me how we worried about you in the time preceding El Alamein! And what a sigh of relief afterwards! But, sadly, the *vivere pericolosamente* [live dangerously] does not seem to have ended yet for you and precisely in these days I have worriedly read the alarming news about Palestine. Are the political troubles having any effect on your fine new field of work, Leo? We saw in advance that your administrative function with the Palestine Orchestra would not be satisfactory in the long run. But what are your plans for the future? If I can do anything for you here, no matter what, please make use of me whenever and however you wish. There is no bigger joy for me. In the meantime, Ruth's baby will have come into the world! Did everything go well? What is the child's name? Altogether — everything that happens with you is of burning interest to me! Please — also photographs of all "participants"! And Rahel's address! I would like to send greetings to her. A further request: Alice Jacob-Loewenson wrote quite nicely to me. I will not be able to reply so quickly. Could you, in the meantime, thank her and give her warm regards?

Forgive this confused letter — head and heart look desolate! — and keep in mind that I am waiting impatiently for further news from you all. I embrace all of you and send regards from the bottom of my heart (naturally also to Tunja!)

Always completely your

Franz W.B

87. FWB to KBG — 1946.01.20

88. Kestenberg (Tel-Aviv) to Beidler (Zurich) 1946.02.17

[handwritten - under letterhead of Music Teachers Training College]

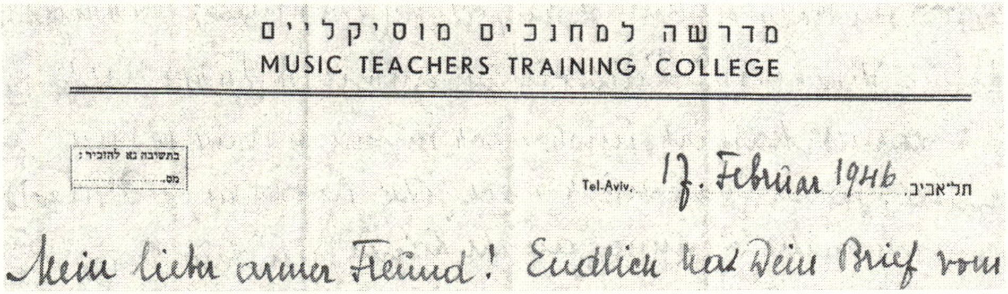
מדרשה למחנכים מוסיקליים
MUSIC TEACHERS TRAINING COLLEGE
בתשובה נא להזכיר: מס.
Tel-Aviv, 17. Februar 1946 תל־אביב.
Mein lieber armer Freund! Endlich hat Dein Brief vom

Music Teachers Training College

17 February 1946

My poor dear friend! Your letter of the 20th of January finally made the terribly cold, shocking, incomprehensible notice of death somehow more humanly comprehensible, although, now too, we still feel Ellen's absence from our picture of the world as a deep and searingly hot and painful wound. Only if we include her in gathering together our early-terminated Mozart and Schubert, Büchner and Alban Berg, if we seek to comprehend death in all its forms as the eternal and as the atemporal, life as the limited, final, almost accidental, can we perhaps find a consolation. This enigma of being and not-being becomes still more significant if we very profoundly plunge into her appearance as a whole, if we envision her with the infinitely tender and simultaneously strong magic of her nature and if we strive to interpret her life and her death in the sense of her always so great, all-encompassing and original personal feeling and thinking. From the first moment that we met, I felt the inexpressible charm of her personality like a unique miracle and therefore I also always felt as if I were under her spell. I still feel it now in this magic circle, whenever I think of her voice, her laugh, her walk, and whenever I bring together all the things she said and the forms of expressing her nature, together with her intellectual, analytical and logical abilities and her persuasiveness. If I got annoyed about anything that Franz, her beloved Franz, had perpetrated or delayed, she only needed to step into my room with a request for absolution on her lips — and everything was forgiven and forgotten.

Now, she has laid on you the difficult responsibility, in its elevated sense, of continuing to live, to strive onward and this infinitely sweet child — how we endlessly rejoiced over her photo — to bring her up in your and her spirit. You will fulfill these responsibilities without petty prejudices and scruples, of that I am certain — and I feel, as if ordered by her, to advise you not to remain alone long, for you and the child absolutely need the sort of human warmth and envelopment, the gifts which only hearth and home can give us. — It is a crying shame that, at this time, we are torn apart at such a distance. I have found very few people along my pathways, with whom I got along so well as with you both. Here, in this land, I have to look for completely new methods of communication, to make myself understood. But precisely this searching — in one sense biblical, understood as language; in another, external — gives me a new boost and leads to a new elasticity, to a rejuvenated and activated, east-west synthesis. Specifically, I find this in a large circle of students, which daily brings me into a more lively and lasting, interaction-based contact with young people. I almost take delight in the isolation, thanks to our geographical and political situation and which, on its own, considered seriously, forces one to an original mindset. I shall write to you in more detail about that in a subsequent letter, but only after you have dedicated to me one of your, sadly, much too infrequent letters — in fact, a small extortion that I reinforce by having to ask you for a few things. — A few weeks ago, Hug & Co. sent me the "New Piano School" by Kugler, which the circle of my students finds interesting. I could easily distribute 10 copies. Please say thank you in my name on the Limmatquai and ask if Hug is in contact with one of the local music shops here — Littauer, Ben Yehuda 67 would be the best. I would especially like to continue to receive the "Swiss Music Paper." It would seem that it is still being sent to my address in the Orchestra office. Please have them change the address. How is my dear and esteemed friend, Mimi Scheiblauer doing? [FWB note: wrote her on 14.IV.46] Please look her up and give her very warm regards and ask her about all things personal and factual from the last years. — I would be very happy if I could receive the smaller, somewhat mini-treatise-like writings — like "On Dealing with Oneself," which I own. [FWB note: wrote him 7.III.46] And do you know anything about Mersmann, Orff, Preußner and all the other ones - past & lapsed, corrupted and seduced? [FWB note: Dopeker? Böttcher? Reichenbach?] With a sadly jovial sidelong glance, I think of our old bone of contention, Moser, who, as proved by his Lexikon, published in 1935, seems to have behaved better than others, e.g. Schünemann. — Yesterday, I received an especially charming letter from Alfred Einstein, who seems to be doing well on a self-built island of industrious peace and work. — And now, realize your dear yearned-for wishes by writing soon, really, as soon as possible, and accept the profound greetings and embraces of

LeoKbg

[The following undated letter of Grete to FWB may predate Nr. 87, 17.02.1946 but is thematically appropriate in this spot.]

My dear Beidler friend,

with your wonderful Ellen a piece of my life also has passed away now — passed into the great, tranquil, so magnificent Eternity. — She was so very much in my life, as I never before knew, until I read the unspeakably sad news of her death and now she continues to live very movingly in my heart, like my Leo, my children, and everything that is "mine," you and your little, boundlessly charming Dagny. And how much she is like her mother in the way she holds her little head! May she be a joyful being, on this – despite everything – nonetheless beautiful earth and good heaven let her grow to be her own person.

Our little Rachel will soon be 7 months old and very sweet. Ruth and Tunja are just as happy with her as are her grandparents. Big Rahel is now: Raquel Vieira da Cunha and lives with her extremely kind-looking husband, Mariv (sociologist and anthropologist) in Sao Paolo in Brazil (Addr: 90 Escola Livre de sociologia e Politica, Largo de Sao Francisco 19), much too far away from our little, lovely Palestine. Strange that it was always our "homeland!"

We live here like Philemon and Baucis in the restlessly blessed hope of a reunion with Rahel, my sisters, and our indestructible beloved friends, above all, naturally with you and Simons.

With all warmheartedness for you and your child, your old Grete Kbg

88. KBG + Grete to FWB — 1946.02.17

89. 1946.05.25 — Kbg (Tel-Aviv) to FWB (Zurich)

[handwritten]

Tel-Aviv, 25.V.46, Adam Hacohen str. 20

My dear friend! Today I must thank you sincerely, first for your good letter of 14 III [not extant], then for the Hanselmann card and printed matter and for your contacting Mimi Scheiblauer. I looked in vain for your Nietzsche article, which I especially was looking forward to. Please do send it to me! — I should have written to you long ago, since my thoughts roam to you incessantly and I have any number of questions that only you can answer. But: – and now I am replying to one of your remarks – : I believe that I have a duty to dedicate myself, limitlessly, to the youth that is growing up here. With a passion that is new even to me, I teach from morning to evening. Here and now, for the first time, my old ideas about teaching music have won real substance. Here, because the east-oriental perception of music and sound are becoming ever clearer to me, the connection of voice and speech, the cultish significance of the instruments reaches me with ever greater vitality. And, with Hermann Hesse's *Morganlandfahrer* and *Glasperlenspieler,* the only thing I now can wrest from the era of romantic music with its arts commentaries is a historical interest, whereas "life" — as you have known a long time (I remind you only of my critical attitude to Mahler) — seems to show many different aspects. But, up to this point, we agree with each other, more or less. — On the other hand, I cannot agree with you if you are of the opinion that, somewhere in the great world, I should strive for and take on a so-called "post" once again. No: *Hic Rhodus hic salta* [here is Rhodes, jump here; i.e. prove what you can do here and now]. Your Pestalozzi, who, like a real *Hans im Glück* [Lucky Hans - from Brothers Grimm], keeps doing with less and less, and advances toward the essential in ever smaller frames of reference, is supposed to be our guide. And above and beyond that — completely and independently separate from any sort of chauvinistic points of view — you must be interested by the Jewish question — which also concerns you — so vigorous in the stirring and stormy immediacy that must have reached you, but which, actually can only be understood in this country. You must grasp the fact that I can only work here, build here, live happily and breathe here. And I am overjoyed that Grete feels the same way, not to mention Ruth and Tunia, who are of a generation for whom all of this is no longer questionable. — But precisely because I want to become ever more deeply rooted here, I must not lose the connection with the West, with the world, with you. I must exert myself in making more time for writing. You in particular can help me in this if you reply to me quickly and if our correspondence takes on the form of a regular and continual linkage.

And naturally, in this connection as well, I would also be happy if I could receive the Swiss Music Newspaper. The English send me their music papers (Musical Times & M. in education), but that is relatively meagre.

I shall write to Prof. Hanselmann very soon, since a remark about his relationship to the "clique" moved me greatly. I have to tell him how great, precisely because of that, his influence and his effectiveness are and how happy he should be about his active dilettantism. — Despite Ruth's attempt, I must also bother you with a similar-sounding request. The art and literature historian Dr. Paul Landau,[1] who was well-known in the former Germany, lives here, very secluded and reclusively. He keeps two very valuable German manuscripts in his desk drawer. I have read one of them: "The Romantics' Picture of the East" or, better stated, The Picture of the East of the last European Centuries. I learned enormously from this not very comprehensive book — and I am sure that a really intelligent publisher could do something with it, especially today, since the picture of the East is becoming ever more prominent. What do you think of Rascher[2] who might perhaps still know me from the Cassirer days? - And one last thing: what do you in Zurich think of the international competition in Geneva? A few young pianists from here want to go there but I fear that it is mostly more or less about a harmless business scheme. At your instigation, Mimi Scheiblauer wrote me charmingly. I also received a query from Mrs. Weingartner-Studer[3] about a possible conducting appearance. — And now, a thousand profound and sincere greetings — also for your Dagny and for your closest friends. Your old Leo [added in Grete's hand] and your old Grete.

89. KBG to FWB — 1946.05.25

[1] Paul **Landau** - (1880-1951) - Jewish-German journalist and writer. After being persecuted by the Nazis, he emigrated to Palestine in 1935, where he worked as a journalist.

[2] Max **Rascher** - (1883-1962) - A publisher in Zurich who had dealings with Thomas Mann.

[3] Carmen **Weingartner-Studer** - fourth wife of conductor Felix Weingartner (1863-1942), married in 1931. She was also a conductor, and author of *Franz Schubert, His Life and Works* and other books.

90. 1946.06.15 — FWB (Zurich) to Kbg (Tel-Aviv)

[typed]

Beidler

Zurich 7: 15. June 1946,
Klosbachstrasse 106,

Prof. Leo Kestenberg
20 Adam-Hacohen-Street,
Tel-Aviv / Palestine.

Dear Leo, Your last letter – it was from the 25th of May – without my being able to describe exactly why, or wanting to, moved us to tears (us, that is, besides myself, Libuše Ott, who now shares my whole life with me, after she had already shared joy and sorrow with me for ten years and now, with such terrible suddenness, so unexpectedly sees herself placed before the responsibility of being Dagny's foster-mother, which, happily works well for both sides, beyond all expectations and which has led to a relationship in which I have new joy every day). Libuše, predominantly an eastern person with a slavic soul, is whole-heartedly of your opinion, without the slightest hesitation. I cannot agree so unconditionally, but I understand you very well and bow to your opinion. Still, something immensely painful hovers over everything, and therefore there were tears. Let us come to a compromise, in good democratic fashion: you stay in your new sphere of activity, but you admit all imaginable connections with the rest of the world — not only with the West! — and you allow your truly unique personality to radiate everywhere — the more people I have met, the more your stature has grown for me, if that was at all possible! What I can do to help, let us say, as letter carrier and facilitator, I shall do with complete joy, that goes without saying. How are things with Czechoslovakia? Have you re-established your contact? Does the Společnost still exist, or again, and, if so, in your spirit?

Above all, accept our congratulations to you and Grete for <u>your</u> granddaughter, Rachel! I wrote Ruth spontaneously four days ago under the impression of Rachel's little picture and won't repeat myself. Dagny had to surrender to Rachel half of the frame in which her picture sits, next to the table at which I read and work. In this and with it, I now have you continually before my eyes. She has already begun to compete with Dagny as Zurich's most popular child.

I am about to leave for a few days for meetings and discussions in western Switzerland and for a performance of "Prometheus" in the French adaptation by André Bonnard[1] with music by Arthur Honegger, in the Roman amphitheatre of Avenches (Aventicum). Your letter, however, should not remain unanswered until my return. Tired and stressed as I am at the moment, I cannot write a "good" letter and must ask you to put up with these miserable jottings. Now to the points contained in your last letter:

I have put your request with regard to Dr. Landau together with Ruth's with regard to Dr. Frankenstein and tried to stress the main point. Instead of further commentary, I include a copy of a letter which represents a first step. Would you please let Ruth see it? I shall keep you up-to-date.

Like you, I tend to class prize competitions as "musical horse races," which Wagner so loathed. Nonetheless, I did discuss the question today — from the perspective of utility and of publicity for the young pianists, about whom you write — with Director Rudolf Wittelsbach of the local conservatory, whom I value as he is (he inwardly rejects the concert business almost the same as we do, if also perhaps not out of the same motivations and convictions). In all impartiality, he was of the following opinion: at present, in Europe, there is no event that guarantees up-and-coming virtuosi such publicity as the Geneva competition. The great opportunity for the prize-winner in the competition consists of being able to play in a public concert under Ernest Ansermet and this concert is broadcast by radio, especially to the United States and finds there a recognition which is not insignificant. Add to this that the monetary prizes offered are not negligible and, at least, cover travel costs, assuming that the contender wins a prize. So, by all means, it can be said that, under certain conditions, for up-and-coming virtuosi, participation opens a really favourable start in an international concert career. There is a whole list of examples of this. But I still want to consult with others in the profession, Scherchen in particular, who is in Vienna at the moment.

I believe that the Swiss Music News is already on the way to you. At any rate, Schuh told me that it was. I will check again and, if necessary, take care of it. I also want to ask Cherbuliez[2] to have the Music Education Journal sent to you. For the rest, I have already begun to collect everything for you that could be of interest, and so, from now on, shipments of printed matter will be sent to you at regular intervals, the first already in the next days with a few newspaper articles, with the yearly report of the Swiss Broadcasting Society (in it, about Scherchen's truly awesome accomplishments!). — As I write this,

---

[1] André **Bonnard** - (1888-1959) - Professor of Greek language and literature. He translated works by Aeschylus, Sophocles, and Euripides. He was a lifelong pacifist, but was accused in the early 1950s of having spied for the USSR, a charge that was mostly dropped in 1954.

[2] **Cherbuliez** - [??]

Mendelssohn's Violin Concerto (Sir Adrian Boult conductor) is playing over the radio, broadcast from England, magnificently as beautiful as on its first day! In every way — Mendelssohn! It is for me as with old Wagner: my admiration for this weightless, transparent music that subsumes pure Spirit in sound increases with every day. Forgive this somewhat dilettantish excursion. — At your request, I am including our Nietzsche article (it was the last work I did together with Ellen — oh, what a horrible crying shame; in spite of all external "composure," it suffocates me incessantly, day for day and night for night!).

Now, quickly, a couple of additional items and questions: the last volume of Ernest Newman's[1] definitive Wagner biography has just arrived here and I am preparing a big review. Newman is unexpectedly hard on Wagner (the years 1940-44 left behind deep wounds!). Admittedly, with regard to political and intellectual history, he makes things too easy for himself. It does not work to draw a line from Gymnastics Father Jahn [*Turnvater Jahn*] to Wagner to Alfred Rosenberg![2] The connective strands are infinitely more complicated and complex, and I believe that my book will be the first to reveal them. Still Newman's work is the first objective, unfalsified presentation, and this is saying something. On my suggestion, the City of Lucerne just delegated me to invite Newman to Tribschen for this summer. He has not yet answered yet (he is 77 years old, but mercurial and enterprising!). [Alfred] Einstein and wife have written in the meantime. If possible, his wife has become even bitchier and nastier than she always was; in him, as well, I miss the somewhat broader points of view; nonetheless I am glad that we have resumed contact. Altogether: every day, letters and signs of life arrive from all parts of the planet, and my correspondence is increasing so much that I hardly know how to cope. Think of it, our Hilde Grunwald-Groening, the loyal secretary of our archive, contacted us. Her husband was in a concentration camp for a long time and then at war. Now he is a prisoner-of-war in Italy. She bravely fought in the anti-fascist movement and is now a top person in the Unity Party, in the Russian zone; she seems to be the dictator of Alt-Landsberg, her home town! I shall send her, as soon as possible, a food package and establish contact with her husband. What ever happened to Miss Rosendorff?? And with Grete's relatives (Kussels) ??

---

[1] Ernest **Newman** - (1868-1959) - English musicologist and critic. Between 1933 and 1947, he wrote the definitive biography of Richard Wagner (Cassell and Knopf) and many other books.

[2] Alfred Ernst **Rosenberg** - (1893-1946) - Nazi, racist ideologist and early Hitler disciple. He was an admirer of Cosima Wagner's son-in-law, Houston Stewart Chamberlain and his racist book, *Foundations of the Nineteenth* Century. Rosenberg wrote *The Myth of the Twentieth Century* as a sequel to Chamberlain's book. He was hanged at Nuremberg.

Another thing: Zeigner[1] is Lord Mayor of Leipzig! Nothing makes me happy at the moment; but that made me happy. Carmen Weingartner-Studer showed great courage in the battle against Furtwänglerism here. If only she were a better musician!

I shall write again soon and embrace you all in profound love and infinite yearning!

Always completely yours

Franz.

90. FWB to KBG — 1946.06.15

[1] Erich Richard **Moritz Zeigner** - (1886-1949) - lawyer, Social-Democratic politician and then East-German communist party politician. He became Minister of Justice in Saxony in 1921. Two years later, he was elected Prime Minister of Saxony. He was jailed several times by the Nazis and did odd jobs. In 1945 he became mayor Leipzig, a position he filled until his death.

91. 1946.09.21 — FWB (Zurich) to Kbg (Tel-Aviv)

[typed]

Background:

On August 28, 1946, Oskar Meyer, the mayor of Bayreuth, wrote to Beidler asking him to lead a renewed Bayreuth Festival. Only later did Beidler learn that the mayor had sent a similar letter to Friedelind Wagner, who was in New York. Beidler drew up a plan for a foundation to replace the Wagner Dynasty. It was a solid plan, in need of some fine-tuning, but workable and featuring leading personalities as participants, all democratic and anti-Nazi. Beidler wrote to Thomas Mann asking him to fill the position of honorary President. Beidler, himself, would act as the Secretary of the Foundation. People like Kestenberg and Alfred Einstein would take on an advisory role. Musicians such as Hindemith, Schoenberg, and Karl Hartmann would look after the musical side of the Festival.

After receiving quite enthusiastic permission from the occupying American authorities in Bayreuth, Beidler travelled there in late December. In a meeting with Wolfgang Wagner and the Mayor in the latter's office, Beidler outlined his plan. Wolfgang was astonished that Beidler seemed to have much more urgent interest in gaining access to the Wagner archives than in taking over the Festival. As late as 1994, when he published his autobiography, Wolfgang somewhat sneered at Beidler, who had died in 1981. What Wolfgang could not understand is why anybody would want to write a book about his grandmother Cosima. A book! A waste of time, as far as Wolfgang was concerned, and, in 1947, definitely an unnecessary diversion from the real business at hand.

Wolfgang was grateful for this diversion. After all, Beidler's intention was to have the Americans dispossess Winifred and her children and replace them with a Foundation that was, as Winifred so inimitably put it, full of Jews — Jews such as Thomas Mann? Hindemith? Karl Hartmann? But never mind. Wolfgang had a few more diversions up his sleeve. First of all, said he, his siblings, himself, and Winifred could not be dispossessed for the simple reason that the Americans were bound to obey laws - unlike the Nazis - and ownership of the Festival was legally settled by Siegfried Wagner's last will and testament. Beyond that, many of the documents demanded by Beidler had been either destroyed or hidden away or blocked for decades by Eva Chamberlain. Finally, he related, because of the relentless allied bombing, the Wagners had hidden their archival possessions all over Germany with trusted people who could not be reached and who, in many cases, were in allied jails. Sorry, said Wolfgang, I never imagined even for a moment that Germany could be divided into four zones of occupation. Gaining access to the family's archival possessions will take years, he stated with the maximum regret he could muster.

Beidler stayed in Bayreuth for several weeks. During that time, he realized that clearing the destruction and doing all the preparation needed to hold a Festival would take years. Furthermore, there had been a large influx of refugees from the Sudetenland, Poland, and Hungary. People were living in camps or being billetted in homes. About a quarter of the population was made up of refugees. The city was having a difficult time coping with all the new people, let alone sustaining indigenous Bayreuthers. Beidler also noticed that the Bayreuthers despised outsiders, including Americans and himself. Wherever possible, they refused to co-operate. It became clear that a Festival could be held only if the Americans continued to occupy Bayreuth.

The final big question was ownership of the Festival. The longer the question lingered in legal limbo, the surer it became that possession would remain with the Wagners. Partially, this was because dispossession depended on Winifred receiving a stiff sentence from the denazification court. As time went on, sentences just kept getting lighter and lighter, even for proven Nazis with black marks in their histories.

By the last months of 1947, Beidler saw the writing on the wall, as did Thomas Mann, and he closed down his idealistic effort to set up a foundation to run the Wagner Festival. He had developed a good and workable plan. He, himself, would have been secretary, responsible for organization. He had a good track record in this, far better than the Wagner brothers who, only a few years later, gave the world New Bayreuth. On August 1, 1947, Heinz Tietjen, who had run the Festival during the years of the Third Reich, wrote that he thought the Festival should remain a family business, as stipulated in Siegfried Wagner's last will.

> If, however, the military government invokes victors' rights and others make the decisions, the only plausible solution is an international Festival Foundation with a Foundation Council at its head. This foundation council will appoint the artistic director of the whole and the head administrator while raising the operating capital.... For the foundation council, personalities such as the following would be considered, among others: Thomas Mann, Ernest Newman, Herbert Peyser, Dr. Alfred Einstein, Jean Chantavoine, Jacque Prod'homme, Dr. Paul Cronheim, Bruno Walter, Thomas Beecham, V. de Sabata, P. Hindemith, A. Honegger, Ansermet, E. Preetorius, Heinz Tiessen, H.H. Stuckenschmidt.[1]

Tietjen was offering a carbon copy of Beidler's plan, with the exception of his addition that the Wagner family should be represented on the Council by its younger generation, namely, Wolfgang Wagner and Franz W. Beidler. The omission of Wieland Wagner

---

[1] Heinz **Tietjen**, 1947.08.01, Adakemie der Künste, Heinz Tietjen Archiv, in Michael Karbaum, *100 Jahre Bayreuther Festspiele* (Regensburg, Bosse, 1976), 134-5.

is traceable to the years of bad blood between Wieland and Tietjen. As with other Dynasties, women like Friedelind Wagner and her sister Verena did not enter leadership considerations. But the presence of Beidler on the council envisaged by Tietjen is a glowing testimony to the feasibility of his plan. In the event, it was not possible for Beidler to surmount the brown sludge which still gummed up Bayreuth, Bavaria, and many other parts of Germany. If Beidler's Foundation idea had proved doable, politically, and if he had been the director, the decades of boring, inartistic, and loutish productions by Wolfgang Wagner and his daughter Katrina could have been replaced by more thought-provoking, more artistic, and more idealistic creations. Bayreuth would also have come to terms with its Nazi past, thoroughly and honestly. But that was not to be.

Zurich 7: September 21, 1946,
Klosbachstrasse 106,
Postal address: Postbox 201, Zurich 12 - Neumünster

Dear, dear Leo,

something has happened which almost has the character of an event (if only of a modest dimension, not to be compared, for instance, with the Palestine Conference)[1] [marginal note by FWB: or with the magnificent speech by Henry Wallace[2] (America's new great man after Franklin D. Roosevelt?)] Enclosed is a verbatim letter from the mayor of Bayreuth and a copy of my reply.[3] I hope that the dignity of mentality and cast of mind which I am to represent, without merit on my part in this branch, reached more or less suitable expression. Outside of you, I am informing only Thomas Mann and a liaison

[1] **Palestine Conference** - Conference in London, 1946, to attempt to sort out all the colliding interests in Palestine: those of the Arabs, those of the surrounding Arab nations, those of the UK and America, those of the hundreds of thousands of Jewish internees in places like Cyprus, waiting to be admitted to Palestine by the British. Both the Jews and the Arabs of Palestine boycotted the Conference.

[2] Henry A. **Wallace** - (1888-1965) - He was Vice-President of the USA, under Roosevelt, 1941-1945. After being replaced as vice-presidential candidate at the 1944 electoral convention, Harry Truman became vice-president and then president after Roosevelt died. Wallace was an open-minded anti-segregationist and a man favouring peace throughout the world.

[3] Oskar **Meyer**, first mayor of Bayreuth, after the war, sent the same letter to both FWB and Friedelind Wagner. In it, he asked them to return to Bayreuth to organize a rebirth of the Festival. He does not seem to have informed either anti-Nazi Wagner descendent that the other had been contacted.

officer in our federal government, because I desire anything other than premature publicity. The name Dr. Benedikt alone already sounds a more than urgent cautionary warning, and I have no occasion to trade the Nazis for the German nationalists whom I hate even more. Professor Engel[1] — is this not the little Engel, at that time a freelance professor [*Privatdozent*] in Greifswald and an iridescent half-communist, which, if I am correctly informed, did not hold him back from energetically co-operating with the Nazis (see his professor title as reward). Was he not the one who "proved" the "teutonic" lineage of Liszt? Naturally, in the Third Reich, despite the alliance with Hungary. We shall see. To reject this out of hand would probably be completely misguided. *Et animam nostram salvavi!*[2] Is that right?

I do not have enough time today to say the thousand things that are weighing on my heart. The first side in my correspondence notebook, your side, is swelling up daily with numerous keywords. But I want you to get your bearings immediately on this change in Bayreuth, if it is one. For now, the main thing, for me, is and remains to break open the Wahnfried archive. That will surely succeed now.[3]

I have greetings for you from Klemperer[4] (a tragic reunion) and Dr. Paul Eger,[5] now director of the municipal theatres in Lucerne. I have owed Ruth a letter for a long time now. Can you give her my apologies and tell her that I am in constant contact with Mi-

---

[1] Hans **Engel** - (1894-1970) - musicologist. His university thesis was entitled *The Development of the German Piano Concerto from Mozart to Liszt.* (1924) He remained a freelance professor until 1944, after becoming a member of the Nazi Party in 1941 (Nr.8,902,866). He was a proponent of Nazi racial theory and methods. During his de-nazification hearing, he claimed to have been an "active opponent of National Socialism."

[2] *Et animam nostram salvavi!* - Karl Marx at the end of his last book, 1875: "I only said that to save my own soul."

[3] FWB was wrong. In the end, very little changed in Bayreuth, including the archive which, in one way or another, remained closed right up to the present day. Even the Richard Wagner archive is only partially "open." The Festival archive is closed. Various family collections, including that of Winifred Wagner, are inaccessible.

[4] Otto **Klemperer** - (1885-1973) - see note in Introduction. FWB calls Klemperer tragic, as he was left partially paralyzed after an operation to remove a large brain tumor in 1939. Starting in 1954, when he reactivated his German citizenship, Klemperer entered a very successful recording and guest-conducting career.

[5] Paul **Eger** - (1881-1947) - Jewish-Austrian theatre director and stage director. He emigrated to Prague in 1932, where he was the diector of the New German Theatre. After fleeing Prague when the Nazis invaded, he did directing on a guest-basis in the Municipal Theatre, Basel (1940-1942). He was the director of the Municipal Theatre, Lucerne 1942-1947.

chal Smoira[1] and can help her, I believe; at the moment, she is in Geneva at a competition (musical, not equine). Miss [?]ranetmann has not contacted me yet. Dr. Frankenstein wrote a very fine letter to me. Could Ruth please thank him for the time being; I am hoping to be able to send him a report soon. At the moment, I am absurdly swamped and hardly find time for private things. Fortunately, Dagny has her Libuše. Enclosed are a few, most recent little photos. I expect, hope for, demand same in return. The little picture of Rachel, as well as both new ones, are entirely captivating!

Profoundest greetings from the heart to you and Grete!

Always completely yours

F.

91. FWB to KBG — 1946.09.21

[1] Michal **Smoira** - (b. Tel-Aviv 1926) - One of Israel's best-known musicologists, daughter of Israel's first Chief Justice, Moshe Smoira, and wife of another Supreme Court Justice, Chaim Cohen. A woman of tremendous energy and many achievements as teacher, journalist, and musician.

92. 1949.01.03 — FWB (Zurich) to Kbg (Tel-Aviv) - *[typed]*

Background:

In this letter Beidler refers to the remarkable place and era in which Kestenberg was living. On May 14, 1948, David Ben Gurion had proclaimed the statehood of Israel. That state was able to fight back the concerted war made to snuff it out by the states surrounding it. Although Kestenberg was a pacifist and a humanist, Israel and its survival were as dear to his heart as to the hearts of most other Jews. Six million Jews had paid with their lives for the founding of Israel. Beidler and Kestenberg were of one opinion — that there was limited hope for the future of a new Germany but that there was great optimism for Israel and its role in a better world.

Zurich 32: January 3, 1949
Klosbachstrasse 106,
Postal address: Postbox 201, Zurich 12.

Grete! Leo! Loved ones, dearest friends!

The new year must break the forced conspiracy of silence! Silence? Not one day goes by without our talking about you. No day begins without thoughts of you, without all the best of wishes for you, without cares about you. No day ends without yearning for you. How many people does one see, day-in and day-out? But those, to whom one uniquely belongs, one does not see. No, this existence is neither carefree nor beautiful.

Only a few words about me. A loss like that of Ellen is something that can never be got over. With her entry into my life, it's path headed upwards; with her disappearance, it plummeted suddenly. You take steps to end what you had started and planned, and that becomes sour enough. Nothing more is expected. The boundaries are defined, the margins measured. And that is good and proper.

But Dagny is growing up with you. Leo and Grete, Ruth, Tunia and Rachel — these are the names with which she is familiar. She is already a "big" girl and has attended school since last Easter. She is totally Ellen but tending to lightness, gaiety, and carefreeness — a source of endless, admittedly also wistful joy. She is now beginning to learn to write in German, very painstakingly, wholly as a foreign language — it is very funny. And good.

That is because nothing can be expected of Germany, at least of the west zones. As you know, I felt myself duty-bound to try to make something out of Bayreuth, in which we — and probably also he [Thomas Mann] — could have taken joy. Naturally, the attempt failed totally. The Weimar Republic was a virtual paragon of progress, compared with what is setting the tone today in the western zones, especially Bavaria. On appeal in court, Winifred was classified as an inoffensive and gullible "follower" and, for all intents and purposes, absolved. In return, she magnanimously renounced directorship of the Festival in order to achieve keeping the Festival a private enterprise into which neither the State nor the City of Bayreuth may meddle. The Bavarian government and the City of Bayreuth — with a Social Democrat as mayor and a Jewish city councillor in charge of cultural affairs (Dr. Karl Würzburger, formerly of the Reich Broadcasting Company - you know him) complied, with obedience and contentment. In future, as ever, only Wagner will be put on — three cheers for tradition. Completely disgusted, I have turned my back on it. Have a look at the enclosed paper. Is it not as if, between 1933 and today, nothing at all happened? From Stuckenschmidt[1] to Klemperer to Kapp — they are all there, the same as ever, and do not know that they, themselves, are their own ghosts. To round out the picture: Tietjen, one hundred percent rehabilitated, is again — General Administrator of the Municipal Opera [later Deutsche Oper Berlin] The game can start over from the beginning. At any rate, I have begun to take up old relationships in the East Zone (among whom, Deiters, whom you will remember). But there too … ! How did Mr. Rust[2] put it? "After us, comes nothing more." He seems to have been right, naturally for Germany only.

You are living in the midst of a remarkably modern and heroic scenery. Remarkable, this synthesis between Old Testament and the most modern technology. Actually, you are to be envied. There is doubtless sense to what you are experiencing around you, and, above all, greatness, at least viewed from a distance, something that does not exist, or hardly so, with us. Israel is a fact, and, with that, our worries about you can lessen, thank goodness. Ruth and her family are probably still with you? I have got whole mountains of greetings to pass on to you, that have piled up, most recently from Dr. Kurt Cassirer and his wife Eva Cassirer-Solmitz[3], who presently are with us in Ticino. Then, of course, from Scherchen; first and foremost, however, from Libuše, Dagny and your,

more than ever completely your Franz.

92. FWB to KBG — 1949.01.03

[1] Hans Heinz **Stuckenschmidt** - (1901-1988) - German composer, musicologist, critic.

[2] Bernhard **Rust** - (1883-1945) - Nazi Minister of Education, his job was to nazify Germany's youth with Nazi thoroughness. Later in the Third Reich, he was responsible for medical experimentation on prisoners, for which the UN War Crimes Commission later indicted him for "human guinea pig vivisection."

[3] Eva **Cassirer-Solmitz** - born Solmitz and married to Kurt Hans Cassirer (1883-1975) - both art patrons.

93. 1949.04.15 — Kbg (Tel-Aviv) to FWB (Zurich)

[typed]

Israel

15.IV.49.

My dear friend! Once again you have really left me waiting a long time for a sign of life from you! With all that is known about the human character, it is really so strange: if I had to reconcile myself with the completely consistent fact that you are a sort of quarter-year person, who has to disappear from time to time, despite all this knowledge, I have a truly difficult time getting over it when you cause such long interruptions in our already so intermittent correspondence. And letters are anyway such a meagre substitute for a direct, personal meeting. How much I would like to showcase all my students for you, for example. How astounded you would be to find in me a completely unministerial person, liberated of all official masquerades and possessed by a passion for teaching! This freedom can be attributed, for the most part, to the way we Jews, here, in our land, behave, with a self-assurance which, in Europe, was mostly foreign to us. Naturally, the new state strengthened even more this feeling of self-assurance and freedom. But do not believe that, after all my experiences of the last 50 years, I regard this form of state as the only saving bliss. All the same, it is an historical hallmark of great consequence.

Your decision to divest yourself of Bayreuth forever has impressed me extraordinarily. Everything that you invoke makes this renunciation even more meaningful and plausible. But, if only a lightly palpitating question is permitted: what is doing with your Cosima book? Personally, as well as impersonally, I have the liveliest and warmest interest in this, your creation, which, in my opinion, you are simply duty-bound to complete and publish — if only in Ellen's remembrance. This is your allotted task on earth. And if I do not exactly fit into the role of a spectrally admonishing old predecessor of Palestrina,[1] you will nonetheless understand that I am standing there with raised index finger.

Happily, everything is going well with us. Tunia is preparing for a trip to Europe. His first stop will be Zurich, where he will surely contact you. He is accomplishing very important development work that is receiving recognition throughout the whole country. His work is closely connected with the whole apprentice system, and he will certainly inform

---

[1] Giovanni Pierluigi da **Palestrina** - (1525-1594) - Italian Renaissance composer of sacred, polyphonic music. He was made master of the papal choir at St.Peter's in 1551. The "admonishing old predecessor of Palestrina" is likely the Spanish composer Cristóbal de Morales, from whom Palestrina drew inspiration and who wrote at least five settings of the *Lamentations of Jeremiah.*

you of this in more detail. Ruth is most keenly continuing her historical work, is also gaining more and more recognition from the local guild. Rahel, in Brazil, already has a second son and our little Rahel in Jerusalem already is showing all signs of a secure and very charming personality. Your sweet Dagny must be imbued with a special magic, by all that you suggest. Send us a picture of her again, soon.

What would you say if I, in the framework of the International Summer-Academy of the Mozarteum in Salzburg, directed by Dr. Preussner, ….. [end missing]

93. KBG to FWB — 1949.04.15

94. 1949.11.20 — Kbg (Tel-Aviv) to FWB (Zurich) - [typed]

Israel
20. XI. 49.

My dear friend! even if I believe with certainty that you owe me an answer to my last letter, I still cannot resist the idea of a moment to send you a very fond and heartfelt greeting and to ask how you, your Buschi [Libuše], and, above all, your Dagny are doing. Tunia recounted so much that was dear and warm about you and yours that we became really homesick for you all! From time to time, we think of making a trip to Switzerland — as far as anyone here thinks back at all of Europe. But, for us, it is always a seesaw, because, counterposed to the thought of Europa is thinking about Brazil and visiting our Rahel.

I must also confess to you that I am now constantly preoccupied by a work that has the deepest connection with my daily activity: I am rhyming a teaching poem about my piano lessons and I concentrate every free minute — and there aren't many of those — on the progress of this "business." To my great joy, a productive interplay with my pedagogical work is emerging, because, when, during my lessons, I think of the poem, my teaching stems again out of the poem's ideas, which continually stimulate me. My students, almost without exception, are gifted and likeable young people. From morning to evening, the day is filled with sounds and illusions.

Now it is your turn to write to me! I should like to know what work is captivating you the most now and what is doing with your book. I took special joy in finding you and your book mentioned in Thomas Mann's "Novel of a Novel." I must tell you openly that this little book is closer to me on a human level than the whole of "Dr.Faustus," which is too contrived and too unmusical in its innermost core. The description of the operation, for instance, in "Novel of a Novel" is incomparably more lively, three-dimensional, and, in this sense, also more musical than the whole of the bulky Faust book. Personally, I am very especially insulted because Thomas Mann does not devote even one single line to Busoni and his "Faust" and because the whole of musical education is wiped off the table with a single sentence that sounds very condescending.

I have not yet spoken with Dr. Millner.[1] Recently, he phoned me and said that he had spent a very stimulating evening with you. He will give me a more detailed account when he comes from Haifa to Tel-Aviv again. With the deepest and fondest greeting for all of you – also from my Grete -

for ever and ever your old

94. KBG to FWB — 1949.011.20

[1] Dr. **Millner** - [??]

95. 1950.03.14 — FWB (Zurich) to Kbg (Tel-Aviv)

[typed]

The Beidler Group [*Die Beidlerei*]

Zurich 31: March 14, 1950
Kirchgasse 25.

Leo and Grete, Grete and Leo, you loved ones,

we are very moved. We just heard Busoni's piano concerto Op.39 with male choir, both of us for the first time, unbelievably. And under this impression, which binds us even closer to you than we always are anyway, you should receive a few completely spontaneous and unpremeditated lines. The credit for giving this work a hearing belongs to our radio — but not to Scherchen, who, at the moment is conducting his way around Italy, but to the organizing of a substitute broadcast by which the sound of the work's reproduction was produced by the Orchestra and Male Chorus of the West-German radio under the direction of Hans Schmidt-Isserstedt.[1] Piano: Gunnar Johansen.[2]

It was spellbinding, right from the first note, spellbinding through the grandiose Dantesque composure, kept by this true cosmogony on the threshold of a new epoch. Astounding, the five-part dimensions reminiscent of Mahler! (Otherwise not the slightest similarity with Mahler, except, it seems to us, for one minor spot in the 3rd part, the *Pezzo serioso*.) Without doubt, the music is the creation of a musician who is primarily attuned to a pianist's idea of sound. Still, the piano is not as overdominating as in other of Busoni's works, the orchestra not so degraded to the role of accompanist and extra, as, sadly, in the *Indian Fantasy* (I am always livid when I hear it, seldom enough, because the simply gorgeous, the wonderfully mysterious rhythm and sound of the first bars of the orchestra are so short, and, after that, are thrown aside in favour of overgrown pianistic embellishment, that just does not say much to me - Buš is not entirely of my opinion in this). Everything full of greatness. Ingenious, especially the 4th part "*All Italiana*" with its phantom and

---

[1] Hans **Schmidt-Isserstedt** - (1900-1973) - German conductor and composer. He was the leading conductor at the Hamburg State Opera 1935-1943 and music director of the Berlin Sate Opera, 1944. After the war, he was the founding conductor of the North German Radio Symphony Orchestra, with which he specialized in performing the music of composers who had been banned by the Nazis; e.g. Bartok and Hindemith.

[2] Gunnar **Johansen** - (1906-1991) - Danish-born concert pianist, scholar, teacher, and composer. He specialize in the music of Busoni, whose complete mature keyboard works he recorded. He also recorded 43 LPs of works by J.S. Bach and 51 LPs of piano music by Liszt. From 1929 on, he resided in the USA.

deeply demonic nature. Outstanding impression, as well, from the outer movements, which are both truly magnificent, magnificent and profoundly gripping at the same time because everything that is purely artistic is banned from it and nothing is set to sound except the searching and foreboding spirit, the heathen spirit of freedom. "Thank God" there is not even a whisper of traditional religion or even Christianity in it. It is regrettable that Busoni's own self, his quintessence, which does always break through in sound, sporadically becomes darkened and unfocussed through the Wagnerian tonal language from the time of the work's creation, which even a Busoni was unable to remain completely free of. Buš found the rhythmic thumping of the deep trumpets at the end of the *Introito* (a kind of organ pedal point) very "*götterdämmerung*-like." But then, from first to last tone, no procession of epigones. Buš has something additional to criticize: Busoni shrinks back, something like Bruckner, from the ultimate consequence and equivocates, mostly with pianistic playfulness, not in childish trifling like Bruckner, with whom he has much less in common than with Mahler. I must agree with her. All things considered, it is completely incomprehensible that a work such as this does not belong to the core stock of our musical knowledge and our programs. People like us, at least, should have it just as memorized as Mahler, Bruckner, Liszt, Schumann, Mendelssohn etc. How is it that a Scherchen so assiduously evades it when he repeatedly swears by Busoni? He will hear about this as soon as he is back here!

Yesterday, we decided to spend a week at Easter in snow and sun in a remote mountain valley 2,000 metres up – a paradise. We shall see no people except for the few locals. Before that, I still have to gobble my way through innumerable meetings, conferences, and banquets until I am at the point of giving up.

To you all — Ruth and Tunja included, of course — much much love!

Dagny Libuše F.

Now Heinrich Mann is also no more! A conscience of humanity has become silent!

Did you actually receive our Chanuka greeting without words, the Kollwitz[1] portfolio (and Tunja the Apprenticeship by Böhny)? [Ferdinand Böhny] How is the Carmen pedagogicum going??

95. FWB to KBG — 1950.03.14

[1] Käthe **Kollwitz** - (1867-1945) - German painter, printmaker, and sculptor. She brought humanistic, socialistic and anti-war themes into her work. The galleries of Paul Cassirer presented a restrospective exhibit of 150 drawings by her in 1917.

96. 1950.05.22 — Kbg (Tel-Aviv) to FWB (Zurich)

[typed]

(Israel)

22. May 50

My dearly beloved friend, your letter of May 14th, the pictures of the three of you, and finally I find the right moment to thank you for all this and your Chanukah gift! But this sounds much too meagre even to hint at how these words come from the heart. I am full of dejected longing for you and for everything that surrounds you, also full of grieving, at bottom, for everything that once made up the life we had in common and now only continues to exist as a very spectral reality. How seldom I now write to you, and yet how happy it makes me that I at least can be near you in this form. Your description of the piano concerto by Busoni made a deep impression on me. Busoni has really become a stepchild of our time, even if it cannot be said that his works ever belonged to the public's favourites. I am convinced that his time will come and it will be recognized how significant his oeuvre was for the aesthetic watershed in the 20th century. I witnessed the genesis of his "Concerto" in the most intimate way. I even pencilled the piano part into the handwritten score. Your intensely insightful, deeply empathetic description of the work brought it back home, very close to me again, and I took the score in hand and combed through it, awestruck. I thank you for that! I am also very moved that your letter, so consummate even in its external form, received a small marginal note in which you asked me about the "Carmen-Pedagogium." Doubtless, you meant our "seminar" in the "Carmel-School," and I'm sending you for your information a small, unfortunately more than half-abbreviated report which appeared in "*Aufbau*" a few months ago. Since it is my only copy, please return it whenever you can. The admiration for the form of your kind letter - even the address - is less mine than Tunja's, in whom you absolutely have found a limitlessly devoted friend who is seriously attached to you.

Grete, Tunja and Ruth have brought forth a proposal which I would need a certain boost to realize. I am already bogged down in its beginnings — but, only when all fear is conquered and the actual depth of a problem is entered, does everything become easier and, as Goethe says, "snugger." And you will now understand when I tell you today that, for about one year, I have been consolidating everything that I want to rescue from the past and bring over into the living present in a "Teaching Poem" of which I enclose the 1st and 2nd parts. This confession is causing my heart to race......... It is an attempt at something that I would like to translate from my musical essence into the act of turning it into words. But why all this explaining and excusing? Everything I have written down has arisen out of a deep need, including even the somewhat cheap form of versification. But I cannot do it any other way – – – – –. What I would like to hear from you, as friend to friend, in complete openness and without ceremony — is how you judge it and if there is any reason to even think of publishing it. Naturally, I am very keen on hearing really soon some word or other about it from you. The 3rd part, about double as long as the two first ones, is dedicated to Busoni, the 4th to the Sonata Op.110 of Beethoven, the 5th to music education, which seems especially current to me, since the "Kestenberg-Reform" is being actively discussed nowadays in Germany. The 6th part belongs to "*Weinen, Klagen, Sorgen, Zagen*" by Liszt and, finally, the 7th and last to my work in Israel.

And now I no longer want to add additional words and I want only to ask you very sincerely to reply very quickly.

In all sincerity and love with a thousand greetings for your Bus, your sweet Dagny, and you,

Always yours,

[handwritten PS]

Copy of the letter fromTh. Mann enclosed
Picture of Rahel
"*Aufbau*" article

96. KBG to FWB — 1950.05.22

97. 1952.11.25 —FWB (Zurich) to Kbg (Tel-Aviv)
[typed]

The Beidler Bunch [Die Beidlerei]

Zurich 31: November 25, 1952,
Zeltweg 65.

Dear, dear Leo,

just this evening, our radio station broadcast Busoni's Opus 44 [*Indian Fantasy*], thanklessly played by Paul Baumgartner.[1] This would not have been necessary to steer our regrettably un-Indian but very central European fantasy (which for me, as opposed to Buš, is hyphenated with -lessness) toward the coast of the once-again Holy Land [*gelobtes Land* - Luther], and, more exactly, to the street which is named after Adam Hacohen [Kestenberg's street], signifying for us the home of Leo and Grete and, with that, more than any other, a point on the planet for which our souls are continually searching. So, the day after tomorrow is the day on which the number of years gets rounded out to a new decade! If I think about it, I am completley undecided whether I should say "already" or "only" about that and it would require lengthier cogitation to figure out that both are right, like the weights of Josef Roth's calibrator.[2] "Already," because the last twenty years have dissipated like a phantom and like water running through fingers, because it is impossible to keep up with the glut of onrushing events, impossible also to resist frightening feelings, as if rooted to the spot. (And so, from time to time, I also cannot get it into my head that I myself have broken through the fifties barrier and, as if overnight, have become an older, more or less "dignified" gent …). "Only," because it is consoling and calming that you are not even higher on the scale of life's years and and that you will be there many more years for all those who love you and have so much to thank you for. And because, for us, plenty of hope remains finally to see you again. (I understood only too well that, in the end, you refused Preussner's invitation to Salzburg — but still, the disappointment was

---

[1] Paul **Baumgartner** - (1903-1976) - Swiss pianist and teacher. After studies in Germany, he took up a teaching position at the Cologne University music school. In 1935, he put the Nazis behind him by returning to Switzerland, where, from 1937 on, he taught at the Basel Conservatory. In 1962 he received the cultural prize of the City of St. Gallen.

[2] Moses Joseph **Roth** - (1894-1939) - Jewish-Austrian writer and journalist. He wrote much about his feeling of loss and aimlessness after the dissolution of his Austro-Hungarian homeland (*Radetzky March*, 1932), as well as the sense of homelessness that came with being a Jew in a non-Jewish world. In 1933, he fled Germany, first to Vienna and then to Paris, where he died penniless and in agony. FWB's reference to "calibrator" points to Roth's *One Night. The History of a Calibration Master* (*Das falsche Gewicht. Die Geschichte eines Eichmeisters*, 1937)

bitter for us!) Prevailing by mail, even to some extent, over the questions and communications that crowd in and impose themselves, day after day, is an impossibility. Already now, I have reached the point of asking myself what I choose out of the abundant selection before me.

There, in the frontmost row, is, without doubt, your teaching poem, this beautiful, great project, courageously taking up the traditions of antiquity. My basic impression, after several readings is: the contents are above and beyond criticism; they circumscribe in what is frequently a profoundly poignant way that world of musical humanism, the ubiquity of human musicality, as only you can portray it, because you are their embodiment in a unique and completely inimitable way that is all-encompassing (embody? - spiritualize is decidedly better - but here, too, both are valid, and, at this moment, I am looking at your picture, the one from Tunia's last visit). Meanwhile, however, the form is not universally worthy of the content and its creator, and this pains me, although, admittedly, I am absolutely conscious that I am demanding much too much because the work is your work alone. I have made many notes, and although I know that it is presumptuous of me, I want to plunge into your work again in the period before New Year's and write down what is welling up within me, despite my estimating my competence in this as slight (until the new year I shall be incapable of freeing up even one quiet hour). I am already living in anticipation of further work on this, which certainly is impaired by my presently being harassed by every dog and hardly know where my head is, which, unfortunately is clearly evident in these lines and their lack of concentration. One thing just must be said now for your seventieth birthday: the similarity of my function with your former activity is so striking that I am often very astounded and I continually seek to be inspired by you, of course without ever coming anywhere close to reaching the level of my paragon.

To you and Grete much love and a thousand heartfelt wishes! F.

Dear, esteemed Professor,

not a day goes by in the Beidler household that the name "Leo" does not come up in one form or another: Franz in grateful memories, and Dagny and I in warmest reverence. To you and your no less loved wife, Grete, our warmest wishes and greetings,

Libuše

97. FWB to KBG — 1952.11.25

98 1953.01.08. — Kestenberg (Tel-Aviv) to Beidler (Zurich)

[typed]

Background:

Kestenberg refers to being invited to participate in a conference in Brussels. Hosted by UNESCO, this conference brought to life an international organization for the improvement of musical education. It was to be call the International Society for Music Education or ISME. To those who were aware of the history of Kestenberg's activities in this field over decades, it was obvious that the organization was a further development of his life's work. That the first President of the ISME was Arnold Walter, a notable follower of Kestenberg, is but one indication of Kestenberg's status as the great man of music education in the 20th century. Arnold Walter's name appears several times in the Beidler-Kestenberg correspondence, relating to Walter's desperate attempts to escape the brutal hands of the Nazis. In the end, he found a safe harbour in Toronto, where he introduced Kestenbergian reforms to dramatically improve the quality and methods of music education not only in that city but across the whole of Canada. Because of ill health, Kestenberg was unable to attend the conference. A speech by him was read to the delegates and he was made the first honorary President of the ISME.

8. 1. 53.

My dear, precious friend,

when it comes to demonstrating expressions of emotion, of experience, of being able to be joyful, our time has become so terribly impoverished, if we think of how former epochs understood how to bring their expression to their feelings, their joys and their grief. These thoughts crowd about me at this moment, when I am about to find the words for you, my dear friend, that are supposed to take over as representatives of my gratitude, since I am not at all able to take your hand in person, to tell you what moves me, with my voice, with my eyes. For you know how fond I am of you, how close to me you have always been and still are and how I always feel the need to see you, to speak to you. It is almost not at all the What, but much more the How, that draws me to you. It is imponderable, ineffable, metaphysical relations that bind us. In the background behind these feelings stands, naturally, your whole personality and your origin, stands what I have experienced with you, with Ellen, stand the Berlin years and our work together. This work, in the gruesome year, 1932, does not represent the end of the line for me, but rather I can say, without boasting, that, in Prague as also here in Israel, I have actually come to true inwardness. The Teaching Poem is only one episode, that I have long surmounted and forgotten, and I ask you not to delve into it anymore and that you really put it aside. Unlike most other people, I really live from the moment outwards, and I do not hold the slightest claim of *scripta manent* [from Lat. "Verba volant, scripta manent" - spoken words fly away, written words remain"]. I live without a care into the so-called day, precisely because I have attained the belief that we are floating in a transcendent eternity, as it sounds out, allegorically, in the music of Busoni's *Dr. Faust*. Now, as well, I ask you to understand me, not through words but rather through sounds and through ideas that are not concrete but rather from out of a world that knows its connection to the cosmic and musical and which wants to recognize musical education as originating in the great eastern philosophical tradition.----- It may seem odd to you that I want to tell you in this connection that directly after my birthday, which was celebrated domestically and internationally with all warmness and panache, I became seriously ill and that I am still suffering from this "old man's sickness" and can not yet foresee when I shall again be well. But: for me, this illness is only an occasion to comprehend spiritual equilibrium in its entire profundity, to make clear to myself, that we can renew ourselves, in the most beautiful and holiest sense and that we must seek inner humility. With this, I have indicated to you that our travel plans have become doubtful, especially my participation in the music education congress in Brussels and Salzburg in this summer of 53, despite my following these plans with all love since the year 1938. Just today, I received a very sincere and warm invitation from UNESCO to the music education congress in Brussels, and it is just now that I must write that I am ill and do not know if I can come. My doctors give me a certain amount of hope, but I fear that it would be foolhardy to expose myself to such an exertion.

The conclusion of your letter, with your assurance that in your work you are sailing fully in the wake of our endeavour of back then, had a vibrant appeal to me. It is the best that you can say to me. It contains the great warning: "difficult duty, daily done" [Goethe: "*Schwerer Dienste tägliche Bewahrung - sonst bedarf es keiner Offenbarung.*"] ! How happy I would be if you would not again activate these long, completely unearned periods of silence which are incomprehensible to me - and if you would write to me again very quickly.

With the most profound, warmest greetings and embraces and the best wishes of the New Year for you and both your dear women,

always and ever your old

Leo

[envellope side of aerogramme - Grete K handwriting]

My dearest Franz, let us hope that it is written in our stars that Leo will recover quickly from this illness and will be the old boy or yore – – – and then we shall come to you for certain, to you and also to Switzerland! How magnificently beautiful that would be in every respect! my special thanks for the snapshot – – with what tender love and loving tenderness you hold your charming Dagny. I cannot look at it enough. Farewell and, above all, be healthy. Warmest greetings and New Year's wishes,

the old Grete K.

98. KBG to FWB — 1953.01.08

99. 1953.06.26 — Kbg (Tel-Aviv) to FWB (Zurich)

[typed]

Background:

In 1953, the government of Konrad Adenauer took up the question of paying compensation to Jews and others who had suffered financial and physical harm at the hands of the Nazis. As Beidler knew all too well, most Germans were not at all in favour of these measures. At the end of December, 1951, for example, only 5% of West Germans admitted feeling any sort of guilt towards the Jews. Nonetheless, Konrad Adenauer pushed through this measure in an effort to convince the international community that Germany had turned over a new leaf in its history. Kestenberg and his wife had lost family members to the Holocaust. Still, he and his immediate family had managed to avoid the gas chambers. On the other hand, a pension was owed him for his years of work in the Ministry of Culture during the Weimar years. He also had a claim for unjust dismissal from his post, from which he had not resigned but had simply been removed. He seems to have been leery of applying for money from the German government. On the other hand, as he notes, all his friends urged him strongly to complete all the formalities required by the German authorities.

My dear friend,

during the last months, our lives have experienced a definite upsurge, above all because of my recovery (wonderful in every sense of the word) from the medical condition which befell me just after my birthday and then because of the prospect of a "a great voyage on the horizon" — to speak in dream-book style. All of our friends in Israel and abroad have advised us urgently to act, in person and resolutely, to put forward our claim to (Jewish) reparations. For that reason, we want to leave already on the 1st of July, and fly and/or drive to Badenweiler by way of Frankfurt a/M. We shall live there in the "Hotel Roemerbad" and we shall likely stay for 2-3 months in the Black Forest.

What makes us happiest is the prospect of green meadows and woods, and the European climate, which we have done without for such a long time, and that we have been unable to forget, despite all our determined efforts to assimilate.

Even if I assume that you yourself are now, in these summer months, on holiday and will drive up to the mountains, we still hope either that we will see each other again in Badenweiler or at your place in Zurich. It is indescribable how warm and cheerful it makes us to think of seeing you again and Buschy and to meet Dagny! In September, we would also like to meet up with Ruth, on her way to London — if everything goes well — also even with our Brazilian Raquel. And now I expect from you, you amazingly stubborn man of silence, a word from you in Badenweiler, from which we shall be able to learn all the details about our meeting.

With all the warmest of greetings to you and your dear wife and daughter, as also from my Grete, who is also writing this letter of mine because my eyes unfortunately have suffered a deterioration in their vision.

Always your old

99. KBG to FWB — 1953.06.26

100. 1953.10.31 — Grete Kbg (Tel-Aviv) to FWB (Zurich)

[typed]

Dearest friend Franz,

how good it feels to be able to write to you once again, since we missed seeing each other even though we were so nearby! We did not find your dear letter, that you sent here instead of to Badenweiler, until our return home here, three months later. What a shame! And so many old and dear friends visited us during the 8 weeks in Badenweiler. It had to be you that we missed! Is it really our destiny never again to see each other in this life? ? ?

At the end of August we had to drive to Berlin to settle Leo's reparation affairs, which we hope was successful — as the immediate future has to demonstrate. In these 4 weeks, which also happened to be the Festival Weeks, Leo, at any rate, was positively coddled by everyone. We were bestowed with many superb performances, and Leo was able to note, with joy and satisfaction, that the seeds which he had sown in Berlin 30 years before. had sprouted fully to maturation, that the "Kestenberg decree" has gone into effect only today. He has been invited again for next year, also by Preussner for Salzburg. Let us see if the stars which have been good to us, that watched over and protected us our whole lives, will remain favourable. At the moment, he is suffering from a serious eye ailment that we hope he will overcome swiftly and completely — his eyes were never his strongest plus-point. At any rate, he is in the hands of a very good doctor who has our full confidence.

Farewell to you, with your two dear women (how much we would have liked to have met them), stay active and healthy; and be most tenderly pressed to my heart!

Your old

100. KBG to FWB — 1953.10.31

101. 1954.02.26 —FWB (Zurich) to Kbg (Tel-Aviv) -
[typed]

Dr. Franz W. Beidler

Zurich 7: Frebruary 26, 1954,
Zeltweg 65.

Grete, Leo - distant but always close friends,

what compels me really to write to you at last, today, after so many beginnings, attempts, and resolutions? Busoni. Just now, probably for only the third or fourth time, I heard his Opus 39, the concerto for piano, orchestra and male chorus — with virtuoso playing — too virtuoso — by the Italian pianist, Pietro Scarpini,[1] unkown to me up to now). Once again I was fascinated, riveted, moved — and torn away from my well-planned everyday work schedule. And instead of doing what I had planned — rendering an expert opinion on a difficult contract having to do with the assignment of world film rights — I am writing to you. Probably because of its tremendously large range, from heroic, often sombre pathos to gentle whimsicality, to the semblance, or better yet, reflection of popular sound; because of its opulence of musical substance, because of the scintillating brilliance of its ornamentation, which never degenerates into the purely playful (as, so often with Liszt); because of its elevated level of spirituality (a level that Liszt himself never reached, even in his best creations! — It remains inexplicable that Busoni, was in his mid-thirties when he created the work, 1903/04. Consider the gap between it and contemporary works, even Mahler's! Perhaps Scriabin might have been the closest?!); because of its resolute unconventionality, and related to that, because of Busoni's very special, keenly-formed Janus head, present in all art — an incredibly interesting and almost daemonically alluring fusion of tradition (formally — much Liszt, naturally, but only formally) with perspectives on, and even clearly formed ventures into, completely new, even undreamt-of areas of musical thought (I say it deliberately: thought1, the term I tend to ascribe to Vladimir Vogel,[2] the most concentrated musical thinker of our time and the

---

[1] Pietro **Scarpini** - (1911-1997) - Italian concert pianist. He saw the high points of his career as playing Beethoven's Fourth Piano Concerto under Furtwängler, the Second Concerto of Prokofiev under Dimitri Mitropoulos, and, what he referred to as the most monumental piece in the entire piano literature, Busoni's Concerto for Piano and Male Chorus, Op.39. There is a fine performance, Scarpini with the Cleveland Orchestra under George Szell - see YouTube.

[2] Vladimir **Vogel** - (1896-1984) - Russian, naturalized Swiss composer. He studied with Feruccio Busoni and taught composition at the Berlin Conservatory 1929-1933. Fleeing the Nazis in 1933, he moved first to Strassburg, then Brussels, Paris, and London. From 1939 on he was in Switzerland, first in Ascona, and, from 1964 on, in Zurich.

Busoni student, who probably evolved the future-facing legacy of his great teacher with the most logic and greatest productivity. The older I become, the more I feel that Busoni, far more even than Mahler, and even Schönberg himself, stands on the cusp between two eras of world music, the discordancy of which defines the fate of our contemporary music and shapes it in a way that is probably more interesting than any generation before us ever experienced (whereby, admittedly, the circle of those who understand it, is inevitably tiny, and, in our "free" world, moreover, atomized, if not virtually proscribed.) That may be why it has to be that I immediately prick up my ears and drop everything as soon as the sound of Busoni reaches my ears. He should receive much more attention, be studied precisely and systematically and I am likely to do just that as soon as I have put behind me certain tasks that are still awaiting completion. People can say what they want in criticism of Adorno. At the present time, among philosophers of music, he is the brightest brain we have. Regrettably, in his "*Philosophy of the New Music*," which you surely know, he forces an exaggerated polarization of Schönberg vs. Stravinsky so far, by means of the black/white technique, the key role occupied and held by Busoni is as good as utterly unrecognizable. There is much to make up for here and weights to be rebalanced!

What should I say about the tragic misunderstandings and disappointed expectations of last year? I thought you would be in Badenweiler much longer — and suddenly, to my horror, a letter arrived, from Tel-Aviv … Now I am hoping for and putting my trust in this year! Please make your plans clear soon so that we can orient things better around them. Fervently and threefold Your F.

101. FWB to KBG — 1954.02.26

102. 1954.06.17 — Kbg (Tel-Aviv) to FWB (Zurich)

[typed]

My dearest friend,

your letter of Feb.26, so worthy of thanks, can be answered easily and gladly. Our theme consists of 3 images: Busoni, during the time of his "Concerto," because I was with him daily and had to write the piano part into the manuscript of the score with which I was so infinitely and intimately familiar, and 2. the memory of Ellen and you in our Berlin years, and finally, I myself, in the contemporary Israeli reality. --- First of all, I have to say, with all power and priority, how happy I am that you have discovered Busoni for yourself and for your studies. Outside of Paul Bekker, Mitropoulos,[1] Gisella Selden-Goth[2] and Scarpini, there are only a few who, up to now, have recognized what a decisively important influence Busoni has exerted on the secular metamorphosis of musical and aesthetic ideas. If I am not mistaken, "*Arlecchino*" is to be produced soon at La Scala, Milan. You will certainly have the opportunity to hear the work in one form or another. Busoni's worldly-wise, ironic, masterful, but Faustian, quintessentially good artistic personality would be an infinitely important mentor, especially for our epoch, if, as far as possible, we would understand him!

And with that, I come to you, my dear Franz, and to the transformations we have had since the time that we, so full of fiery ardour, championed our socialist convictions, of which, in my opinion, only the dialectical method has endured. All the more do we enshrine the memory of this period, with all our love. For our generation, it was truly the best that we could develop from within us. And when I recall today the skepticism with which Busoni confronted my socialism, this whole polarized era comes alive once again. And alive is also your person and your form, with all their virtues and idiosyncrasies.

But now I must tell you about myself and, here, I must begin with antithesis: antithesis is certainly the actual, creative foundation of all existence. The witches' kitchen is the nursery of all renewal and regeneration. An apparently horrific illness, a complete retinal detachment, impedes me from all reading and writing, from reading music, from seeing piano keys. Only with Grete's help can I manage to preserve what I am thinking and what

---

[1] Dimitri **Mitropoulos** - (1896-1960) - Greek conductor, pianist, and composer. Busoni was one of his teachers. In the 1950s, he was the principal conductor of both the New York Philharmonic and the Metropolitan Opera. He was one of the most gifted conductors of his era.

[2] Gisella **Selden-Goth** - (1884-1975) - Jewish Hungarian composer and author. She was a pupil of Busoni's and one of only two pupils of Bartók. She wrote a biography (1964) of Busoni. She donated most of her impressive collection of musical manuscripts to the Library of Congress in 1940.

I want to save. And precisely this defect and this adversity favour me with an unimaginable abundance of visions and inner experiences. Add to this that, since my illness, my hearing has improved markedly and become more refined, enabling me to acquire a completely new technique for playing the piano and for promoting, teaching, and therefore educating my unusually gifted students, with all zeal and dedication, and, so, with success.

You Swiss have a magnificent pedagogical past, which I directly associate with Pestalozzi[1] and Nägeli,[2] with C.G.Jung and Ernst Kurth, about which I must write you a letter sometime. Above all, I should talk to you in greater detail about your remarks concerning your great-grandfather Liszt, because you do him a bitter injustice by judging everything that he wrote by one standard. He is of such a sublime opulence that he could afford to jot down the most significant thoughts beside the cheapest. And if I think back to the time when I played all the *harmonies poétiques et réligieuses*, I once again become conscious how fundamentally deep my roots in the religious sphere were and are. For me, today, in Israel, all that is cloaked in a new form and a new significance.-----

Travelling abroad, my dear, is something which is utterly impossible for me to think of anymore. I have to limit myself to the shortest of walks in my immediate neighbourhood, but these are a completely satisfactory substitute for "the great wide world." In August, we shall only go to our good old sanatorium on Carmel. But we shall be with you in our thoughts, if, perhaps, you meet with all the Gladsteins.

Warmest greetings to Buschi, Dagny and you,

Your old

102. KBG to FWB — 1954.06.17

---

[1] Johann Heinrich **Pestalozzi** - (1746-1827) - Swiss pedagogue and educational reformer. Having founded several institutions of learning in Switzerland, he almost completely eradicated illiteracy in Switzerland by 1830.

[2] Hans Georg **Nägeli** - (1773-1836) - Swiss composer and music publisher. He composed much music for use in educating students. He was also important in promoting choral music-making in Switzerland. As a publisher, his most important contribution was publishing for the first time J.S. Bach's *Well-Tempered Clavier*.

103. 1956.04.06 — Kbg (Tel-Aviv) to FWB (Zurich)

[typed]

My dear, good, old friend,

despite my frequent painful regrets about long gaps in our correspondence, I feel very happy once again when a letter from you arrives to confirm our bonds of friendship. And now even this triple conversation about your great-grandfather Liszt, that speaks to me so from the heart, which, in my opinion, could betray a touch more great-grandsonish love that, even more, would underline our common, almost familial, bond! Busoni brought home Liszt's greatness to me, infinitely so. Still today, I have a renewed feeling for his genius, his incomparable goodness, and his love, at every instant. I continually go through all his works with all of my students and I have learned as well to see merit in his so-called weaknesses, the same as required for all of us, with our disadvantages and advantages. The magnificent chivalric richness of Liszt's creative power, which, was expressed particularly in his lifelong pianist-essence and pianist-fame, also occasionally caused him to jot down works of the moment that can be explained only as improvisational gestures. If I only think of what Liszt achieved for Schubert, how he was the one who brought Schubert to the world, and when I then remember how he behaved to Smetana, and that is only to mention two relatively small instances, my heart just goes all warm and fuzzy and I could fall to my knees before him in thanks and songs of praise! In addition, the older I become, the more his very special kind of religious faith, that underwent so many transformations, is steadily more obvious to me. For, here in this Land of Israel, only with our own special kind of belief can we manifest and substantiate our right to exist. In his own, completely personal form of Zionism, Liszt again contributed something to us — despite his tendency to a certain, instinctive anti-Semitism, probably a result of the influence of the Princess Wittgenstein. But who desires to test and investigate this? My dear Franz, here I wanted only to thank you for your kind letter and for sending the trio-talk, which certainly was was brilliant in fulfilling its task.

We are doing well, even if I am often severely disabled by my eye affliction --- but thanks to my Grete, I am rarely conscious of this condition.

Farewell and best greetings and hugs to all three of you from both of us.

Always your old

All of our dear ones, Ruth, Tunja and Rachel, and our Brazilian Rahel and her family are happily also doing well.

103. KBG to FWB — 1956.04.06

Afterword

When you read the twenty-three years of Kestenberg letters contained in this collection, you might be forgiven for imagining from his balanced and circumspect tone that he sailed through life, blessed by enormous good luck. Here was a man who grew up in a highly cultivated environment, one that gave him every opportunity of education, especially in music. He met people who helped him at the right time. He had a long and profoundly significant friendship with Feruccio Busoni, one of the leading keyboard virtuosi of his day, a man with a broad philosophical horizon.

Through his achievements up to 1918, Kestenberg came to the attention of other patrons, powerful men who brought Kestenberg into the Prussian government to take musical matters in hand. For ten years, he had almost complete support from the governmental minister to whom he was responsible. He was able to introduce reforms and new projects almost at will.

Bad luck struck Kestenberg for the first time, it would seem, when the Nazis took over in German. Nonetheless Kestenberg landed on his feet in Prague where he found new, exceptionally cultivated politicians who believed in his work and vision and made it possible for him to form an international organization of music pedagogy which, after World War Two, developed into the ISME (International Society for Music Education).

Bad luck again when the Nazis invaded Czechoslovakia. Miraculously good luck when the virtuoso violinist Bronislaw Huberman saved Kestenberg and his family from a concentration camp by giving him the opportunity to move to Palestine as the Managing Director of the Palestine Symphony Orchestra.

Yes, Kestenberg's life was blessed. But was the going so smooth as the style of his letters would indicate? Unflappability was one of the valuable character traits with which he was born, one that helped him to weather the storms that every Jew had to surmount even after Germany and Austro-Hungary emancipated the Jews in the mid-1860s, about fifteen years before Kestenberg's birth.

Born in the Hungarian part of the Austro-Hungarian Empire, he moved with his parents, first to Prague and then to Reichenberg. From the age of seven, Reichenberg was his home. Although in Czech territory, Reichenberg was populated by Sudeten Germans. Kestenberg grew up in a German-speaking environment. He had a strong feeling for this, his homeland. But, as he indicated in his memoirs, this feeling was not only profound and beautiful but also stressful:

> … I viewed the Reichenberg countryside as my true homeland which I loved immensely. But this love was seldom returned. On the contrary, I had to suffer at the hands of the horribly anti-Semitic Sudeten German population many curses and much hatred.[1]

Because he was a Jew, reports Kestenberg, he was screamed at by teachers and beaten up on a regular basis.

These experiences of constant, active discrimination was a normal part of life for Jews throughout Europe. In some places it was worse; in Russia and Poland, for instance. In some places it was less harsh; in England, the Netherlands, Scandinavia, and Italy. No matter the gradations, Jews found ways of dealing with the problem. Some emigrated to North America or Australia. Others converted to Christanity, a solution that sometimes backfired because the rednecks refused to recognize Jewish conversion. Others studied assiduously in order to gain entry to occupations that would allow them to exist within a society that was sometimes hostile even to doctors, lawyers, dentists, academics, and journalists but less often to top-notch performing musicians.

In the case of Kestenberg, opting to solve his racial problem by becoming a musician came naturally. In his own way, it was a solution already partially practised by his father., who was a well-regarded cantor in a succession of important synagogues including temples in Prague and Reichenberg. Kestenberg's father Adolf. played a central role in forming his son's interests and character. Adolf was first and foremost a musician, practising at home for hours a day, during which he spent much time expanding his growing repertoire of German Lieder. At the same time, he worked diligently to improve his command of the German language.

Adolf was a man of broad interests, some of them not necessarily what many temple members would endorse. When Leo was only nine, for instance, Adolf decided to become a vegetarian, on ethical grounds. Little Leo, much taken with observing biblical protocol, had to be held back by his mother from denouncing his father in the synagogue.

On May 1, 1892, Adolf took his son to his first mass socialist demonstration, something that proved an epic event for Leo's life. "At that time," he wrote, "I was filled with a feeling of belonging to this mass, something that certainly resulted from the socialist education given me by my father."[2] Afterwards, continues Leo, during his piano lesson, he played one of Felix Mendelssohn's *Lieder ohne Worte* (Songs Without Words),

---

[1] Kestenberg, *Bewegte Zeiten*, p.7.

[2] Kestenberg, *Bewegte Zeiten*, p.9.

> and, more or less consciously, I sought to express, in sound, the fundamental feeling of freedom, equality and fraternity. Already at that time, the unity of socialism and music was beginning to dawn on me in a way that was still diffuse but which I worked toward for the whole rest of my life and which I made every effort, step by step, to bring to realization.

Indeed, this was Kestenberg's mission in life and he did work to realize it with a single-mindedness that left no room to heed racism of any sort.

That the racist hatred that disturbed Kestenberg's childhood did not let up during his adulthood is something that does not emerge from the present correspondence. He does mention it, however, in his memoirs, in the form of the political racism of the Nazis"

> Looking back, I see that from the earliest years of my entry into the Ministry [of Culture] right up to my last working day there, I had to swim against the current. The political development of the Weimar Republic, from its beginning up to its shameful demise, went differently from anything that could have been predicted. It is clear to me that all my reforms had to be enacted without any supporting foundation. And the strong opposition to my work which originally came from the rightwing parties, increased more and more as the National Socialist Workers' Party grew stronger so that, in the end, it was no miracle that in the year 1930, people were already saying: "Kestenberg is a dead man."[1]

Given the pressures and opposition that Kestenberg underwent his whole adult life in Germany, it is amazing what he nonethelesss achieved. His reforms have survived and still influence music educators and institutions of learning to this day. Thankfully, his work outlived the Nazis who attacked him with their own special brand of brutality.

One of the techniques of the Nazis used against the Jewish community of Germany was to form a deliberately uninformed image of the Jews of Poland, Russia and other slavic countries of the East, the sort of stereotype which could be seen as caricatures in Nazi publications such as the *Völkischer Beobachter* or *Der Stürmer* but also, to maximum effect, in the movie *Jüd Süss*. This stereotyping had been done in 1850 by Richard Wagner, in his *Judaism in Music*, where he implied that real Jews, the ones he viewed with most disgust, were those of the Orient, i.e. of the East and that Jewish Germans such as Heinrich Heine and Felix Mendelssohn, not to mention Giacomo Meyerbeer, could never escape the inborn, rotten characteristics of the East.

As long as he could, Kestenberg, like other German Jews, coped with the hateful slops spilled on their heads with various more or less effective techniques. For virtually all Ger-

---

[1] Kestenberg, *Bewegte Zeiten*, p.76.

man Jews the first and foremost technique was to delve into German literature, music and visual arts. They did this with a singular passion. Waves of excellent German musicians enriched the German culture that they so loved: Mendelssohn, Mahler, Schoenberg, among many others. Great German Jewish novelists, critics, academic writers, artists, and art historians developed, out of all proportion to the number of Jews living in Germany and Austria-Hungary. This method of coping worked well both for Jews and for Germany/Austria — until it didn't.[1]

In essence, the literary and artistic concentration achieved by the Jewish intellectuals, most of whom had to flee Germany in 1933 or Austria in 1938, was a form of compartmentalization. It allowed the Jews in question to think they were disarming idiotic criticisms of them as a "race" by showing that, culturally, they were more German than the majority of other Germans. At the same time, they had made the obvious signal compromise of distancing themselves from the Yiddish and Hebrew languages and culture. This was supposed to show their dedication to their German homeland and culture in that they abandoned the culture and languages of their antecedents from the East or wherever.

Compartmentalization is the tactic that Kestenberg used in giving himself the space to achieve his reforms and many other projects despite the deadly opposition of the anti-intellectual thugs from the right. A small but telling instance of Kestenberg's compartmentalization arises from a remark made by Beidler that Rachmaninoff had commented that modern music was a mystery, so incomprehensible as to be non-existent for him. So incensed was Kestenberg that he declared Rachmaninoff to be dead, as far as he was concerned.

Another such case was that of the writer and Jewish political activist Theodor Lessing (1872-1933). In 1925, Lessing warned against the election of von Hindenburg as President of Germany, saying that the old General was a zero, and that after a zero there could follow a Nero, which, of course turned out to be true. In addition to many books concerning Zionism and other jewish themes, with the inclusion of Yiddish and Hebrew terminology, Lessing published a much-read book entitled *Jewish Self-Hatred*. Self-hatred may have afflicted the odd troubled Jew here or there but Leo Kestenberg was anything but afflicted by Jewish self-hatred. Like other enemies of the Nazis, Lessing fled Germany. Like Kestenberg, he settled in Czechoslovakia. Soon after Hitler's takeover, Nazi agents broke into Lessing's house and assassinated him in cold blood. Beidler was horrified by this act. Kestenberg's only reaction was to commet that he had no regard for authors who

---

[1] see Michael Haas, *Forbidden Music*, Yale University, 2013.

wrote narrow-bore Jewish-themed books. Lessing and Rachmaninoff. And then there was Wagner.

Wagner was territory where Kestenberg's and Beidler's compartments came into something of a friendly ricochet. Like Sam Goldwyn[1] who famously said, "include me out," Leo Kestenberg simply excluded the rabid anti-Semite Wagner from his life. As he explained to Beidler, the whole of Hitler's staging of his Nuremberg *Reichsparteitage* could already be seen in Lohengrin's grand entry via swan in the first act of the opera *Lohengrin*. While recognizing Wagner's technical genius as a composer, Kestenberg refused to let such a base human into his life.

This sort of view was not something that Beidler could share, at least not before 1945. Like so many Wagner enthusiasts, Beidler wrestled with how to allow himself to surrender to Wagner's magic as a composer without leaving any room for Wagner's written ideas, especially his racist proto-Nazi "theories." As the only long-time anti-Nazi among the Wagners, Beidler had an inborn right to defend his grandfather if anyone did. For a time, he leaned, half-heartedly, to the argument that Wagner would never have gone along with Hitler and his thugs. The Nazis merely made use of the great composer for their own horrific ends. People are still making use of this argument to excuse Wagner, only with more enthusiasm than Beidler could muster. Significantly, fairly soon after World War Two ended, Beidler adopted Kestenberg's position of excluding Wagner from his life.

It is not only Beidler and Kestenberg who have had to deal with their own core beliefs in approaching Wagner. The Nazis made subsequent generations of musicians uneasy about co-operating with Wagner in taking a bath, not only in the Rhine, but also in the pure joy of losing oneself in his world of ecstatic sound. Every Jewish musician, and many non-Jewish ones, find themselves having to justify to themselves any connection they might have to Wagner, to Bayreuth, to Hans Sachs or Lohengrin or Parsifal. Some seek to relativize Wagner's hatreds. Others repeat endlessly that Hitler had made use of Wagner and warped the composer's only mildly anti-Semitic utterances for the sake of Nazi racism. Others seek to force Israelis to ban their boycott of Wagner in Israel.

Wagner demands forms of self-justification from thinking and feeling Wagner enthusiasts who glory in his magic while detesting his hatreds. At any rate, and in comparison, when Kestenberg took over management of the Palestine Symphony Orchestra, he immediately banned Wagner from the orchestra's programs. There is reason enough to keep that ban in place. "Lest we forget." In any event, it is a problem that should be resolved by

[1] Samuel Goldwyn - (1879-1974) - Hollywood film studio executive and producer.

the inhabitants of Israel.

The skirmishes caused between Kestenberg and Beidler over Wagner involved a corollary, continuing skirmish — over Wagner's father-in-law and Beidler's great-grandfather, Franz Liszt. Although some anti-Semitic writing was published under Liszt's name and the Nazis rather liked him, Liszt never suffered the sort of widespread controversy attached to Wagner and his dynasty. After all, it was ostensibly Liszt's companion, the Princess Sayn-Wittgenstein who bore responsibility for the anti-Semitic pages in his book about the "gypsies".

For Kestenberg, there was no nobler, more admirable, no more visionary composer than Franz Liszt. Kestenberg was completely smitten by the holy Liszt worshipped by so many to this day. Not inclined to irrational ecstasies, Beidler occasionally played the curmudgeon in pointing out, with brevity, that Wagner was the greater composer and that certain works of Liszt showed compositional weaknesses. In this Beidler was in agreement with Liszt's own daughter, Beidler's grandmother, Cosima, who maintained that, as a composer, Liszt had missed his train and it had left the station without him.

What Kestenberg worshipped about Liszt was his outreach to fellow humans, his openness, his idealism - as well, of course, as his greatness as a piano virtuoso In view of these qualities, Kestenberg could forgive Liszt everything. When Beidler needled his friend about Liszt's affairs and his irresponsibility with regard to his children by d'Agoult, Kestenberg replied that artists like Liszt, living as they did in a flamboyant era, were required to break bourgeois boundaries and to live free of constraint in order to show their uniqueness, their fire, and the profundity of their emotions.

On one artist both Kestenberg and Beidler were in full agreement. Their admiration for Busoni both as soloist and composer knew no bounds. Beidler did allow himself to criticize what he saw as Busoni's arrogance with regard to the USA. But, in Zurich, he had the opportunity occasionally to hear Busoni works in concert performances, in the hall or on radio. He took pleasure in describing these at length because he knew that Kestenberg took such joy in reading about Busoni.

For Kestenberg, his compartmentalized approach, his life-tactic, dissolved almost immediately upon his landing in Palestine in 1938. He wrote jubilantly that he had rediscovered his father in the Jewish homeland. Later he recounted how he had finally understood his father's repeated emphasis on the greatness and value of Jewish literature, both in Yiddish and Hebrew. Finally, said Kestenberg, he no longer had to weigh his words and tailor them to the degree of anti-Semitic opposition he expected from any given listener. He was finally fully at home. He had rediscovered his roots and his beloved father. That he was able to bring his whole immediate family to Palestine as well, including his mother, was a blessing since they would not have been safe in occupied Czechoslovakia - to put it mildly. After the war, when Beidler urged Kestenberg to return to Germany to resume his former activities as a reformer, Kestenberg refused. He had found his homeland and his happiness, he said, and would remain there to the end.

The life story of Leo Kestenberg, forms a wonderful arch, like a bright rainbow, full of his glowing missions and ideals, mostly accomplished despite great difficulty One colour of the rainbow is German, as is shown by a growing interest in Kestenberg's work in the Federal Republic of Germany. Another colour is Jewish, starting in his father's synagogue and ending in the Land of Israel. There is no room on the Kestenberg rainbow for hatred, neither self-hatred nor Nazi hatred. It is a real rainbow, radiating a message of light and goodness.

If Franz W. Beidler's life can be compared to a rainbow, it is one that is high up in the Swiss Alps, sometimes obscured in mists and weather. His grandfather Richard Wagner-talked a lot about blood, or, as Nietzsche remarked about *Parsifal*, "too much blood and not enough meat." Franz carried Wagner's blood in his veins, literally and figuratively and that sometimes turgid liquid determined many aspects of his life. Franz W. Beidler could not spend his last decades in the sort of magnificent afterglow that Kestenberg experienced. He was not able to simply slough off Wagner, for instance. He had been born into the heart of Wagnerdom, after all, the son of the Wagners' first daughter, Isolde. His birth was greeted by the clan with jubiliation. They celebrated him as the future male heir to the Wagner legacy, something for which they had lost all hope because they expected that Wagner's son Siegfried was so keen never to marry.

As is all too well known, everything having to do with Richard Wagner is superdimensional. Everything connects with everything else and seems to stretch into infinity. That goes for the Wagner family of which Franz W. Beidler was a part. Where Kestenberg's family was a haven of love and culture, Beidler's was a place of strife and chaos. "The family," often described as a clan, had expelled him from "Monsalvat" after winning a pyrrhic victory in a German court of law in 1914. The Wagners won the right to call his mother von Bülow and falsify the patrimony of her son. Bad luck for Franz W.? For his part, Franz refused to bear a grudge against his relatives for their cold-blooded behaviour towards him. Like his grandmother Cosima, he rejected small-mindedness as beneath his dignity.

After his Beidler's mother, Isolde, died in 1919, he returned to Bayreuth at times. Despite not being granted an audience with his grandmother, he did strike up a friendship with Siegfried Wagner's young wife, Winifred, who also happened to be Franz's aunt (shades of Anna Russell).[1] As a former orphan child, Winifred knew what being an outcast was like. Treated like a Wagnerian Cinderella, Winifred found understanding and companionship mostly from the elderly and bed-ridden Englishman, Houston Stewart Chamberlain but also from the young Franz W. Beidler.

Winifred was a fanatic Nazi and Beidler a leftist. No matter. Even after Winifred had become "the mightiest (Nazi) woman in Germany," Beidler retained his positive feelings for her on a strictly personal, non-political level and told her so. At the same time, he let her know how much he detested her politics and compartmentalized them off to one side so that he could continue to value the private person. Even as late as the early 1950s, he publicly honoured Winifred for the rôle she played in advancing and permitting the publication of the complete correspondence of Wagner with King Ludwig II of Bavaria. As he noted, this publication was unprecedented in the history of the Wagner family for its openness, lack of tendentiousness and thorough academic preparation by Winifred's chosen expert, Dr. Otto Strobel, who, although a dedicated Nazi, showed equal dedication to objectivity and thoroughness in his work on the correspondence.

It is quite astounding that Beidler retained a special feeling for the Wagners and their world. While despising all the Nazis for their dense intolerance and brutality, he continued to feel himself part of a family that he cared about. Athough sickened by the German invasion of Poland in 1939, for instance, Beidler worried about Wolfgang Wagner who had been wounded in Poland. As already noted, Franz roundly berated the anti-Nazi Friedelind for writing a book that he found gratuitously trashy in style and content. Maintaining decency and dignity in dealing with the family, despite the way they had mistreated him, was more important for Franz than pummeling them beneath the belt, even for the sin of their fanatical Naziism.

Franz had celebrated ridding himself of his German citizenship. As we have seen, he had demanded this schism and applied for it through official German channels. Intoning how everything about Germany nauseated him, he gave every sign of never wanting to return there in the future. After the war, however, following an invitation from the mayor of Bayreuth, Franz did return to Bayreuth. It was not his family feelings that caused him to return to Germany but his conviction that he could serve the artistic cause that had been so important to his ancestors, including above all Richard Wagner. Franz's dedication to "the Cause" proved stronger than his rejection of his family's shameful Nazi past. He saw it as his special responsibility as a Wagner untainted by Nazism to help rebuild the

[1] In 1919, Siegfried was 50, Winifred 22.

Festival especially since, in 1947, it seemed as if people like Winifred might be prevented by denazification penalties from further participation in the family mission, something that he would have approved of. At any rate, Beidler, like Kestenberg, was not a man to nurse a grudge or a hatred. That would be both unproductive and harmful to a socialist's yearning to improve mankind for its own sake.

Wolfgang Wagner, with whom Franz had the most dealings after the war, was not capable of thinking in the sort of intellectual or philosophical ways of a Franz Beidler. As Wolfgang himself said, he was cut out to be a farmer more than anything else. Perhaps unjustly, the stereotypical farmer is seen as land-hungry and calculating. Wolfgang was good at contracts, money-making, and bonhomie, bad at thinking big thoughts. A typical example should suffice here. Not long before he died, family intimate Hans von Wolzogen (1848-1938), editor of the house propaganda organ, *Bayreuther Blätter*, gave Wieland Wagner a complete edition of the works of Goethe as a gift. At the same time, he gave Wolfgang an old spring-wound wall clock with the specific instruction that Wolfgang enjoy himself taking it apart to see how it worked.

Wolfgang laughed at Franz for wanting to see source documents about Cosima Wagner. Franz needed them for the biography he was writing, he told Wolfgang. Writing in 1994, Wolfgang still expressed astonishment at Beidler for bringing up the idea of a book in 1947 when he was in Bayreuth to bring the Festival back to life. When Friedelind introduced me to her brother and told him that I was researching the history of the Wagners, he shook his head and said he felt sorry for me. It was my impression that he did not feel sorry for me because of the theme of the work (his family) but more for the waste of time involved in doing such useless work as archival research — for a mere book. The way Wolfgang saw things in early 1947, Beidler was making problems for him and his siblings and his main purpose at that time was to make Franz return, empty-handed, to Switzerland — forever.

In the event, Franz W. Beidler had gone to Bayreuth with some excellent ideas in his briefcase. He wanted to start a foundation to run the new Festival. There would be a number of internationally-recognized, very distinguished intellectuals, including at least one Nobel Prize winner (Thomas Mann) on the advisory council. Works by Wagner would be performed as always, but also works by other composers. The dynastic succession principle would be done away with. Anyone familiar with Beidler's letters to Kestenberg and his biography will be persuaded that Franz was capable of leading such a foundation. Over the difficult 1930's and early 1940s, he had shown great energy and an impressive aptitude for organization. With his knowledge of the history of the Wagners and the Wagner Festival, he should have been predestined to fill a leadership rôle.

Certainly, the circle of rightwingers, still much in contact with Wahnfried, chose not to take Beidler and his ideas seriously. In the years that followed, most people simply dismissed Beidler's foundation idea. For them, it was as if the dynastic succession principle was chiselled on a hunk of granite somewhere in heaven. After Winifred, Wieland would come and then Wolfgang, then Wieland's or Wolfgang's progeny. For the prewar Wagnerites who were also postwar, only Wagner could be played in the Wagner Theatre.

The Wagners and their Bayreuth are surrounded in myths of magnificence, many of them invented by themselves. What is the Bayreuth Festival if we look at it objectively and historically? From 1876 until 1882, it was really an experiment with which to give the *Ring des Nibelungen* and *Parsifal* the ideal performances for which their composer had longed all his life. *Parsifal* was the greater artistic success. Wagner had composed it specifically for the Festival theatre, after all. Both the premiere production's stage direction and design were widely admired in their time and better integrated than those in the original *Ring* of 1876.

During Cosima Wagner's directorship of the Festival, from 1883 to 1906, the Festival turned into a museum for the preservation of the unpreservable. Cosima, the lady who let nothing be changed "upon which the Meister's glance had alighted," busied herself with trying to remember exactly how Wagner himself had staged his works. Everything had to be as close as possible to the originals because everything about Wagner was holy, so it seemed. And where nobody could remember exactly how Wagner had wanted his staging, Cosima took over with her own predilection for nobility of movement and studiously accurate historicism in both costumes and scenery.

To make matters worse, Cosima insisted that singers place great emphasis on exaggerating consonants, leading to something George Bernard Shaw called "the Bayreuth bark." At the same time, she rejected great conductors such as Ernst von Schuch and Gustav Mahler because she thought them both of Jewish origin. Instead, she had her son Siegfried fill in as conductor in preference to Mahler or Schuch. Siegfried couldn't, but he did it anyway, for mama. In the Wagner family, Siegfried was worshipped as a theatrical and musical genius. And beyond Wahnfried's fence? Musicians such as Claude Debussy scoffed.

When Adolphe Appia, the brilliant Swiss theoretician of stage design (lighting is everything), presented his ideas for Cosima's consideration, she handed down to him her final and infallible verdict that, since Wagner had tread upon the boards of the Festival Theatre and staged his works there, there was nothing further to be learned, nothing to be improved, nothing more to be thought about. During Cosima's years, the Festival became a family hobby run by opinionated and very conservative family members. Isolde designed costumes, Daniela and her husband, art historian Henry Thode, researched historical detail, Eva took notes, son-in-law Franz Philipp Beidler taught in Cosima's school, coached singers and conducted, Siegfried conducted and worked on stage design and lighting. Backing up these amateurs in their efforts were professional theatre people. With only one major exception, Hermann Levi, no Jews were allowed to participate. Non-Germans had to be extraordinary to find their way into the Festspielhaus. The closed minds of the Wagner family could only present a Festival that was acceptable musically but otherwise shoddy.

After 1906 an ailing Cosima retired — to spend more time with her family — including such hoary additions as the syphilitic racist, Houston Stewart Chamberlain. Son Siegfried, more fancy-free in Monte Carlo or Rome, now accepted his mission as dynastic keeper of the Wagnerian mysteries. His sisters adoringly praised the way he improved Act II of *Parsifal* with more flowers, but were otherwise deliriously grateful that he kept a lid on other changes. They praised every note that he composed even though their quality was questionable. Thankfully, the world-class level of singers and orchestral players helped to keep Festival attendance at a financially healthy level.

After Siegfried's death at 60 in 1930, the former orphan Winifred took over the Festival leadership and started running things on the Führer principle. Why not? She had long been Germany's most rabid female supporter of Hitler, well on her way to becoming the mightiest woman in all of Germany. Many writers kneeled down before *Führerin* Winifred and extolled her one-woman rule over Bayreuth as the further extension of the Cosima era.

Never mind that Winifred, ever cognizant of her duty to the Führer principle, fired Wilhelm Furtwängler and alienated Arturo Toscanini, the two greatest conductors of the era. She found it more important to assert her total command over the Festival, including its artistic side than to keep Furtwängler as the Festival's artistic director and main conductor. She did bring up Karl Elmendorf and Heinz Tietjen as conductors, thereby continuing the old Bayreuth tradition of letting routiniers and family-related stage designers do the conducting in the *Festspielhaus*. Tietjen, who had been raised to his place of power in the Prussian theatres by Kestenberg, had latched onto Winifred as a way of protecting himself against the ravenous brownmen who remembered his Kestenberg connections. During the Third Reich, Tietjen had a permanent place on the Festival stage and podium but also in Winifred's bed while taking out additional insurance as legal guardian of Winifred's children.

Meanwhile, even family members such as son Wieland Wagner began to complain about Tietjen's set designer, Emil Preetorius, a fine man whose Japanese tea-garden style infuriated Wieland while, admittedly, being nowhere near as unfortunate as Wieland's own early attempts at stage design. Winifred's fabled era was put to a definitive end by the victory of the Allies which, by the way, also put an end to the Führer Principle in Bayreuth — for a while — and cleared her bed of Heinz Tietjen who dropped Winifred and took up with a young ballerina.

Into this vacuum walked Franz W. Beidler in 1947 with his rational plan for the resurrection of a revamped, creative, and progressive postwar Bayreuth Festival. For many reasons, he failed. This proved a bigger blessing for him than for Bayreuth. He did not have to waste his best years fighting off old Nazis and super-rich, arrogant "friends" of Bayreuth, the donor class. Had Beidler been able to gain the leadership of the Festival and drag the Festival into the second half of the twentieth century, he likely would have recognized Wieland's enormous talents and put them to use while steering Wolfgang to the Press Office, the fundraising department, or agriculture.

One thing must be underlined: despite the lack of Beidler's leadership and assistance, there has been one, and only one golden age in the history of the Bayreuth Festival, one period when Bayreuth became the centre of all operatic developments all over the world. That period extended from 1951 to 1966, the years when Wieland Wagner was the centre of all attention because of his stage designs and direction. For once, in the history of operatic production, one person found a way to make Wagner's music visible, to make the visible audible, by expert, revolutionary, thoroughly organized use of lighting. Wieland's productions of *Parsifal* and *Tristan und Isolde* were epoch-making. His other productions were also not only beautiful, meaningful, and trend-setting, but also simply magnificent and often overpowering. These productions disseminated an ethical message to the rest of the world. Things were changing even in Bayreuth and the loud protests of the old Nazis proved it. In addition, Wieland found the right artists, strong personalities with great voices, to embody his new and reformed vision. As Wieland's great soprano Martha Mödl said to me: "What would Wieland have done without us?" Wieland's strong and individualistic singers were people , scenery, and props on Wieland's empty stage. They were both liberated and challenged and proved remarkably successful. In addition to fine performers, Wieland also found distinguished progressive intellectuals to engage in postwar dialogue with the Bayreuth Festival as its anchor. Theodor Adorno is a prominent example.

Wieland had one big, continuing problem. That turned out to be his brother Wolfgang's ambition to be a stage director and scene designer just like his big brother, an ambition which was justified neither by his intellect nor his aesthetic competence. His 1960 production of *The Ring*, for instance, with its gigantic elephant-tusk shapes as scenery, was a low point. His *Ring* of the 1970s was an improvement. It was quite tolerable in places, such as Act III of *Die Walküre* which was closely modelled on the instructions outlined by none other than Adolphe Appia.

With the early death of Wieland in 1966, the Bayreuth Festival went into a sort of desperate hibernation. Wolfgang took over. Whatever he did not understand and could not deal with, he called a "workshop." What did the word mean? Seemingly: a talisman and promise that next year productions would not be as bad as this year because there would be more time to experiment, to repair things. The press came to like the sound of the word workshop and started referring to the whole of Wolfgang's festival as a workshop, a place in which a lot of capable people filled in for Wolfgang wherever possible. Recognizing his own deficiences, Wolfgang brought in more stage directors to populate his workshop instead of himself: East Germans like Götz Friedrich and Harry Kupfer, Frenchmen like Patrice Chéreau and Jean-Pierre Ponnelle, and Britons such as Sir Peter Hall, as well as more conservative directors such as August Everding.

Gradually, during Wolfgang's decades as director, the Festival lost its relevance to the world of art and even to its own blemished history. It was during this period that anyone familiar with Beidler's postwar plan could have seen that he was right. But those who knew remained silent — perhaps fearing that they might be erased from Wolfgang's hard drives and go ticketless for the rest of their lives.

In the early 1970s, Wolfgang and his mother, at long last allowing themselves to be inspired by Franz W. and their own mortality, took up his foundation idea and negotiated a dynastic version with the various levels of German government. With the mayor of Bayreuth ensconced as the managing director of the foundation, Wolfgang was able to have his friend, Mayor Hans Walter Wild, help him to become director-for-life of the Bayreuth Festival. That is how Wolfgang managed to remain director well into his eighties. He refused to leave the scene until his daughter Katarina and her mother, Wolfgang's second wife Gudrun, were appointed his successors. Surprisingly, the wife died before Wolfgang; and two daughters took over, Katarina (by the second marriage) and Eva (by the first).

Katarina, especially, has done an excellent job at rehabilitating the eminently shopworn legacy of father Wolfgang. In his heyday, he had been the most affable opera director in the world, beloved by singers and technical people alike. His own evident deficiencies as a stage director and designer were camouflaged by capable people on his staff. In her short but well-publicized career, daughter Katarina has followed in her father's footsteps, thereby convincing Wagnerians that Wolfgang need not go down as the worst

Wagnerian stage director of all time.

Franz W. Beidler might not have approved of everything that I have written here about his family. He did not take well to people who showed the Wagners disrespect. On the other hand, he himself was heard to refer to his Bayreuth relatives in breathtakingly uncharitable terms. Who can blame him? All of us need to call a spade a spade from time to time.

It was in Israel that Kestenberg found the antidote to the ignominy and humiliation suffered by his soul in Europe. Beidler, too, found succor for the wounds he had suffered. In Switzerland, the land of his ancestors, he was able to take his place on the battlements in the 1940s, confronting the Nazis, with his rifle if need be. He was able to live in a free land unblemished by the inevitable, unanswerable reproaches invariably lurking just around the next corner in postwar Germany. As Secretary of the Swiss Writers' Association, he served Swiss writers well and had the privilege of avoiding the dark and dismal, cutthroat world of operatic intrigue and machination (which Bayreuth was a part of).

After being rejected and spat out by a brutalized Germany, these two men immediately went to work on establishing new lives. Like wanderers in a maze, they moved with extraordinary energy, being unfazed by barriers, backing off, then starting again. They were lucky and they were intelligent. They survived, where others, without their qualities, succumbed. As intrepid and stubborn survivors both Leo Kestenberg and Franz W. Beidler effectively foiled Hitler. Not only that, however. While confounding the universally infernal intentions of Hitler, both men served their fellow men well. Both Leo Kestenberg and Franz W. Beidler left the world a better place while keeping their own personal, ethical integrity intact.

Acknowledgements

Special thanks to Dagny R. Beidler for making most of the present correspondence available to me and for giving me permission to publish it. Thanks also to Rachel Epstein for allowing me to publish the letters of her grandfather. To Ann-Kathrin Seidel, who has done yeoman work at the Kestenberg Institute (Tel-Aviv) and elsewhere, great gratitude for sending me scans of additional letters. Thanks go to Hans H. Habluetzel for many a helping hand, both with this publication and many other matters in the past. Many people have helped me in many ways: Dr. Manfred Eger, Dr. Sven Friedrichs (RWA), Susanne Kutschera, Mr. and Mrs. Gunther Fischer (Bayreuth), Dr. Dietmar Schenk, Dr. David and Martha Appleby, Birgit Rasel, and Dr. Daniel and Patricia Leung. Last, and always first, Carmen. Thank you.

Index— by letter number

24809157R00193

Made in the USA
Charleston, SC
04 December 2013